THE CHORAL EXPERIENCE

The Choral Experience

LITERATURE, MATERIALS, AND METHODS

Ray Robinson
WESTMINSTER CHOIR COLLEGE

and

Allen Winold
INDIANA UNIVERSITY

HARPER & ROW, PUBLISHERS
New York   Hagerstown   Philadelphia   San Francisco   London

Text design: Christine Aulicino
Cover design: Robert Aulicino
Text composition: American Book–Stratford Press, Inc.
Music composition: Music Typographers, Oyster Bay, New
   York
Printer and Binder: Halliday Lithograph

Library of Congress Cataloging in Publication Data

Robinson, Ray, 1932–
     The choral experience.
     Includes bibliographies.
     1. Choirs (Music) 2. Choral singing—Instruction and study.
I. Winold, Allen, joint author.   II. Title.
MT88.R7   783.8   75-23349
ISBN 0-06-161419-X

ACKNOWLEDGMENTS

The authors wish to express their appreciation to James Bryant, Gerald Custer, and Christina Emra for their assistance in the preparation of the manuscript. And to Ruth Robinson for the posture diagrams throughout the book.

Grateful acknowledgment is also made to those publishers listed below who have given permission to use music examples and materials presently under copyright:

Belmont Music Publishers, Los Angeles, California; Boosey and Hawkes, Inc., New York, New York; Theodore Presser Co., Bryn Mawr, Pennsylvania; G. Schirmer, Inc., New York, New York; and Universal Edition, Vienna, Austria.

CONTENTS

Contents · ix

PREFACE

This book is designed specifically for the practicing choral conductor and the student training for a career in choral music. It presents the fundamentals of the choral experience—vocal production, choral diction, ensemble singing, basic musicianship, and performance practices—that will be useful to the choral conductor who seeks to create a meaningful learning environment for his singers.

Most conductors would agree that the choral experience should not only provide the participants with an opportunity to develop vocal technique and to master a number of works from the choral literature, but also to develop skills in basic musicianship and insight into the performance practice and musical style of various periods of music literature. Even when rehearsal time is severely limited, the time devoted to basic musicianship and performance practice will be justified in terms of the eventual gain in efficiency, enthusiasm, and excellence in both rehearsal and performance. More importantly this study will enable the singer to extend his musical experience beyond the immediate rehearsals and performances of the choral ensemble to other realms of music. The knowledge, skills, and appreciation gained in the choral experience will enhance the student's understanding of other choral literature and of literature from other musical works, such as symphonic music, opera, ballet, or chamber music.

The fourfold organization of this book reflects this allegiance to a broader concept of the choral experience. Part one places the choral experience in historical perspective. Part two covers the essential aspects of rehearsal and performance. Part three presents fundamental concepts of basic musicianship, and part four introduces both general principles and specific application of performance practice. Chapters one to three present a short survey of the history of choral performance with special emphasis placed on the emerging role of the conductor and the function of the individual participant in choral singing. Chapters four to six present an introduction to the practical aspects of rehearsal and performance. Chapter four provides a systematic exposition of many of the principles of vocal production and breath control as they relate to the production of choral sound. Choral diction is the topic treated in chapter five, and chapter six covers such matters as voice classification, common vocal faults, placement, and seating plans in choral singing. Also of special interest in chapter six is a detailed analysis of the performance arrangements used by such conductors as F. Melius Christiansen, William Hall, Norman Luboff, John Nelson, Robert Shaw, Gregg Smith, Roger Wagner, Fred Waring, and John Finley Williamson. Many points discussed in these chapters will require experimentation by the conductor-teacher, and in some cases modifications may be employed to meet particular situations. However, the material given here will provide the basis for an understanding of the practical aspects of choral performance.

Chapter seven introduces concepts of rhythmic interpretation that should improve the choral singer's rhythmic sight reading ability. Chapter eight presents concepts of pitch organization applicable not only to music organized according to major-minor tonality but also to music structured according to other modes of pitch organization. Chapter nine identifies a limited number of broad concepts about harmony and texture as structuring forces in music of various periods, and chapter ten introduces basic concepts and terms used in the study of musical form.

No attempt is made in these four chapters to give a complete theory of music; the emphasis is rather on the organization of concepts of basic musicianship to help the conductor improve the quality of the musical experience of his choral singers. The terminology is kept as simple as possible, and relevant points are illustrated by musical examples in the text, the anthology, and the singer's manual.

The concluding five chapters offer an introduction to the literature and stylistic practice of choral music from various periods. This study not only focuses upon examples but also includes some discussion of other works and of parallel developments in instrumental music.

The authors hope that the use of this text will not only increase the choral conductor's effectiveness and understanding but will also make the participation of the choral singers more meaningful as well as deepen their appreciation for all music. Throughout the centuries choral music has been a vehicle for the expression of man's most deeply felt emotions; it can also be the vehicle for the development of his musical ability and understanding.

THE CHORAL EXPERIENCE

In a world of political, economic, and personal disintegration, music is not a luxury but a necessity, not simply because it is therapeutic nor because it is **the** "universal language," but because it is the persistent focus of man's intelligence, aspiration, and good will.

ROBERT SHAW

PART ONE

THE CHORAL EXPERIENCE

Introduction to Part One

OF ALL THE FORMS of musical expression, choral singing is the most accessible to the amateur. Because extensive and serious musical study is not an essential prerequisite for a satisfying choral experience, many children, teenagers, and adults throughout the world find delight and fulfillment as regular participants in this form of musical endeavor. It is the one art form that can provide for the nonprofessional a glimpse of transcendental beauty and musical self-fulfillment usually reserved for those who have devoted years of practice and study to their instrumental or vocal specialization.

What is the choral experience? Stated simply, it might be defined as an interaction between a singer and a piece of music within a group setting under the guidance of a conductor. More accurately, it is an unusual experience of communication between a composer and a singer, in which the singer is able to perceive the universe in a new perspective—through the eyes of the composer. This extraordinary act is accomplished through an empathic relationship between the singer and the conductor which allows both, at least for the moment, to participate with the composer in the creative act. Termed a "peak experience" by Maslow, this moment is the actualization of a cosmic awareness of the place, history, and nature of man in what often appears to be a disorderly, chaotic existence.

Intimately bound up with the communicative aspect of the choral experience is its educational function. Equally essential to the nature of choral singing is its function as a learning experience, in which the singer not only learns about his relationship with the macrocosm but also becomes better acquainted with himself. Most importantly, this encounter with aesthetic beauty exhibits a primary characteristic of any great learning experience: it leaves the participant forever changed. Naturally, then, the choral experience is one of those deep emotional encounters whose existence is only discovered after the fact and whose results are the only real record of its occurrence.

It seems hardly necessary to mention that the choral experience is also a physiological and sociological phenomenon. Obvious physical changes manifest emotional events of any depth, and choral singing is no exception: changes in pulse rate, respiration, adrenalin flow, and similar symptoms are present, as well as a feeling—at the end of a good rehearsal properly sung—of satisfying physical exhaustion.

Finally, the choral experience is a corporate event: the sensitive choral ensemble possesses a group psyche, and the presence of many minds all bending their intellectual and emotional energies toward a common goal is a powerful force on the experience itself.

Part one of this book places the choral experience in historical perspective and relates its essence to its most important participants: the conductor and the individual singer.

Chapter One

The Choral Experience
in Historical Perspective

With the power of speech the great Diviner separated man
from all the other animals and with the gift of song raised him
to a level one rung lower than the angels. The human soul was
modeled and attuned to the spiritual harmony of a perfectly
ordered world so that man alone, of all the creatures on the
earth, possesses the capacity to imitate celestial harmonies in
musical sounds.[1]

CHORAL SINGING as a formal group activity involving more than a few singers in
public performance is a recent phenomenon in the history of music. Prior to the
eighteenth century the choral art was practiced primarily by professional singers
who performed in small groups in the church, the court, and schools like the
schola cantorum.[2] While certain types of group singing accompanied man in practical exploits—in wars, in athletic events, and in celebrations—long before coming
to the cathedral and the concert hall, the idea of singing in a choir for cultural
and aesthetic pleasure and personal growth is little more than two centuries old.

The term *chorus* or *choir* is derived from the Greek word Χόρος and refers to
any body of singers whose performance is corporate as distinguished from solo
singing. Originally used in Greek drama, chorus is now synonymous with the
French *choeur*, the German *Chor*, the Italian *coro*, and the English *quire*, and applies to unison as well as polyphonic singing.[3]

From earliest times the choral experience has been a natural outgrowth of man's quest for worship, beauty, and communication, and in this connection its development has been nurtured by three important institutions in Western culture: the church, the school, and the singing society. By far the most influential of these has been the church.

THE INFLUENCE OF THE CHURCH

The Biblical narrative in the book of Genesis informs us that the God who created man also gave him the power of expression and communication through speech and song. Man was created with a voice with which to praise his Creator and to communicate with other human beings. This physical characteristic of man soon became a means of expressing thanks for victories won in battle. The human voice, the very basis of the choral experience, was thus an attribute bestowed on man by his Maker to set him apart from all other forms of life.

The theory that singing grew out of impassioned speech is actually Greek in origin, as is vividly described in Plutarch's summary of Theophrastus's discourse on music:

> Theophrastus lays down three causes of music—grief, pleasure, and enthusiasm; for each of these changes the usual tone, and makes the voice slide into a cadence; for deep sorrow has something tunable in its groans, and therefore we perceive our orators in their conclusions and actors in their complaints, are somewhat melodious, and insensibly fall into a tone.[4]

Singing and praise were a vital element in Hebrew culture. The battle of Jericho, the exultation that burst forth following David's victory over the Philistines, and the symphony of praise recorded in Psalm 150 are but three instances of this affinity for corporate vocal expression. Even in captivity the Israelites, whose fame as singers had undoubtedly spread to other lands, were required by their conquerors to sing a song of their homeland:

> By the rivers of Babylon, there we sat down,
>   Yea, we wept, when we remembered Zion.
> We hanged our harps upon the willows in the midst thereof.
>   For there they that carried us away captive required of us a song;

And they that wasted us required of us mirth, saying,
  Sing us one of the songs of Zion.
How shall we sing the Lord's song in a strange land?[5]

This excerpt from the Psalms demonstrates dramatically that some form of corporate singing was very much a part of Jewish culture.

When King David ascended to the throne of Israel, a systematic musical culture developed around the program of the temple. The Levites were appointed to supply musicians (as well as priests and porters) for the worship services:

And David spake to the chief of the Levites to appoint their brethren to be the singers, with instruments of music: psalteries, and harps, and cymbals sounding by lifting up the voice with joy.[6]

Massed musical forces numbering as many as four thousand persons participated in these services, creating an impressive cacophony of sound which the Chronicler describes as possessing impeccable ensemble:

Also the Levites who were the singers, all of them of Asaph, of Heman, of Jeduthun, with their sons and their brethren, being arrayed in white linen, having cymbals and psalteries and harps, stood at the east end of the altar, and with them a hundred and twenty priests sounding with trumpets: It came even to pass, as the trumpeters and singers were *as one* [our italics] to make one sound to be heard in praising and thanking the Lord.[7]

The choir was indeed an important part of the temple program. Its professional singers were furnished homes and paid for their services. The prophet Ezekiel writes that they lived in chambers between walls and windows with southern views.[8] The total choral resources available for temple activities numbered approximately two thousand singers—and included women in David's temple and young boys in Herod's temple.

These early choral performances consisted of antiphonal and responsorial renderings of the Psalms with instruments added on festive occasions. The method of singing was probably simple and straightforward:

1. The leader would intone the first half of the psalm verse, whereupon the choir (or congregation) would repeat it. Then the leader would sing each succeeding half line, while the congregation repeated the same first half line, which thus became a refrain throughout the entire psalm.

2. The leader would sing a half line at a time, and the choir or congregation would repeat what he had sung.

3. The leader would sing the whole first line, whereupon the congregation would respond with the second line of the verse.

In ancient times the congregations seldom joined in the singing but would respond with one word as a refrain to laudations and supplications: typical one-word responses were *Amen, Halleluyah, Hosh(i)'āhnnā* (Oh help!), *Aneau* (Answer us!). Later we find more sophisticated responses, such as the one below from Psalm 136:

Oh, give thanks unto the Lord, for he is good;
For his mercy endureth forever.
Oh, give thanks unto the God of gods;
For his mercy endureth forever.
Oh, give thanks to the Lord of lords;
For his mercy endureth forever.

The terms *antiphonal* and *responsorial* have had significance in choral singing throughout the ages, from the earliest intonations of Hebrew culture to the sophisticated double chorus and polychoral style of the Venetian school (c. 1527–1612). The introduction of the antiphon and response in temple worship is important because soloistic and virtuoso elements appeared in sacred music even during the primitive developmental periods.

While the choral music of the Hebrews was impressive because of its grandeur and timbre, that of the Greeks depended for its effect on refinement and perfection of detail. The information that has come down to us concerning Hebrew music deals principally with the external features of temple services and musical celebrations. The treatises on Greek music, however, are of a theoretical nature and are concerned with the most complicated problems in rhythm, meter, scale construction, modes, and with questions regarding the relationship between music and poetry.

Greek choral music was closely associated with the annual religious festivals in city-states that honored a particular deity. These celebrations employed choral music for their effectiveness, with choirs of singers praising the gods, musicians playing the kithara and aulos, and musico-gymnastic contests in which both individuals and choruses participated. In these activities two distinct tendencies were apparent: the first had its origin in the worship of Apollo and was national and ethical in character, while the second had as its source the cult of Dionysius and emphasized more individual and sensual expression.

Although few examples of early Greek music have come down to us, we know that the choral forms associated with the worship of Apollo included hymns of praise, hymns of thanksgiving, dirges, and lamentations. The festivals of Dionysius eventually became the basis of Greek drama, and choral music accompanied the orgies, processions, and games during these early celebrations. Instrumental music was later included, actors were added, spoken dialogue became part of the setting, and the elements of the Greek drama were now complete.

To appreciate the importance of choral participation in the dramatic presentations in ancient Greece, we must realize that these celebrations were not private undertakings intended for the amusement of the public but festivals of a semireligious character which were considered essential to the political and moral welfare of the nation. The organization of the choruses was provided by law. If a poet wished to mount a dramatic production, he had to apply to a magistrate. If his request was granted, the best singers in each district were sought out and given an examination. Once the singers were chosen, wealthy citizens furnished the financial support necessary for the sustenance, instruction, and equipment of the choir. The singers were generally trained by a chorus master who was assisted by the leader of the orchestra. On certain occasions the poet chose to perform this duty.

Greek choral singing, like the Hebrew, was in unison and octaves. When performed with the aulos or kithara, independent melodic material was probably introduced according to strict theoretical principles. It is doubtful that a true contrapuntal texture (consisting of several individual melodies occurring simultaneously) was practiced by the Greeks.

Roman culture, occupied as it was with the extension of the empire and the establishment of a political power base, contributed little toward the development of choral art. When Greek singers and instrumentalists were brought to Rome, there was an abundance of choral music, but only music that pleased and vitiated the taste of a culture delighting in excesses. Choral performances were popular in Rome, but it was the music of the Greeks—native music, simple in melody and rhythm—that was played on these occasions. Choral and instrumental music on a grand scale was indeed the order of the day when twelve thousand singers and instrumentalists assembled in Rome in public celebration at the time of Julius Caesar (102?–44 B.C.).

It is thus little wonder that singing was the only art form admitted at the services of the early Christian church. The excesses of the Greeks and Romans created the climate that led to spiritual and artistic reform. The commandment "thou shalt not make unto thee any graven image, or any likeness of any thing" ruled out architecture, sculpture, and painting as legitimate artistic expressions of worship in the formative years of the Christian church. Instrumental music was prohibited, and for more than fifteen hundred years the history of sacred choral music was synonymous with the history of music in Western culture.

The popularity of singing among the early Christians is well documented in the writings of church leaders of the time. Pope Leo I, who lived during the fifth century, related that the "Psalms of David are piously sung everywhere in the Church." As late as the thirteenth century St. Thomas Aquinas defended the prohibition against instrumental music on ethical grounds:

> Instrumental music as well as singing is mentioned in the Old Testament, but the Church has accepted only singing on account of its ethical value: instruments were rejected because they have bodily shape [*figuralia sunt*] and keep the mind too busy, induce it even to carnal pleasure, and consequently the Church refrains from musical instruments in order that by the praise of God the congregation may be distracted from concern with bodily matters.[9]

Philo, the Jewish philosopher, described the singing of the new Christian congregations as similar to the chanting of several Hebrew sects. It is probable the choral music of the early Christian church included the singing of antiphonal and responsorial psalm texts in a style similar to that practiced in the temple.

There is also evidence that the difficulty of this worship music changed from the simple intonation of Biblical (psalm) texts to a more florid style of singing by the end of the fourth century. This change in style, along with a similar development in responses which grew considerably longer in text and music, created the need for better trained singers. The natural outgrowth of this need was the *schola cantorum*.

The choral singing of the Middle Ages was marked by one important characteristic: it was closely linked to specific nonmusical functions. The idea of music as an "absolute" art form is a nineteenth-century concept. The very thought of a concert, at which large numbers of people would gather for the purpose of listening to a performance, would have seemed strange to the medieval mind. The value of music rested in the fact that it served activities other than those with a strictly musical purpose; choral music as subordinate to the worship service is perhaps the best example of this characteristic of medieval culture. Carrying this thought one step further, Wilhelm Ehmann speaks of the relationship between choral singing and the drama in the Middle Ages:

> The liturgy of the Middle Ages . . . was conducted by those who acted, and all acting groups were considered to have direct access to God. The choir did not think of itself as singing to a listening audience, but it took part in various parts of the liturgy . . . the music which it produced, represented a direct link to eternity.[10]

The manner in which choral music was performed prior to 1600 is a subject that deserves attention in any historical survey of the choral experience. The only type of choral singing generally practiced during the Middle Ages was that of the choir in unison led by a singer-director who was trained in one of the singing schools. With chant serving as the melodic and formal basis for the choral literature in medieval times, the art of contrasting solo and choral singing in antiphonal and responsorial musical forms became highly developed. The practice of alternating solo and choral forces also influenced the performance of polyphonic music. The first great achievements of polyphonic vocal writing—the *organa quadrupla* of Perotin and the motets of the thirteenth and fourteenth centuries—were composed not for large choral groups but for soloists. With the introduction of polyphony only the sections intended for soloists in the performance of chant were composed for two or more voices; the other sections remained choral monophony. This practice continued until the beginning of the fifteenth century. These early attempts at polyphonic writing were less effective than pure chant composition because the element of contrast, which existed between the solo singer and the choral group or congregation, was not present when performed by two groups of singers. However, it was not long before composers found new and effective ways to contrast monophonic and polyphonic sections, and a new form of choral composition—the polyphonic setting of the mass—was born.

According to Bukofzer, choral polyphony as an idiomatically composed musical form for group performance developed about 1430.[11] At this time the first clear distinction between solo and choral composition became apparent, and for the first time in the history of music we find two styles developing side by side: the liturgical and chorus-conscious music of Joannes Okeghem, Jacob Obrecht, and Josquin des Prés, the polychoral extension of the choral idiom with Adrian Willaert and Andrea and Giovanni Gabrieli, and the synthesis in Giovanni Pierluigi da Palestrina and Orlando di Lasso; and the music for solo voice, leading to the secular literature of the French *chanson* and the Italian *madrigal* and ultimately to a chamber music choral style. This new choral idiom, however, was still very closely related to the style of Gregorian chant, which explains why the earliest polyphonic choral music comes out of a liturgical setting.

The introduction of polyphonic music into the church service did not replace the established practice of performing plainsong in the worship service. It is probable that the number of trained singers available for polyphonic performances of choral music in the fifteenth and sixteenth centuries was limited, and only those large and important churches were able to afford a coterie of trained singers. Chant, therefore, continued to play an important part in the liturgy of the Catholic church well into the twentieth century.

Prior to 1600 the manner in which the various functions of choral music were performed was usually determined by the size of the church and the importance of the occasion. Festival services were obviously ideal opportunities for polyphonic music, and in the fifteenth and sixteenth centuries were also occasions for performances combining instruments and voices. In the post-Reformation Protestant churches a distinction developed between the congregation, the untutored element, and the trained choir. As further demands were made upon trained singers to perform solo parts in cantatas, anthems, and masses, there was a further division of the functions of the choral resource within the church.

The Protestant Reformation in the first quarter of the sixteenth century had a far-reaching effect on the development of choral music. By allowing lay participation in the service, and by admitting the use of vernacular texts in the liturgy, the reformers brought the choral experience to every member of the congregation. Singing thus became an activity in which all could participate, and eventually led to the establishment of the amateur choral societies of the eighteenth and nineteenth centuries. The *chorale*, which replaced chant at the heart of the new liturgy, brought such new compositional forms as the *cantata* and the *passion* into the Protestant service. In the early years of the Reformation, these chorale tunes were probably sung unaccompanied and in unison. When treated polyphonically by the German composers of the sixteenth century, they formed the basis for motets with vernacular texts. Toward the end of the century, as the melodic part gradually shifted to the top voice, a chordal accompaniment was added and the familiar hymn style emerged. Wherever these new hymn tunes appeared—first in Germany and later in England—they were easily learned and readily recognized by the average church member who could lift his voice in praise to his God in a language with which he was familiar.

The influence of the Church in the development of choral art reached an apex in the sixteenth century. The ideal of "ecclesiastical art as the servant of the church" found its fullest polyphonic expression in the liturgical music of Renaissance composers. The new Protestant attitudes concerning the role of music in the Church, combined with the reforms dictated by the Council of Trent (1545–1563), created a musical climate in which chant was discarded in favor of polyphonic settings of the Mass. The pristine beauty of the choral music of Palestrina and his contemporaries passed the test of the church hierarchy:

> All things should indeed be so ordered that the Masses, whether they be celebrated with or without singing, may reach tranquilly into the ears and hearts of those who hear them, when everything is executed clearly and at the right speed. In the case of those Masses which are celebrated with singing and with organ, let nothing profane be intermingled, but only hymns and divine praises. The whole plan of singing in musical modes should be constituted not to give empty pleasure to the ear, but in such a way that the words may be clearly understood by all, and thus the hearts of the listeners be drawn to the desire of heavenly harmonies, in the contemplation of the joys of the blessed. . . . They shall also banish from church all music that contains, whether in the singing or in the organ playing, things that are lascivious or impure.[12]

This action by the Council, as well as other trends, led to the eventual decline of chant as the basic form for the liturgy and to an increasing demand for polyphonic settings of the Mass.

With the questions of polyphony resolved, Catholic choral music reached its culmination in the beautiful cathedrals of Rome and Venice in the late fifteenth and early sixteenth centuries. The Sistine Chapel and the Capella Giulia of St. Peter's, the church of St. John Lateran, and Santa Maria Maggiore became the settings for the musical creativity of Palestrina (c. 1525–1594), and the cathedral of St. Mark's of Venice, with its two separate choir lofts and two organs, served to inspire the polychoral works of Willaert (c. 1490–1562), Andrea Gabrieli (c. 1510–1586), and Giovanni Gabrieli (c. 1555–1612).

Although Catholic choral music began to decline in importance in the seventeenth century, the church in England and Germany still exerted a significant influence on the choral art for another one hundred and fifty years. The English composers who alternately wrote music for the Anglican and Catholic churches in the late sixteenth and early seventeenth centuries made a new and distinctive contribution with the *anthem*. Because the reign of Henry VIII (1509–1547) was such a period of unrest, anthems were not permitted as a part of the worship service until Queen Elizabeth granted permission for the use of a "hymn or such like song in churches" during the period of her reign (1558–1603).[13] With the ascendancy of Charles II (1660–1685) the anthem was given a permanent place in the liturgy —after the third Collect in both the morning and evening services—and placed in the 1662 edition of the Book of Common Prayer. The list of important English anthem composers is quite extensive, including John Redford (1491–1547), Christopher Tye (c. 1499–c. 1573), Thomas Tallis (c. 1510–1585), Richard Farrant (d. 1580), William Byrd (1543–1623), and Orlando Gibbons (1583–1625).

While interest in choral composition declined in most European countries in the late seventeenth and eighteenth centuries in favor of opera and instrumental music, the popularity of the *chorale* and the participation of the congregation in worship kept choral art very much alive in the German Protestant church. This new liturgical setting provided the musical environment for the development of four important choral forms: the oratorio, the passion, the cantata, and the motet.

The early history of choral art in America is almost entirely related to the needs of certain religious groups. With the exception of the Moravians and the Huguenots, who brought their European musical culture with them to the new land, the choral experience in Colonial times consisted almost exclusively of the singing of psalms and hymns. Because John Calvin's views about the place and role of music in the religious service exerted such an important influence, the music of most Protestant groups during this period was limited to singing metrical versions of the Psalms and simple hymn tunes. Secular music (or concert music in any form) was not generally accepted by the early New England settlers, who were more concerned about the basic problems of survival in their new environment rather than developing a musical culture.

Beginning about 1720 a number of eminent New England clergymen, including Cotton Mather, Jonathan Edwards, Thomas Symmes, Timothy Dwight, and John Eliot, began an ardent campaign to improve the state of music in the church. Singing schools were established, and the itinerant singing teacher made his appearance on the American scene. Two important books, published in 1721, aided this reform movement in the development of choral music in the church: John Tuft's *Introduction to the Art of Singing* and Thomas Walter's *Grounds and Rules of Music*. By the time of the Civil War (1861), more than 375 tune books had been published. These books, which generally contained a few pages on the rudiments of music and the elements of singing, thus served as a primary force, along with the itinerant singing teacher, in the establishment of an early American choral culture.

The first important American psalm tune composer was William Billings (1746–1800), a native of Boston and a tanner by trade. He was entirely self-taught, and because his means for acquiring musical training were limited—theoretical treatises in English were rare in eighteenth-century America—his accomplishments were necessarily of the most superficial quality. Yet, his natural endowments and instincts led him to try his hand at harmonizing, then at composing, and finally in 1770 he published his first collection of compositions consisting of psalm tunes, anthems, and canons. Encouraged by the success of this first book, he was inspired to write English-influenced "fuguing tunes" and patriotic songs. By composing, publishing, teaching, and organizing choirs, he created a new and vital interest in church music and choral singing and exerted a profound influence on the choral art in America.

With these important eighteenth-century developments, and the concomitant emerging skill in singing and directing, a separation occurred in the worship service between the trained choir and the congregation. Evidence of this cleavage appeared in the 1830s when two types of hymn books appeared in American churches: one included the dignified and artistic hymns of the present day; the other the camp meeting, revival service, and Sunday school songs of the nineteenth century. The result was a pluralism of taste and musical practice in which black spiritual and folk music, white folk music, the English anthem and "fuguing tune," and European-influenced church music all began to develop side-by-side to create a special and unique religious musical culture in America.

Thus while the churches of New England and the Middle-Atlantic states were singing metrical Psalm tunes, or the new hymns of Isaac Watts, the black and white churches of the South their camp meeting and revival songs, and local artisans such as William Billings were composing Americanized English fuguing tunes, a group of European-transplanted Moravians were composing elaborate, concerted anthems in Bethlehem (Pennsylvania) and Winston-Salem (North Carolina), which were modeled after the choral works of central European composers of the period. These Moravian pieces were in fact the earliest examples of concerted, sacred choral music written in America.

The American Moravians were without doubt the finest composers of sacred music this country had known up until the end of the nineteenth century. Because of European rather than English influence, Moravian anthems and arias were conceived as extended, concerted compositions encompassing the stylistic traits of preclassical composers on the European continent. Yet at the same time these works have a remarkable and pronounced individuality. As an example of the Moravian's affinity for the music of the Viennese classical composers, Haydn's *Creation* received its first American performance in the Moravian *Collegium Musicum* in 1811, two years after the composer's death. (Handel's *Messiah* received its first performance in this country in 1770 under the direction of William Tucker in New York.)

With the choral music of Bach, Beethoven, and Handel and the Viennese Classical composers—Haydn and Mozart—the influence of the church on the development of choral art reached its climax. From the middle of the twelfth century to the beginning of the nineteenth century the church had served as the primary patron of choral art. In the nineteenth and twentieth centuries this role shifted to the school and the amateur choral society.

THE INFLUENCE OF THE SCHOOL

Because the school was so closely associated with the church in its early history, it is virtually impossible to separate the influence of each upon the other in the development of choral art prior to the seventeenth century. Instruction in music in early times was an outgrowth of religious necessity, of the need for trained singers and instrumentalists to participate in activities connected with religious rites. The earliest examples of this practice are found in the cultures of the Hebrews and the Greeks.

Musical training in Hebrew culture was limited to those members of the Levitical tribe who participated in temple worship services. Because King David believed that music should play an integral part in the temple, a rigorous instructional program was established in which a Levitical musician studied as an apprentice in a guild (or course of instruction) that contained twelve trainees. The Biblical account in Chronicles lists twenty-four such guilds under the direct supervision of the three master Levitical musicians: Asaph, Heman, and Jeduthun. These 288 trained musicians in turn were expected to lead the less-skilled body of assistants which numbered some 3,712 singers and instrumentalists. Of the twenty-four guilds in existence at the time of King David, four belonged to the family of Asaph, fourteen to Heman, and six to Jeduthun.[14]

The important Greek sacrificial festivals, an annual occurrence in most city-states, depended upon trained singers and instrumentalists for effectiveness. And, while the training of the singers for these great religious choirs was primarily a state function and relied heavily upon the oral tradition handed down from one generation to the next through individual participation, there were also private schools for the teaching of music. Terpander, for example, is reported to have had his own school of singers and instrumentalists.[15]

The Greeks placed a high priority on choral participation as one mark of an educated person. Plato (*Laws*, VI and VII) and Aristotle (*Politics*, VIII) write of the state of music in ancient Greece and inform us that Greek education included music among its basic elements so that in later life a person would possess discriminating taste and learn to make efficient use of his leisure time. Musical studies continued until age thirty and participation in annual choral dances in the theater was required of everyone.

The increasing difficulty of worship music in the early Christian church, especially the florid style of liturgical music that developed after the fourth century, created the necessity for some kind of training program for singers. The response to this need was the *schola cantorum*. Founded by Pope Sylvester between the years 314 and 335, and reorganized by Pope Gregory (590–605), the *schola* exerted a profound effect on the development of choral art in Western civilization.[16]

From earliest Christian times the Church had used special singers in the musical part of the liturgy. The schola cantorum thus became the practical vehicle for training such singers, an important band of musical pioneers who would become the leading force in the development of choral music in Western culture. Similar in program to the Greek schools which trained singers who performed in religious rituals, the schola became the model for similar institutions in monasteries and cathedrals in the Western world. In fact, it is possible to trace the development of choral music from the Roman schola to the early monasteries and cathedral schools, to the medieval and Renaissance universities, and finally to the various court chapels throughout Europe. In each case the common ingredient in the development of choral art was the professional singer-director, who was trained in Rome (or in a school influenced by the Roman schola) and disciplined in the style of chant. To his basic knowledge of plainsong the director applied the compositional experiments that led to later choral developments in organum and polyphony and subsequently to the flowering of the musical renaissance.

Consequently, singers trained at the schola were not only responsible for the cultivation of chant in Rome and in the surrounding city-states but also for the spread of the Roman liturgy—and with it a new choral tradition—to other parts of Europe to people not familiar with the style of Gregorian chant. For example, the Roman liturgy was established at Canterbury in 596 by the Benedictine Augustine, who was sent to England by Pope Gregory. Under Augustine a school, modeled after the schola, was developed, followed shortly by others at Wearmouth and York. Thus began the choir school tradition which has been such an important influence on English choral art throughout its history.[17]

It was only a matter of time until the Roman liturgy was introduced in France. Roman-trained singers appeared during the reign of Pepin (751–768), and song schools modeled after the schola and directed by men trained in the papal school were established at Metz and Rouen. Charlemagne, following in the footsteps of Pepin, and anxious to unite all Christians in his empire by means of the same religious ritual, founded *scholae cantorum* throughout the empire. These schools then trained other singer-directors who established singing schools at Toul, Dijon, Cambrai, Chartres, and Nevers.

As important as it was, the schola cantorum was not the only educational institution to influence the development of choral art in medieval Europe. An ordinance of Charlemagne in 787 directed that the monastic schools should include a broader curriculum and include the study of music within the context of its liberal arts education. Two years later his order was more specific—that "psalms, notes, chants, and grammar" be taught in each monastery and bishop's house. By the tenth and eleventh centuries the monasteries of Ferrieres, Auxerre, St. Amand, St. Germain, and Fulda all became important institutions for the cultivation of chant as well as the study of the liberal arts. Perhaps the most influential center for the study of choral music in medieval times was the monastic school at St.

Gall, where such students as Ratper, Balbulus, and Tuotilo first learned chant and later composed tropes and sequences to add to the musical wealth of the liturgy.

With the decline of monastic instruction after the tenth century, the cathedral schools assumed the important role in the development of choral art. Chant was still performed and studied in the monasteries (the monastery at Solesmes remains to this day an important center for the study of Gregorian chant), but it was in the cathedral schools, such as those in Chartres, Paris, and Rheims, that musical studies emphasizing ecclesiastical chant became a regular part of the curriculum. Again the close relationship between the church and the school is evident in the development of choral literature.

The rise of the universities as learning centers in thirteenth-century Europe brought a new dimension to the growth of choral art. One of the best examples of the influence of a medieval university upon the cultivation of choral art is the University of Paris. Because the University developed out of the Cathedral School of Notre Dame, and since in its early years it remained closely integrated with the cathedral, which became an important center of culture for all Europe, a close connection between the two was natural. It is not surprising to learn that Notre Dame's choir school served as the preparatory school for the University, and many singers in the royal choir and masters of the children of the king's private chapel were enrolled in the University either as students or teachers. The two most important musical figures of the twelfth and thirteenth centuries, Leonin and Perotin (whose innovations in *organum duplum* and *triplum* and various forms of *discantus* laid the foundations for the choral literature of the Renaissance), were probably associated with the University in some kind of teaching capacity. The musical studies in the universities thus continued a practice noticeable with the ancient Greeks, evident in the Roman rhetorical schools, and cultivated in the monastic and cathedral schools of the Middle Ages: the association of studies in choral music with religious needs and uses.

For the most part, however, musical study in the European universities was theoretical rather than practical. Performance was considered an informal and extracurricular activity. University choral organizations developed under student influence with very little faculty supervision except in the English universities of Oxford and Cambridge. In Germany especially, the congregational singing in the Protestant churches provided the stimulus for informal university choral organizations—the forerunner of the modern collegiate glee club.

In organizing and establishing his new musical liturgy, Martin Luther

(1483–1546) incorporated music into the curriculum of Reformation schools by placing "singing and music as a part of the full course of mathematics." It was his intention that all children receive instruction in chant and in the elements of music theory. The children who were trained in these schools formed excellent choirs which performed in church and community functions throughout Germany and in the Scandinavian countries. These choral groups, called *Kantorei*, sang at weddings, funerals, and various town functions, and eventually became one of the important forces in the performance of polyphonic works of German Protestant composers of the sixteenth and seventeenth centuries. With the inauguration of this system of musical instruction for all children in Germany around 1530, the *Schulkantorei* developed into an increasingly significant vehicle for the growth and development of choral art.

Just as the schola cantorum was the practical result of the need for trained singers in the early development of the Catholic church, and the Schulkantorei for the training of singers in the new liturgy of the German Protestant church, the *singing schools* fulfilled a need to provide instruction in notation and rote singing for Colonial Americans. Taught in most instances by itinerant singing masters, these classes exerted an important influence on the eventual development of American choral singing. Beginning in the early eighteenth century (c. 1720) and maintaining their influence for well over a hundred years, the singing schools vitalized singing in early American churches and eventually served as the forerunner to the public school music programs which emerged in the 1830s in New England. In a land more concerned with economic and physical survival than the development of a musical culture, the singing schools served two vital functions: they brought people together on a regular basis to participate in the corporate act of singing, and they developed a basic music literacy among their participants that would lead them to enjoy a meaningful choral experience in worship and community singing activities.

The earliest choral groups in American colleges and universities were established primarily for social reasons: to sing college songs for amusement. These choirs and glee clubs traditionally wore formal dress and gave concerts in a minstrel show atmosphere. Frequently they sang for campus alumni activities and sometimes went on tour primarily for the purpose of bringing publicity to the alma mater.

University choral unions and various choral societies appeared in American colleges in the second half of the nineteenth century, when musical studies were beginning to gain a foothold in higher education. These early groups often included persons from the community, as well as students at the college, with the campus serving as the focus for the organization's rehearsals and performances. Usually these choruses sang the better-known works of Handel, Haydn, Mozart, Beethoven, and Mendelssohn. Two of the earliest choral unions of this type were the University Choral Union of the University of Michigan (1879) and the sixty-voice chorus at Northwestern University (1892).

The A Cappella Choir of Northwestern University, the first college or university choir to use the title "a cappella," was formed in 1906 by Peter Christian Lutkin, as a result of a request for singers who could illustrate a lecture on the music of Renaissance composers. The St. Olaf Lutheran Choir was established in 1912 when the St. John's Church choir, composed mostly of students and college faculty and directed by F. Melius Christiansen, toured Wisconsin and Illinois. The Westminster Choir, which served as the stimulus for the establishment of the Westminster Choir College in 1926, developed from a church choir at the Westminster Presbyterian Church in Dayton (Ohio) and toured extensively beginning in 1922.

By the middle of the 1930s a cappella choirs were present in abundance in high schools and colleges across the country. The tours of the St. Olaf and Westminster choirs, together with those of a number of professional touring groups from Europe, were influential in the spread of the movement. The a cappella fad began to decline after World War II when professional choirs like the Robert Shaw Chorale and the Roger Wagner Chorale began to tour throughout the United States with a balanced program of accompanied and unaccompanied repertoire.

THE INFLUENCE OF THE SINGING SOCIETY

While an interest in choral singing for the nonprofessional had been apparent in the congregational singing of the Protestant church and the student and alumni choruses of the German universities, it was not until the end of the eighteenth century that the organization of choruses independent of these two institutions became significant in musical performance. Up to this time choral works were composed for the practical and utilitarian purpose of enhancing the worship service or the entertainments of royalty and aristocracy. And, for the most part, choral music was performed by specially-trained professional church choirs, boy choirs studying at a cathedral school, or members of the musical staff of a royal court.

The scarcity of public concerts added to the incentive for amateurs to meet together for the performance of choral music. Such gatherings were encouraged by the conductors of church choirs, and in some cases these spontaneous music-making occasions led to the establishment of permanent concert organizations. The group of students, for example, that assembled each week in Zimmermann's coffeehouse in Leipzig to sing and play (with the encouragement and assistance of Johann Sebastian Bach[18]) provided the impetus for the formation of concerts out of which the Gewandhaus concerts and orchestra developed.

As musical performance became more and more independent of the church and theater in the nineteenth century, similar amateur societies for the perform-ance of choral music sprang up throughout Europe and America. In the early years their purpose was largely social in nature. A social and dance almost always followed the musical program, which was often arranged to provide an opportunity for a display of the talents of certain individuals. For these and similar reasons many of the early societies were short-lived. For those that sur-vived, however, the musical reasons for which they were founded assumed greater importance, and eventually many of these societies attained an impressive degree of artistic accomplishment.

The dissolution of many of the royal chapels during the last half of the eighteenth century was another factor in the development of the amateur singing society. Certain noblemen, who were especially fond of promoting these types of performances, established concert societies involving the participation of the citizenry at large. Under the patronage of Baron Gottfried Von Swieten, for ex-ample, performances of the choral works of Bach, Handel, and Hasse were given in Vienna, commissions were extended to composers like Mozart to add accompani-ments to Handel oratorios (especially *Messiah*), and translations of English works like *Creation* and *The Seasons* were prepared for German-speaking audiences. It was this type of cooperation between the nobility and middle-class society that established the pattern for twentieth-century support of the arts in America and provided another impetus for the development of the amateur singing society.

These early societies were obviously incapable of a high degree of musical achievement because they lacked the lofty aims and artistic standards that were eventually to become a part of musical life in the nineteenth and twentieth centuries. Symphonies were often played at sight and choral works suffered from a similar lack of preparation. In the words of the eminent critic Eduard Hanslick, "they did not, as they perhaps hoped, make the whole population musical, but certainly themselves." These early societies of dilettante singers and instrumentalists nevertheless survived and flourished because of their social purpose, their support by the nobility, and their provision of concerts for the general public.

Meanwhile the choral society in England was developing more slowly than its counterpart in Germany. Church music in the British Isles remained under the exclusive control of the professional choirs of men and boys for much longer than in other parts of central Europe. In Germany, for example, the Protestant church was substantially more flexible in terms of its liturgical restrictions and thus allowed a degree of simplification which in turn allowed the participation of the congregation. This fact alone led to the popularization of choral singing among the people and created a desire for choral groups that included women as well as men.

The Church of England, on the other hand, insisted that trained choirs perform at all worship services, a practice that automatically excluded women from participation in the liturgy. The status of these seventeenth-century professional choral groups was further enhanced by demands for their services in theaters and other public places, particularly during Advent and Lent. Public choral concerts, open to anyone on the payment of a nominal admission fee, were instituted in England as early as 1670, long before such concerts were a regular practice in Germany.

The most influential force in the establishment of a choral culture in England was the music festival. In the beginning, these festivals were little more than special church services scheduled by two or more church choirs to raise funds for charity within an area of geographical proximity. The earliest events of this type were the Festival of the Sons of the Clergy (1655), which took place in London's St. Paul's Church, and the Three Choirs' Festival (1724), involving the church choirs of Gloucester, Worcester, and Hereford. The latter festival, an annual affair, was particularly influential in spreading an interest in amateur choral performance throughout the English counties.

There can be little doubt that the oratorios of Handel also exerted a positive influence on the growth and development of the amateur choral society in England and eventually in America. It was inevitable for the further development of choral singing among the people that choral forms, which had been the exclusive domain of the church for centuries, were now introduced into the concert hall. Handel was aware that events in sacred history, with which the church-going English public were thoroughly familiar, would appeal to the understanding and sympathy of both the singer and the audience.

One of the most famous oratorio performances in England during the eighteenth century was the "Grand Commemoration of Handel," which occurred in Westminster Abbey in May, 1784. With the combined choirs of St. Paul's, Westminster Abbey, Windsor Castle, and the Royal Chapel, a total of 525 performers were conducted by three time-beating directors. W. T. Parke described the performance in the following account:

> Now as the orchestra seemed to ascend to the clouds, and unite with the saints and martyrs represented on the painted glass in the west window, which had all the appearance of a continuation of the orchestra, I could hardly refrain from imagining that this orchestra was a point or segment of the celestial circles: and perhaps no band of mortal musicians ever exhibited a more imposing appearance to the eye or afforded more ecstatic and affecting sounds to the ear than this.[19]

Once the ability of Handel's music for performance on a grand scale had been demonstrated on occasions such as this, Handel festivals became a common occurrence.

A turning point in the development of the amateur choral society occurred with the establishment of the European professional orchestral associations. Instrumental performances were immediately elevated to a level of quality with which the amateur orchestra could not compete. These concerts educated the concert-going public to demand the same standard of excellence from choral performances since the amateur choral societies eventually collaborated with the professional orchestras in the performance of choral literature. These standards were not necessary prior to the nineteenth century because amateur choral societies were not performing for the concert-going public.

The influence of Haydn's two important choral works, *Creation* and *The Seasons*, on the development of taste for choral music in Germany was similar to that which Handel exerted in England with his composition of *Messiah*. Choral societies were organized in cities, towns, and villages for the special purpose of performing these works. The success of these sacred choral compositions created the demand by amateur choruses for similar works.

The first choral society that achieved significant musical and artistic success was the Berlin *Singakademie*. Founded in 1791 for the specific purpose of providing an opportunity for singing for its members, the Singakademie soon found it impossible to resist the many invitations it received for public performances. Among the vocal academy's many accomplishments, the one which was perhaps of greatest historical significance was the performance on March 11, 1829, of Bach's *St. Matthew Passion*, under the direction of Felix Mendelssohn (1809–1847). This event, which led eventually to the discovery and revival of the music of Bach, was another important way in which the amateur choral society played a key role in the development of choral art.

In Vienna the *Singverein*, which was established in 1858 as an adjunct to the Gesellschaft der Musikfreunde, served a similar purpose and could count among its early conductors the composer Johannes Brahms.

The Romantic movement in music, which found its most natural compositional outlet in instrumental music and in opera, nevertheless influenced a number of important composers to write works which were popularized by the developing choral societies. The emphasis upon the picturesque expression of emotions, fantasies, and literary works provided the stimulus for a number of successful nineteenth-century choral works, including those of Mendelssohn, *St. Paul* and *Elijah*; Charles Gounod (1818–1893), *The Redemption*; Franz Liszt (1811–1886), *Christus, The Legend of St. Elizabeth, Psalm XIII*; Hector Berlioz (1803–1869), *The Damnation of Faust, Requiem, Te Deum*; Robert Schumann (1810–1856), *Paradise and the Peri*; Giuseppe Verdi (1813–1901), *Requiem, Four Sacred Pieces*; Johannes Brahms (1833–1897), *Alto Rhapsody, German Requiem, Song of Destiny*; Antonin Dvorak (1841–1904), *Requiem, Stabat Mater*; and Sir Edward Elgar (1857–1934), *The Dream of Gerontius*. While this is by no means an exhaustive list of nineteenth-century choral works, it does demonstrate the important fact that the focus of choral activity after 1800 shifted from the church to the public choral concert, an activity in which the amateur choral society played a prominent and active role.

With the choral festivals in England and the Singakademie in Germany leading the way, public societies for choral singing began to appear in many countries where Protestant congregations had developed the habit of hymn singing. European choral music entered modestly on the American scene during the last few years of the eighteenth and early nineteenth centuries, as the result of the singing schools and hymn singing in Colonial churches. The Handel and Haydn

Society, modeled after similar organizations on the European continent, was established in 1815 in Boston for the purpose of "cultivating and improving a correct taste in the performance of sacred music, and also to introduce into more general practice the works of Handel, Haydn, and other eminent composers."

Amateur choral activity in the United States was not limited to the Handel and Haydn Society. Other singing societies which appeared around the same time included the Stoughton (Massachusetts) Musical Society (1786), Worcester Music Festival (1858), Cecilia Chorus of Boston (1874), Apollo Musical Club of Chicago (1872), Oratorio Society of New York City (1873), Cincinnati May Festival (1873), and the Bethlehem Bach Choir (1900). Associations of this type became more and more prevalent as singers increased in number and efficiency, and musical performance became more and more independent of the church and the stage.

The twentieth century signaled the beginning of considerable professional activity in the choral field in this country and abroad. The first American choral group of this type was the Musical Arts Society of New York City, founded by Frank Damrosch in 1893, "for the express purpose of bringing to artistic performance the immense treasury of ancient and modern *a cappella* music." Similar choral ensembles were established throughout the United States and included the Choral Art Society of Boston (1902), the Cecilia Choir of Pittsburgh (1932), the Madrigal Club of Chicago (1900), and the MacDowell Chorus (1912), which began as an adjunct to the Philharmonic Society of New York and later (1912) assumed the title of The Schola Cantorum of New York City when Kurt Schindler became its director. Radio choruses in Munich, Paris, Stockholm, and other cities created an important outlet for the professional choral singer.

The most important professional and community groups to emerge in the mid-twentieth century were the Fred Waring Glee Club (originally called The Pennsylvanians when founded in 1923), the Collegiate Chorale (1941), the Robert Shaw Chorale (1947), the Roger Wagner Chorale (1945), the Norman Luboff Choir (1963), and the New York Pro Musica (1953).

It is thus obvious the amateur choral society has had an important influence on the development of choral art. When the influence of the church began to wane in the eighteenth century, choral societies in England, Europe, and eventually America provided an impetus for composers to influence the development of a broader base of music culture through public concerts. Yet, the most important beneficiary was the individual singer, who was given the opportunity of a personal encounter with the composer—a benefit that is so aptly described by A. F. Hermann Kretzschmar (1848–1924) in a monograph published in 1879:

Yet as much as art profits by the singing societies, and notwithstanding that through their influence it has entered upon a new phase of life, the greatest good accrues to the members themselves. In no other art are amateurs privileged to enjoy spiritual beauties of a creation in the degree that music offers to choristers. Whoever belongs to a singing society in which the study is well conducted, at each performance accomplishes a work and receives an artistic reward analogous to that of the painter who has copied a masterpiece. And he who has spent a generation in such a society can cherish his recollections like an entire museum.[20]

In summary, the choral experience in Western European and American culture has been firmly rooted in three important institutions: the church, the school, and the singing society. For nearly two thousand years the church has provided an opportunity for choral singers, professional and amateur, to express their deepest thoughts as an act of worship and praise to their Creator. The means of this response to the Almighty have been many and varied: monks chanting in a medieval monastery; Palestrina writing for the papal choir at the Sistine Chapel; Monteverdi composing for St. Mark's in Venice; Bach supplying choirs for five churches in Leipzig; William Billings pioneering a refreshing style of choral music in a new land; and singers in a black church in Georgia improvising on a familiar folk tune.

With the diminution of church influence in the nineteenth century, the school became the patron of the choral art, with composers turning to its singers for the performance of their choral literature. In countries where the Protestant church had already encouraged hymn singing, the singing society became an important force in the development of choral music. The impulse behind these groups which sprang up in England, Germany, and America was that ordinary people could be led into an uncommon experience within the existing society by the ennobling cultivation of choral art.

NOTES

1. Julius Portnoy, *Music in the Life of Man* (New York: Holt, Rinehart and Winston, 1963), p. 1.

2. School of singers.

3. *Grove's Dictionary of Music and Musicians*, ed. Eric Blom, 5th ed. (New York: St. Martin's Press, Inc., 1954), 2:277.

4. Plutarch, *Symposiacs.*

5. Psalm 137:1–4.

6. I Chronicles 15:16.

7. II Chronicles, 5:12–13.

8. Ezekiel 40:44.

9. St. Thomas Aquinas, *Summa theologica*, Question 91, Art. II.

10. Wilhelm Ehmann, *Choral Directing* (Minneapolis: Augsburg Publishing House, 1968), p. 7.

11. Manfred Bukofzer, *Studies in Medieval and Renaissance Music* (New York: W. W. Norton and Company, 1950), p. 189.

12. Edward Dickinson, *Music in the History of the Western Church* (New York: Charles Scribner's Sons, 1953), p. 175.

13. Myles Birket Foster, *Anthems and Anthem Composers* (London: Novello and Co., Ltd., 1901), p. 15.

14. I Chronicles 16:4–6, 39–42.

15. Nan Cooke Carpenter, *Music in the Medieval and Renaissance Universities* (Norman: University of Oklahoma Press, 1958), p. 4.

16. Willi Apel, *Harvard Dictionary of Music* (Cambridge: Harvard University Press, 1944), *schola cantorum.*

17. Carpenter, op. cit., p. 16.

18. Hans T. David and Arthur Mendel, *The Bach Reader* (New York: W. W. Norton and Company, 1945), p. 149.

19. W. T. Parke, *Musical Memoirs* (London: Henry Colburn and Richard Bentley, 1830), Vol. I, p. 41.

20. H. E. Krehbiel, *Notes on the Cultivation of Choral Music* (New York: Edward Schuberth, 1884), p. 15.

Chapter One
RECOMMENDED READING LIST

Apel, Willi. *Harvard Dictionary of Music.* Rev. ed. Cambridge: Harvard University Press, 1969. A thorough but relatively brief compendium of technical terms; especially important is the article on "Editions, Historical."

Baker's Biographical Dictionary of Musicians. Edited by Nicholas Slonimsky. 5th ed. New York: G. Schirmer, Inc., 1958. The standard reference work on biographical information for composers, theorists, instrumentalists, and conductors.

Carpenter, Nan Cooke. *Music in the Medieval and Renaissance Universities.* Norman: University of Oklahoma Press, 1958. The definitive work on the historical development of music study in European monasteries, cathedral schools, and universities during the Middle Ages and the Renaissance.

Grove's Dictionary of Music and Musicians. Edited by Eric Blom. 5th ed. New York: St. Martin's Press, Inc., 1960. A thorough collection of articles on musical notation, ornamentation, composers, compositions, and historical periods.

The New English Bible. New York: Oxford and Cambridge University Press, 1970. This version of the Holy Scriptures is a must in every personal library; ". . . not a revision of any previous version." It also contains the Apocrypha.

New Oxford History of Music. Edited by J. A. Westrup, Gerald Abraham, Edward Dent, Anselm Hughes, Egon Wellesz. London: Oxford University Press, 1957. 11 volumes. Signed articles on all phases of musical development; includes profuse musical examples.

Portnoy, Julius. *Music in the Life of Man.* New York: Holt, Rinehart and Winston, 1963. A well-written work that brings into focus the different functions music performs in our daily lives.

Chapter Two

The Conductor and the
Choral Experience

The skill of conducting can be learned,
but not the art.—CARL BAMBERGER[1]

CONDUCTING IS a many-sided art, and its essential nature is viewed in different
ways by the listener, the amateur choral singer, and the professional orchestral
instrumentalist. To the average concert-goer, the time-beating function of conducting is the most apparent, and the competence and effectiveness of the conductor are judged on the basis of physical appearance and gestures. In the eyes
of the amateur choral singer, these characteristics are seen as a means of communication evoking a certain empathic response that results in a satisfying choral
experience. For the professional musician who has been directed to an inspired
performance, the time-beating gestures may seem less important than the conductor's ear, knowledge of the score, and ability to interpret the intentions of
the composer.

Conducting is a complex matter, and the mastery of its physical technique,
though important, is still but a small part of the total art. Sound training, technical
conducting skill, musical talent of the highest order, thorough knowledge of
musical style, consummate musicianship, and experience are indispensable ingredients for development of a good conductor. However, even these qualities may
not ensure that a person will be a successful and inspiring conductor. The intangi-
ble qualities of personality, which are essential for forceful leadership in other
fields, are also necessary ingredients in musical leadership, because many per-

sonalities with heterogeneous emotional characteristics and intellectual capacities are to be merged into one homogenous sounding musical unit. Added to these leadership imperatives, the distinctive vocal and musical demands of choral performance bring yet another dimension to the complexity of the choral conductor's art.

THE EMERGING ROLE OF THE CONDUCTOR AS INTERPRETER

Little is actually known about the origin of the conductor in choral performance, but it is safe to speculate that musical direction, even in its most primitive form, evolved from a need to control instrumental and vocal forces rather than from a desire for expression and interpretation. The conductor did not become a significant figure in the interpretative aspects of musical performance until the nineteenth century, when the size of orchestras and choruses, the combined musical and dramatic forces of opera, the demands of the composer for special musical effects, and the complexity of the rhythmic element made a single source of direction a necessity.

The Conductor in Early Times

While conducting per se and the conductor as an interpreter are nineteenth-century phenomena in musical performance, it is inconceivable that large instrumental and vocal groups in ancient times could have made an acceptable uniform effect without some central direction. Our lack of knowledge of ancient cultures makes it possible for us to glance only briefly at the period of music history which could be called pre-Greek. Most of our information about performing habits comes from the extant art of the period.

There is evidence to support the claim that the Sumerians probably had a highly developed musical culture. Sachs[2] and Galpin[3] devote considerable space in their writings to the music of the Sumerians and their successors, the Babylonians and Assyrians. From the study of bas-reliefs, wall paintings in tombs, and musical instruments of the time, we can almost be sure that singing and some form of conducting were a part of musical performance of the Sumerians and the Egyptians.

In the representation of a Sumerian feast in c. 2700 B.C. which appears below, we have an example of vocal and instrumental music. Note that the musicians at each end of the top row are probably keeping time by clapping their hands.

Sumerian banquet with music and song. From the Royal Standard at Ur; c. 2700 B.C. (The British Museum)

Although there is no direct evidence that the leader of the entertainment at this feast was actually conducting, this is the earliest example which we have that suggests some kind of central control in musical performance.

Galpin supports this hypothesis in his description of the practices of the priests and other liturgists in the religious rites of the Sumerians.

> The musical establishment consisted of liturgists and psalmists, who were charged with the proper conduct of daily services and their ordered chanting. In the great temple of Ningirsu, at Lagash, so splendidly restored and equipped by the king-priest Gudea, c. 2400 B.C., they were under the direction of a special officer, who was responsible for their training: with him was associated another official, who was in charge of the choir.[4]

The research of Sachs and Galpin would seem to leave little doubt that the musical art in the Sumerian civilization was developed to the extent that choral and instrumental performances were under the formal leadership of trained musicians. We can only speculate what methods of direction were used, but it is evident that hand clapping, foot stamping, and possibly head nodding were all present in the relief pictured above.

References to choral performances in Egyptian culture are fairly numerous in the writings of Sachs[5] and Wilkinson.[6] Choral music at a Bacchic festival is described by Wilkinson as follows:

> In the Bacchic festival of Ptolemy Philadelphus, described by Atenaeus, more than 600 musicians were employed in the chorus, among them were 300 performers on the *Kithara*.
>
> Sometimes the harp was placed alone, or as an accompaniment to the voices, and a band of seven or more choristers frequently sang to it a favorite air, beating time with their hands between each stanza.[7]

The waving of hands to which Wilkinson refers was quite refined. The wall relief (shown below) was painted during the 18th Dynasty.

Egyptian wall painting showing musicians at a banquet. Reign of Tuthmasis Ty. (The New York Public Library Picture Collection)

Another example of one who seems to be simultaneously snapping the fingers of both hands and stamping the foot while leading four other musicians would give evidence of some kind of audible time-beating method in Egyptian music.

Egyptian arched harp, lute, double oboe, and lyre. Tomb painting in Thebes;
c. 1420–1411 B.C. (The New York Public Library Picture Collection)

Schünemann has found reference to another type of conducting, a sort of *chironomy*,[8] in the performance of the Vedas in India.

> In the Vedic music the leader of the singing would during the singing of the sacred chant indicate the pitch on the knuckles of the right hand and thereupon strike it with the index finger of the left, a method which might have served as an aid to the memory of the singer.[9]

This type of hand gesture undoubtedly assisted the singer in recalling the direction of the melody. In later performances of early Christian music, similar hand signals served to guide the singer's melodic interpretation, especially in the rhythmically free style of chant. The presence of gestures in early cultures is significant in that they indicate rather conclusively the existence of some kind of central control in primitive choral performances.

The enormous forces to which the Bible refers in the Hebrew temple—

4,000 Levites in musical service—would also hint toward some type of central control. The use of cymbals at most musical events in the Old Testament would lead one to speculate that the cymbal player(s) in the Hebrew temple served a function similar to the hand director, foot stomper, and finger snapper in other cultures. This practice is consistent with the present-day custom in Eastern cultures where one person, usually the player of the rhythmic instrument, establishes the tempo and then brings the performance to a close.

The tradition of the cymbal player-director in the Hebrew temple is described in the Talmud:

> On a sign given by the cymbals, twelve Levites, standing upon the broad steps of the stairway leading from the place of the congregation to the outer court of the priests, playing upon nine lyres, two harps, and one cymbal, began the singing of the Psalm, while the officiating priests poured out the wine offering. Younger Levites played other instruments, but did not sing; while the Levitical boys strengthened the treble part by singing and not playing. The pauses of the Psalm or its divisions, were indicated by blasts of trumpets by priests at the right and left of the cymbalists.

The earliest accounts of time-beating in Greek music indicate that various audible and visible techniques were used to control a choral performance; the most common device being use of the foot. The musical director, or *coryphaeus*,[10] was placed in the middle of the performing group on an elevated and conspicuous location where he could be seen and heard by all. Sachs paints a vivid picture of this audible method of direction:

> . . . the chorus . . . held his men together with the obtrusive voice of the kròupalon (Latin scabellum). This odd contraption was, in the words of the present author, "a kind of thick sandal, tied to the right foot and consisting of a block of wood cut out to form an upper and under board, fastened together at the heel. Each board had a kind of castanet inside. In stamping, the boards with the castanets were clapped together with a sharp cracking sound." The coryphee marked the *thesis*, quite as its name implies, by a noisy downtread, and the *arsis*, by a silent lift. Aristides Quintilianus, indeed, describes the *thesis* as "noise" or *psophos*, and the *arsis*, as "silence" or *eremia*. Other Greeks called the sound of the *thesis* a *krotos* or "rap," and the Romans, *ictus* and *percussiv*.[11]

In addition to foot beating there were other devices employed by the Greek chorus leaders. Finger snapping and the clapping of oyster shells and bones were used to establish audible control of the singers. Wallace informs us that "the foot beat and snap of the fingers is referred to by Quintilian, who says that time is measured mentally and intervals marked by the beat of the foot or fingers."[12] Such evidence would lead us to speculate that when the foot and fingers were used together, the foot probably marked the strong accents (the *thesis*) and the fingers the unaccented part (the *arsis*).

The earliest description of arm and hand gestures for time beating dates from 709 B.C. Murchard, in a translation from ancient Greek tablets, indicates that a central time-beater used some kind of directing stick to control a large group of performers:

> Pherekydes had stationed himself in the center, and had placed himself on a high seat, waving a golden staff, and the players on the flute and cythara were placed in a circle around him. Now when Pherekydes with his golden staff gave the signal, all the art-experienced men began in one and the same time, so that the music resounded afar, even to the sea.[13]

Medieval and Renaissance Practices

The earliest polyphonic music was usually performed by soloists and a conductor per se was not necessary. The chief singer of the professional choir—probably trained at the Roman schola cantorum—was responsible for the musical direction in the church services.

Music at this time consisted either of one line performed with the free rhythm of chant or of the interaction of contrapuntal voices in which a steady motion was dominant. In the free rhythm of chant the motions of the leader were intended to guide the singers and to remind them of the direction of the melody. When the melodic line did not conform to any categorical method of control, these simple gestures were effective because they conveyed the various melodic inflections, the rhythmic freedom, and the overall shape of the performance.

If the music was rhythmically strict and at times very complex, as in the vocal literature of the fourteenth and early fifteenth centuries, the most efficient method of control of the complicated cross rhythms, syncopation, and frequent metric changes was a type of "metronomic conducting," an up-down motion of the hand that indicated the normal pulse without any conscious attempt to convey accents or phrasing. These motions were consistent with the contemporary concept of the *tactus* (English, time or stroke). Sachs informs us that the term *tactus* "appeared for the first time in Ramis de Pareia's *De Musica* (1482)," and denoted a unit of time consisting of a downbeat and upbeat.[14]

In the choral music of the late sixteenth century in which the rhythmic structure was generally less complex and the underlying pulse was usually consistent, a circular motion of the hand was used to guard against destroying the essential independence of each line thereby avoiding a false accent. The importance of an absence of stress in the music of this period is emphasized by Morley in his definition of a *stroke:*

> It is a successive motion of the hand directing the quantity of every note and rest in the song with *equal measure* [italics ours], according to the variety of signs and proportions.[15]

Thus we learn that in the music of the fifteenth and sixteenth centuries the director served a minimal time-beating function. Since most of the music performed was vocal, the lead singer of the professional choir was in charge of the performance. He conducted one of two ways: When directing chant he used hand signals that outlined the shape of the melodic line. In polyphonic music, he established the basic tactus by either silent or audible up-and-down (or circular) motions in which the duration and stress of each gesture were equal. The hand, a long wooden stick, or a roll of paper were used interchangeably by the time-beaters of the period.

The Conductor in the Seventeenth Century

The seventeenth century was marked by a decline in polyphonic composition and an emergence of keyboard instruments as a part of the accompaniment. Interpretative conducting as we know it was not yet a factor in musical performance, and the sixteenth-century practice of directing with some kind of stick, or roll of paper, was replaced in most churches by the keyboard player who directed while playing the harpsichord or organ. In the early Baroque period, harpsichord accompaniment proved effective because small instrumental and choral groups could depend on its distinctive and percussive tone for any necessary unifying direction.

In contrast to the conducting gestures of the sixteenth century, in which the hand remained motionless following each beat, the seventeenth-century time-beater used a more distinctive motion on each beat. The simple, up-down motions of the previous century evolved into a definite beat pattern that moved from one point in the gesture to another, thus creating a situation in which one beat was distinguished from another by the shape of the gesture.

Both audible and silent systems of directing were used by seventeenth-century conductors. Singers at the Pontifical chapel in Rome were so well schooled that they could perform the music of the sacred services without any direction, and thus the gestures were silent. However, when larger choral and instrumental groups were brought together in churches like St. Mark's in Venice, and especially after the introduction of *stile concertato* in the last half of the century, a system of audible time-beating was necessary simply to hold the musical forces together.

It is very difficult for the twentieth-century conductor to conceive that performances in earlier times were probably given amid pounding, stamping, singing, and shouting on the part of the director. This practice, however, continued even into the nineteenth century in isolated places like the Paris Opera.

Since the emphasis during the period was upon the composer who sat at the keyboard and directed his own works, it is clear that the function of the leader in the seventeenth century was simply to control performances from the standpoint of tempo and rhythm. What conducting technique that existed was individual and not codified into accepted practices.

The Conductor in the Eighteenth Century

The eighteenth century brought a number of changes in the style of musical composition and these innovations eventually led, in the nineteenth century, to a new concept of conducting. Choral music began to lose its predominance as the primary compositional idiom. From Italy came the *concerto grosso*, which in time formed the basis of the symphony, the trio and solo sonatas out of which grew the modern sonata form, and the new, free, melodic style of Italian *opera buffa*. Eventually a style emerged in which melody supported by a harmonic structure replaced polyphony, and a contrast to the concept of the primary melodic figure was established. The balancing of main themes against sustaining voices gave an entirely new dimension to the musical texture.

Tempo and rhythm also underwent a fundamental transformation during the eighteenth century: the steady, regular motion made way for an ebb and flow of movement. Thus perspective, the third dimension, slowly came into being, with a foreground, middle ground, and background in the pictorial sense. These developments brought with them the need for balance and counterbalance, weight and counterweight, stress and restraint. As music began to tend away from its former chamber-music give-and-take, it became necessary to have a watchful eye outside the performing group.

The melodic structure of music also underwent a change. The style based on regularly repeated note values reached its climax in the work of Johann Sebastian Bach (1685–1750). At this point melody started developing dramatic suspense. This new mixture of note values, supported by changing harmonies in a three-dimensional sound texture, gave melody a completely new freedom. As melodic elements acquired prominence, a personal expressive value became a part of musical interpretation.

The conductor in the eighteenth century was almost always a composer. As *Kapellmeister* or *Maestro di Capella* in a church or court he was concerned primarily with the performance of his own compositions, and those of his contemporaries which he arranged and altered freely. His main functions in the early eighteenth century were to start the singers and instrumentalists and to keep them together during the performance. The only interpretative function performed was determining the tempo.

The eighteenth century was a period when music was scored for relatively small vocal and instrumental ensembles. The transparency and simplicity of the musical texture allowed the singers and players to hear one another without much difficulty. The structure of the music was such that the necessary freedom existed within the framework of the expected, but without destroying the natural pulse of the music. This combination of factors—the small ensemble, the uniformity and familiarity of style, a rhythmically consistent musical texture, and a melodic structure that did not require elaborate control—created an art with which a group of performers could achieve an acceptable ensemble out of their innate musical sense. With few exceptions, the music's inner momentum could carry the performance from beginning to end. In this type of musical environment the conducting responsibilities of the Kapellmeister were minimal.

Time-beating as a continuous motion of the hand first appeared in the early eighteenth century. Thomas Janowka, a Bohemian organist, published an article on "Tactus" in 1701, in which he described the modern cross-beat pattern as it was used in early opera:

> The means of measuring an ordinary beat is that the first quarter is traced by lowering the hand, the second by carrying it to the left moderately higher, the third by going again to the right a bit higher, and the fourth by raising it to the height of the shoulder. And this is to be understood as concerning the right hand.[16]

By the end of the century the beat patterns in use today were well established among orchestral directors. Still lacking however were the attributes of the interpretative conductor. Conducting was still a metrical rather than an interpretative procedure.

In the eighteenth century dual conductors were employed if there were combined performances of singers and instrumentalists. The audible time-beater was usually in charge of the chorus while the concertmaster, or lead violin, supervised the instrumental parts. The Kapellmeister, who was usually the composer, also directed from the keyboard using gestures which controlled the entire performance.

There are instances later in the century when the leadership is shared by the Kapellmeister and the *Konzertmeister*. The Maestro di Capella or Kapellmeister sat at the keyboard and was responsible for the singers and the overall supervision of the performance, while his assistant, the violin leader, was in charge of the instrumentalists. This was the first hint that the violin leader—the Konzertmeister—would emerge in the nineteenth century as the silent time-beater and interpretative conductor.

For large choral festivals in England and Germany there was often triple control of a performance: the Kapellmeister at the keyboard, the violin leader, and a time-beater to guide the singers. The famous "Grand Commemoration of Handel," which took place in Westminster Abbey in May, 1784, is one of the best eighteenth-century examples of this type of control. The direction of the 525 performers, one of the largest groups ever assembled, was shared by Mr. Bates at the organ, Mr. Cramer, the violin leader, and three time-beating subdirectors. In a contemporary account of this performance, Charles Burney described the function of the subdirectors:

The design of appointing *subdirectors* was to diminish as much as possible, the trouble of the noblemen and gentlemen who had projected the undertaking as well as that of the conductor; diligence and zeal, not only in superintending the business at the doors of admission, but in arranging the performers, and conveying the signals to the several parts of the wide-extended orchestra.[17]

Such a system of dual control was not without its hazards. It was inevitable that sooner or later temperamental directors would demand complete control of the performance. W. T. Parks reported the following anecdote related to the famous Handel commemoration of 1784:

When this great event was in contemplation, two very pompous gentlemen, Dr. Hayes of Oxford and Dr. Miller of Doncaster, came to town to give their gratuitous assistance as conductors by beating time. After several meetings and some bickerings, it was at length agreed that Dr. Hayes (Mus. Dr. Oxon.) should conduct the first act and Dr. Miller the second. With regard to the third, I suppose they were to toss for it. When the time of the performance had arrived, and Mr. Cramer, the leader had just tapt his bow (the signal for being ready), and looked around to catch the eye of the performers, he saw to his astonishment, a tall gigantic figure, with an immense powdered toupee, full dressed with a bag and sword, and a huge roll of parchment in his hand. "Who is that gentleman?" said Mr. Cramer. "Dr. Hayes," was the reply. "What is he going to do?" "To beat time." "Be so kind," said Mr. Cramer, "to tell the gentleman that when he has set down I will begin." The Doctor who had never anticipated such a *set-down* as this took his seat, and Mr. Cramer did begin, and his majesty and all present bore witness to his masterly style of leading the band.[18]

Both the violin and the keyboard instrument began to assume an important role in direction during the eighteenth century. Spitta informs us that the harpsichord was first used in 1660 to hold the vocal and instrumental forces together in Easter performances at Torgau:

. . . it ceased to be the fashion for the conductor to stand, and beat time all through the piece, and in time it became more usual to conduct from the harpsichord, that is now to mark the time with the hand, and now to play the piece with the others, according as it was necessary so that order was preserved, not merely by mute signs, but by audible musical influence. In very large performances alone, with a great number of executants, the older method remained in vogue, because it was indispensible.[19]

This is the method that Bach used in performances at the Nikolaikirche and Thomaskirche from 1732 to 1750. Spitta has also quoted Johann Agricola (1720–1774) and Carl Philipp Emanuel Bach (1714–1788) in their descriptions of J. S. Bach's facility in conducting: "He was very accurate, and in time which he generally took at a lively pace, he was always sure."[20]

C. P. E. Bach, writing in his *Versuch*, articulated the many reasons why the Kapellmeister should direct from the keyboard:

> The keyboard, entrusted by our fathers with full command, is in the best position to assist not only the other bass instruments, but the entire ensemble in maintaining a uniform pace. . . . The tone of the keyboard, correctly placed, stands in the center of the ensemble and can be heard clearly by all. . . . It is easy to make minor changes of tempo.[21]

In fact, a performance of eighteenth-century music without the support of the keyboard continuo—except, of course, in certain liturgical settings like the Pontifical chapel in Rome—was almost unthinkable. C. P. E. Bach makes this point emphatically:

> The emptiness of a performance without this accompanying instrument is, unfortunately, made apparent to us far too often. . . . No piece can be well performed without some form of keyboard accompaniment. Even in heavily scored works, such as operas performed out of doors, where no one would think that the harpsichord could be heard, its absence can certainly be felt.[22]

With the elimination of the continuo in works of the late eighteenth century, the violin-conductor soon emerged as the key musical leader of orchestral concerts. And, while the organist still maintained control over choral performances in churches, as well as those not involving orchestral forces, the violin-leader established a silent conducting style much like one would find today in

European restaurants in which an orchestra plays for dining entertainment. It is thus not surprising that the early nineteenth-century conductors, like Spohr, were string players.

The Conductor in the Nineteenth Century

By the nineteenth century, music, with its subtleties, its treatment of personal and philosophical matter, and its vast vocal and instrumental forces, was removed from the objective chamber-music style of earlier periods. The expansion of form, the new freedom of melody, and a rhythmic structure that established a need for balance and counterbalance created a music texture which required interpretation by a force outside the ensemble. The interpreter thus emerged as a third figure in a musical environment previously shared by only the composer and the performer.

Because composers were not including a keyboard part in the score, the responsibility for direction and control rested with the concertmaster, except, of course, in choral music where the organist continued to direct from the console. Since the violin bow was too delicate to beat on the music stand, a silent conducting technique returned to ensemble performance.

The technique of the conductor also became a serious concern of writers in the nineteenth century. Hector Berlioz (1803–1869) was one of the first conductors to codify the conducting practices of the period and to develop a systematic approach to the teaching of conducting.

The nineteenth century also brought a divergence of opinion over the concept of *rubato* conducting. The idea that modifications of tempo within a given metronome marking were necessary to a "living rendering" of the music was emphasized by Richard Wagner (1813–1883). Felix Mendelssohn (1809–1847) representing the opposite viewpoint, believed in absolute purism in interpretation. In spite of the romantic nature of his compositions, Mendelssohn respected classical form and its interpretative principles. Wagner, who believed that the conductor not only had the right but the clear duty to add his intuition in a performance, recommended tempo modification within a movement or section and based this practice on the doctrine of *Affektenlehre*.

Although the two points of view were diametrically opposed to each other, the controversy which surrounded this aspect of musical interpretation significantly influenced conducting practices in the nineteenth and twentieth centuries.

Since each view was carried too far, the end result was a controlled rubato that became a factor in the development of the virtuoso conductor of the twentieth century.

The Conductor in the Twentieth Century

The conductor in the twentieth century has emerged as a virtuoso in his own right. The demands which the composer has placed upon the conductor of contemporary music have required a program of extensive training. The stop watch, the electronic tape, and the percussion battery have added an entirely new dimension to the necessary skills and required knowledge of the conductor.

An examination of contemporary scores reveals an increased use of many of the composition devices which have been developing during the past century: negation of the bar line, negation of the beat, polymetrics, distintegration of metrical regularity, continually changing time signatures, free rhythms based on speech patterns, and various attempts to make rhythm look like it sounds. These devices have contributed to the emerging indispensable role of the conductor in the twentieth century.

THE REQUIREMENTS OF A GOOD CONDUCTOR

One of the most important elements necessary for a healthy experience for every choral singer is the well-trained, competent conductor. The choral conductor should be, first of all, a sound musician, schooled in the traditional disciplines of the orchestral conductor, but also trained as a specialist in the choral field in addition to his basic musical education. Choral music is unique: it is an activity unlike any other in the arts, or even in music itself for that matter. As the leader of a communicative-educational experience, the choral conductor must be trained as a facilitator—one who is able to create and control a special kind of learning environment and evoke an empathic response from the participants in the choral experience.

Like any good conductor, the choral specialist must possess certain personal characteristics of leadership as neatness and personality and be a competent, extemporary verbalizer. He should be well-read, well-rounded, and exposed to and interested in a variety of nonmusical disciplines. Since a stable psychological makeup is basic to any leadership role, the choral conductor must also learn about group dynamics and the psychology of working with people by observing master conductors. Especially important is a dramatic ability, indispensable not only because it enables the conductor to communicate the mood and style of a musical work, but also because it allows him to assist the singers vocally through empathic facial expressions and appropriate body gestures. Equally important is an intense commitment to people—a commitment much more vital than one at first might think necessary. There are two basic reasons for this: First, the choral conductor deals with people who *are* the instruments. As singers grow under the care of the dedicated and competent conductor, they develop as total physical and musical personalities. A true commitment to the music itself is thus impossible and inseparable from a commitment to the singers, to their growth both individually and corporately. Secondly, the choral conductor deals almost exclusively with participants whose training and overall musical exposure are for the most part on a nonprofessional level. Without a strong commitment to the worth and potential of the singers under his leadership, the love, patience, and faith that are so necessary in dealing with amateur choral singers often are missing in the choral conductor, to the consequent detriment of both the singers and the music itself.

The choral conductor must also be a competent educator. If real learning is to take place in the choral rehearsal, regardless of level, the choral specialist must be able to teach. A highly developed sense of pacing, timing, and delivery are essential elements in the coherent and creative rehearsal. The similarities between good lesson planning and classroom discipline and good rehearsal technique are obvious. Since much of the choral conductor's career will be spent working with nonprofessionals, the successful choral specialist must be able to communicate with singers at any level without condescension. Thus training the conductor as an educator helps to develop this self-serving facet of musical leadership—the ability to diagnose the proper level of expectation for a particular group of singers will contribute significantly to the impact of the choral experience.

The choral conductor must be thoroughly competent in the elements of basic musicianship—theory, harmony, sight-singing, music history, and literature—and demonstrate this knowledge in his score preparation and rehearsal manner. Equally essential is a good ear and a sensitivity to musical style as expressed through an understanding of proper performance practices applied in the musical literature entrusted to him. The conductor should also be responsive to the demands of tempo—its determination, establishment and maintenance—as well as to the accuracy of rhythm, both internal and external, as manifested in the choral results of his direction. He must be especially strong in communicating theoretical concepts and conclusions of pitch, rhythm, and dynamics to the nonprofessional singer in a concise and complete manner.

Karl Gehrkens, a twentieth-century writer, has spoken of the necessity for a conductor to be able to transmit the subjective experience of music making to the ensemble:

> . . . the conductor must have general musicianship, a specific and detailed knowledge of the composition he is conducting; he must possess not only the ability to understand and feel many different kinds of music but the power to express each one so vividly, so dynamically that he can lift the performers to emotional states amounting to exaltation.[23]

Often overlooked but absolutely necessary are the vocal requirements of the choral conductor. In response to the unity of the singing instrument with the individual personality, the conductor must be one with his choir, both in mind and in body. The conductor must possess a thorough and practical knowledge of vocal production and pedagogy, and must be able to reinforce his verbal instructions in a vocally competent manner. Perhaps the most important reason for this vocal understanding is that choral music is so intimately wrapped up in sound: vocal sound, choral sound. Thus any conductor, while basically involved with interpreting the intentions of the composer, is nevertheless equally concerned with the total means of musical expression. The corporate sound—the choral *tone*—becomes the tool with which the conductor builds phrases along the outlines suggested by the harmonic, melodic, and formal structure of the music. A choral conductor who is thus unable to produce, control, and shape the sound (or sounds) he requires from his singers will ultimately be unable to obtain optimum musical results.

The choral conductor bears one other important responsibility: the vocal health of every singer in the choral ensemble. This is especially true in church, community, and school situations, where the only vocal encounter is the weekly rehearsal and performance. This responsibility is especially present when there are daily rehearsals. Although a singer may study voice privately on a weekly basis, that person is still under the care of the choral conductor anywhere from two to five hours each week. Thus, it is possible that the choral conductor may exert three to five times the influence upon the student that the private teacher may have.

Even the eighteenth-century Kapellmeister was expected to understand the voice. The description of a Kapellmeister by the violinist and author Heinrich Christoph Koch (1749–1816) underscores the importance of vocal training for every choral conductor:

> . . . at the same time he [the Kapellmeister] has to be a singer himself, not so much as far as a beautiful voice is concerned, but rather with regard to correct and good singing. He also has to know exactly the nature and quality of all the instruments used in the orchestra and especially their effect when used alone or in combinations.[24]

The importance of the choral rehearsal as the class voice lesson thus becomes apparent, because a conductor without a firm knowledge of the voice and a well-developed vocal technique may fail to perform his duties adequately, and also may run the additional risk of doing vocal harm to his singers. The satisfying choral experience is dependent upon the vocal freedom of every singer. In essence, while choral singing is a corporate expression, it is nonetheless essentially an individual affair. The excellence of any choir rests upon the ability of each singer to cope with the technical demands of the music. When the singer is totally dependent upon the choral rehearsal for his or her vocal growth, it is obvious that the vocally prepared conductor is not only a positive force in the prevention of bad vocal habits, but with proper training is able to diagnose, correct, and continually improve the vocalism of his choral group, both individually and collectively. The result is a growth experience for everyone concerned.

THE TRAINING OF THE CHORAL CONDUCTOR

Hector Berlioz set a very high standard for conductors when he wrote in 1844:

> The conductor should *see* and *hear*; he should be *active* and *vigorous*, should know the *composition* and the *nature* and *compass* of instruments, should be able to *read* the score, and possess other almost indefinable gifts, without which an invisible line cannot establish itself between him and those he directs.[25]

From this quote it is clear that conducting is a many-sided art, and therefore any program of training must possess breadth as well as depth.

The conductor bears a large responsibility: interpreting the intentions of the composer, guiding the performance musically, training the chorus in rehearsal, delineating the musical style, and finally shaping the public performance so that the music communicates its message to the audience.

In all the arts except music the creator's work, once completed, retains its essential unity independent of any interpreter. The meaning of a painting or sculpture, the message of a play, the shape of a building is at once apparent to the viewer. When we return to it, we find it essentially unchanged in form and structure. This is not the case with music, however. The notes on the page are meaningless to all but the trained musician until they are transformed into sound.

In a choral performance, two intermediaries are necessary before the genius of the composer finds its fulfillment in the ear of the listener: the performer (the choral singer) and the interpreter (the conductor). Thus the conductor has a serious problem. The quality of his interpretation is dependent upon the performing ability of his singers. He must draw from them the sounds which his inner ear requires. The choral group is his intermediary in the projection of his concept of the technical, intellectual, and emotional demands of the music to the audience. He must therefore be able to communicate his ideas to the singers, influence them by drawing out an empathic response, and lead them in such a manner that they will perform as he wishes.

How can a program of training be developed to prepare choral conductors to get the most out of their singers? What are the elements of such a program? What makes one conductor great, another only adequate, a third poor, even though the three may be similarly trained and beat time in much the same manner? Why is one performance of a work exciting, even monumental, while another is dull and lackadaisical, although both performances consist of the same notes?

For some reason there has developed a polarization among those who have been charged with the training of the choral conductor. Some hold that musicianship training is the most important element in the training of a conductor: if the musicianship is there, everything else will fall into place. There is another approach that focuses the training of the choral specialist on the production of choral tone at the sacrifice of musicianship. A third group leans toward scholarship as the sine qua non of choral preparation and virtually ignores the vocal development.

Obviously *all three* elements *are essential* if the choral conductor is to be a thoroughly prepared professional. Sound musicianship is the basis of all successful music making; yet, if the individual singer is not able to cope vocally with the demands of the music, the musicianship of the conductor will be crippled in the performance. For a performance to be stylistically correct, the principles of style and performance practice in all periods of music literature must be understood and applied.

While the methods, techniques, and approaches expounded by the teachers of conducting probably have as many variations as there are students, the training of the complete choral conductor must include certain basic skills: a thorough understanding of vocal production as it applies to the choral singer; a sound program of basic musicianship training; and a comprehensive grasp of those principles of style that lead to the proper performance for choral literature of all periods.

The following recommendations reinforce these observations and serve to highlight further areas of study:

1. The training of the choral specialist must emphasize a vocal approach to choral conducting. Like any other craftsman, the choral conductor should possess a thorough knowledge of the mechanics of his craft. An orchestral conductor must understand the nature of orchestral instruments; likewise, the choral specialist must know and understand the instruments of his ensemble—the individual voices of his singers. As an integral part of his study he should receive intensive, personalized vocal training and learn to diagnose and correct vocal problems in other singers. He must be exposed to a systematic approach to singing diction in several languages. In short, the choral specialist must become equipped to fulfill the vocal responsibilities of the singers entrusted to his care.

2. The training of the choral specialist must provide the best musical education possible. Thorough musicianship training in sight-singing, keyboard skills, and analysis must be combined with a comprehensive understanding of music history and literature. The musicianship training must be of sufficient depth to allow the choral conductor to make discriminating musical judgments.

3. The training of the choral specialist must emphasize the service dimension of choral performance: every conductor must learn the importance of teaching and relating to others. Only those persons whose personal philosophy and lifestyle exhibit a concern for and a commitment to others should be encouraged to pursue a career in choral music.

4. The training of the choral specialist must include intensive study in musical styles and their relationship to the performance practices of all periods of music literature. This necessarily includes a continuing effort throughout one's career to become knowledgeable of recent developments and discoveries.

5. The training of the choral specialist must provide varied opportunities to learn repertoire as well as gain practical teaching experience. A close coordination should be maintained between conducting classes and internship opportunities.

6. The training of the choral specialist must provide positive stimulation for the nonmusical interests of the student: it should at the very least serve as a stimulus to shape an inquisitive mind about a number of topics outside the field of music. The training program should excite and expose the young musician to the world into which he will project his musical life.

7. The training of the choral specialist must provide a learning environment which will allow the young conductor to become thoroughly familiar with both the aesthetic and historical perspectives of the choral experience. He should be challenged continually to search for the best available new ideas in choral singing and conducting. He should develop a personal philosophy about vocal production and its relationship to choral singing. Most importantly, he should be involved in daily music-making experiences, preferably in one or more choral groups, but in instrumental ensembles as well, if this is possible. Regular participation in the experience of choral singing will give the young conductor the opportunity to experience on a physical-personal level the choral experience under the direction of master conductors, noting how they fulfill their dual responsibility toward music and musicians.

NOTES

1. Carl Bamberger, ed., *The Conductor's Art* (New York: McGraw-Hill Book Company, 1965), p. 3.

2. Curt Sachs, *The Rise of Music in the Ancient World East and West* (New York: W. W. Norton and Company, Inc., 1943), p. 58.

3. Francis W. Galpin, *The Music of the Sumerians and Their Immediate Successors the Babylonians and Assyrians* (New York: Macmillan, 1937), pp. 62–63.

4. Ibid., p. 53.

5. Curt Sachs, *Die Musikinstrumente das alten Ägyptians* (Berlin: Karl Curtius, 1921), p. 16.

6. Sir John Gardner Wilkinson, *The Manners and Customs of the Ancient Egyptians.* Revised by Samuel Birch (Boston: S. M. Cassino and Co., 1883).

7. Ibid., pp. 441–442.

8. A type of choral directing in which hand motions were used to indicate the progress of the melody.

9. Georg Schünemann, *Geschichte des Dirigierens* (Leipzig: Breitkopf and Härtel, 1913), p. 2.

10. *Croyphaeus* means chorus leader.

11. Curt Sachs, *Rhythm and Tempo* (New York: W. W. Norton and Company, Inc., 1953), pp. 140–141.

12. William Wallace, "The Conductor and His Fore-Runners," *Musical Times* (Jan.–Dec., 1923): 609.

13. Professor Murchard, "Ancient Greek Tablets," *Harmonicon*, 3 (April–May, 1825): 76.

14. Curt Sachs, *Rhythm and Tempo* (New York: W. W. Norton and Company, 1953), p. 216.

15. Thomas Morley, *A Plain and Easy Introduction to Practical Music (1597)*, edited and annotated by R. Alec Harman (New York: W. W. Norton and Company, 1948), p. 19.

16. Hugo Löbmann, *Zur Geschichte das Taktierens und Dirigierens* (Dusseldorf: Schwann, 1913), pp. 81–83.

17. Charles Burney, *An Account of the Musical Performance in Westminster Abbey and the Pantheon, in Commemoration of Handel.* Quote taken from Clyde William Holsinger, "A History of Choral Conducting" (Ph.D. diss., Northwestern University, 1954), p. 240.

18. W. T. Parks, *Musical Memoirs*, Vol. I (London: Colburn and Bentley, 1830), pp. 39–40.

19. Phillip Spitta, *Johann Sebastian Bach*, translated by Bell and Maitland. Vol. II. (London: Novello and Co., 1899), p. 327.

20. Ibid., p. 329.

21. Carl Philipp Emanuel Bach, *Essay on the True Art of Playing Keyboard Instruments*, translated and edited by W. J. Mitchell (New York: W. W. Norton and Company, 1949), pp. 34–35.

22. Ibid.

23. Karl Gehrkens, "The Psychological Basis of Conducting," *Musical Quarterly*, 21 (1935): 437.

24. Heinrich Christoph Koch, *Musiklexikon* (Frankfurt am Main: August Herman dem Jungern, 1802), *Kapellmeister*.

25. Hector Berlioz, *A Treatise on Modern Instrumentation and Orchestration*, translated by Mary Clarke (London: Novello, Ewer and Co., 1856), p. 245.

Chapter Two

RECOMMENDED READING LIST

Bakaleinikoff, Vladimir. *Elementary Rules of Conducting*. New York: Boosey, Hawkes, Belwin, Inc., 1938. A short treatise which is required reading for every conductor.

Berlioz, Hector. *A Treatise Upon Modern Instrumentation and Orchestration.* Translated by Mary Cowden Clarke. London: Novello, Ewer, and Co., 1858. While primarily concerned with orchestral instruments and their proper use in scoring, the role of the conductor is discussed at some length in a special section of the treatise.

Ehmann, Wilhelm. *Choral Directing.* Translated by George D. Wiebe. Minneapolis: Augsburg Publishing House, 1968. One of the best-known and most practical books on choral conducting.

Gehrkens, Karl Wilson. *Essentials in Conducting.* Boston: Oliver Ditson Co., 1919. An early book on conducting by a pioneer music educator. It is especially helpful in the area of practical suggestions.

Wagner, Richard. *On Conducting.* Translated by Edward Dannreuther. London: W. Reeves, 1887. A good resource on the late-nineteenth-century view of the conductor's role in musical interpretation.

Chapter Three

The Individual Singer and
the Choral Experience

Since singing is so good a thing, I wish that all men
would learn to sing.—WILLIAM BYRD, 1588[1]

THE CHORAL EXPERIENCE offers many and varied benefits to the individual singer.
For some, it provides a forum for involvement and an opportunity for personal
commitment. Others enjoy the social aspects of choral singing: attracted to people
of similar musical taste, they enjoy sharing with them and with the listeners their
own musical expression of the composer's intentions. Choral singing is also a
satisfying activity, a meaningful use of one's time and energy. The intense feeling
of community—a special esprit de corps—fostered by an exciting conductor creates a powerful bond of fellowship that is attractive to the individual participant
in the choral experience.

There are a great many people who sing in a choir for cultural and aesthetic
pleasure and for personal growth. Many are attracted by the literature itself, and
others sing for the emotional and psychic fulfillment that comes through contact
with basic human emotions communicated in a new and transcendent manner.
Still others participate in choral singing because they regard the experience as an
offering of worship to their Creator.

Regardless of the initial motivation, most choral singers return again and
again as participants in this musical act of recreation. In a technological society,
persons seldom, if ever, participate in truly creative endeavors. There is often little
relation between what a person does and who that person is: and only rarely does

one purchase the fruits of his labor. This situation is typical of the spiritual divorce that turns contemporary men and women into consumers and spectators.

Thus it is not difficult to understand why choral singing is so popular with participants of all ages: no other musical activity accessible to the nonprofessional offers the promise of such direct involvement with the creation of beauty; no other can stimulate such a rebirth of mystery and wonder; no other can offer the individual the same liberation of the human spirit that results from the re-creative activity we call the choral experience.

The key to a satisfying choral experience for the individual singer is a conductor who can create a performing environment in which each singer can realize his or her inherent vocal potential. This experience is possible when the conductor understands the principles of vocal production and is able to apply this knowledge in the rehearsal and performance of choral literature. The elements of vocal production as they relate to the development of the individual choral singer are theoretical and intended for use as background information for both the choral conductor and singer.

THE VOCAL MECHANISM

The human body is composed of a wonderful collection of interrelated structures and organs, which are composed of many materials and utilized for various life-supporting purposes. The organs which are used in vocal production are part of the respiratory tract: the larynx, pharynx, mouth, tongue, jaw, lips, and teeth, together with the complex muscular organization binding them together as a unit (see diagram 1). When viewed conceptually, the entire skeletal framework of the

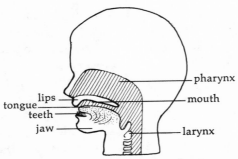

1. Organs of the vocal mechanism

2. Larynx or voice box

individual singer, with its locomotor and nervous systems, may be considered part of the vocal mechanism. If conceived in a more limited sense, the vocal instrument may accurately be understood to be the larynx, because it is here that vocal sound originates.

One of the exciting things about choral singing is that it touches directly on the entire life of the individual singer. From birth to death we are vocal, rhythmic creatures: our rhythms are synonymous with nature's rhythms—the heartbeat, the seasons, the tides, the weather. We celebrate our lives vocally—we laugh, cry, shout, sing. We are provided with a natural means of communicating our spiritual state. Our physical bodies cultivate life at the same time that they sustain art.

No other bodily instrument has the organic location of our voices, placed as they are at the center of the life-sustaining functions of respiration and digestion. No other musical activity embraces the body directly and completely in the expression of psychic reaction to mood. Ehmann graphically relates this concept to the individual and the choral experience when he writes: "through music-making, the body is awakened and supported in its original proportions; its parts are harmoniously related to each other, and . . . all mental and physical inhibitions are dissolved."[2] The voice is indeed the unique manifestation of our total individual personality, and its use in choral singing is very much a natural expression of man's unique role in contemporary culture.

Vocal tone—as well as the tone of speech—is produced in the larynx. The larynx, or voice box as it is often called, is situated between the back of the mouth cavity and the top of the trachea or windpipe (see diagram 2). Placed as it is in this strategic position, the larynx forms the upper part of the tube of communication between the mouth and the lungs. Because of its location it opens directly into the postnasal, the nasal, and the oral pharynx, the primary cavities of resonation for the sound vibrations that are produced in the larynx. When viewed from above, the larynx is somewhat triangular in shape (see diagram 3). Its front angle, sometimes called the Adam's apple, can be seen in the front of the throat of the male singer.

Within the larynx are situated the vocal cords, two narrow elastic fibrous bands enclosed in folds of mucous membrane (the lining tissue of the larynx) which serve as the vibrator in the production of vocal sound. The vocal cords lie horizontally within the larynx, running from the front to the rear of the lower throat area. The front ends of the cords are virtually stationary as they are at-

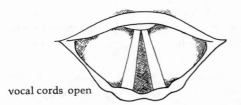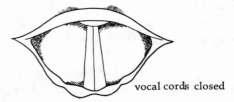

vocal cords open   vocal cords closed

3. Triangular shape of the larynx

tached close to one another just behind the Adam's apple. The back ends are fixed
to two movable cartilages, which by the action of two sets of small muscles can be
rotated inward and outward or pulled backward or forward. Because the vocal
cords are flexible, they can be made to vibrate by directing air against them. It is
this action which establishes pitch. Because the larynx in the adult male is larger,
the larynx cavity larger, the thyroid cartilage more pronounced, and the vocal cords
longer and thicker, the vocal sound produced is lower in pitch than in the voices of
the female and the child.

The relative position of the vocal cords at any given time is determined by
the response of the muscles of the larynx and pharynx as they adjust to a mental
concept composed of pitch, intensity, and the vowel. This mental concept, which
in choral singing is the result of a skillful rehearsal technique on the part of the
conductor, is the key to a free and natural use of the vocal mechanism.

These adjustments in the vocal cords as the result of a mental concept of
correct tone production cannot be seen except by the use of special mirrors. If you
were to look into the throat, you would see two narrow muscular folds with a
small opening, called the *glottis*, between them. In its natural state of rest the
glottis is V-shaped, with the point of the triangle pointing forward. When the
cartilages at the back of the cords are rotated inward, the cords are drawn together. This is the proper position for tone production. If the muscles are rotated
in an outward direction, the cords are drawn apart—the V-shape is opened out—
and the vocal cords are then in a position for inhaling and exhaling. When the
cartilages are pulled forward, the vocal cords are relaxed; when they are pulled
back, the cords are tightened in their length and are then ready for vocalization.

The resonators in vocal production are the pharynx, mouth, nasal cavities,
and the sinuses or air cavities of the face and head (see diagram 4). There are some
writers who believe that the chest is also a vocal resonator of importance, but to
what extent has not yet been proven convincingly. Because some of the resonance
cavities are adjustable, skillful positioning through carefully chosen vocal exer-

cises will result in a fully resonant vocal tone. When the vocal mechanism is working to its fullest potential (i.e., when the positioning of the vowel is ideal), the tone is acoustically reinforced, a condition which adds not only volume to the voice but gives it a feeling of freedom and natural beauty as well.

Since the size and shape of the resonance cavities are natural endowments and thus determined by genetic combinations, vocal potential is actually predetermined in each human being. For this reason each individual singer possesses a distinctive vocal sound in keeping with other physical endowments and mental concepts.

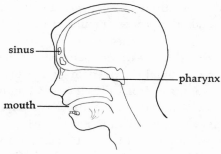

4. Primary cavities of resonation: postnasal, nasal, and oral pharynx

Of special importance to a fuller understanding of the principles of vocal production is the relationship that exists between the vocal cords (together with their surrounding resonators) and the respiratory tract, which are, in effect, one and the same and must be conceived as such.

The organs of the voice serve as an integral part of the respiratory tract. For example, the vocal cords fulfill a number of life-sustaining functions as part of the respiratory system. Like many of the body's organs, they are capable of efficiently performing a variety of tasks in everyday life although their primary responsibility is to allow the transfer of air to and from the lungs through a breath cycle. It is little wonder that the vocal mechanism possesses the basic elements common to most instruments capable of producing sound. The voice is an amazing phenomenon. In the words of Portnoy, "any other instrument can only be inferior, for the human voice is the natural instrument of God's own creation, man."[3]

THE BREATHING MECHANISM

No other aspect of the study of singing has received more attention and caused more controversy than breathing and breath control. A survey of some of the methods or so-called schools of vocal pedagogy will quickly show the disagreement among authorities regarding the importance as well as the method of this phase of vocal development. For example, there are those who believe that establishing a correct breathing technique is the first and basic step to good singing. Another group insists that breathing is relatively unimportant; that the emotional set of the singer will provide the proper amount of breath. The truth lies possibly somewhere in between these two extremes.

Most choral singers spend years of their lives in high school, church, and community choirs striving to obtain a freedom of the breathing mechanism that will lead to comfortable vocalism. Ironically, it is something that few choral singers actually achieve. Those who have it seem to have acquired it naturally; those who work hardest to achieve it often find the goal elusive. Yet, a correct use of the breathing mechanism is essential for the artistic performance of choral music because breathing and breath control are part of the basic technical equipment of every accomplished choral singer.

In the most basic sense the breathing act consists of two obvious and relatively simple actions: the transferring of air from outside the body to the lungs and the reverse process of returning the inhaled air to the exterior. Breath enters the body by the mouth or nose,[4] passes through the larynx in the neck, proceeds down into the trachea and bronchial tubes, and finally reaches the lungs in the thoracic cavity. It is exhaled by the reverse process (diagram 5 illustrates this activity).

Why do we breathe? Regardless of the intended purpose—singing, speaking, or running the mile—we breathe essentially for one reason: to remove carbon dioxide and other wastes from the blood and to replace them with oxygen. The breathing act, which is essentially the same in all physical activities, is controlled by nerves originating in the *medulla oblongata* at the base of the brain. This center sends nerve impulses to the diaphragm and intercostal muscles, causing them to contract, and it is this action, triggered by a certain minimum level of oxygen in the blood, that initiates the process.

The result of these muscular contractions is a lowering of the breath pres-

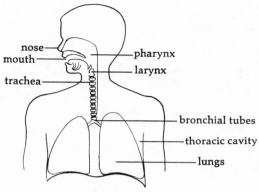

nose — pharynx
mouth — larynx
trachea —

bronchial tubes
thoracic cavity
lungs

5. Breathing mechanism

sure within the lungs, causing the breath to enter the body. It is important to note that this is essentially an involuntary action, much like the flowing of water into an empty glass. It is possible, of course, to stop inhalation momentarily and turn "blue in the face," but ultimately the body rebels and normal breathing must resume.

The complete breathing cycle consists of two separate but related acts: inspiration (the taking of air) and expiration (the expulsion of air). Since a number of muscles are involved in the process, it is important for the choral conductor to know which muscles participate and to understand how they work.

Inspiration

Like all muscles of the body the muscles of inspiration are paired into agonist and antagonist groups: the rib raisers and the rib depressors. The primary rib raisers are the *diaphragm* and the *intercostals*. These muscles lift the ribs during inspiration and suspend the ribs during expiration. The rib depressors, of which the *quantus lumborum* is the most important, exert a downward pull on the rib cage, moving the lower border of the cage out and up during the breath cycle. In this process, the diaphragm is the key muscle.

The diaphragm is a band of tissue forming an almost complete partition between the thorax and the abdomen and is double-domed in shape, somewhat like an inverted basin (see diagram 6). The sides of the dome are composed of muscular tissue and are attached around the lower circumference of the thorax—

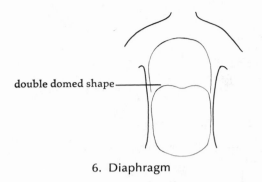

6. Diaphragm

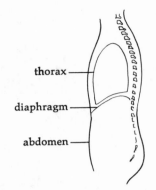

7. Diaphragm as floor of thorax
and roof of abdomen

to the lower ribs and the cartilages on either side, to the lower part of the sternum in front, and to the lumbar vertebrae behind. The upper central part of the dome is tendenous and is not attached to any bone structure. The pericardium (the sac containing the heart) is attached to the upper surface of the central tendon and thereby helps to maintain the shape of the dome. The diaphragm thus forms the floor of the thorax and the roof of the abdomen (see diagram 7).

Although the diaphragm may appear at first glance to be a continuous sheet of muscle and tendon, it actually is made up of two separate muscles: one muscle rises at the back from the first three lumbar vertebrae and is connected to the central tendon; the other muscle rises from the central tendon and is connected to the lower six ribs and cartilages and the lower part of the sternum. When the first contracts, under involuntary nerve impulses from the brain, it pulls down the top of the dome; when the second is activated it pulls up the sides of the dome and flattens out the arch of the diaphragm. The combination of the action of these two muscles is to lower the floor of the thorax, stretching the lungs and resulting in the intake of air.

The intercostal muscles occupy the spaces between the rib-arches. In each space there are two muscles, one internal and the other external. And, although anatomists still disagree over the voluntary or involuntary nature of these muscles, they do serve an important function during inspiration by expanding the upper rib cavity during the breath cycle.

The *quadratus lumborum*, the other important muscle in inspiration, rises from the back part of the crest of the hipbone and from the lower lumbar vertebrae. The muscle fibers proceed upward to the inner half of the lower part of the last rib and to the upper lumbar vertebrae. While only a small portion of this muscle is used in inhaling, it assists in establishing the critical point of suspension between inspiration and expiration.

In summary, the diaphragm is attached to the lower rib-arches, sternum, and vertebral column, and is shaped like an inverted basin, the highest part of which is tendon and the sides muscle. As a functioning organ in the process of inspiration, the diaphragm consists of two separate muscles: the vertebral muscles, attached to the lumbar vertebrae, and the costal or rib muscle, which is attached to the rib-arches and sternum.

When inspiration takes place, the vertebral muscles come into action and pull the top of the diaphragm dome downward and forward, and the whole dome descends (see diagram 8). The resultant lowering of the floor of the chest brings an

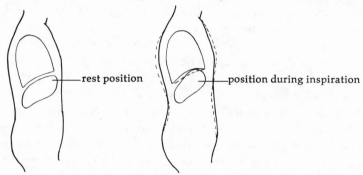

8. Action of diaphragm in breathing

increase in the chest diameter from top to bottom. The lungs, which then adjust to the upper surface of the diaphragm, follow its movements and also increase in vertical diameter. This expansion causes the spaces within the air sacs to expand and the pressure within them to become lower than the outside air. To equalize this pressure, air rushes into the lungs and this results in the taking of a breath. The expansion of the lungs does not take place equally throughout but is probably confined largely to the lower portion.

When the diaphragm descends during inspiration, it causes a slight forward and downward protrusion of all the organs which lie below it. Because the back of the abdomen and the upper parts of its side are confined by the bone structure, the greater amount of expansion takes place in the front and sides. With the pronounced forward and lateral expansion of the abdomen, which continues until a comfortably taut feeling occurs, the diaphragm reaches its normal limit of expansion. This is the extent of diaphragmatic expansion that is necessary for most physical activity of a healthy person. It is perfectly adequate for ordinary work and should be more than sufficient for the purpose of choral singing.

Expiration

Since artistic choral singing is dependent upon the ultimate control of the breathing mechanism, it is the strength and control of the abdominal muscles that give the singer this ability. The physical action during the taking of a breath, which is more mental than physical, may be adequate, but since it is the inspired air with which a choral singer actually works in the performance of choral literature, a physical control during expiration is critical. The greater the control, the easier vocal work becomes: the nuance of dynamics, the power of attack, and the power or emphasis and sonority all depend upon the control of the breath. This is especially true in very quiet singing and where an intensity of the melodic line is required.

Because tone production in singing is the result of the pressure of air forced by the abdominal muscles through the vocal cords, the manner of exhaling air thus becomes of great importance in choral singing. Even after singing an extremely long musical phrase in one breath, there is always some amount of air, called residual air, remaining in the lungs, and no physical effort of exhalation can expel more than a portion of it.

Consequently, as long as the contraction of the muscles of the diaphragm is maintained, the inspired air will remain in the lungs. But the moment the muscles are relaxed, normal expiration begins. This phenomenon is caused by three factors: the return of the diaphragm to its dome-shaped position of inaction; the recoil of the abdominal wall which pushes back the abdominal organs to their previous position; and the return of the chest walls and bone structure to their position prior to inhalation. It is this action which creates the column of air that leads to the vibration of the vocal cords.

As a result of these physical movements, and without any special muscular effort, the size of the chest is reduced by just the amount of its expansion, the pressure of the air in the lungs is then increased above that of the atmosphere, and, as a result, air is expelled from the chest. No additional muscular effort is necessary for the purposes of normal breathing. However, since it is apparent that the breath is expelled at a very slight pressure that is just sufficient to carry it from the lungs, in such physical activities as coughing, sneezing, sobbing, or blowing, more air pressure is required. Likewise, when the voice is used for expressive choral singing, increased air pressure must be generated.

It is here that the abdominal muscles come into play and the phenomenon of breath support is created. A careful analysis of the physical action will show that in activities such as coughing the effect of contracting the abdominal muscles is a drawing in of the abdominal wall. This is easily simulated by holding the four fingers of the hand against the soft spot below the breastbone while clearing the throat or shouting "hey." The result of this action is that the abdominal organs are pushed up against the diaphragm, an activity that is just the reverse of the action that takes place during inspiration.

One further observation should be made at this point. It is important to realize that the action of the abdominal muscles, while essential, is not the whole story. Ultimate control in singing is the result of coordinating the action of many more groups of muscles, both thoracic and abdominal. It is this coordinated muscular action that the singer must strive to master. It is this synthesized control that is one mark of the accomplished choral singer.

THE PRODUCTION OF VOCAL SOUND

The human voice possesses certain basic properties which are characteristic of all sounds: *intensity* or loudness, *timbre* or quality, and *pitch*. The intensity of a vocal sound depends on the amplitude of the vibrations of the vocal cords, which in turn depend on the force of the column of air that moves past them. Timbre is determined by the number and intensity of the overtones or harmonics, which is the result of the shape and size of the resonating chambers. Pitch is the result of the length, tension, and thickness of the vocal cords, factors which affect the frequency of the vibrations of the cords. Because women and children have shorter vocal cords than men, their voices are more highly pitched.

There are three basic elements that are common to most musical instruments that are capable of producing sounds: a *vibrator*, which sets the air particles in motion and thus becomes the source of the sound; a *generator*, the force which sets the vibrator in motion; and a *resonator* (one or more) or amplifier, which reinforces or multiplies the original vibrations. Since the human voice is similar in its mechanism to most tone-producing instruments, it is helpful in the understanding of the production of vocal sound to discuss how sound is produced in other instruments.

The Percussion Family. The timpani is perhaps the most familiar orchestral example of the percussion family. The skin of the drumhead is the vibrator, the stick wielded by the player is the generator, and the body of the timpani is the resonator.

The String Family. The violin is typical of this type of instrument. In a stringed instrument the string is the vibrator, the bow drawn by the performer is the generator, and the body of the instrument is the resonator.

The Wind Family. The oboe is a good example of the wind family. The vibrator in the oboe is the enclosed column of air which is set in motion by the reed. The generator is the breath of the player, and the resonator is the body of the instrument.

In the production of vocal sound, the larynx serves as the vibrator. The force which sets the vibrator (the vocal cords) in motion is the breath exhaled from the lungs. The resonators are the pharynx, the mouth, and the nasal cavities, which function in the amplification of the sound vibrations initiated at the level of the larynx.

When comparing vocal production with the production of sound in other musical instruments, it is at once apparent that the vocal cords (the vibrator) most nearly resemble a stringed instrument, and the breath (the generator) of the singer relates it to a wind instrument. Vocal sound is obviously a combination of the two principles. And, when combined with a system of resonation that includes the cavities of the head, mouth, and throat, the result is a musical instrument of magnificent structure that far excels anything that science and the genius of mechanical construction are capable of inventing.

The mechanism of the human voice differs from most tone-producing instruments in that it possesses a series of articulators which modify the tone into specific sounds. These articulators are the lips, teeth, tongue, the hard and soft palates, and the walls of the resonating cavities.

The actual production of vocal tone in the larynx occurs when a current of air passes through the glottis. On either side of this opening the parallel edges of the vocal folds vibrate and produce the sound waves that are amplified in the resonating chambers. Immediately before a tone is produced, the edges of the vocal folds come together. The contraction of the abdominal and thoracic muscles increases the air pressure in the lungs. When this pressure reaches a certain level, the glottis opens and the current of air passes out through the narrow opening, causing the vocal folds to vibrate with the resultant production of vocal tone.

The changes in position and in tension of the vocal folds are brought about principally by the movement of two small triangular cartilages (the *arytenoid cartilages*) to which the posterior ends of the vocal cords are attached. The anterior ends of the folds are attached to the thyroid cartilage. Through the movement of these cartilages, the cords can be brought close together (which increases their tension and decreases the size of the glottis) or they can be moved outward toward the sides of the larynx (which decreases their tension and greatly widens the air passageway). In ordinary breathing, the cords occupy the latter position and no sound is produced during the respiratory process.

THE NATURE OF VOCAL REGISTERS

Another controversial aspect of vocal study surrounds the subject of registration: its existence, its nature, and the terms used for its description. Practically all writers on the vocal art acknowledge the existence of vocal registers in one form or another. The more common terminology includes such terms as head and chest voice in women, falsetto and chest voice in men, heavy and light registers, low and high voice mechanisms, and thick and thin registers. Some writers argue that registers simply do not exist; some believe that proper vocal training will eliminate registers; while others have worked out a complicated system that classifies voices and establishes specific terminology on the basis of vocal registers.

Most instruments possess some kind of register change. The timpani player changes registers each time he changes instruments to play a higher or lower note on the scale. A violinist experiences a register change that requires some kind of technical adjustment each time he crosses over to another string. The clarinetist changes registers, and thus varies the pressure and position of the embouchure, whenever he plays above or below the treble clef b flat on his instrument. Likewise the singer experiences a similar sensation as he or she performs diatonic scale passages during vocalization.

A vocal register can be defined as that section of the tessitura of the voice where the vocal cords readjust themselves for pitches of faster or slower frequencies. This change is reflected in a homogeneous tone quality, a different resonance placement of the voice, and a noticeable change in amplification. The change in timbre reflects the adjustment in the size of the resonating cavity.

The term *register* comes from pipe organ terminology and was originally used to describe the changes in qualtiy which resulted from the setting of different combinations of stops. Because the vocal organs are also capable of making sounds of diverse qualities, it was only natural for writers to refer to each group of similar or homogeneous sounds as a vocal register. Like the organ, the vocal registers appeared to owe their peculiar and distinguishing characteristics to a special type of technical action.

A number of factors contribute to the confusion and disagreement concerning the subject of vocal registers, but the most important seems to be faulty nomenclature. The terms *head* and *chest* are actually misnomers. From a physiological standpoint, the vocal organs are neither in the head nor in the chest, but in the throat. Since there are no vocal organs in the head or chest, only cavities, no physiological action related to vocal production can possibly take place there. The illusion of head and chest voice is caused by a sympathetic vibration which appears to be located in one of these areas each time an adjustment in the vocal cords is made.

The most convincing evidence to support a theory of registers in the voice is the "break," "change," or "lift" that occurs about an octave above the speaking voice of the average person. This modification, which is especially prominent in adolescent and untrained voices, is called *passagio* by the Italians, *break* by the British, and *lift* by some American schools. We will refer to it simply as register change. This sensation, which can fluctuate according to the intensity or form of the vowel used in a vocal exercise or scale passage in a choral work, generally occurs somewhere in the area just above the speaking voice. The sensation of the tone lifting is the result of a change in the vocal cords themselves, an adjustment that directs the sound waves postnasally. The register change signals the end of the so-called low (or chest) voice and the beginning of what may be called the middle voice, mixed voice, or high voice, depending upon whether one believes that there are two (chest-head) or three (low-middle-high) registers.

What happens at the level of the larynx is that when the pitch is low, and the cords vibrate along their full length and thickness, the sounds that result belong to the low or chest register. As the pitch moves higher, the vibrations move toward the outer lips of the cords, the length and thickness of the cords are reduced, the vibrations pulsate along a shorter, thinner surface, and the vocal sounds that emanate are called the head or middle voice.

Much of the existing confusion is due to the fact that register change can be negligible, smoothed over by careful vocal training, absent entirely because only the head register is used, or raised higher or lower depending upon the level of intensity being sung and the condition of the voice. One other circumstance must also be considered: the chest voice will react differently for different vowels even at the same level of intensity. For example, an "ah" vowel will function differently than an "ee" vowel, even though the two are sung at the same pitch and with the same level of intensity. For these reasons the position of the register change is variable and may shift to meet changing circumstances.

In theory there are two vocal registers: a chest (or low) voice and a head (or high) voice. There is also an area in the voice where the two registers meet and blend, a phenomenon we will call the *mixed* voice. The adjustments, or lifts as they are sometimes called, are actually changes in resonance placement, a sensation that gives the singer the illusion that there is a third register (or middle register) in the male voice and as many as five different registers in some female voices.

Consequently the ultimate goal of vocal training is to combine the action of the two registers so that they perform as a single functional unit, with the kind of gradual tonal change that one finds in the piano or any other well-played instrument. The ideal coordination—a correctly produced and fully resonated vocal tone—smooths over the register change and provides the singer with a legato scale throughout a wide tonal compass without obvious changes in quality. This ideal is difficult to achieve in the choral rehearsal unless the individual singer studies voice privately, possesses exceptional talent, or sings in a choral group where the conductor takes the time to nurture the vocal development of every singer.

However, since artistic choral singing is dependent upon a freedom and flexibility of the vocal mechanism of every singer, so that the ensemble can meet the technical and musical demands of a broad range of choral literature, a part of every choral rehearsal should be devoted to vocal development to insure that each singer will have sufficient technique to enjoy a satisfying choral experience.

NOTES

1. Edmund H. Fellowes, *William Byrd* (London: Oxford University Press, 1948), p. 149.

2. Wilhelm Ehmann, *Choral Directing*, translated by George D. Wiebe. (Minneapolis: Augsburg Publishing House, 1968), p. 2.

3. Julius Portnoy, *Music in the Life of Man* (New York: Holt, Rinehart and Winston, 1963), p. 4.

4. The authors recommend mouth breathing for singing as not only the most quiet but also the most natural of the two methods.

Chapter Three

RECOMMENDED READING LIST

Appelman, Dudley Ralph. *The Science of Vocal Pedagogy.* Bloomington: Indiana University Press, 1967. A highly detailed and scientific study of the tangibles of vocal pedagogy.

Bacon, Richard Mackenzie. *Elements of Voice Science.* Rev. edition. Champaign: Pro Musica Press, 1966. The view of the nineteenth-century vocal pedagogue with respect to scientific method and voice teaching.

Ehmann, Wilhelm. *Choral Directing.* Translated by George D. Wiebe. Minneapolis: Augsburg Publishing House, 1968. The initial four chapters of this book contain specific and helpful information on vocal technique.

Fields, V. A. *Training the Singing Voice.* New York: King's Crown Press, 1947. An analytical study which attempts to compare the various methods of training the singing voice.

Reid, Cornelius L. *Bel Canto.* New York: Coleman-Ross, 1950. A well-written volume on the elements of the traditional bel canto method of singing.

Vennard, William. *Singing, the Mechanism and the Technique.* Los Angeles: University of California, 1964. One of the finest books on vocal technique by a highly respected teacher.

REHEARSAL TECHNIQUE

Introduction to Part Two

AMONG THE QUALITIES that make a choral group successful in the performance of choral literature of all periods are a vital and flexible tone quality, a clear enunciation of vowels and a crisp articulation of consonants, and clean ensemble singing. These attributes, which rarely come instinctively, must be taught in a systematic manner by the conductor during the choral rehearsal. Just as the band and orchestral director must understand and be able to communicate to the members of his ensemble the principles of bowings, fingerings, and embouchures, likewise the choral director must understand the principles of vocal production, breath control, choral diction, and ensemble singing if he or she is to develop a group capable of performing great choral literature with sophistication and understanding.

The material in the next three chapters is designed to provide the conductor with principles which when applied to regular rehearsals will help to produce a sound rehearsal technique.

A clear understanding of vocal production, breath control, and registration is absolutely indispensable for a choral conductor. Most choral singers are either young people or adult amateurs for whom choral singing is a pastime in which they participate for personal and musical fulfillment. Some are endowed with superior vocal equipment and substantial musical talent, while a few are almost entirely lacking in these characteristics. But the majority will derive a great deal of enjoyment from choral singing if they are able to gain a vocal technique that is sufficient to perform the standard choral literature. Thus the choral conductor becomes a teacher of voice and the choral rehearsal a class voice lesson, and the manner in which the subject is presented will determine the ultimate quality of the choral experience to the average singer.

Diction also becomes an important element in the choral experience because choral music is always (or nearly always) associated with some kind of text and is written and performed on the assumption that the text will be heard and understood by the audience. The clear enunciation of vowels and the crisp articulation of consonants thus become basic requirements for artistic choral singing.

The success or failure of a public performance of any choral group can usually be traced to the rehearsal technique of the conductor. A fine performance is invariably the result of careful and systematic attention to musical detail, something that rarely happens by chance. Many conductors waste valuable rehearsal time because they simply do not know how to rehearse a group in order to achieve the musical discipline that produces outstanding ensemble singing. The final chapter in this section deals with the problems encountered in rehearsal and performance.

Two notes of caution must be raised at this point. First, the authors recognize that no book can be a substitute for the individual conducting technique and musicianship of the conductor. This volume therefore makes no attempt to be a manual of conducting technique. The ultimate stamp which each conductor places on his choral ensemble will be the result of long training and careful musical discipline.

Finally, never forget that the interpretation of the music is the ultimate goal of the choral experience. Vocal and rehearsal technique is never an end in itself, but a means toward the interpretation of the composer's intentions. Any exercises employed for the purpose of technical vocal development must be used to accomplish this end and no other.

Chapter Four

Choral Sound

There is not any Musicke or Instruments whatsoever,
comparable to that which is made of voice of Men, where the
voyces are good, and the same well sorted and ordered.
—WILLIAM BYRD, 1588[1]

A VITAL, FULLY RESONANT, yet musically flexible choral sound, which should be the goal of every choral conductor who works with adolescent, college, and adult voices, is the result of a free and coordinated vocalism on the part of every member of the ensemble. Unfortunately, vital choral singing does not just happen by chance—unless, of course, one is blessed with a choir of professional singers, or advanced students who are studying voice on a regular basis. It is rather the result of applying certain fundamental principles of vocal production to the regular rehearsal routine. A choir that is capable of performing a cross section of choral repertoire in a musically competent and stylistically appropriate manner is usually built by a knowledgeable choral specialist, in much the same manner that a fine coach will mold a group of high school, college, or professional athletes into a championship team.

Vocal exercises which are purely mechanical in nature and not meaningfully related to a specific musical or vocal deficiency are not advised, since every conductor should develop a rehearsal technique that will lead to a satisfying experience for each member of the ensemble.

Such problems in the practical areas of choral technique that are so essential in the development of choral sound will now be examined, beginning with an aspect of choral technique that is often neglected—the auditioning and classifying of singers. Material on posture, breathing and breath control, resonance, and registration will be offered, and a survey of some of the common vocal problems that arise in the regular choral rehearsal will conclude the section.

AUDITIONING AND CLASSIFYING VOICES

A vital choral sound is very much dependent upon a well-balanced, carefully selected group of singers. Yet this phase of choral activity is often neglected by conductors who simply do not take the time to audition and classify their choir members. Robert Shaw would personally audition up to six hundred voices to select the thirty members who would tour annually with the Robert Shaw Chorale. If a conductor of this stature would take the time and expend the energy necessary to audition this many singers, the value of auditioning and classifying voices should be obvious.

Voices are classified for choral placement according to a number of methods. Since many untrained singers have more than one possible singing quality, and since the effective range of a singer who has not had formal vocal training is often misleading, using quality and range as the only means of classification is hardly satisfactory. There is also a psychological factor involved in auditioning. Singers usually have very definite opinions about the type of voice they think they have, or would like to have. For example, many sopranos think they are altos because they can read music and are able to sing the alto part. By the same token, many tenors think they are baritones, and baritones think they are basses because they are not properly trained to sing the higher range comfortably. These judgments are often based on what the singer thinks he or she hears. A singer hears his voice in two ways: through air and bone conduction. This is one reason why he does not recognize his voice when he hears it played back for the first time on a tape recorder; he is hearing it only by air conduction through the outer ear. This inability of a singer to hear his voice as it actually sounds emphasizes the necessity for a choral conductor who knows what to listen for when he is selecting his choir.

Four criteria are generally used in determining sectional placement in choral groups: quality of the voice, pitch of the speaking voice, range of the voice, and vocal registers. Some conductors use all four so that they can gain a complete profile of the voice; others only one or possibly two. We will begin this discussion with the quality of the singing voice.

Quality of the Voice

Quality is perhaps the most problematic profile on classification because vocal sound is such a complex phenomenon. Every tone that is sung has a distinctive quality. This quality is determined by the mental image the singer has of his own voice, the anatomical structure of the larynx and resonance cavities, the characteristics of the vowel that is sung, and the partials or overtones that lie outside the vowel range itself but impart additional characteristics of sound to the tone—brilliance, shrillness, thickness, etc.—according to their dispersal in the harmonic spectrum. When a conductor auditions singers, he should determine sectional placement with an ear to the type of quality (or timbre) which will add color and tonal variety to the group, i.e., thickness or heaviness in the alto and bass sections, resonant or ringing quality in the tenors, brilliant and pure quality in the sopranos. These characteristics are only a few of the possibilities of tonal variety or flexibility that can enhance sectional placement.

Pitch of the Speaking Voice

The average normal pitch of the speaking voice may be used as another indication of the type of voice that a singer possesses. If a person speaks on a pitch that is below B flat, he generally has a low voice; between B flat and D, a middle or mezzo voice; on D or above, a high voice. This is a general method of classification and should not be considered definitive. However, auditions based on this data would lead to the following categories:

FEMALE		MALE	
High voices	—First sopranos	High voices	—First tenors
Middle or mezzo	—Second sopranos —First altos	Middle voices	—Second tenors —High baritones
Low voices	—Contraltos	Low voices	—Baritones —Basses

Range of the Voice

While range represents yet another profile that is helpful in classifying and placing the singer according to section, the conductor must be careful not to use this method as the sole criterion. Voices can only be classified accurately when the production is absolutely natural and unaffected; the apparent range of untrained singers is often misleading if used as the only gauge. Consequently, the classification which follows should be taken as an approximation, not as the rule.

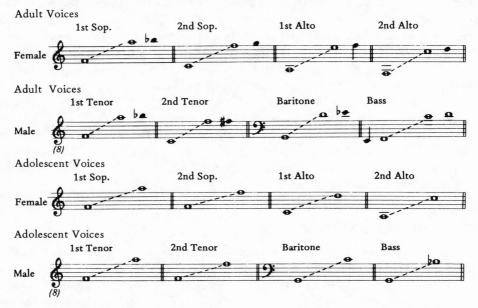

Register of the Voice

Another useful method of choral placement is called classification according to register. When a choral singer performs an ascending diatonic scale, as in one of the polyphonic choruses of Bach or Handel, there is a definite and recognizable register change in the quality and intensity of his voice when a certain point in the range is reached. For a more complete discussion of registration, refer to chapter three and the section on this subject later in this chapter.

Many choral conductors and teachers of voice dispute the existence of registers; however, since there is enough evidence—both theoretical and practical—to support their existence, the application of the principle of registration in auditioning and classifying voices can be a useful exercise for the choral conductor.

A register change is that section of the tessitura of the voice where the vocal cords readjust themselves for pitches of faster frequency. This adjustment is reflected in a change of tone quality, a different resonance placement, and an increase in volume. In addition, the notes sung in each ascending register require the expenditure of less breath to maintain the same volume. When the point is reached where the vocal cords adjust themselves naturally for notes that are higher in the range, a new register begins, and a different quality or resonance placement results.

It should be noted that this adjustment is a natural phenomenon and will be automatic if the vocal mechanism functions correctly. Register change can be prevented, however, either through physical manipulation or mental control, causing the vocal cords to separate violently in order to avoid injury, resulting in the familiar "cracking" of the voice. If this unnatural condition continues, the result will be a hoarseness or laryngitis.

The existence of registers can be easily demonstrated by slowly vocalizing, with the aid of a piano, on the vowel sounds *ah* or *ee*—if the *ah* sounds dark or swallowed—in five-note diatonic scale patterns in the appropriate octave, beginning on E above middle C for high voices (sopranos and tenors) or B flat below middle C for low voices (alto-bass). To facilitate recognition of the register change, it is important to begin these scales below the point where the change is expected to occur so that the conductor may be familiar with the original quality of the voice.

Soprano / Tenor (octave lower)

Alto / Bass (octave lower)

In high voices this change in resonance occurs between C and E; in low voices between G and C. If the average pitch of the speaking voice is used as the basis of the starting pitch, a change in resonance placement occurs about an octave above the starting pitch. If the vocalization is continued, another change will take place a perfect fourth above the first break, and a final change will happen a major third above the second change in the female voice.

This classification by register change is considered by many to be the most accurate method of determining the placement of singers in choral groups. It is an especially attractive tool for classifying singers with unusually large or underdeveloped voice ranges, or when incorrect vocalism produces a false "color" in the voice.

The first register change occurs approximately one octave above the average pitch of the normal speaking voice, and marks the beginning of a middle voice range of approximately a fourth or fifth. The singing voice then has a rather natural division of a low voice of approximately an octave, a middle voice of a fourth or a fifth, and a high voice of a third or fourth. With extended training the low range and the high voice may be expanded in their respective directions. The chart that follows will serve as a guide to the choral conductor who wishes to classify and place singers in sections according to register.

VOICE CLASSIFICATION ACCORDING TO REGISTER CHANGE

Male Voice

	CHORAL SECTION	SOLO REPERTOIRE
E flat	First tenor	Lyric tenor
D	First tenor	Lyric tenor
C sharp	Second tenor	Dramatic tenor
C	Second tenor	Heldentenor
B	Baritone	Baritone
B flat	Baritone or bass	Basso cantando
A	Bass	Basso cantando or bass
A flat	Bass	Basso
G	Bass	Basso
F sharp	Bass	Basso profundo

Female Voice

E	First soprano	Coloratura soprano
E flat	First soprano	Coloratura or high lyric soprano
D	Second soprano	Lyric soprano
C sharp	Second soprano	Lyric soprano
C	First alto	Mezzo soprano
B	First alto	Mezzo soprano
B flat	Second alto	Alto
A	Second alto	Alto
A flat	Second alto	Contralto
G	Second alto	Contralto

The importance of a careful and systematic approach to the auditioning and placement of choral singers cannot be overemphasized. When the voice is classified correctly and the vocal mechanism is working properly, and is guided by a careful conductor, choral singing will become a greater joy to the individual singer because he will be able to express musical ideas with complete freedom. Ideal choral placement is one of those basic elements of rehearsal procedure that will contribute to mastery of the choral art.

POSTURE

Since one of the goals of the choral rehearsal is to develop a free and vital vocalism in every singer, the process must begin with posture. Good posture is a fundamental element in correct singing. Repeated or even daily insistence on good posture is one of the musts in any kind of vocal training. Correct singing posture seldom happens by chance; and this is especially true when you are dealing with groups of singers who may become tired and listless during long rehearsals. Good posture must be practiced until it becomes second nature to every singer.

A dramatic example of the damage caused to the sound of a choral group by poor posture can be heard when a conductor allows his singers to slump into bad posture during the rehearsal or performance of a technically demanding work. Breath support disappears, tone quality deteriorates, and intonation becomes a problem. It is amazing to hear the difference in the sound when the conductor insists upon a body posture that is upright and expansively vital. A state of vocal readiness results which is at once evident in the vocal sound that emanates from the choral ensemble.

Thus it is extremely important for the choral singer to understand that the necessary physical development for singing begins with correct posture, proceeds through carefully selected vocal exercises that establish proper resonance efficiency and breath control, and is applied to the regular singing of choral literature.

Before presenting a model of correct posture that can be applied to the choral rehearsal, it might be helpful to examine the misconceptions about the terms *tension* and *relaxation*. The word *tension* is often used to imply that all tension in singing is wrong, while *relaxation* is sometimes considered to be the cure-all that insures correct use of the body.

Do not confuse *tension* with *rigidity*. Whenever there is any kind of muscular movement, there must be tension because it is an integral part of every muscular process in which coordination is involved. Without tension in singing there can be neither pitch nor tonal amplification. Thus the task facing the choral conductor is one of developing ways to influence and improve the coordinative process of vocal production in the choral singer: to induce the right tension while insisting on correct posture, and to avoid creating the wrong tension so that the muscles of the laryngeal and pharyngeal tract work harmoniously and without conflict. It is this correct affirmative action—tension within the coordinative process without wasted energy—that gives the appearance of relaxation and ease of execution.

Producing a vocal sound is only possible because of muscular movements that occur as a response to a mental concept. As these movements cannot be made without some tension, the suggestion to relax while moving is obviously a contradiction of terms.

One of the best ways to avoid unnecessary tension in the choral rehearsal is to refrain from any reference to muscular tension. This should be a standard procedure for all choral conductors; the mere suggestion of muscular tension will tend to create tension in the minds of the choral singer.

To establish correct posture the following exercises should be practiced until they become a regular part of the rehearsal behavior of every singer.

1. Have the choir stand erect, hands on hips, one foot slightly in front of the other, with feet placed a comfortable distance apart (see diagram 9). Do not permit locking of the knees because this stance is too rigid and may, if continued through a concert, cause fainting. The posture for singing must be upright and expansively vital, ready to function, but neither rigid nor flabby.

2. While the choir is standing in this position, have them stretch their arms above their heads as if they were reaching for the ceiling, bringing the upper chest to a high position. The purpose of this exercise is to raise the chest to a comfortable position for the intake of breath, while at the same time keeping the shoulders free from tension (see diagram 10).

3. While maintaining the same relative position of the chest, have the choir slowly bring their arms down to their sides, comfortably away from the body in a position of relaxed readiness. The shoulders must be relaxed otherwise a large amount of energy is wasted and the shoulders will become very sore.

4. The head and neck should be resting comfortably in a position perpendicular to the shoulders. If the chin is lifted too high, the result will be a con-

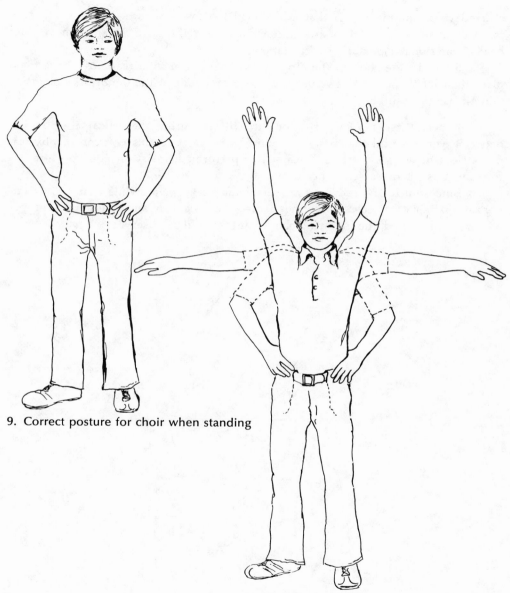

9. Correct posture for choir when standing

10. High chest position

stricted vocal sound; a chin that is dropped too low causes a "dark" or throaty tone. To insure that the neck and chin are not too rigid, have the choir move their heads from side to side during vocalization.

5. While the choir is standing in this position of vital readiness, have them place their left hands on the upper chest as a reminder of the importance of maintaining a high position.

Repeat these exercises two or three times during the rehearsal—possibly between works—until the choir automatically moves into this position of physical readiness whenever a work is rehearsed or performed. Insist on good posture before any music is rehearsed or performed.

Since much of the choral rehearsal may take place while seated it is important to insist on correct seating habits. To establish and maintain a proper posture while seated, the following checkpoints should be observed.

11. Correct posture for choir while sitting

1. Have the choir sit on the front half of their chairs, without resting against the back, with the position of the head, shoulders, and chest the same as when standing. Insist that the choir assume this posture whenever vocalizing or rehearsing (see diagram 11).

2. While sitting in this position, have the choir lean forward slightly, with both feet on the floor, one slightly ahead of the other, applying slight pressure on the balls of the feet.

3. Remind the choir that they should not cross their legs under any circumstances. Such a position inhibits the natural coordination of the muscles involved in the act of singing.

4. Again have the choir check the high chest position by placing their left hands on the upper chest while exhaling.

Remember it is much easier for singers to maintain a correct posture while standing than it is when they are seated. The amount of time a choir spends seated in rehearsal is probably far greater than standing, unless the conductor insists that the choir stand during rehearsal. There is thus a natural tendency for singers to slump in their seats, to lean back, or to cross their legs when seated. The task facing the conductor during every rehearsal is one of teaching the singers the importance of correct posture and then insisting that they maintain good standing and sitting habits.

BREATHING AND BREATH CONTROL

Before describing some of the prominent approaches to breathing, it might be helpful to discuss some of the requirements that choral singing places upon breathing and breath control. Though it is true that there are good and bad methods of breathing, no single approach is a cure-all for the vocal problems of the singer who does not possess vocal freedom. When posture is correct, and when there is sufficient resonance and coordinated registration, very little is actually demanded of the breath, and not much attention should be directed to it in the choral rehearsal.

Breathing exercises practiced separately from the choral rehearsal are not generally advised, unless the purpose of such exercises is to introduce a correct approach to the choir. The choral singer should avoid any system of breathing that emphasizes a purely mechanical approach. Breathing for singing is different in terms of the quantity of intake and control of release than breathing for speech. Therefore, only exercises dealing with the coordinated act of singing should be used to improve the choral singer's breath support. Specialized effort directed to the physiological aspects of breathing generally interferes with coordination; this is one of the chief dangers of focusing too much attention on this subject during the choral rehearsal.

However, when vocal problems do arise, it is helpful to know which method to recommend to the choral singer in order to restore the effective and natural coordination of the vocal organs.

What are the traits of a sound method of breathing? In essence, no approach should interfere with the natural motions of the body as it breathes at rest. Breathing should provide enough air and sufficient freedom of control to sustain and shape any phrase that the choral singer might encounter. The following additional guidelines should be especially helpful to both singer and conductor.

1. Good breathing should integrate easily into the singer's posture, enhancing his stance and in turn be improved by it. It should not interfere with, nor should it contradict, the state of flexible tension that is necessary for the singer's vocalism. It should not cause tenseness nor drain the energy of the singer unnecessarily.

2. Good breathing should allow the muscles and the organs of the body to move freely and naturally. Any manner of breathing that cramps or hinders the muscular movements previously outlined in chapter three should be discarded. The ribs and back should be free to expand, the diaphragm should move easily, the abdominal organs should shift naturally without force. The muscles of the abdomen should be free to control the expulsion of air from the lungs.

3. Good breathing should provide maximum expansion of the lungs. Obviously, the greater the area of expansion, the greater the quantity of breath the singer has for singing. At no time should this feeling of expansion become rigid or inflexible; the buoyancy of the rib cage must be maintained at all times.

4. Good breathing should assist in the freedom and relaxation of the total vocal mechanism. It should allow the larynx to function in a low, stationary position. In addition, the greater the compression of air—through thoracic buoyancy —below the level of the larynx, the less strain the singer will feel at the level of the larynx. The best approach to breathing is one that allows the larynx to float freely and function without pressure. This condition is produced by a good posture, a high and buoyant rib cage, and sufficient room for thoracic expansion.

5. Good breathing should be sensitive to the artistic demands of the singer. Any breathing process that forces the singer into a rigid mold limits that singer's potential for growth as an artist and gives an artificial, stilted appearance to the audience.

6. Good breathing should provide an additional means of artistic communication for the singer. Not only should it supply the choral singer with sufficient air for the nature and length of the phrase being performed, but it should also allow freedom for the use of the body, the chest, the face, the eyes—the whole personality—in communicating the musical essence and style of the literature being sung.

In summary, an effective method of breathing will provide the maximum amount of air for the minimum effort, with freedom, flexibility, and little exertion on the part of the body. With these guidelines in mind, let us examine the principal approaches to breathing. Practically all methods conform to one of the following types: clavicular, diaphragmatic, costal, or diacostal. Since clavicular breathing is the least desirable, we will begin with it.

Clavicular Breathing

Clavicular breathing is a type of respiration in which the upper parts of the chest (the *clavicles* are the collarbones) are raised during inspiration and collapsed during expiration. Often called the "breath of exhaustion," because of the exaggerated heaving of the shoulders, its great disadvantage to the singer is that it actually limits expansion in the thoracic cavity and thus adversely lowers the breath capacity. It ultimately interferes with the effective coordination of the vocal mechanism.

Three important reasons make clavicular breathing undesirable for the choral singer: (1) by lifting the shoulders, the muscles of the neck are brought into a state of tension; (2) by raising the shoulders only partial inspiration can be completed; and (3) by a strenuous misdirection of effort physical exhaustion occurs which results in the loss of vocal control, the creation of vocal strain, and the limitation of the tessitura. Clavicular breathing virtually renders the choral singer useless to any choral organization to which he or she may belong.

Diaphragmatic Breathing

Diaphragmatic breathing, the natural respiration for everyday life, is sometimes called "abdominal" breathing because it is characterized by a slight protrusion of the stomach with every breath. While sufficient for most activities in everyday life, diaphragmatic breathing is somewhat deficient for singing purposes because it fails to build up enough pressure to sustain any musical line that demands intense singing or singing in an exceptionally high tessitura; in musical literature of this type more power (or support) is required.

The diaphragmatic method of breathing does, however, provide the basic foundation for a solid breathing technique; it adapts easily to a posture of energized relaxation, it demands little additional physical exertion, and it is unobtrusive in appearance. Diaphragmatic breathing is the healthiest, easiest, and, in some ways, the most efficient type. Yet, alone it is unable to provide the necessary breath support for artistic choral singing.

Costal Breathing

Costal or rib breathing is really an auxiliary form of respiration; it is an additional means for obtaining air for purposes of unusual physical activity. This type of breathing is accomplished by lifting and widening the lower ribs through the use of the intercostal muscles, a muscular action that is usually accompanied by a visible pulling in or flattening out of the upper abdomen and an extension of the back up to the level of the shoulder blades.

Diacostal Breathing

The most efficient method of breathing for the choral singer is one that combines features of diaphragmatic and costal breathing. In this approach the breathing mechanism expands to utilize its full pressure potential and receives assistance by the outward movement of the lower ribs. This combined movement thus increases the dimensions of the thoracic cavity in three directions: length, width, and depth. The effect is to create a feeling of expansion around the entire middle part of the body that will include the small of the back and sides, as well as the abdominal wall. Deep breathing of this type results in a naturally high sternum and rib cage, maintained by muscular control rather than by inflation with air. It also allows for greater freedom of the upper part of the body, thereby relieving pressure on the muscles of the neck and thyroid areas around the larynx, preventing constriction in the vocal mechanism itself.

At this point the importance of good posture must be reemphasized. Correct posture and proper breath control are closely related. Good posture is the key to free, coordinated singing. When the body is bent forward or the shoulders are slumped, the ribs become shoved together and their free expansion for maximum breath capacity is considerably inhibited. Similarly, if the body is bent backward or the shoulders pulled backward to an overly rigid position, the rib arches are spread apart and their movements are restricted. Any position of the body other than one in which the body is held comfortably erect results in a constriction of the ribs and limits the full expansion of the thoracic cavity. The best position for breathing is one in which the body is held erect with a comfortably high chest, but without any exaggerated pulling back of the shoulders. The body must always be in a position of poised relaxation to insure full respiratory development.

Certain physical checkpoints may be recognized when the physical aspect of diacostal breathing is correct. The expansion can be felt and tested at the following places:

1. There should be a slight expansion at the front of the waist.

2. There should be noticeable expansion at the sides of the abdomen at the level of the lower ribs.

3. There should be some expansion in the upper chest at the level of the upper rib cavity.

While none of these areas should be expanded by force, all three checkpoints are necessary for optimum breath capacity.

When any breathing exercises are practiced in the choral rehearsal, the choir should be encouraged to check each area of expansion, even if the movement seems slight. The expansion of the upper chest must be achieved without drawing the front wall of the abdomen; if contracted it is an indication that the singer is forcing the breath.

One final point should be emphasized: correct breathing is *not* the result of forcing the muscles to expand but is rather the natural development of the above sets of muscles in coordination with the mood of the choral work, the intensity of the melodic line, and the degree of volume desired. It is in the coordination of the physical and musical aspects of vocal production that the true essence of the choral experience rests for every singer.

Breathing Checkpoints

In summary the following nine steps may be used as a guide for use in a choral rehearsal:

1. To discover the proper position of the upper chest and shoulders during respiration, have the choir lie down if possible with the back flat against the floor. This is the proper position of the upper chest and breastbone for vital choral singing.

2. While standing in the vital and buoyant posture described earlier in this chapter, have the choir inhale a deep breath and then blow it out, but always maintaining the position of the upper chest and shoulders that they experienced while lying on the floor.

3. After they have exhaled, have the choir lift both arms quickly, and as they reach above them take a quick breath so that the breath is simultaneous with the act of reaching.

4. As the choir members slowly lower their arms, exhaling slowly at the same time, they should experience the feeling of the arms floating down while maintaining the proper position of the upper chest and shoulders. There should be no collapsing of the chest in the process.

5. Once this position of vital buoyancy has been achieved, it can be checked by placing the left hand on the upper chest during exhaling to insure that the chest does not fall. If a slight lowering is detected, have the choir think of pushing up against the hand while they exhale.

6. Another check on the expansion of the lower rib cavity can be made by having the choir place their thumb and fingers (upside down) around the lower ribs during inhalation to establish the feeling of the floating rib cavity. If no expansion is experienced, the breath has not been taken deeply enough.

7. Another checkpoint is the soft spot just below the sternum. While they are breathing deeply with the proper posture, have the choir place the thumb against the soft spot to experience the expansion there.

8. If the choir is having difficulty experiencing this full expansion of the diaphragm and costal area, the correct action can be simulated by having the choir pant deeply in the manner of a winded animal. When the choir has experienced this muscular action without moving the upper chest, have them slow down the panting until it approximates the normal inhaling and exhaling that is necessary in singing.

9. The breathing technique can be further refined by having the choir ease the deep breath in and out quietly with such careful control that a lighted candle held in front of the mouth will not go out.

Breathing and Artistry

Throughout this chapter the emphasis has been placed on the physical side of breathing and breath control—the actions of the muscles and the manner in which they relate to the singer's supply of air. However, that is not the total picture. Just as the impulse to breathe originates involuntarily in the mind of the singer, it is also here that the voluntary psychological decisions are made that constitute artistic breathing for singing. By this we mean the subtle response to mood that is the mark of the artist: the distinction between the mechanical and the creative. And, while research has shown that the physical process of breathing and phonation is identical regardless of the character of the music, minute deviations can be identified in the manner and style with which the breath is taken. It is this variation in the physical process that enables the artist to communicate meaning to the listener as he interprets the intentions of the composer.

This can be demonstrated to the individual singer by having the choir participate in the following exercise:

1. Have the choir place their hands—thumbs pointing to the back—on the bottom of the rib cage at the place where it meets the abdomen.

2. While in this position have the choir inhale several times, preceding each breath by mentally conceiving a different mood: love, joy, surprise, sorrow, anger, confusion.

3. Note that the conducting gestures are also influenced by the mood being simulated.

An exercise of this type can dramatically demonstrate that while in each case the same physical response took place, the rate and dimension with which they occurred varied. When translated into musical language, the mood has determined the tempo and the pace of each preparation for attack.

This exercise should be repeated at subsequent rehearsals by calling out individual members of the choir and having them simulate these moods in front of a mirror. (Be careful to construct the mood clearly before the breath is taken.) Another interesting variation on this exercise is to repeat the same mood—surprise, for example—while conceiving of it at two different dynamic levels.

While subjects of this type defy written explanation, the implications should be clear: good breathing for the individual singer—and for the choir as well—is the coordination of the body in a vital and healthy manner through careful mental preplacement of mood on the part of the singer. This process begins with the conductor who establishes this mood through physical posture and facial expression. This empathic relationship between the individual singer and the conductor creates an instant form of communication and establishes a choral sound that is in sympathy with the style and mood of the musical work.

Practical Breathing Exercises

The following excerpts from Handel's *Messiah* are presented for use in developing the breathing techniques of the choral singer. While it will become immediately obvious that the primary goal of these exercises is the ability to sustain these long phrases, further use may be made of them in developing vocal agility (the "leaping" from pitch to pitch that establishes clarity) and in homogenizing the vocal registers, as almost every example includes passages both in chest and head registers. This is by no means the limit to such exercises: the conductor should search in the choral repertoire for passages such as these for use in his choir's vocal development. It is necessary to make the warm-up count as much as possible toward the finished product—an artistic and well-sung performance.

TENORS:

shall be _____ ex - alt - ed, and He shall pu - ri - fy _____ the sons of Le - vi. His yoke is eas - - - - - - - - - - - - - y, if he de-light, _____ if he de-light in him,

BASSES:

and He shall pu - ri - fy ____

____ the sons of Le - vi.

but the Lord shall a-rise ____ up-on thee,

For un-to us a child is born ____

____ un-to us,

and we shall be chang'd ____

and we shall be changed

RESONANCE

In the previous chapter we discussed the conditions that lead to the production of sound in a musical instrument: a *vibrator*, which causes the air particles to vibrate (in the case of the singer, the vibrator is the vocal cords); a *generator*, which sets the vibrator in motion (the breath of the singer); and a *resonator*, which amplifies the original vibrations (the cavities of the head, mouth, and throat of the singer). It is the resonators with which we are concerned in this section of the chapter.

The manner in which vocal "sound" or tone is produced by the human voice is one of the more interesting aspects of the study of the choral art. A subject that could be confusing and difficult to understand is, in fact, a relatively simple and easily understood process. Vocal sound is produced at the level of the voice box (or larynx). A simple, almost "toneless tone" of insignificant volume and quality created by the vibration of air through the vocal cords is transmitted to all the resonance cavities that it can reach, and this strengthening process produces musical tone in the case of singing and speech tone in the case of speaking.

A close examination of the vocal mechanism will show that the area above the larynx contains resonance cavities in two locations: one in the area leading from the throat to the mouth, the other in the passage to the nose. The throat is actually a tube or passage that branches at the pharynx into the two resonance cavities that contain the primary resonators: the mouth, the laryngeal pharynx (the top of the throat), the oral pharynx (the back of the mouth), the postnasal cavities (those of the nose), the less influential trachea and bronchi, and the sinuses of the head. Since all of these cavities, with the exception of the trachea, bronchi, postnasal cavity, and sinuses, are adjustable with the proper vocal exercises, it is the task of the conductor to develop a rehearsal routine that will produce the maximum resonance potential in every singer.

For this reason the selection of the proper vowel for vocal exercises in the choral rehearsal is also important. For example, it is possible to change the shape of the resonance cavity, and therefore the nature of the choral sound, by having the choir vocalize first on the vowel "ah" as in *father* and then having them change to the vowel "ee" as in *see*. When singing "ah" in the lower (or chest) register the mouth is comfortably open and the tongue is relaxed and lying comfortably in the mouth. If "ee" is sung, there is a natural tendency for the tongue to rise in the middle and for the mouth to close slightly. What is actually happening in the change of vowel is that by singing "ee" we are restricting the resonance potential of the mouth cavity just enough to change the "ah" into an "ay" or even "ee"; or to view it another way, by raising the tongue we are decreasing the size and changing the shape of the mouth so that it is dampened slightly as a resonator.

Resonance development is such an important part of the vocal technique of the individual choral singer that some attention should be directed to it at each rehearsal. The exercises that follow are designed to accomplish four purposes: to establish a fully resonant sound, to coordinate resonance with breathing and breath support, to develop resonance through vowel formation, and to build facility through vocalises that are constructed to establish resonance.

1. To produce a rich and fully resonant choral tone we must be sure that the vibrating column of air reaches the primary resonance cavities: the mouth, the top of the throat, the back of the mouth, and the postnasal cavities. To accomplish this when singing, have the choir begin with a "hum" that is characterized by an open throat, and mouth and lips that are loosely closed:

The basic vitality of this "hum" is important and must be continued in other exercises. If the sound is thin or nasal, it may be necessary to check individual voices to insure that each member of the choir is producing a fully-resonant sound—regardless of dynamic level this vitality must be present. Once the sound is satisfactory, have the choir continue this basic "hum" on the following vocal exercises:

2. To coordinate resonance with breathing and breath support we must insure that the fully resonant "hum" is tied to the support and flow of breath. The following exercise, which emphasizes a diaphragmatic attack on each note, will help this process along if care is taken to insure that every singer is involved physically and mentally.

Repeat slowly one step higher until the key of D major is reached.

Mm _____

If the choir is large enough to allow eight-part singing, the same exercise can be sung in the following manner:

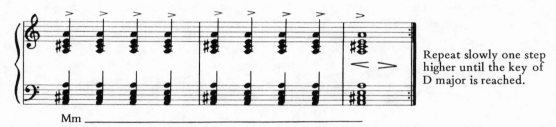

Repeat slowly one step higher until the key of D major is reached.

Mm _____

Care must be taken to insure that each member of the ensemble sings with an open mouth, open throat (in the position of a beginning yawn), and gently closed lips that experience a tingling sensation from the resonance of the hum.

As soon as the coordination of resonance and breathing has been securely established (this may take the warm-up period of two or three rehearsals) other vocal exercises may be used to develop facility.

Repeat slowly one step higher until the key of D major is reached.

Mm _____

The sixteenth-note variation of this exercise should only be used when the choir is far enough along technically to profit from it.

Mm

The exercise that follows—termed the *messa di voce* by eighteenth-century Italian pedagogues—is effective in developing control of rising and falling dynamics. Beginning singers will tend to lose support on the decrescendo rather than carefully controlling the release of breath. For this reason it is better not to use the term "soft" when referring to *piano* or *pianissimo* singing: Singers need to be reminded to "keep it energized!"

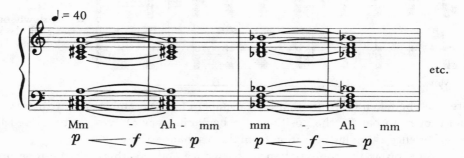

etc.

3. To develop resonance through vowel formation, vocal exercises such as the following will help the choral singer move smoothly from the hum to the actual vowel sound.

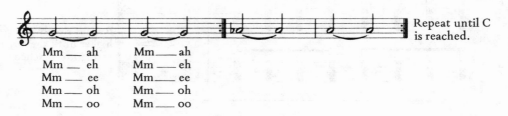

Repeat until C is reached.

This exercise should be sung as legato as possible with a slight crescendo leading toward the whole note.

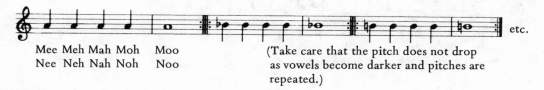

Mee Meh Mah Moh   Moo
Nee Neh Nah Noh   Noo

(Take care that the pitch does not drop
as vowels become darker and pitches are
repeated.)

For variety in the choral rehearsal the same vocalise can be sung in either four- or eight-part harmony.

Mee   Meh   Mah   Moh   Moo
Nee   Neh   Nah   Noh   Noo

4. To develop vocal facility and still maintain a fully resonant sound, begin with exercises that are diatonic in nature and then move carefully to those using intervals. In each case check the individual singer from time to time to insure that the sound is correct. The exercises that follow should be used in the rehearsal on a selective basis, over a period of weeks or months, for the purpose of developing vocal facility and a fully resonant choral sound.

mee   mah   mee   mee   mah   mee
mah   moh   mah   mah   moh   mah
moh   moo   moh   moh   moo   moh

nah   nay   nah   nah   nay   nah
nee   neh   nee   nee   neh   nee
noh   noo   noh   noh   noo   noh

mah _____ ah ha ha ha mah _____ ah
may _____ ay hay hay hay may _____ ay
moh _____ oh ho ho ho moh _____ oh

yah ha ha ha yah   hah   yah   hah   yah
yoh ho ho ho yoh   hoh   yoh   hoh   yoh

(8) lah _____   lah _____
lay _____   lay _____
lee _____   lee _____

REGISTRATION

Registers in the singing voice are similar in their behavior to registers in other instruments. A string player changes register each time he plays on a different string. This change can be delayed by extending the melodic line on the same string, but sooner or later the violinist will have to change the string when the melody soars into the upper tessitura.

In this sense the voice is very much like a stringed instrument. The vocal cords—like violin strings—vibrate at different lengths and thicknesses to accommodate the changing patterns of pitch and intensity. As the string change is one of the most difficult technical problems for the beginning string player to solve, with special exericses designed to overcome it, so it is with vocal study. The teenage or adult amateur usually comes to the choral rehearsal with a divided registration: the transition from the low or "chest" voice to the high or "head" register is distinguished by a "break" or change of quality that destroys the legato or "blended" character of the voice. The voice is also characterized by a quality above the break that is soft and buoyant, while the quality below the register change is heavier and less flexible. One of the purposes of any kind of vocal study is to develop a legato scale that bridges the upper and lower registers and virtually eliminates the register change.

The first step in establishing a smooth, legato scale in each choral singer is to establish the exact location of the register change(s). The "break" or "change" can be easily demonstrated by having the individual singer vocalize on the vowel sounds "ah" or "ee" in five-note diatonic scale patterns in the appropriate octave —E above middle C for high voices (soprano-tenor) and B flat below middle C for low voices (alto-bass). The chart for classification of voices according to register change is found on page 78.

Bridging the registers and developing one legato register is accomplished by the proper use of pitch (scale patterns), intensity (interchangeable use of loud and soft vocal exercises), and vowel. While it is necessary to sing loudly in the lower tonal range to establish the chest quality by using the vowel "ah," it is usually more effective in developing the upper register to sing quietly on either an "ee" or "oo" vowel. There are of course occasions when a moderately loud yell (hey!) can be effective in building the upper register, especially when there is a lack of intensity or an absence of diaphragmatic action.

It is best to begin with the upper register because the object is to extend its range as far as possible without distortion. And, since the human voice is capable of encompassing two octaves, it is best to begin with four-note diatonic scale passages, followed with triads, and then arpeggios and extended scale exercises. Remember that the "ah" vowel is the most effective vowel for the lower (chest) register; in the upper register any vowel can be used.

When performing this exercise there should be a crescendo with each rise in pitch and a descrescendo with the descending line. Begin quietly with the vowel "oo" and use other vowels, especially "ee."

A descending diatonic scale of five and eight notes can also be helpful in bridging the break between the upper and lower registers.

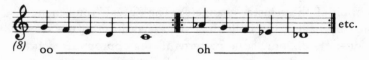

If the choir—or an individual choral singer—is having trouble bridging the registers with a fully resonant and vital choral sound, preceding the vowel exercise with a half-yell is often effective in tying the vowel to correct diaphragmatic action. For example, precede the following exercise with four extended half-yells (i.e., a vocal sound that has the intensity of a yell but only half of the normal volume of a yell).

(8) Hey!   Hey!   Hey __   Hey__
    Hoh!   Hoh!   Hoh __   Hoh __

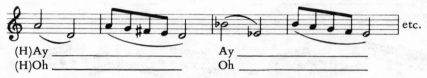

(H)Ay _____   Ay _____
(H)Oh _____   Oh _____   etc.

This vocal exercise is especially helpful with men's voices and with the coordination of the total vocal mechanism.

The exercises that follow should be used selectively for the purpose of bridging the break between the registers and building greater facility with the choral ensemble. The greatest danger with vocalises of this type is the temptation for the singers to practice them thoughtlessly or incorrectly. Therefore, great care should be taken so that they are not used for "warm-ups" unless there is a specific musical or technical problem that they can help solve.

(8) Mah   moh   mah   moh   mee   mah   mee   mah
    Nah   noh   nah   noh   nee   nah   nee   nah

(8) Lah _____ Lah   Lah _____ Lah
    Loh_____ Loh   Loh _____ Loh
    Lay_____ Lay   Lay _____ Lay
    Lee_____ Lee   Lee _____ Lee

(8) Lah _____ Lah   Lah _____ Lah
    Loh _____ Loh   Loh _____ Loh
    Lay _____ Lay   Lay _____ Lay
    Lee _____ Lee   Lee _____ Lee

(8) Mah _____   lah _____
    Moh _____   loh _____
    Mee _____   lee _____
    Moo _____   loo _____

(8) Dah _____ doh _____ dah   dah _____ doh _____ dah

COMMON PROBLEMS IN CHORAL SINGING

Choral singing is a corporate experience and as such is dependent upon the full and competent participation of each member of the ensemble. The old adage "a chain is only as strong as its weakest link" is a truism that is appropriate when applied to the choral experience. Ironically, it is often a vocal or musical problem with a relatively simple solution that prohibits a choral group from realizing its full potential as an ensemble.

Since the conductor must assume the ultimate responsibility for the success or failure of his group, he must find ways to control all aspects of choral performance. When standing before the choral ensemble, the conductor must become a diagnostician whose primary task in rehearsal is the solution of vocal and musical problems which, if left unattended for even an instant, will spoil the corporate result. For instance, if a note is learned incorrectly, it is virtually impossible to correct it. If the conductor is familiar with the cause of some of the common problems in choral singing, and can prescribe a cure during the rehearsal, the group will have a better chance of achieving impressive musical results.

Many common problems in choral singing are the result of sloppiness or laziness on the part of the singer; others can only be detected by the sensitive ear of the conductor. Since the physical action of the vocal organs are below the level of consciousness, it is often impossible for the individual singer to know that he has a problem.

If the conductor knows the chief cause of the problem, he can lead the singer to a solution through a mental concept which will alter the sound and cause the singer to hear and feel the change. If the problem is a vocal one, the simple change in vowel placement might be all that is necessary. Often interferences such as poor posture, undue tension, closed mouth position, or other problems with relatively easy solutions will prevent the vocal mechanism from working naturally, thereby changing the normal sound spectrum on which good vocal quality is dependent.

These are a few examples of the types of problems that can prevent good ensemble singing. For the purpose of clarity the discussion of common problems will be treated in two parts—visible problems and audible problems. Artistic choral singing is dependent upon vocal freedom. When properly produced, the singing voice has a satisfying quality, a psychological effect of being free. Any hindrance to this freedom must be removed. Many of these visible symptoms of poor vocalism can be handled during the rehearsal. Since music is an aural art, the final proof of quality in choral singing is the sound of the ensemble. Many directors sacrifice a vital vocal sound for musical interpretation and, consequently, put up with audible faults in their choral singers that have relatively simple solutions.

Visible Problems

1. *Poor posture* is perhaps the most common problem in choral singing. A choir which exhibits good posture will usually sing well. Poor posture is almost always due to carelessness, laziness, or lack of training. (See page 80 for exercises to develop correct posture.)

2. *Protruding jaw* tends to establish an unnatural head position and thus creates undesirable tension and stiffness about the mouth and neck. This undue tension will prevent the free vibration of the vocal cords and resonance cavities and thereby change the normal sound spectrum on which good vocal quality is dependent. The usual result is a shrill or thin vocal sound.

The best solution to this problem is a jaw that is comfortably relaxed. To achieve relaxation have the choir move the jaw from side to side as they vocalize to establish the feeling of a "floating" lower jaw. The best position of the head and chin is one that is perpendicular to the shoulders.

3. *Chin turned up* is a common fault caused usually by an unconscious reaction to singing high notes—the attempt to "reach" for high notes. When this vocal fault is detected, it should be cured by having the choir move their heads from side to side and up and down until an easy, relaxed position is obtained. Choral singers should be taught to think low on high notes and to think high on low notes. If the problem persists, have the choir bend over when vocalizing high notes to break the habit of "reaching."

4. *Chin turned down* in a singer—most often an alto or bass—is an attempt to establish a stronger or more resonant tone quality in the lower register. A practice that is effective in keeping the singer from turning the chin up is often a bad habit when used to "reach" for low notes. Singers should be encouraged to keep their heads in the same position (without constriction) on all notes. A consistently turned-down chin will result in an excessively dark or throaty quality.

5. *Raised or hunched shoulders* on inhaling is a natural reaction of the untrained singer. Technically called clavicular or upper chest breathing, this method is the least desirable of the three types of breathing commonly practiced. The exercises on pages 80–83 will help to develop correct posture and achieve effective diaphragmatic-intercostal breathing, and an explanation of the principles of breathing should be referred to on pages 58–63.

6. *Singing with a blank expression.* Since choral music is usually composed with some sort of text, it is assumed that the composer is trying to communicate a specific message to an audience. Communication is virtually impossible without some kind of expression on the face of the individual choral singer, i.e., joy, sadness, fear, praise, etc. When the face of the singer is blank, it is usually an indication that the conductor has not developed an empathic relationship with his singers. Choral singers normally reflect the facial expression of the conductor.

The face of the conductor should reflect in some way the message the work intended to convey. It might also be helpful to read or translate the text in rehearsal so that the singers are aware of its meaning. Conductors who do not convey expression to their singers should work in front of a mirror to improve their facial interpretations. The director can create a dramatic quality in his singers by insisting on absolutely clear enunciation, by stressing the poetic value of the lyrics, and by adapting the color of each musical phrase to the mood of the word it accompanies.

7. *A wrinkled forehead* is usually an unconscious habit or mannerism which reflects either vocal problems or a lack of coordination within the vocal mechanism. If this is a characteristic of only one or two singers, the director should take them aside after the rehearsal and work with them privately. Care should be taken not to embarass individual singers during the rehearsal. Staccato and legato exercises on octave arpeggios will help to restore the coordination within the vocal mechanism. It is also helpful to ask the singer to look into a mirror while vocalizing to see if he can determine why he wrinkles his brow.

8. *A tongue which rises up* in the back of the mouth can reduce the size of the resonance cavity in the throat. This retracted tongue position is a common problem and affects the quality of tone production in the chest voice. Its cause is either a weakness in the muscles of the tongue or a lack of balanced coordination between the pressure flow of the breath and the openness of the vowel sounds.

The singer who is afflicted with a protracted tongue should practice exercises to develop flexibility of the tongue: extend and retract the tongue rapidly, then change the motion to a side to side movement. A simulated yawn will also help to lower the tongue and open the throat.

To develop a balanced coordination between the pressure flow of the breath and the open vowel, the singers should place the tips of the fingers on their midsections below the breastbone and above the waistline. Ask them to clear their throats or call "hey." Then have them call "hey," and sustain the vowel sound "ey" on one pitch by maintaining the pressure flow of the breath. With this same technique have them sing arpeggios (triads and octaves) up and down the scale, legato and staccato.

9. *Bulging neck muscles* in choral singing are the result of excessive tension in the neck and jaw muscles and is probably caused by forcing the tone. The exercises on page 96 to develop proper tone production should be combined with the exercises to establish nasal resonance and those to loosen the lower jaw.

10. *A flushed face* is the result of forcing the voice beyond its technical capabilities and is usually due to a lack of proper registration, or trying to sing too loudly without the proper coordination of the vocal mechanism.

The best solution to this vocal problem is for the conductor to take the singer aside and give him a series of private voice lessons to establish a basic vocal technique. It is also most important to have the student avoid singing with a full voice until proper vocal production has been established.

Audible Problems

1. *Nasality* is a tonal quality, a vocal trait of many untrained singers. It is the result of a small mouth opening, weak pharyngeal resonance, and a low, soft palate (or any combination of the three) which causes the breath to pass through the nose during singing. Nasality is considered to be an objectionable quality for choral singers, not only because it is unpleasant for the listener, but also because it interferes with normal vocal production.

To eliminate nasality, open the mouth and throat. Yawning or simulating a yawn during vocalization is a physical device that is effective in raising the soft palate. Then also, singing with a slight smile will give additional help in this effort. Beyond this be certain that there is a consistent flow of breath pressure throughout the vocal exercises. Using the vowels "ee" and "ay," place the prefixes "h" and "m" in front and call loudly in the middle of the register "hee" and "hay." Repeat several times. Then use "mee" and "may." Once the proper flow of breath pressure has been established, the following exercises can be used effectively:

Hee _____ Hoh   Hay _____ Hoh   Mee _____ Moh   May _____ Moh

The nose test—holding the nose closed with the thumb and forefinger—should reveal, by a change in quality, whether or not breath is passing through the nose during vocalization on open-vowel sounds—arpeggio fashion. The use of the vowels "ah" and "oh" sung with the lips and mouth in an open position will also be helpful in eliminating nasality if practiced regularly.

2. *A tone quality lacking nasal resonance* creates a dull and muffled sound. A properly produced vocal tone is characterized by strong vibrations in the nasal cavities, i.e., nose and sinuses. This condition differs from nasality in that the same resonance vibrations are felt but with the breath passing through the nose during tone production.

Vocal exercises built on the "hum" should establish a basic nasal resonance, provided that they are practiced slowly and with a feeling of openness in the mouth and throat. Use bright "ee" and "ay" vowels in the following patterns, even exaggerating the brightness to the point of being ugly to overcome the dull tone. Later the sound should even up with the correct balance of nasal and mouth resonance.

Hmm
(Ee)

Hmm
(Ah)

3. *"Hooty"* classifies two types of vocal sound: one in which there is an overemphasis of mouth resonance for the purpose of making a big sound; and one in which there is a straight tone resulting from a weak diaphragmatic breath pressure in a rigid or inflexible throat. Both may also be the result of a poor conception of tone quality. In both cases normal nasal resonance must be established through humming exercises and pure vowel vocalises. Omit the "oo" vowel because it most nearly resembles the sound to be changed.

To project the vowel sounds away from the throat, use trilling exercises of alternating half steps and whole steps in the middle or lower tessitura. These exercises should accelerate in tempo to develop flexibility.

Half-step
trills

Ah _____
Oh _____
Eh _____
Ee _____

Whole step trills

Mah _____
Moh _____
May _____
Mee _____

4. *A tight, pinched-sounding tone* quality is the result of a small, tight throat position, a small mouth opening, or a lack of breath support. This problem is especially common in high school and church choirs.

To open the mouth and throat, use humming and modified yawning exercises which will establish a nasal resonance with an open throat position. If the pinched quality is found only in connection with the upper voice, treat it as you would the development of smooth registration. Where the problem is generally found throughout the range, the singer should practice exercises in the lower part of his range before trying to master the changes necessary for the upper register. Because there is often a special inhibition associated with an inner expansion of this type, the singer must be encouraged to exaggerate both the expansion of the mouth and throat and the volume of the sound produced as he sings down the scale. In this way, the correctly produced tone will seem more natural.

5. *Throatiness* (or throaty quality) is a lack of full resonance caused by an overemphasis on open tone singing and a deficiency of diaphragmatic action. Use humming exercises that emphasize an open throat to establish nasal resonance; vocalize "ee" and "ay" vowels with nasal prefixes "m" and "n." Employ vocal exercises which build up breath pressure such as those found on page 97.

6. *Guttural quality* is a condition usually the result of constriction in the throat, resulting in a heavy quality that is lacking nasal resonance. It might also be caused by an overemphasis on the neutral vowel "uh" in vocalization. Normally it is a problem especially prevalent in altos and basses.

To establish a normal quality, vocalize on the brighter vowels "ee" and "ay" and add the prefixes "h" and "m" (hee, hay, mee, may). If the quality does not improve, vocalize slowly and carefully on a "hum" and emphasize proper breath pressure at the level of the diaphragm.

7. *A strident quality* is usually caused by singing in the upper register with a throaty sound quality that is lacking in sufficient breath pressure. This condition may also be caused by the position of the head in relation to the shoulders and body. When the head is tilted too high, the resulting vocal sound tends to be shrill.

Establish head voice register by vocalizing on "ah," "oo," and "ee" vowels with prefixes "h" and "m" in descending scale patterns. Sustain strong breath pressure throughout the vocalise. Simulate a feeling of yawning during exercises to open throat and nasal resonance cavities. Use humming techniques to create the illusion of head voice production.

8. *A tremolo* is a rapid pulsation of pitch fluctuation that is usually caused by a throaty tone production. Throatiness results from an unnatural function of the vocal mechanism. In order to avoid discomfort, the vocal organs seek relief by distributing the tension over as wide an area as possible. For this reason the tension spreads to the muscles of the jaw and tongue and does not remain confined to the throat itself. By continuing this practice over a long period of time, the tension that builds up causes a fluttering of the entire vocal mechanism. It is this fluttering that is heard as a tremolo.

The cure for the tremolo involves rebuilding the vocal technique. The production is obviously incorrect and must be changed by establishing vowel purity, resonance, and proper registration. As soon as proper registration is established, the tone quality will change and the tremolo will gradually disappear. These exercises should be combined with a planned relaxation of the neck, chest, and shoulders. When these conditions have been established, the tonal flutter will disappear and the tremolo should no longer be a problem.

9. *Wobble* is one of the more undesirable vocal sounds from the standpoint of artistic choral singing. A wobble is a pitch change whose width and unevenness of amplitude and periodicity are its distinguishing characteristics. Like the tremolo —but unlike the vibrato—there is no relationship between the amplitude of the pitch change that takes place in the wobbly tone and the intensity of the sound produced. The vibrato is a perfectly even pulsation whose amplitude is governed by intensity. The tremolo is an irregular tonal flutter whose cause can be traced to some kind of vocal constriction. The wobbly tone is a slow, wide pitch change that is usually caused by "driving" or forcing the voice. It also may be caused by a deteriorating physical condition or old age, for which there is little cure.

Correcting the wobble in most voices is a relatively simple process. Since forcing the tone for volume is normally the cause, the first step is to reduce the energy expended so that all "push" is eliminated. The second step is to give the male falsetto and female chest register the prominence in vocalization which will return the voice to its natural quality. Refer to the exercises to develop the registers on pages 101–103.

10. *Lack of intensity* when considered on its own tends usually to be equated with loudness. However, intensity is obviously more than volume. A vocal sound can be loud either because of sheer physical vitality or because of intense emotional involvement. Because musical interpretation is a projection of the emotional through the physical, it is quite evident that the two are to some degree inseparable. Thus, the cause of a "thin" vocal quality can usually be attributed to the following factors: inadequate diaphragmatic action, and fear of oversinging or forcing the voice. Pure physical weakness of the entire body is also a major cause, as well as a negative attitude toward inserting one's self into a dramatic portrayal of musical emotions.

A fully resonant vocal tone is dependent on an increase of breath pressure which in turn causes a muscular involvement that engages the entire respiratory tract. Another factor is the resonance adjustment made in order to amplify the tone to the fullest possible extent. A good vocal technique maintains optimum resonance at all times, regardless of the level of volume being sung. Most choral singers fail to do this: they decrease the volume by shutting off or constricting, and increase by pushing or forcing the tone. A fully resonant and vital tone quality is the sound of a vocal mechanism that is completely coordinated. To allow the singer to experience the strength associated with singing at any volume, have him place his fingertips against your sternum as you crescendo and diminish a vocalized sound. He should feel expansion rather than collapse of the chest. For example, have the singer push down slightly on the top of a grand piano or table to arrive at that slight feeling of resistance as he sings. Explain that this feeling should be experienced at all times. Of course, this must not become a detached act, rather it comes eventually from physical involvement with the line and tension of the musical structure.

11. *Noisy breathing,* which is a common problem in choral singing, might be represented either by a gasping for breath or obvious nose breathing. The former may be caused by an insufficient breathing method that will sustain long phrases, poor breath pressure, or nervousness. Nose breathing is often caused by a mouth that is not opened widely enough or a tongue that is not relaxed.

Use the exercises on page 88 to restore proper breathing for singing. Since very few choral conductors recommend nose breathing, the singer who is having this problem should be encouraged to breathe through the mouth exclusively.

NOTES

1. Edmund H. Fellowes, *William Byrd* (London: Oxford University Press, 1948), p. 149.

Chapter Four

RECOMMENDED READING LIST

Christy, Van Ambrose. *Expressive Singing.* Dubuque, Iowa: W. C. Brown Co., 1961, 4 vol. A comprehensive source that includes the most useful ideas bearing on the problem of singing and the teaching of singing.

Dodd, George Robert, and James Dunlop Lickley. *The Control of the Breath.* 2nd edition. London: Oxford University Press, 1935. Two English doctors write on the physiology of the breathing mechanism.

Lamperti, G. B. *The Technique of Bel Canto.* Translated by Theodore Baker. New York: G. Schirmer, Inc., 1905. The traditions and precepts that developed the great voices of the Golden Age of Song are presented by a famous teacher.

Ross, William Ernest. *Secrets of Singing.* Bloomington: Indiana University Press, 1959. An objective approach to the teaching of singing. The comparison of various schools of vocal technique is especially valuable.

Witherspoon, Herbert. *Singing; A Treatise for Teachers and Students.* New York: G. Schirmer, Inc., 1925. One of the most important American teachers of the first half of this century presents a middle road between the scientific and empirical approaches to the teaching of voice.

Chapter Five

Choral Diction

The whole plan of singing in musical modes should be
constituted not to give empty pleasure to the ear, but in such a
way that the words may be clearly understood by all, and thus
the hearts of the listeners be drawn to the desire of heavenly harmonies, in the contemplation of the joys of the blessed.
—COUNCIL OF TRENT (1562)

CHORAL DICTION IS the clear and accurate articulation of the phonetic elements of
the text of a musical work for the purpose of communicating its meaning to the
listener. Prior to the establishment of regular polyphonic singing in the Church,
there was little problem communicating the text in choral singing; not only were
the liturgical texts generally known to most of the congregation but the words were
clearly audible because of the simplicity of the texture of the music with which
they were associated. Before the availability of the printed Bible, the reinforcement
of spoken scripture by singing was the aim of the style; in fact, the very pattern
of plainsong is in great part a result of this need for clarity.

The introduction of polyphonic music alongside this simpler transmittal of
text in the liturgy posed a problem that has not been completely solved by any
subsequent change in compositional style. This new musical utterance created a
musical texture in which different syllables of text or even different words were
sounded at the same time. Confusion was often multiplied as musical styles—
secular as well as sacred—continued to develop utilizing different phrases or entire
poems that were pitted against each other in the musical texture. One result of all
this was a series of decrees, such as the one found at the head of this chapter.

The problem of communicating the text in choral performance faced an even greater challenge when the addition of instrumental forces—often in vast numbers—created a musical texture that threatened to completely sacrifice the text for new and colorful musical sonorities. The large nineteenth-century orchestra and the dissonant compositional practices of the twentieth century made it absolutely imperative that the individual choral singer understand the mechanics of singing diction. Execution of clear, definitive, and consistent vowel sounds and consonants would thereby fulfill the intentions of the composer who assumed that the text would be heard and understood by the audience.

John Finley Williamson, founder of the famed Westminster Choir, wrote that "correct pronunciation in singing helps to create the mood which the composer intended." This is a fact because the several vowels, due to their acoustical spectra, excite different images within the mind of the listener. The careful acknowledgment by the choral singer of the difference between vowels helps to sustain interest in the audience and, of no less importance, aids in keeping the vocal mechanism relaxed. Most faulty vocal production is due to poor mental awareness of vowel sounds. Therefore, it should be remembered that all good singing is conceived in the mind before it is produced by the vocal apparatus.

Generally it seems that a singer's vocal technique may be judged by the vowels he sings, while his sensitivity and artistry are evident by the manner in which he treats the consonants and weaves the whole into musical phrases. It is the responsibility of the teacher and conductor to nurture the complete development of his singers. Choral diction thus becomes one of the important elements in the choral experience.

This chapter seeks to emphasize the importance of choral diction. After presenting some coverage of general diction rules and their application to the English language, five other languages will be explored (Latin, Spanish, Italian, German, and French), in terms of English whenever possible. Difficulty often arises when different letters or combinations of letters are used to represent like sounds. The explanations and examples given in the individual language sections will be of help in this area. The singer and conductor must learn to recognize sounds which are common in several languages, especially where English equivalents are appropriate. Especially useful in this area is the alphabet of phonetic symbols that was devised by the International Phonetic Association before the turn of the century. The majority of these symbols are presented in the chart (together with word examples from the languages to which they apply) on pages 148–151. Following the discussion of each language, an excerpt is included from a choral work employing that language.

VOWELS

Singing has been defined as intensified or sustained speech. In all languages this sustaining process is accomplished through the vowel sounds. The vowels are used in vocalization to condition the voice to this sustaining nature of singing. The open-throated "ah" is often used for purposes of voice building, since studies have shown that in forming this vowel the vocal cords are in a position nearest to their normal "at rest" position. This suggests that vowel sounds are actually initiated by vibrations of the vocal cords. In a rough form, they are then clarified and intensified by the changes in relative sizes of the resonators. For instance, the vowel "ah" is most clear when the tongue is loose and flat, thus allowing a large mouth cavity; whereas, the vowel "ee" is most colorful when the tongue is arched in the middle, leaving little mouth opening. However, the most important guide to the pronunciation of vowels is the ear. This is a dangerous statement because far too many singers judge their sound by what they hear inside their heads. This practice can be avoided by using a good tape recorder to evaluate individual growth. In choral performance, the conductor must develop his ear so that he can make quick adjustments of faulty production of the vowels. For instance, singers often tighten their lower jaw when singing, thus creating tension which will adversely affect the choral tone.

The basic vowels used in the singing of the English language are listed below, together with common word examples containing these words. Whenever possible it is most effective to relate any desired vowel (even in another language) to these few sample words. This brings to mind a standard mental concept of vowel placement and quality.

	IPA SYMBOL
a, o as in *psalm, sod*	[ɑ]
e as in *set*	[ɛ]
i as in *sit*	[ɪ]
e as in *see*	[i]

a   as in *sat, lamb*   [a]   (Note that this is not the
                                                        flat "a" like the sound of
                                                        sheep. Rather it is a more
                                                        intermediate sound, more
                                                        appropriate for sustained
                                                        singing.)

a, as in *say*   [ei]

o, u as in *soon*   [u]

o, u as in *soot*   [ʊ]

a, o as in *saw*   [ɔ]

yr, ir, er,
or, ur, as in *earth*
(without the "r")   [ɜ]

o, oo, ou, u
as in *sung*   [ʌ]

[The neutral vowel]
as the "a" in *sofa*   [ə]   (This vowel occurs only in
                                                        unstressed syllables, and is
                                                        not exactly like ʌ since a
                                                        tinge of the printed vowel
                                                        is present.)

o (in an unstressed syllable)   [o]   (This vowel is neither a
   such as in *obey*   broad "aw," nor the diph-
                                                        thong as in *so*, but it is
                                                        used in accented syllables
                                                        as the sustained vowel of
                                                        this diphthong.)

One way of approaching the principle of vowel formation in the English language is to think of their open and closed characteristics and of their relative placement when articulated. The "oo" (*soon*) vowel can be considered the most open vowel and the "ee" (*see*) the most closed. Thus the sound spectrum (as visualized) proceeds as follows:

When conceived in terms of placement from back to front when articulated, the visualized spectrum looks like this:

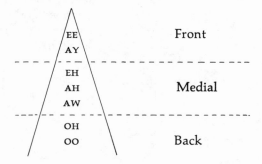

Beginning at C in the low voice and E in the high voice, "see" gradually opens toward "sit" (IH), and "soon" opens toward "soot" (UH). Thus, all vowels modify to two vowel sounds in the singer's very high tessitura. This follows the register principle explained in chapters three and four. In the upper range, the strident quality that would be present if chest-voice vowels were carried into the upper register is eliminated. This is very much a matter of coordination on the part of the singer and a measure of the conductor's ability to distinguish vowel colors. When handled correctly, the natural buoyancy and agility of the body takes away any tension from the jaw and throat muscles in the extreme ranges.

DIPHTHONGS

A diphthong is a sound consisting of two vowels, one sustained and the other treated as a vanishing vowel, within the same syllable. The vanishing vowel is treated as a consonant in terms of the time value alloted to it, depending on the dramatic quality of the word in question. The five principal diphthongs are:

	IPA SYMBOL		
vɑ as in *vie*	[ɑɪ]	vɑ ——————— ɪ	
sɛ as in *say*	[ɛɪ]	sɛ ——————— ɪ	
bɔ as in *boy*	[ɔɪ]	bɔ ——————— ɪ	
vɑ as in *vow*	[ɑʊ]	vɑ ——————— ʊ	
so as in *so*	[oʊ]	so ——————— ʊ	

A slightly different kind of diphthong occurs when the letter "u" appears in such words as *use;* when "u" or "ew" follows one of the consonants—d, n, l (itself preceded by a vowel), s, t, th; and when "y" begins a syllable such as *you*. In these cases, the vanishing vowel (really an initiating vowel) appears first (iu). Other words having this sound include *dew, view, tune, Tuesday*.

Several diphthongs and triphthongs (three vowels) are occasioned by the neutral vowel which replaces the "r" or "re" in words such as:

*ai*r [ɛə]

*ea*r [ɪə]

*o*re [ɔə]

*su*re [ʊə]

*i*re [ɑɪə]

*ou*r [ɑʊə]

The special problem in diphthongs and triphthongs must be explained to choral singers to ensure their clear enunciation in choral literature.

CONSONANTS

Various noises and humming sounds serve to delineate vowels and thus give character to the words themselves. These consonants are produced by vibrations of the vocal cords or the breath in the mouth and the stoppage of the lips, teeth, tongue, or palate. This stoppage may be complete, as with the "m" and "n," or partial as with the sibilants (f, s, etc.). The consonants fall into five categories:

I. Vocal Consonants Having Pitch

m	zh
n	th (as in *thee*)
ng	w ⎫ function
l	y ⎭ as vowels
r	b (subvocal
v	at beginning
z	of word)

II. Voiced Explosives

b ⎫ voiced by addition
d ⎬ of *-uh* at end of
g ⎭ word
j = dg

III. Pure (Voiceless) Explosives

p
t
k

IV. Sibilants

    f, s, sh, ch, th (as in *thin*)

V. Aspirate

    h

Most consonants have IPA symbols which are consistent with their spelling: b, d, f, g, h, k, l, m, n, p, r, s, t, v, w, z.

A few basic rules for the articulation of consonants are listed below.

    1. Vocal consonants are sung on the same pitch as the vowel to which they are joined. Often syllabication in singing is different from that given in the dictionary. For instance, spir-it-u-al is sung spi-ri-tu-al.

    2. The most beautiful consonants (and vowels) are those sung with complete relaxation of the throat muscles and an active tongue.

    3. The time value of the consonant is proportionate to the drama of the word. The more dramatic the word, the longer the consonant.

    4. When a nasal consonant "m," "n," or "ng" occurs at the end of a word set above the pitch C in the low voice and E in the high voice, it is treated as a voiced consonant. When sung on high pitches, these consonants tend to modify to "uh" and "ih."

    5. Madeline Marshall cites three basic rules for omitting and sounding "r":[1]

a. "R" should never be sung before a consonant.

b. "R" should not be sung before a pause.

c. "R" should always be sung before a vowel sound. It is flipped gently (not a prolonged roll as in Italian opera) in English words of action, and between vowels. In other instances it is sung as the regular American "r," but without dialectical prolongation.

    6. Beginning consonants should precede the beat much in the manner of a grace note so that the vowel sound occurs at the beginning of the note value. For example:

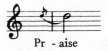

Pr - aise

For further study, the choral conductor should consult *The Singer's Manual of English Diction.*

O God, Thou Art My God

Henry Purcell (1659–1695)

LATIN

In this book the Latin pronunciation according to Roman usage will be used because most of the choral music in Latin was written for the Church, and the Roman dialect was authorized in a decree of Pope Pius X, *Motu Proprio* (1903). The rules which follow reflect the point of view that liturgical works should be sung in Church Latin. The definitive publication on this subject is *Latin Pronunciation According to Roman Usage*, William D. Hall, editor.

Vowels

There are six vowels in the Latin language: a, e, i, o, u, y. Their pronunciation is simple because each is a pure and open vowel sound, that is, one produced most effectively when the jaw is relaxed and the uvula is lifted as when yawning.

		EXAMPLE
a	is pronounced as the "a" in *father*.	*Alleluia*
e	is pronounced as the "e" in *set*.	*Kyrie*
i	is pronounced as the "ee" in *see*.	*Christe*
o	is pronounced as the "aw" in *saw*.	*Gloria*
u	is pronounced as the "oo" in *soon*.	*Factum*
y	is pronounced as the "ee" in *see*.	*Kyrie*

In instances where diphthongs, consecutive vowels, and double vowels appear in the text, it is common practice to enunciate each vowel distinctly. The two exceptions to this rule are "ae" and "oe," which both have the sound of "e" as in *set* (Ex. *saecula*, *coelestis*). Diphthongs include the following:

	EXAMPLE
au is pronounced as the "ow" in *vow*.	*laudate*
ua is pronounced as the "wa" in *water*.	*quam*
ii is pronounced as two consecutive "ee" sounds.	*filii*

Most American singers are unaware of the fact that they rarely sing pure vowels. At the end of vowels they insert a brief "uh" (ʌ) sound, which, in effect, transforms a monophong (single vowel) into a diphthong (double vowel). Singers must first be made aware of this tendency, and then taught to avoid it when singing the pure vowels of foreign languages.

Consonants

Consonants serve the important purpose of framing the vowels in Latin. They should be articulated quickly and never be allowed to obstruct the vowels. Double consonants are treated, as in Italian, by slight prolongation and suspension where they occur. Time must be taken from the vowels which precede these double consonants. The consonants b, d, f, k, l, m, n, p, s, t and v are pronounced almost as in English. D, t, and k are not strongly exploded as in English; they are gently enunciated, almost as suspended consonants. S is never pronounced as z.

c	pronounced as "k" when it precedes the vowels a, o, u; and before consonants; and at the end of a word. Ex. *credo, nunc.*
	pronounced as "ch" as in *church* when it precedes the vowels e, i, y, and the vowel combinations ae, oe, eu. Ex. *luceat, crucifixus.*
cc	pronounced as "tch" as in *which* before e, i, ae, oe, and y. Ex. *ecce.*
ch	has the hard "k" sound before any vowel. Ex. *charitas.*
g	pronounced as the "g" in *general* when it appears before e, i, oe, ae, and u. Ex. *genus, regina.*
	has a hard sound as in *give* in every other case, except when followed by n. (See below.) Ex. *gloria.*
gn	is pronounced as the "ny" in *canyon* when it occurs within a word. Ex. *agnus.*
	has the English sound when at the beginning of a word. Ex. *gnaeus.*
h	is silent in most cases—never aspirated as in English. When joined with "p," it is pronounced as an "f." Ex. *hominibus.*
	has the sound of "k" in words such as *mihi, nihil,* etc.
j	is pronounced as the "y" in *you.* (It is often written as *i*). Ex. *ejus, Jesu.*
ph	has the sound of "f." Ex. *phrenetici.*
qu	has the sound of "koo" as in *quiet.* Ex. *quam.*
r	rolled when it occurs at the beginning of a word; lightly flipped when it occurs at the middle or at the end of a word. Ex. *Requiem, Kyrie.*

sc	has the sound of "sh" as in *show* before e, i, y, ae, oe, and eu. Ex. *suscipe.*
	has the sound of "sk" as in *scare* before a, o, or u. Ex. *obscurentur.*
sch	has the "sk" sound, as in *school.* Ex. *schola.*
th	is pronounced as a pure "t." Ex. *thema.*
ti	is sung as "tsee" when followed by a vowel and preceded by any letter except s, t, or x. Ex. *gratia.*
	retains its sound as in English, when followed by a vowel and preceded by s, t, or x. Ex. *modestia.*
x	has a softer sound of "gs" when it is preceded by *e* and followed by a vowel. Ex. *exaltabo.*
	has the sound of "ks" in every other instance. Ex. *rex.*
xc	has the sound of "ks" before a, o, and u. Ex. *excarnificare.*
	has the sound of "sh" before e, i, y, ae, and oe. Ex. *excelsis.*
y	is a vowel (i).
z	is sung as "dz." Ex. *Lazaro.*

Occasionally, works composed by Germans or Austrians are sung with a German pronunciation of Latin, requiring only a few necessary adjustments:

1. ae, oe, and y are treated as umlaut sounds: ä, ö, and ü respectively. Ex. *Kyrie, saeculi.*
2. "c" is pronounced as "ts." Ex. *coelis; pacem.*
3. "g" has the sound of "g" as in *give,* even before *n.* Ex. *Agnus, agimus.*
4. "s" has the sound of "z," before vowels. Ex. *Sanctus, Sabaoth, Osanna.*
5. "qu" has the sound of "kv." Ex. *quia*

O Magnum Mysterium

Tomás Luis de Victoria (1549–1611)

ITALIAN

Because its vowel sounds are the purest of any of the Romance languages, and therefore most easily produced, the Italian language is considered the most musical of all the languages. The occurrence of diphthongs in Italian is rare. Italian words achieve their patterns of stress by the relative lengths of the vowels contained in the syllables. Furthermore, it is important to remember that every vowel is pronounced. Even a vowel which concludes a word is clearly pronounced and not minimized as in English. For instance *forte* is pronounced (for'-tɛ) and not (for'-tə). There are eight vowel sounds in Italian:

Vowels

a	is always pronounced as "a" in *father*.
e	has the sound of "e" in *set* when it occurs with stress: (1) in the third-from-last (or fourth-from-last) syllable of a word. Ex. *medico*. (2) in the next-to-last syllable when the last syllable is spelled with two vowels. Ex. *vecchio*. has a sound more closed than the "a" in *say* (without diphthong) in all other situations. Ex. *cine, temere*.
i	has the sound of "ee" in *see* when it is the only vowel in a syllable or follows another vowel in the same syllable. Ex. *di, idea, eroico*. has the sound of "y" as in *you* when it is unstressed and is followed by another vowel. Ex. *più, giocare*.
o	has the sound of "o" as in *obey* when it occurs with stress: (1) in the third-from-last (or fourth-from-last) syllable of a word. Ex. *povero*. (2) in the next-to-last syllable when the last syllable is spelled with two vowels. Ex. *goccia, gloria*. has a sound more closed than the "o" in *so* (without diphthong) in all other situations. Ex. *nove, piccolo*.
u	has the sound of "oo" in *soon* when it is the only vowel sound in a syllable or follows another vowel in the same syllable. Ex. *uno, più*. has the sound of "w" in *way* when followed by a vowel in the same syllable. Ex. *nuovo, guerra*.

The five basic vowels of the Italian language occur in about every possible combination as diphthongs. The more common of these combine a *strong* vowel (a, e, o) with a *weak* vowel (i and u). The strong vowel is sustained and the weak vowel is treated as a vanishing sound: e.g., *mai, causa, uomo.* When the two weak vowels combine to form a diphthong, the "u" is usually stressed: e.g., *più.* However, the "i" may be stressed, and then the "u" has the sound of *w:* e.g., *guida.* Consultation of a good dictionary is recommended in order to determine whether two contiguous vowels are intended as a diphthong (in one syllable) or as elements of two separate syllables.

Triphthongs are found occasionally, occurring as combinations, such as: "aio," "iei," "iuo," "uai," "uia," "uoi." The accentuated vowel gets the longest part of the note under which it stands. Each of the vowels should be pronounced clearly but connected in a legato manner.

Consonants

Speakers and singers of the Italian language render the consonants clearly and definitely, with a distinct action of the articulators. Single consonants are pronounced crisply but lightly. It is especially important that the p, t, and k should not be strongly aspirated as they are in English. It is only necessary that they be differentiated, by the listener, from their respective counterparts b, d, and g. Special rules for the pronunciation of certain consonants follow. The others (b, d, f, l, m, n, p, q, t, v) are pronounced much the same as in English, with the three exceptions noted above.

c	has the sound of "k" when it is followed by the letters a, o, u, h, l, or r. Ex. *caro, corpo, cuore, che, classe, credo.*
	has the sound of "ch" as in *chair* when it is followed by e or i. Ex. *cena, cielo, ciao.*
g	has the sound of "g" in *get* when followed by a, o, u, h, l, or r. Ex. *gamba, gola, gusto, ghiro, globo, grande.*
	has the sound of "g" as in *gem* when followed by e or i. Ex. *gente, gigante.*
gi	has the sound of "g" in *gem* when it is followed in the same syllable by a, o, or u. Ex. *già, giubba.*
	has the sound of "gee" as in *genial* when it is not followed in the same syllable by another vowel. Ex. *dogi.*

gl	has the sound of "gl" as in *glad* when followed by a, e, o, or u. Ex. *glaciale, globo*.
gli	has the sound of "lli" in *million* when it is followed in the same syllable by another vowel (a, e, o, u). Ex. *foglia, biglietto, figlio*.
	has the sound of "l ye" as in *will ye* when it occurs at the end of a word. Ex. *gli, egli*.
	has the sound of "glee" when it is followed in the same word by a consonant. Ex. *negligenza*.
gn	has the sound of the "ny" in *canyon*. Ex. *bagno*.
h	is always silent.
r	is always rolled by rapidly vibrating the tip of the tongue against the base of the upper front teeth. Ex. *caro, rosa, tardi*.
s	usually has the sound of "s" in *set* when: (1) it is initial. Ex. *sabbia, si*. (2) it is between two vowels of which the first one belongs to a prefix. Ex. *risuono*. usually has the sound of "z" as in *zeal* when it stands between two vowels or before another voiced consonant (b, d, g, l, m, n, r, v). Ex. *usare, rosa, slanciare*.
sc	has the sound of "sh" as in *share* before e or i. Ex. *scena, scimmia*. has the sound of "sk" as in *scare* in all other cases. Ex. *scusa, schema, scritto*.
sci	has the sound of "sh" as in *share* when it is followed by another vowel. Ex. *scialle, scienza*. has the sound of "she" when it is not followed in the same syllable by another vowel. Ex. *sci, scibile*.
z, zz	usually has the sound of "dz" as in *suds*: (1) at the start of words. Ex. *zio, zuppa*. (2) in all verbs ending in -izzare (-izzante, -izzato, etc.). Ex. *scandalizzare*. *usually* has the sound of "ts" as in *let's* when it occurs elsewhere. Ex. *altezza, azionare*.

Exceptions are numerous so dictionary consultation is necessary for "z" words. For instance, "zz" has the sound "dz" in *mezzo*.

Double consonants are always strongly stressed, in contrast to the gentle stress given to single consonants. Distinctive pronunciation of a double consonant is the only way to mark the difference between similarly spelled words, e.g., *fato-fatto, casa-cassa, lego-leggo*, etc. Double consonants are pronounced like one prolonged consonant, they are not to be divided. They necessarily shorten the vowel that precedes them and give intensity, impetus, and character to the words that contain them. In their execution, the tongue or lips form the double consonant at the end of the tone that has just been sung. In the case of pitched consonants (ll, mm, nn, etc.), the double consonant gets even more time, as a sort of anticipation to the next note, than does the single consonant. This will have the effect of a suspended consonant. In the case of occlusive and semiocclusive consonants (dd, gg, zz, cc, etc.) which, because of their nature, are over as soon as the occlusion breaks, a minute interruption of the vocal line occurs at the point of suspension. This interruption is inevitable and serves to stress the double consonant. When one word ends with the same consonant as the next word begins, the words are treated as double consonants, e.g., *nel libro*. Care must be taken that all consonants and especially the double consonants are made only with the articulators (and not the jaw), otherwise the vowel which follows will be jawed and a break in the musical line will result.

Accentuation

In most Italian words the stress is placed on the next-to-last syllable, which makes pronunciation fairly simple (e.g., *rotondo*). Occasionally the stress falls on the last syllable, and when this occurs, the syllable is always marked with an accent (e.g., *virtù*). This accent is also used over the vowels of one-syllable words to distinguish the meanings of identical spellings (e.g., *è = is; e = and*). Other words are stressed on the first or second syllable, but these are much fewer in number (e.g., *flaccido*).

Ecco Mormorar l'Onde

Claudio Monteverdi (1567–1643)

SPANISH

The valuable and rather extensive collection of choral literature by Spanish, Mexican, and Latin American composers sounds best when it is sung in its native language. This is especially true of the music of the nineteenth and twentieth centuries in which composers have been influenced by the desire to emphasize national and ethnic characteristics in their music. A few moments of rehearsal time devoted to the principles of Spanish diction can thus result in a satisfying and rewarding experience for the individual choral singer.

Vowels

Spanish vowels include a, e, i, o, u, and y, and are always clearly pronounced, as in Italian.

a	is pronounced "ah"
e	is pronounced like "ay" (without the diphthong)
i and y	are pronounced "ee"
o	is pronounced like "oh" (without the diphthong)
u	is pronounced like "oo"

When two strong vowels (a, o, e) are found together, they are pronounced separately and form two different syllables (e.g., *deseo, real*). If one of the vowels in a pair is "i" or "u" (so-called weak vowels), the other vowel takes precedence (e.g., *viaje*). In this case a true diphthong exists and the unstressed vowel, in this case "i," loses much of its identity and receives less duration. If "i" and "u" occur together, the stress is on the one which comes last, the two again counting as one syllable, the first vowel being passed over rapidly (e.g., *rudio, viuda*).

Consonants

In Spanish, consonants are often somewhat suppressed. The consonants f, k, l, m, n, p, and x are pronounced as in English. The letters k and w occur only in words of foreign origin: the letter w is pronounced according to the rules of the foreign language of the word's origin.

b	is not as strongly sounded as in English. Ex. *bueno, bastante*.
c	has the sound of "th" as in *thin* when followed by e or i. Ex. *centro, vecino*.
	has the sound of "k" in other cases. Ex. *contar*.
ch	is pronounced like "ch" in *church*. Ex. *mucho, muchacho*.
d	is pronounced as in English when it is the first letter of a word or is immediately preceded by n or l. Ex. *diente, donde*.
	is more lightly pronounced in word endings, such as -ado or -ido. Ex. *mando, entregado*.
g	has the guttural sound like the German "ch" as in *Buch* when followed by e or i. Ex. *gigante, general*.
	has the hard sound of "g" as in *gate* in other cases. Ex. *gato*.
h	is not pronounced. Ex. *hablar, ahora*.
j	has the guttural sound like German "ch" as in *Buch*. Ex. *jugar, bajo*.
ll	has the sound of "lli" in English *million*. Ex. *caballo, calle*.
ñ	has very much the sound of "ni" as in *onion*. Ex. *niño, mañana*.
q	is always followed by "u" and has the sound of *k*, as in English. Ex. *quiero*.
r	is rolled, especially at the beginning and end of words. Ex. *rio, tomar*.
s	always has the sound of "s" as in *sat*. Ex. *seso, sabado*.
t	is pronounced more vigorously than in most English words. Ex. *trabajo, traer*.
v	is often pronounced less strongly than in English, especially in some areas of Spain or Latin America. Ex. *vida*.
z	sounds like "th" as in *thin*. Ex. *zapato, brazo*.

In Spanish only the acute accent (') appears. It is used in the following manner:

(1) to indicate that the emphasis or stress is to be laid on the vowel over which it is placed.

(2) in words like *cuando* (when) and *donde* (where) to make them interrogative. Ex. *¿Cuándo?, ¿Dónde?*

(3) to distinguish between words spelled alike but of different meaning.

There are three basic rules for determining stress of words:

(1) In words ending in a consonant, the last syllable is stressed.
(2) In words ending in a vowel, the next-to-last syllable is stressed.
(3) In words conforming to these rules, the printed accent mark is not needed as a guide to pronunciation.

The consonants n and s, when added to form plurals, do not affect the stress.

Liaison

In speaking English we do not always pronounce each word in a sentence separately and are apt to run some of them together. While this is often a mark of carelessness in English pronunciation, Spanish speakers and singers employ this running together of words to produce pleasant, smooth sounds. This *liaison* is most evident in the French language as we shall see, but also occurs in all Romance languages when two vowel sounds come together, as a general rule. For instance, *mi abuelo* would sound *mia-bue-lo; una iglesia* would sound *u–nai–gle–sia.*

Por Unos Puertos Arriva

Antonio de Ribera Fl. 1514

GERMAN

The choral singer should not encounter unusual diction problems in the German language because most of the sounds which occur in German are easy for the English-speaking person to comprehend. A small number of sounds which do not have direct English counterparts will be explained so that their use may become more natural and unaffected. While tradition and experience figure heavily in the forming of laws for pronunciation of Italian and French, the rules for German diction are presented in an official publication, *Deutsche Hochsprache; Bühnenaussprache,* by Theodore Siebs. The foremost experts in phonetic and stage (singing) diction are among its contributors.

Vowels

As is the case in the Romance languages, the vowels are again the main elements on which the tones are built. German has long and short vowels, as well as diphthongs. All single vowels are pure, i.e., they are monophthongs, and therefore have no diphthongal glide as in the English letters a and o. The distinction between long and short vowels is very important but is not always indicated by spelling. Generally, however, a vowel is short when it is followed by a double consonant (*bitte*), or by two or more consonants (*binde*). A vowel is usually long when followed by an h in the same syllable (*gehen*), or when followed by a single consonant (*den*). This long-short differentiation is based on the proportionate duration of the vowel to the consonants, and affects the actual sound of the vowel to a greater or lesser degree.

VOWELS	LONG: AS IN	SHORT: AS IN	UNSTRESSED ONLY: AS IN
a	Saat (Eng. *father*)	satt (Eng. *cot*)	
e	Beet (Eng. closed "a" as in *say*, but without the diphthong)	Bett (Eng. *set*)	
-e (at end of word)			gebe (like Eng. *sofa*)

-er (at end of word)			Geber (like Eng. *sung*)
i	ihn (Eng. *see*)	in (Eng. *sit*)	
o	Ofen (Eng. closed "o" as in *so*, but without the diphthong)	offen (Eng. "aw" as in *saw*)	
u	Buhle (Eng. *soon*)	Bulle (Eng. *soot*)	

Umlaut

The two dots over ä, ö, ü, are called Umlaut. Occasionally, especially in names, these sounds are spelled out ae, oe, ue (e.g., Goethe = Göthe). This is particularly useful to know when a mass is performed with Germanized Latin employing such words as *coelis*, rendered *cölis*. These vowels are also classified as either long or short.

VOWELS	LONG	SHORT
ä	Fähre (like Ger. *Beet*)	ertränken (like Ger. *Bett*)
ö	höflich (like Ger. *Beet*, but with lips rounded)	göttlich (like Ger. *Bett*, but with lips rounded)
ü	müde (like Eng. *see*, but with lips rounded)	füllen (like Eng. *sit*, but with lips rounded)

Notice that the same rules for determining length of vowels apply here. The letter "y" occurs in words of Greek derivation (e.g., *Kyrie*). It sounds like ü and follows the same rules for length, although both usually tend closer to *see*.

Diphthongs

There are three German diphthongs, two of which can be spelled in two different ways: ei (ai), eu (äu), and au.

ei (ai)   has the sound of "ie" in *vie*

eu (äu) has the sound of "oi" in *voice*
au has the sound of "ow" in *vow*

Like all German vowels, these must be pronounced more precisely and more clearly than their English counterparts. Incidentally, notice that "ie" is pronounced *ee*, but "ei" is *ah-ee*. In English terms, one pronounces the second vowel in these two German combinations.

Consonants

There is a widely held misconception that German is the language of harsh consonants. Today German is usually sung according to the principles of classical Italian singing. While the characters of the consonants are not slighted in the least, they are handled lyrically so that the diction remains primarily based on pure vowels. Most consonants in German are pronounced in a fashion similar to their English equivalents. The German consonants b, d, f, h, k, l, m, n, p, t, and x are nearly the same as in English. B, d, and g are often given special treatment:

b at the end of a syllable or before t is pronounced "p." Ex. *Lob, habt.*
d at the end of a syllable or before t is pronounced "t." Ex. *Tod.*
g at the end of a syllable containing a long vowel, or a short vowel and an r or l, is pronounced "k." Ex. *Burg.*
   in a word or syllable ending in -ig is pronounced like the forward "ch" described below. Ex. *König.* However, if another soft "ch" appears in the same word, the -ig retains its lightly voiced form. Ex. *Ewiglich.*

The following consonants also need special care in pronunciation:

ch is pronounced as a forward sibilant (produced by exaggeration of the aspiration of "h" in *hue*) whenever it follows ä, e i, ö, ü, ai, ei, äu, l, r, or n. Ex. *Bächlein, sprechen, Licht, feucht, mancher.*

is pronounced as a guttural sound (produced by aspiration between the back of the tongue and the soft palate) whenever it follows a, o, u, or au. Ex. *Bach, hoch, Fluch.*

is pronounced as "sh" in words of French origin. Ex. *Chef.*

is pronounced as "k" in words of Greek origin. Ex. *Chor.*

g	is occasionally pronounced (in words of French origin) as the "s" in *measure*. Ex. *Genie*.
j	is pronounced like "y" in *you*. Ex. *ja, Jahr, Jugend*.
	is pronounced (in words of French origin) as the "s" in *measure*. Ex. *Journalist*.
r	is trilled in singing. Ex. *Krieg, Burg*.
s	is voiceless (as in *sat*): (1) at the end of a word or syllable. Ex. *das, loskommen*. (2) when the spelling β is used. Ex. *Fuß, mäßig*. (3) in the middle of a word after consonants other than r, l, m, and n. Ex. *Erbse, sechse*. is voiced (as in *rose*): (1) if it is an initial sound. Ex. *Salome, so, Segen*. (2) if it appears between vowels in the middle of a word. Ex. *Rose, Hase*. (3) if it appears between an m, n, l, or r on one side and a vowel on the other side, or after a prefix. Ex. *unser, Ab-sicht*. (4) when a word ends with -sal, -sam. Ex. *langsam, Schicksal*
sch	is pronounced like the English *sh*. Ex. *schön, Busch*.
st/sp	pronounced as written in the middle or at the end of word. Ex. *bester, lispeln*. pronounced as "sht" and "shp" at the beginning of a word or after a prefix. Ex. *Spinne, gesprochen*.
th	is always pronounced as a pure "t." Ex. *Theorie, Muth*.
-tion	is pronounced tseeon.
v	is usually pronounced like the English "f." Ex. *Vater*. is pronounced as the English "v" in words of foreign origin. Ex. *Villa*.
w	is pronounced like the English "v." Ex. *warum*.
y	See ü in the section on vowels.
z, tz	always pronounced as "ts." Ex. *Herz, Kreuz, Platz*

Based on the Italian practice, sung German treats double consonants by giving them double time value when the drama demands. Therefore, one must shorten the preceding vowel and close to the consonant sooner. This is not natural to the German language, according to Siebs, so it is necessary that the performer be careful to limit this practice to certain characteristic words such as *Himmel* (heaven), *Sonne* (sun), etc.

When two explosive sounds (not double consonants) occur together (t-t, d-d, t-d, etc.), the first is not exploded but suspended, and then the second is exploded well. Ex. *ist das*.

There are several situations in which final consonants and initial vowels, or two vowels, must be separated: (1) if a word must be isolated for euphonic reasons [Ex. Eng. *slumbers not*]; (2) if rhythmic or dramatic emphasis demands it; or (3) for general clarity of diction in large choral works. Where such separation is called for, the glottal stroke is necessary. Contrary to the teaching of some pedagogues, the gentle use of the stroke will never hurt a singer who has correct vocal instruction. In fact, gentle glottal strokes are regularly employed in any kind of staccato singing and are quite unlike the violent attacks which indeed do create hoarseness, thickening of the vocal cords, and even nodes on the cords. If you neglect to use the glottal stop, you may find yourself in an embarrassing situation. For instance, if your choir does not use the stop in front of *-au*, the audience may interpret the name of the village of *Himmelsau* as Celestial Pig instead of Heavenly Meadow.

Roses, All Blooming

Johannes Brahms, Op. 112 (1833–1897)

FRENCH

French is a much more complicated language phonetically than all the others except English. There are sixteen different phonetic vowel sounds in French. The English-speaking singer will find the whole group of vowels and nasal sounds difficult to master. In general, French singing diction conforms to the rules of Italian singing, with the unavoidable exceptions of the unique French vowel sounds. For vocal purposes, the nasal sounds also must be adjusted, because if the velum is lowered too much, as in speaking, the resonance switches from the mouth to the nose, and an uneven vocal line results. Notable French artists themselves make these language modifications.

Vowels

French vowels, with the exception of combinations involving the semivowels y and w, are clear-cut and should not be altered by changes in the position of the tongue, lips, or jaw. This prevents the vowels from gliding into diphthongs, which never occur in French.

The choral singer will notice certain written "accents" in the French language. These are not for the purpose of indicating accentuation. Rather, they are actually parts of the spelling which serve to change the pronunciation or differentiate two words which are spelled alike otherwise.

(1) *Accent aigu* (′), or acute accent, is used only on the letter e. It gives it the sound of a closed "a" as in *say*, but without the diphthong. Ex. *cité*.

(2) *Accent grave* (`), or grave accent, when placed over the letter e gives it the open sound of the "e" as in set. Ex. *prophète*. When placed over the letter a, it designates a short, intermediate sound as in *task*. Ex. *voilà*.

(3) *Accent circonflex* (^), or circumflex accent, gives the letter e the same sound as *è*. On a or o, it indicates that the vowel is long. On i or u, it does not change the pronunciation of the vowel, but merely indicates that these vowels were formerly followed by an s. Ex. *île* was *isle*.

(4) The diaresis (¨) over i or e means division of syllables in pronunciation. Ex. *haïr, Noël*.

a	is pronounced as in *task:* (1) when it has the grave accent. Ex. *voilà.* (2) in the endings *-ac, -ak, -ague, -at, -ap, -af, -ache.* Ex. *arracher, flaques.* (3) in monosyllabic words. Ex. *ma, la.*
a	is pronounced as in *psalm:* (1) in final syllables ending in *-ar, -age, -ave, -asion, -ation, -ase, -aze, -able, -acle, -asse, -ail, -aille.* (2) in nouns and adjectives derived from *-as.* Ex. *las, passer.*
e, é, ai	are pronounced as in *say* but without the diphthong: (1) when é is used. Ex. *été, désir.* (2) in words ending in *-er, -ier* (mute *r*). Ex. *leger.* (3) in words ending in *-ez, -ied, -ieds* where the consonants are mute. Ex. *pieds.*
e, è, ei	are pronounced as in *set:* (1) when è or ei occurs. Ex. *près, mère, neige.* (2) in monosyllables. Ex. *mes, tes.* (3) in words ending with *-et, -ets, -ect.* Exception: *et* (and) is pronounced like *é.*
ai, aî, ei, ey	are pronounced before consonants in the same syllable with the sound of *e.*
i, î	are pronounced as in *see.* Ex. *pipe, île.*
au, eau, ô	are pronounced as in *so,* but without the diphthong. Ex. *chaud, l'eau, trop.*
o	is pronounced as in *obey.* Ex. *coq, poste, homme, abord.*
ou	is pronounced as in *soon.* Ex. *toujours, doux, trouve.*
eu	is pronounced like the German ö (long and short forms as in German). Ex. *peu, Dieu.*
u	is pronounced like the German ü (long and short forms as in German). Ex. *pur, lune, plus.*
e	is pronounced as in *earth* (approximately without the "r") in syllables ending with e. Ex. *je, retour.* (Some words have normally mute e's that are sung when they occur on long notes.)

Whenever ui occurs, the pronunciation is not "(oo)-ee," but "(ü)-ee." This diphthong usually gives beginning singers difficulty. Words spelled with the vowel combination oi are pronounced as "wa" in *water.* The semivowel y occurs in a few French words, such as *yeux,* and is pronounced as "y" in *you.* The letter w occurs in only a few words. Sometimes it has the sound of "v" as in *vow* (Ex. *wagon*). Other times it has the semivowel sound as "w" in *water* (Ex. *warrant*).

The four nasal vowel sounds found in French do not exist in other languages. They should be produced for singing by a slight lowering of the velum which will not adversely affect the tone. Thus a singer uses as little nasality as possible, while still preserving the identity of the vowel.

an, en, am, em, (rarely) aon	like "ah" in *psalm,* with velum slightly lowered. Ex. *tempo, blanche, faon, paon.*
in, im, -ien, -ient, ain, aim, oin	like "eh" in *set,* with velum slightly lowered. Ex. *timbre, vainqueur, chien, bien, loin.* (Initial *in-* and *im-* are usually not nasalized when followed by a vowel or by another n or m. Ex. *image, immensité.*)
on, om	is the French "eau" with the velum slightly lowered. Ex. *ombre, onde.* (*Om* and *on* are not usually nasalized when they occur before another n or m. Ex. *somme, homme.*)
un, um	is the French "eu" as in *peu,* with slightly lowered velum. Ex. *un, lundi, défunte.* Only one nasalized word ends in -*um*: *parfum.* Other words ending in -*um* are not nasalized. Ex. *rhum, album.*

Consonants

There are a number of consonants in French which have substantially the same sounds as their English counterparts. These are b, d, f, k, l, m, n, q, t, v and z. Care must be taken because many consonants are mute in French. A dictionary should be consulted when there is doubt concerning the pronunciation. Some rules are listed below, but the list is not inclusive. French consonants conform in general to the crispness and gentleness of the Italian model, with one difference: double consonants in French receive no additional stress; they are sung like single consonants. P, t, and k are likewise treated gently.

c	sounds as "k": (1) before a, o, ou, u, [ɑ̃], [õ], [œ̃], and all consonants. Ex. *carillon, cortège, candeur*. (2) after any vowel except nasals. Ex. *bec, avec*. is mute after a nasal vowel. Ex. *banc, flanc*. sounds as "s" when it appears before e, i, or y; or when written with a cedilla (ç) before a, o, or u. Ex. *ciel, français*.
g	sounds as "g" in *go* before a, o, ou, u, [ɑ̃], [õ], and all consonants with the exception of n. Ex. *gloire, agonie*. sounds as "s" in *pleasure* before e or i. Ex. *argent*.
gn	sounds as "yn" in *canyon*. Ex. *agneau, digne*.
h	is *never* sung: (1) It is always mute in words of Greek or Latin origin. (2) It is aspirated, which simply means that it allows no elision (see page 145) in many words of Teutonic origin. (Obviously, a dictionary must be consulted.)
j	is sung as "s" in *pleasure*. Ex. *jaloux, déjà*.
l	is sung as "l": (1) at the beginning of words. (2) in the endings *-al, -el, -eul, -ol, -oil, -oul*, and *-ul*.
ll	is sung as "l": (1) in combinations *-all, ell, -oll, -ull*. (2) in a few words with *-ill: ville, mille, tranquille*, and their derivatives.
l, ll	are sung as the "y" in *you* in combinations *-ail, -aille, -eil, -eille, -euille, -ouil*, and *-ouille*. Ex. *travail, deuil, accueillir*; and in most words ending in *-ille*. Ex. *famille, fille*.
ph	is sung as "f."
r	is rolled in singing, as with Italian and German. before mute e and after a consonant, it is pronounced lightly, as in *notre, être*. is silent at the end of *-er* infinitives, and at the end of nouns and adjectives ending in *-ier, -cher*, and *-ger*. Ex. *chanter, premier, danger*.
s	is sung as "s" in *sung*: (1) when it is followed by a vowel and preceded by *a-, anti-, co-, contre-, entre-, para-*, or *pro-*. Ex. *prosaïque*.

(2) when it is followed by a vowel and preceded by a consonant. Ex. *versez.*

is sung as "z":
(1) before b, d, g, j, and y. Ex. *sbire.*
(2) between two vowels of which the first is not a nasal. Ex. *visage, raison.*

sc	is pronounced as "s" before e or i. Ex. *scène, cygne.*
th	is sung as "t."
ti	is sung as "s" in *sung* in combinations such as *-tion, -tieu, -tien, -tie.* Ex. *nation, patient, diplomatie.*
x	is sung as "gz" in *eggs* when it occurs between two vowels. Ex. *exile.*

is sung as "ks" when followed by a consonant. Ex. *excuser.*
is occasionally pronounced as "s." Ex. *dix.*

Liaison

The most complex aspect of French diction is the phenomenon known as liaison. A liaison is the connection of the final mute consonant of one word and the initial vowel or semivowel or mute h of the following word. (This suggests that the French language does not require glottal stops to clarify the beginning of vowels.) Except for a few established rules, however, the use of liaison is controversial, even among the French. Where s or x are involved in liaison, they have the "z" sound. D and f become t and v when they are allowed to form liaisons. Certain letters are not allowed to form liaison: b, c, f (except for *neuf*), l, m, and nouns with the n-nasal spelling (*an, on,* etc.).

Forbidden Liaison:
(1) No liaison is made before an aspirate *h.* Ex. *les haines.*
(2) Liaison is to be avoided between words separated by punctuation marks. Ex. *Si vous voulez, amis, . . .*
(3) Liaison must be avoided where it would create a misunderstanding or change the meaning.
(4) Liaison is forbidden after the following words: *et, oui, huit, onze, oh! ah!*
(5) Nouns ending in a nasal vowel are not to be connected by liaisons. Ex. *Le printemps est venu.* (See 3 under Required Liaison.)

(6) No liaison should be made after the pronouns *ils, elles,* and *on* in a question. Ex. *Sont-ells arrivés?*

Required Liaison:

(1) Liaison is made between articles or pronouns (such as *les, des, ces, un*) and the following noun or adjective. Ex. *ces etoiles.*

(2) Liaison is made between personal pronouns and the verbs to which they belong. Ex. *Vous arrivez.*

(3) Liaison is made between words in familiar phrases, such as *mot à mot, nuit et jour, de temps en temps,* etc.

(4) Liaison is made between *en* and *tout* and the verb to which they belong. Ex. *tout est fini.*

(5) Liaison is made between possessive, indefinite, and qualifying adjectives (including numerals) and the word to which they refer. Ex. *deux esprits, tes ailes.*

(6) Liaison is made between prepositions and the words which follow them. Ex. *dans un, sans amour.*

Mon Coeur se Recommande à Vous

Orlando di Lasso (1532–1594)

PHONEMIC CHART IN SIX LANGUAGES

IPA	CHURCH LATIN	ITALIAN	SPANISH	GERMAN	FRENCH	ENGLISH	MERRIAM WEBSTER
ʌ						sung	'ə
i	Christe	minuti	sí; y	ihn	prix	see	'e
ɪ				mit	lyre	sit	i
e		vero	sé	spät; meer	été; nez; pied; et	(like "ay" but more closed and without diphthong)	ee
ɛ	saecula; coelis	vecchio		Messen; hätte	vrai; est; lait	set	e
æ						sat (not considered good for singing)	a
a					tabac; femme	task (sat)	aa
3						earth (with dropped "r")	əi
3˞						earth (with some "r" present)	'ər
ɑ	agimus	amare	sala	Vater	lave	psalm; sod	a
u	solus	ultimo	su	gut	toujours	soon	ü
ʊ				Mutter		soot	u
o		voce	lo	schon	sabot	(like "so" but more closed and without diphthong)	oo

IPA	Latin	Italian	Spanish	German	French	English	Key
ɔ	Dominum			doch	aube; notre; côte	saw	o
e				freude; Ehre	je; te	above	e
w		uomo	puerto; cui		wallon	well	w
ʍ						which	hw
j	Jesu; ejus	ieri	vienen; Yo	Jungfrau	joyeux; pieu	view; you	y
ɑʊ	laudamus	causa	autór	auch		vow	au
oʊ						so	o
eɪ						say	a
ɔɪ			estoy	heute; Träume		voice	oi
ɑɪ		mai	donaire	Haide; Mein		vie	i
l	laetatus	lasciare		Lied	lent; bacille	love	l
r	regni	rapida	cera	herrlich	roi; terre	raw	r
h				heilig		hot	h
hj						huge	hy
ʔ				(between vowels)		oh!	
p	pleni	popolo	peso	Pausa; lieb	part; appel	pet	p
b	benedictus	basso	baca	bauen	bas	bet	b
t	tollis	tasto	tú	tief; Magd	thé; sotte	to	t
d	Deum	dolce	seda	darum	dame	do	d
k	cum	canto; che	cafe; quesco	Trug; Kreuz	kaki; écho	keep; class	k
g	gloria; ergo	gusto	persigue	geben	second; gris	got	g
f	filia	forza		verlagen	fin; aphte	fall	f
v	vitam	vivace		wachen	vent; wagon	vow	v
θ			diez			thin	th

IPA	CHURCH LATIN	ITALIAN	SPANISH	GERMAN	FRENCH	ENGLISH	MERRIAM WEBSTER
ɚ						the	th
s	sanctus	sempre	soy; estoy	Vaters	déclaration	sing	s
z		casa; (never spelled as "z")		sanft; Rose	rose	zero	z
ʃ		lasciare		sprechen; schliessen; Stimme	chat; schisme	mission	sh
ʒ				Journal	jamais	vision	zh
tʃ	ecce; luceat; crucifixus		charro; mancha		tchèque	church	ch
ʃt				stehen		rushed	sht
dʒ	genitum; regina	gentile			bridge	judge	j
ʒd						merged	jd
m	mundi	molto		Motif	mime; gemme	more	m
n	nomine	naturale		Nacht	nef; automne	no	n
ŋ		ancora	nunca; ningun	Engel		sung	ŋ
ɲ	magnam	ogni	señor; mañana			canyon	ñ
y				fühlen; müde	flux; jus	("see" with rounded lips)	ue
ʏ				füllen; Hütte	ruse; usure	("sit" with rounded lips)	ue

Symbol	Examples	Description	
ø	boeuf; eux — Goethe; Hölle bleu	("say" with rounded lips)	œ
œ	öffnen; Höhle seul; oeuf	("set" with rounded lips)	œ
ç	selig; ich	(sibilant similar to exaggerated "h" as in "huge")	k
x	Juan; hijo — ach; Loch	(scraping sound produced by back of tongue and soft palate)	k
œ̃	Parfum	nasalized [œ]	
ɛ̃	faim; vin; vingt; sein	nasalized [ɛ]	
ɑ̃	camp; bane; sang	nasalized [ɑ]	
õ	don; onde	nasalized [o]	
r	sur (flipped at end of word)		
ɣ	gli — orilla — will ye million		

NOTES

1. Madeline Marshall, *The Singer's Manual of English Diction* (New York: G. Schirmer, Inc., 1953), p. 9.

Chapter Five

RECOMMENDED READING LIST

Angelis, Michael. *The Correct Pronunciation of Latin According to Roman Usage.* Edited by William D. Hall. Anaheim: National Music Publishers, Inc., 1971. The definitive guide to the singing and speaking of Latin in liturgical functions.

Colorni, Evelina. *Singer's Italian.* New York: G. Schirmer, Inc., 1970. A concise guide to the pronunciation of Italian as applied to performance of Italian vocal literature.

Cox, Richard G. *The Singer's Manual of German and French Diction.* New York: G. Schirmer, Inc., 1970. A brief presentation of the sounds of French and German, based on the IPA; familiar song texts serve as the example material.

Heffner, Roe-Merrill S. *General Phonetics.* Foreword by W. W. Twaddell. Madison: University of Wisconsin Press, 1949. An introduction to phonetics which contains the International Phonetic Alphabet.

Kenyon, John Samuel, and Thomas Knott. *A Pronouncing Dictionary of American English.* Springfield, Massachusetts: G. & C. Merriam Co., 1944. One of the standard works in the area of American English diction; an important source for the conductor.

Marshall, Madeline. *The Singer's Manual of English Diction.* New York: G. Schirmer, Inc., 1953. A detailed approach to the pronunciation of English that is a must for every singer and choral conductor.

Siebs, Theodore. *Deutsche Hochsprache; Bühnenaussprache.* Berlin: Walter de Gruyter and Co., 1961. An official publication that presents rules for German diction by the leading authorities in phonetic and singing diction.

Chapter Six

Rehearsal and Performance

The object of art is expression.
The essence of expression is imagination.
The control of imagination is form.
The "medium" of all three is technique.
—HERBERT WITHERSPOON[1]

THUS FAR IN THIS BOOK we have dealt with what might be called the technical aspects of choral training. But to write of choral technique without relating its functional significance to the interpretation of music in rehearsal and performance would omit the very purpose and capstone of musical study. Music is an aural art and as such finds its true expression in performance. Consequently, unless the theories and practical suggestions presented in these pages lead to the achievement of better choral performances in the church, school, and concert hall, their validity is obviously open to question.

Choral conducting requires a combination of theoretical analyses and specific directions that enable the choral singer to translate symbols from the printed page into a meaningful musical expression of the composer's intentions. The former exercise is diagnostic; the latter finds its fulfillment in a systematic, yet flexible, rehearsal technique. How successful the conductor will be in his analysis of the ensemble sound will depend on many factors: his understanding of the voice, his musicianship, his knowledge of style and performance practices, and his concept of and preparation for the rehearsal and performance. It is hardly to be expected that a conductor will be able to teach breathing and breath control unless he is reasonably efficient in his own breathing technique; the same can be said of his knowledge of music reading and musical style. His success as a conductor will be dependent on the manner in which he can combine a clear and precise conducting technique with a consummate knowledge of the choral art.

Choral singing thus becomes more than just an exercise in musical interpretation. It is the ability of the conductor to equip himself and his ensemble with the technical competence and mastery—vocal and musical—that will allow both to become channels through which the inner essence of the choral experience can truly reveal itself. This lofty goal—toward which every choral conductor should strive—can only be achieved if the conductor and the ensemble are one, musically and spiritually. Its prerequisites include careful musical preparation on the part of the conductor, functional freedom of the individual singer, and empathy between the conductor and singer. The entire process begins in the rehearsal.

THE REHEARSAL

While choral singing reaches the audience or congregation in the public performance, it is, in reality, in the regular rehearsal that the choral experience finds its true identity; put more simply, the location of the choral experience is the rehearsal. It is here, under the direction of an inspiring conductor, that the sensitive choral ensemble develops a group psyche. The presence of many minds blending their intellectual and emotional energies toward a common goal becomes a powerful force on the individual singer. The performance, the ultimate goal of choral singers at every level, is thus best understood when conceived as the communication of truths and insights discovered and internalized during the period of rehearsal preparation. It is in this respect that the choral performance differs from the professional orchestral performance, where much less rehearsal time may be spent in preparation for a public concert.

The rehearsal, thus conceived, becomes an end in itself, as well as a means. In addition, it shifts the focus of the choral experience from the audience to the participating singer, who becomes more than a simple servant of the music: the individual singer *is* the audience, first and foremost. This is an important, even critical, distinction that makes the choral experience something special. By stressing the individual and corporate importance of the singer as the ultimate beneficiary of his own creation, a powerful bond of responsibility is forged within the ensemble and among the individual participants, reinforcing the communication within the group and the emotional involvement of its members.

Locating the choral experience within the rehearsal clearly requires a restructuring of our thinking about it. No longer is it simply a work session where a conductor (or accompanist) mechanically "pounds out" parts toward a performance goal. Instead, each rehearsal becomes precisely what its name implies: a rehearing of the work—its nature, its essence, as well as its musical elements. Each rehearsal presents conductor and singer alike with a new and exciting musical encounter with the composer; ultimately, there are *no* rehearsals as we know them, only performances of the work "in progress" as the participants (conductor and singers) seek to express and to recreate the intentions of the composer.

Our cue for restructuring the rehearsal so that it becomes the focus of the choral experience comes from an understanding of the inherent value and nature of choral singing and choral music. Recognizing its potential power, we treat every music-making session with expectation: we do not permit ourselves or our singers the luxury of leaving our intellects or emotions at the door of the rehearsal room. We do not allow the emotional experience of music-making to become separated from an understanding of the music and its style; in this sense, choral singing becomes a vital and living experience, not merely a journey through a museum.

In this new rehearsal attitude the individual singer is encouraged to learn on his own as much of the fundamental material of the music—notes, diction, dynamics—as possible. The conductor then reinforces this dedication on the part of the singer by his own meticulous musical preparation; he knows the music so well that constant eye contact is maintained between himself and the choir and immediate and continuous empathy is established. This kind of corporate dedication allows both singer and conductor to realize the full potential of the choral experience musically, emotionally, and spiritually.

Preparation for the Rehearsal

Planning the rehearsal is one of the most important responsibilities of the conductor, yet it is probably also one of the most neglected. The preparation begins with the serious study of the works that will be "performed" during the rehearsal: they should be studied carefully from the standpoint of their form, musical style, text, tempo, rhythmic complexity, harmonic structure, and phrasing. Warm-up and sight-singing exercises should be planned—even composed—anticipating the technical and musical demands of the works that will be sung in the rehearsal.

The preparation of the accompanist is also important. All music to be studied during the rehearsal should be given to the accompanist in advance of the rehearsal so that valuable practice time will not be lost because of technical difficulties in the piano or organ part. When working with an orchestra, especially union musicians, the time spent in preparation of the orchestra parts, such as adding bowings, checking mistakes, making rehearsal numbers consistent, etc., will prove to be a valuable investment of time and energy.

Important rehearsal time can also be saved by selecting an efficient librarian who will place the music to be sung in the individual folders prior to the rehearsal. Even though this job should be delegated to the librarian, it is the responsibility of the conductor to check prior to each rehearsal to make certain that this task has been accomplished.

Finally, the rehearsal should be planned with consideration for the approximate amount of time that will be spent on each work.

Organizing the Rehearsal

A well-organized rehearsal begins with the music in the folders and the sequence of numbers to be studied written on the blackboard, allowing the singers time to arrange their music in advance. It is also important to make sure that all necessary equipment (piano, tape recorder, etc.) is in the room and ready for use prior to the beginning of the practice session. Assign each section leader the responsibility of taking the roll for that particular section so that the conductor will be free to concentrate on the music.

Planning the Warm-up

A good rehearsal begins with a well-planned warm-up period. The purpose of the warm-up in choral singing is the same as for any other physical activity: to tone up the muscles and improve the coordination; in short, to exercise the voice. Because singing is first and foremost a physical activity, the muscles must be "loosened-up" so that the rehearsal or performance that follows will have the advantage of maximum vocal efficiency. It would be unthinkable for an athlete to begin an intense practice session without some kind of warm-up activity; the same is true of the choral rehearsal. A carefully planned and efficiently executed warm-up period is a necessity if the continuous musical growth and vocal development of the choral ensemble is to be assured.

One reason that the choral warm-up is neglected by some conductors is that it is sometimes thought of as a period of meaningless vocal exercises required of bored singers. An attitude of this type misses the point. In fact, it is possible to devote the entire warm-up period to the improvement of the music that is currently under study. The primary purpose of the warm-up is to exercise the voice. Its object is not to push the voice to the limits of pitch and dynamics so that every singer will be hoarse during the rehearsal. It is rather a very special time when the conductor brings the choir together and each singer finds his or her identity in the choral ensemble. It is a wonderful time when the unity and esprit de corps begin to emerge in a musical and spiritual environment.

With this extra-musical goal in mind, the warm-up period should accomplish the following purposes: (1) It should establish good posture. (2) It should establish the basic principles of vocal production. This is an ongoing process that must be emphasized at every rehearsal. (3) It should improve the basic musicianship of each singer. (4) It should correct errors of vocal technique and diction. (5) It should prepare the voice for extended use. Every exercise used during the warm-up period must be carefully planned and designed to facilitate the musical growth of the choral ensemble. Behind each vocalise there must be a specific objective or series of objectives.

Conducting the Rehearsal

The responsibility for the effectiveness of the rehearsal rests squarely on the shoulders of the conductor. This is why planning and pacing are so important. There must be a critical balance between verbal instructions and music-making: directions must be given clearly and precisely; verbal comments and instructions must be kept to a minimum. A good rule of thumb to follow is "talk little, sing a lot."

When verbal instructions are given it is helpful if they are presented in a consistent and logical sequence: page, line, measure, and beat. Instrumental parts are most often cued by letters and occasionally measure numbers. Be acquainted with the system used in the work you are preparing and alert the chorus.

Every time a section is repeated in rehearsal it is good for the morale of the choir if a reason is given. Singers respond better if they know specifically what needs to be improved or corrected. Is it a vocal problem? The diction? The rhythm? The pitch? The phrasing? The effective conductor is one who can "diagnose" a musical or vocal problem and then immediately "prescribe" a solution. Valuable rehearsal time should not be wasted by repeating a section without suggesting a specific solution to the problem.

The efficient conductor anticipates musical problems, and the following simple rules for conducting can result in a stimulating rehearsal:

1. Do not avoid rehearsing difficult passages.
2. Correct mistakes immediately to avoid bad habits.
3. Rehearse slowly when difficulties arise; this will allow singers to experience success in sections that are technically demanding. Increase tempo gradually. If the choir becomes tense or flustered when working out a problem passage, go on to something else.
4. Hold chords or intervals double their length to allow the singers to hear relationships of chords.
5. Speak words in rhythm to establish a relationship between the text and the musical texture.
6. Rehearse a difficult passage until the singers have rhythmic and pitch patterns securely in their ear. Do not proceed until these fundamentals are mastered.
7. Avoid fatigue by drilling passages with high tessitura an octave lower.
8. Rehearse loud passages softly from time to time to insure that the choir is singing the right notes in the correct rhythm.
9. Practice each number without accompaniment at some time to insure that the ensemble can hold its own without the supporting instrument.

When one particular section is having difficulty with a passage, it is important to find ways to assist those singers without neglecting the rest of the choir.

1. Have the entire choir sing the problematic passage.
2. Have the weak section sing loudly while the others sing softly or hum.
3. Have the accompanist play only the part of the weak section, while the others sing their parts without accompaniment.
4. Have the weak section sing the passage with words, while the others sing on neutral syllables or hum their parts.

A good conductor will always prepare every entrance of the choir. A clear preliminary beat is the key to a clean attack. The preliminary beat is the beat just prior to the entrance and must be executed clearly and on the beat pattern, and reflect the tempo, dynamic level, style, mood, and character of the musical entrance. Eye contact with the choral ensemble and a model of the facial expression and posture desired in the singers will improve the attack. Often subdividing the beat in slow passages will help to avoid rushing and general rhythmic instability. Sometimes varying the accompaniment will improve the ensemble of the choir. For example, use a percussive accompaniment when pulse is needed; double the bass in octaves to give a firmer support; play the accompaniment an octave higher to clarify the texture; or drop the accompaniment altogether in key passages to encourage the choir to sing on its own.

Pacing the Rehearsal

The pace of the rehearsal is extremely important when working with singers at any level, but it is especially critical with adolescent voices. If the conductor is to have an alert choral ensemble, he will need to keep the rehearsal moving.

1. Alternate easy and difficult numbers in the rehearsal schedule.
2. Keep all sections busy as much as possible during the rehearsal.
3. Ask other sections to hum their parts while working with a given section.
4. Require other sections to follow their parts while working with one section.
5. Limit the time spent on one piece of music. Do not spend excessive time rehearsing the easiest part of the most difficult work on the program.
6. Leave a work for another rehearsal if it is not going well. Often changing pieces will improve the spirit of a rehearsal.

There are a number of other ways to put variety into a rehearsal:

1. Combine warm-up exercises with sight-singing sessions.
2. Have all sections sing a part that is proving difficult for one section.
3. Have all sections (or homogeneous sections like soprano-tenor or alto-bass) sing the theme of a polyphonic or fugal passage to save time while learning the notes, phrasing, and articulation (diction).
4. Have members of a large section sing their part by rows. This is especially useful in eight-part or double chorus works.
5. Schedule short sectional rehearsals from time to time for the purpose of learning especially difficult passages. These sessions should be limited to fifteen or twenty minutes.

6. Vary the tempo of a work from time to time to keep the group alert and to maintain eye contact.

7. Schedule a "stretch break" or recess in the middle of the rehearsal to keep the group fresh.

Energizing the Rehearsal

The alert conductor is sensitive to the general rehearsal attitude of his choral ensemble. Discipline problems will not normally become a factor if the rehearsal is well-planned and well-paced. However, when a practice session does drag, the conductor should recognize the symptoms and view them as an opportunity to take specific steps to energize the rehearsal.

1. Vary the pattern of the rehearsal procedure to avoid monotony. For example, change the seating or performing arrangement. (See pages 162–165.) If the choir normally rehearses while seated, have them stand up occasionally, or when a performance date draws near.

2. Change the warm-up exercises on a regular basis. Create warm-ups from the music that is under study. However, avoid extended warm-up periods and get to the music as soon as possible. Always have a specific purpose behind every vocal exercise.

3. Insist on attention and respect. Instructions should not be given to an inattentive group of singers.

4. Obtain recordings of the works that are in rehearsal and play them when the piece is being introduced to give the ensemble a conceptual view of the work. This is especially helpful if the work is either difficult or written in a contemporary idiom.

5. Use a tape recorder to encourage the choir to develop a positive self-criticism of their musical development.

6. Conclude rehearsals on a familiar or enjoyable work to give the choir a feeling of accomplishment and exhilaration at the end of an exhausting session.

Building Technical Facility

One of the important by-products of locating the choral experience in the rehearsal is that it becomes a time of musical growth and vocal development for each member of the ensemble. For this reason the conductor must conceive of every rehearsal as a class voice lesson as well as an important music-making experience. Warm-up exercises and vocalises should be constructed with a view to the individual vocal development of each singer. In some cases the vocal problems may warrant the individual attention of a private voice lesson. If a singer shows special promise, the conductor should recommend a private teacher who can guide the vocal development of that singer. However, in most instances, the carefully planned and skillfully executed choral rehearsal can serve as an effective class voice lesson and contribute significantly to the musical growth of every member of the choral ensemble.

In building the vocal technique and facility of the individual singer, the conductor should strive for the following goals: (1) a posture characterized by vital readiness; (2) a fully resonant and flexible vocal sound; (3) a breath support that involves the action of the diaphragm; (4) a range that is expanded; and (5) a vocal control that is capable of considerable nuance.

Introducing a New Work

The manner in which the conductor approaches the introduction of a new work will often go a long way toward determining the choir's initial enthusiasm for the work. Sometimes it will even affect their willingness to study the piece seriously weeks and months later. The following suggestions are designed to improve the singer's attitude toward a new work:

1. Discuss the work briefly by presenting background information on the composer, the compositional setting, the musical style, the meaning of the text, the form, etc.

2. Play the work on the piano (or a recording if available) while the group follows with the music.

3. Play the work a second time and have them follow the text.

4. Play the work again and have them hum their parts.

5. Have them sing through the work on neutral syllables so that they can concentrate on the notes and rhythm without the added confusion of the text.

6. When notes and rhythm are secure, then have them sing in parts with the text.

7. Rehearse individual parts in various combinations such as soprano-bass, tenor-alto, soprano-alto, tenor-bass, etc. Encourage them to listen to the other sections while singing.

8. Have the choir speak the text in rhythm to emphasize the rhythm, diction, style, dynamics, etc.

Maintaining Human Relations

Each choral ensemble has its own special group ethos. This corporate character is the result of many factors (the group's purpose, its age level, its success, its performing environment, etc.), but one of the most important of these factors is the relationship between the conductor and the singers. Positive human relations begin with eye contact between the conductor and the members of the choral ensemble. They are fostered by a warm, friendly attitude, by humor during the rehearsal, by fairness in judging the relative abilities of the singers, and by genuine respect for the hard work and accomplishments of the group. The enthusiasm of the director is often contagious.

Social relationships among the singers will also help in developing and maintaining human relationships. After-rehearsal refreshments and special parties on a regular basis will help group morale and spirit.

Evaluating the Rehearsal

The preparation for the next rehearsal actually begins with an evaluation of the practice session just completed. The alert conductor will make notes concerning the manner in which the next rehearsal can be improved. If a recording is made, it should be studied with score in hand as a means of both evaluating the rehearsal just completed and preparing for the next one.

REHEARSAL FORMATIONS

The most important consideration in the arrangement of singers in rehearsal is the placement of the singers so that they are able to hear each other. Unless each section can hear the other clearly, the ensemble cannot develop as a cohesive musical unit. In many ways the ideal formation for rehearsal is the circle, because all singers can see and hear each other constantly. Ehmann reminds us that the circle preserves the "choir's awareness of its corporateness."[2] This attitude is especially important in rehearsal because it is here that the ensemble is created and the esprit is developed.

The idea of rehearsing in circles may be expanded to allow each section to practice in a circle formation. In this way the unity of sectional sound that is so critical in music of the Renaissance and Baroque periods can be preserved. Spreading the sections around the rehearsal hall may also help improve the aural sensitivity of the individual singer. For example, instrumentalists are taught the importance of listening to other sections, and this ability develops to a very high level as the individual player applies this principle to the improvement of the ensemble's performance. Similarly in choral singing, musicianship must begin with the discipline of hearing the other parts, especially the inner parts and the bass line. Rehearsing in a circle formation from time to time will be an aid in improving the sound of the choral ensemble.

The inherent value of the circle formation in the development of musicianship as well as esprit is aptly described by Ehmann:

> To open this "closed circle" to a listening audience would have been inconceivable to early musicians. The liturgy of the Middle Ages, for instance, was conducted by those who acted, and all acting groups were considered to have direct access to God. The choir did not think of itself as singing to a listening audience, but as it took part in various parts of the liturgy, the unending circle, the unending spiral of music which it produced, represented a direct link with eternity. In our day the ideal circular formation is preferred whenever a music society sings for itself, i.e., singing without an audience.[3]

The traditional block arrangement is also effective in the rehearsal of certain kinds of music. Since there are many variations of the block seating formation, the specific type may depend upon a number of considerations: the style of music being rehearsed, the acoustical properties of the rehearsal room, or the relative balance of sections. For example, in Renaissance music containing a predominance of polyphony and equality of voice parts, the seating plan will probably depend more on acoustical properties and conductor preference. In a rehearsal hall where the lower voices have trouble penetrating, the conductor may adopt a block arrangement that will bring the men's voices closer to the front. This may also be the case when there is a shortage of male voices to balance the choir adequately.

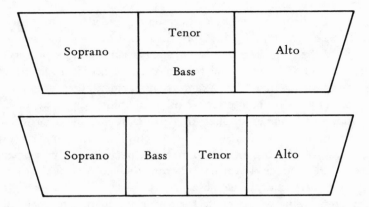

Sometimes a conductor will prefer to seat the tenors in the front.

In music with a definite soprano-bass orientation, that is, choral literature in which the soprano section sings the important melodic material and the bass section sings a musical line that is doubled by the keyboard instrument or continuo part, it is advisable to seat the basses behind the sopranos. The soprano section will probably sing with a better sectional ensemble, and their intonation will improve because they will be able to hear the basses.

Often a conductor of a large amateur chorus will utilize other methods to achieve the blend and balance that is desired for outstanding ensemble singing. Some conductors will use voices of one section to strengthen another section in especially transparent writing. For example, second sopranos may be borrowed to assist the altos in especially high passages. Or, altos may be used to assist the tenor section when there is a shortage of men. In cases when there is a very low bass line, it is often necessary to move some baritones who possess the range to the bass part to insure that these low notes will be heard and thus provide balance to the musical texture.

COMMON REHEARSAL PROBLEMS

This section is not by any means an exhaustive list of the problems that are encountered by the choral conductor while rehearsing choral literature. The purpose here is to identify some of the more common problems that occur in the choral rehearsal and to suggest some easy solutions. We will begin with faulty intonation.

Faulty Intonation

Accurate pitch in choral singing is dependent upon two factors: (1) the mental ability to hear the tones being sung, and (2) the physical ability to translate the mental image into reality. Often throat tension can affect the functioning of the ear, as well as the jaw and the tongue. Many choral singers who are guilty of faulty intonation are not deficient in pitch perception; it is rather that tension interferes with and prohibits the accurate adjustment of the vocal mechanism as its parts move in response to instructions from the brain. The net effect is a situation in which the accuracy of the mechanical response is upset and the result is poor intonation. This condition is almost always due to an imperfect muscular coordination, seldom to hazy mental concepts.

For the average pitch problem in choral singing the quickest remedy is to have the choir or section sing a phrase staccato, at the rhythmic value of one-quarter of the written note value:

$$\text{♩} = \text{♪} ❞ ❬, \qquad \text{♩} = \text{♪} ❞❞, \qquad \text{♪} = \text{♪} ❞❞ \text{ etc.}$$

This exercise is most effective if sung at the dynamic level of piano.

Because bad intonation may stem from a number of causes (a poor ear, an inferior vocal mechanism, singing in the wrong tessitura, poor musicianship, or lack of adequate breath pressure), it is advisable to give special attention to the individual singer who is experiencing pitch problems. When there is doubt as to the ability of a singer to hear, devise some kind of pitch matching test or administer one of the standard musical talent tests. Individual voices should also be classified as to whether the tessitura is low, medium, or high. (This problem is discussed at length on page 75.) Vocalization should be prescribed first to develop the registers and then to bridge them. The basic musicianship should then be checked to determine whether the singer actually knows how to read music. Finally, a continuing effort should be made to develop stronger breath pressure.

Flatting is almost always caused by either some form of constriction in the vocal mechanism or by an absence of diaphragmatic action. Sharping may be due to nervousness, forcing the breath, oversinging, or overdramatization of the choral literature.

More specifically, flatting may be caused by one or more of the following situations:

1. The tone production is poor.
2. There is a lack of breath pressure (or support).
3. The singer exhibits poor posture.
4. There is a lack of physical involvement, especially at the level of the diaphragm.
5. The vowel quality is not uniform.
6. There is mental or physical fatigue.
7. The singers are scooping or slurring notes from below.
8. The rehearsal room (most important) has poor acoustics or ventilation.
9. The composition may be pitched too high (or too low).

Rhythmic Instability

Rhythmic instability is invariably caused by a poor concept of rhythmic pulse and the relationship of pulse and pace (tempo) to the rhythmic patterns which the composer has written. To establish rhythmic stability, first develop a sensitivity to the pulse of a given piece of choral literature. This can be accomplished most effectively by having the choir clap to establish the pulse. Often by clapping out the rhythms vigorously and simultaneously with the steady underlying pulse, an understanding of the rhythmic organization of the work will develop that will allow the singers to perform the music with confidence. This exercise should be used for every piece of music where there are rhythmic intricacies. (A complete discussion of rhythm is presented in chapter seven.)

Poor Phrasing

Poor phrasing is usually the result of a misunderstanding by the singer as to the shape of the phrase, where it begins and ends, and where it reaches a point of climax. Sometimes it is due to the lack of sufficient breath to complete the phrase.

This critical aspect of musical performance can be improved easily if the conductor will take the time and make the effort to point out definite places where phrasing should occur according to text meaning, climax, and musical line. As a reinforcement in musical performance these points of musical articulation should also be conducted by gesture. If a lack of breath is the main problem, exercises should be constructed that will improve the pressure of the breath. (Refer to the Resonance section on page 97.)

Remember that phrasing in choral singing is influenced by both musical and textual factors. Sometimes the two coincide and the phrasing is obvious. In the following example, a selection from the "Hallelujah" chorus of Handel's *Messiah*, the phrasing is clearly signalled by such musical factors as the rest and the arrival at tonic. This is reinforced by the obvious punctuation of the text.

On the other hand, in the following example from the same work the musical phrasing and the textual phrasing are not identical.

Without a text the musical phrasing would strongly depend upon the change in tessitura. With the text, however, it is clear that the line should be carried over.

Cutting Off Ends of Phrases

This musical fault is usually caused either by the absence of a clear gesture or cut-off by the conductor or by a lack of poise on the part of the singer. Rests must often be inserted in polyphonic literature when the various parts end phrases at different points; a clear release from the conductor is usually sufficient for pure homophonic literature. A sure cure for this rhythmic problem is for the conductor to insist that each note value be held until the beginning of the next note, i.e., when a note ends a measure or a piece, the cut-off should be conceived as taking place at the beginning of the next measure.

Scooping and Slurring

The scooping and slurring of notes is most often the result of mental laziness and musical sloppiness on the part of the choral singer. When caused by poor musicianship or uncertainty in changing from one pitch to another, the best solution is to concentrate more rehearsal time on certain aspects of rhythm and pitch organization. (Discussions of these musical fundamentals are included in chapters seven and eight.) If the problem is primarily laziness, or if the scooping and slurring of pitches are vocal mannerisms of certain choral singers, the most effective remedy is to use staccato exercises on open vowel sounds in arpeggio fashion as part of the regular choral warm-up. The same staccato technique used to improve the intonation—singing a phrase staccato at the rhythmic value of one-quarter of the written note value—is equally effective when scooping and slurring is a continuing problem. In this way more thought is given to pitch placement rather than actual vocal production.

Dropping Final Consonants

The careful articulation of the consonant at the end of the word makes the speech understandable and thus communicates the message of the text to the audience. This is especially true of sustained tones ending in a consonant. When consonants are dropped at the end of a word or musical phrase, it is usually due to an imprecise cut-off by the conductor or to the carelessness of individual singers. Another cause may be the result of placing too much emphasis on the enunciation of vowel sounds to the neglect of articulating the consonants, although this problem is somewhat rare in nonprofessional groups.

The ear of the conductor is usually the best means of detecting this deficiency in the ensemble sound. The conductor must listen constantly and consciously to the words as they are sung. Too often the conductor neglects the words because of his zeal to interpret the music correctly. If the constant reminder of the conductor does not solve the problem, the use of a tape recorder will serve as a dramatic means of pointing out this deficiency to the chorus.

THE PERFORMANCE

In the public performance a third party is added to the music-making process— the listener. The composer conceives his work in the ideal and expects that it will reach the audience. He creates a musical structure which stands by itself on the printed page, yet it must be heard to transmit its message to the listener. The performer (the choral ensemble in this case) and the interpreter (the conductor) thus stand between the score and the listener. Music comes alive through performance. And, just as the composer expects his work to stand alone as a valid exemplar of musical creativity, the performer also creates his own edifice of sound which must also reach the listener. Whether the public performance fulfills this function or not depends on a number of factors: the performer's conception of the work, the listeners' background and musical capacity, the preparation of the conductor, the ability of the chorus, the acoustics of the hall, the readiness of the audience to respond to the performance, and the ethos of the particular occasion. All of these are vital parts of choral performance.

The Nature of Performance

The public concert as a form of social behavior is a relatively recent phenomenon in Western culture. In primitive times man would intone and improvise his vocal expression as individual praise to the gods. Musical activity in the early church also took place without regard for an audience. The motive of corporate worship was to bring praise and adoration to the Creator, the giver and sustainer of life. Even in the reformed liturgy of Luther, in which the congregation became an active participant in the worship experience, there were no spectators, only participants. The early music-making activities of the court were likewise marked by participation. Every royal family had its chest of viols and its family of recorders (see chapter eleven for the instrumental and vocal participation in the wedding of Count Cosimo I and Leonora); the madrigals and glees were intended for informal singing by the family around the table after dinner. It was not until the late eighteenth and early nineteenth centuries, when the public concert was made available to the man in the street, that a distinction developed between the performer and the audience.

The public concert, however, is only one aspect of choral performance; it is simply the culmination of a long and complex process which actually begins with the musical score. The score is a script, much like the script of a play. And just as the playwright does not provide the actor with complete instructions regarding make-up, voice inflections, stage gestures, or movements, in a similar manner the composer usually does not prescribe how loud, how soft, or how accented all notes of a work should be, how long a hold or ritard or an acceleration should be, or what quality or timbre a choral tone should have (except of course in avant garde choral works where special effects are desired). All these matters and many others like them are left to the discretion of the conductor.

Performance therefore can be considered as an effort on the part of one or more players or singers to interpret the intentions of the composer on the basis of the script or score. A musical performance is not the score but simply one idea of the interpretation of the score. Because no two performances are exactly alike, there are as many ideas of the score as there are performers.

It is thus not difficult to see that the relationship of the performer and the composer is a very special one. The performer is at the same time coauthor and re-creator of the work he performs. This is a relationship that calls for a special sense of responsibility. There is no place for carelessness or insufficient study on the part of the conductor or performer; hence one reason why well-planned and efficiently run rehearsals are such an integral part of the total process. As the primary agent of re-creation, the conductor must apply his imagination to the task of discovering the composer's intentions. And once he has discovered the inner essence of the music as well as he can through study and practice, he must then apply himself to the task of reproducing the music with the utmost conviction. In the words of Roger Sessions, "without fidelity a performance is false, without conviction it is lifeless." The choral conductor then must determine, on the basis of his training and ability, the intentions of the composer and then project them, according to his own convictions, in the musical performance.

The relationship of the listener to the performance is even more complex than that of the performer to the composer. In any given audience there are listeners who possess various musical tastes and who proceed from different stages of sophistication in their understanding of music. This creates a serious problem in performance because listening to music, as distinct from participating in its reproduction, is the product of a relatively late stage of musical sophistication. Up until the middle of the nineteenth century the musical public consisted almost exclusively of people whose primary relationship with music was through active participation in corporate worship or through playing or singing in the privacy of their own homes. For them even their occasional role as listeners was one of participation; they were better eqiupped to listen because their experience as regular participants in the act of musical production gave them a special understanding of the total process.

It is clear that the major problem facing the conductor in public performance today is the involvement of the listener as an active participant to insure that the cycle of composer-performer-listener is indeed complete. To do this the listener must be challenged by the performance; active involvement as a listener means that he "performs" the work in his imagination as the actual performance takes place before him. Listening will then become an act of real and vital participation, a sharing in the work of the composer and performer, an awareness of the individual and specific sense of the music performed. When the conductor can create this kind of concert environment by careful study, effective programming, and exciting music-making, the performance will no longer be an incident or an adjunct, but an independent and self-sufficient medium of expression that will thoroughly involve the score, the performer, and the audience.

Building the Program

Building the choral program is one of the most important and satisfying responsibilities of the conductor. Selecting the "right" program for the right occasion can be a most rewarding experience for the conductor, but it does not happen by chance. Into successful program building goes an immense amount of planning and study. Many factors contribute to the process: knowing the individual voices of the choral ensemble, understanding the purpose of the concert, defining the audience, determining the acoustical properties of the hall (or halls if the choir is on tour), etc. Obviously program building is a complex matter which must be approached with care.

Many conductors build choral programs in a vacuum; they approach this responsibility from the standpoint of the ideal as opposed to the practical point of view. They will program one difficult work after another until they have exhausted the choir vocally. Or they will put together a program that is perfectly fine from a musical standpoint but one that wears out the audience.

Today's choral conductor is faced with a special problem in program building that his forerunner of two hundred years ago did not face: a pluralism of tastes. Today's choral groups are singing before audiences that are conditioned by the entertainment industry and the mass media. Many teenagers and young adults have been entertained throughout their entire lifetime by the television screen. The problem is obvious: for someone who has grown to expect movement (choreography), color, and infinite variety in an evening's enjoyment and relaxation, the idea of spending two hours in the same seat listening to a choir dressed in formal attire and singing without moving from their set arrangement can be a dismal experience. It is thus not difficult to understand why program building is such an important element in the success of a choral performance.

Since choral performances encompass such a broad spectrum, it is important to consider at least three basic rules of program building: knowledge of the audience, purpose of the program, and planning for encores and substitutions.

Knowledge of the Audience

Knowledge of the audience is perhaps the most important element in program building. Many choral concerts have turned out to be utter fiascoes because the conductor failed to consider the nature of the audience. The conductor who presents a full program of sixteenth- and seventeenth-century Italian and German music for a concert of teenagers in a Romanian youth hostel is doomed to failure. A collection of American spirituals, nineteenth-century Brahms folksongs, or sixteenth-century English and Italian madrigals would be much more effective if sung with expression and vitality.

However, this does not mean that a conductor should play down to an arbitrarily assumed audience level in small town concerts; neither does it mean that he should attempt to lift public taste up to the level of a sophisticated large city musical culture in one evening. There is obviously a middle ground between these two extremes and both alternatives are fraught with danger.

Purpose of the Program

There are several kinds of programs that should be considered in what might be called concert situations, as opposed to occasions that are entertainment-oriented (i.e., the service club concert to raise money for a special tour or project, the annual Christmas sing for the local ladies' club, etc.): the tour program, the concert series on campus or in a church, the one-composer concert, the topical concert, and the critic's recital.

The tour concert presents a special kind of problem because it usually has commercial implications. Tours are successful when they make money, satisfy various audiences, and result in a return invitation. Yet, the conductor may also want to display his group in the best possible way musically and thus collect favorable reviews that will be useful to further his career and that of the choir. Consequently, the program must present the group at its best in technical facility, interpretation, handling of styles and languages, stage appearance, poise, and every other characteristic that makes a group look and sound professional. The program must also be built in a manner that will satisfy the professional critic as well as the public-at-large. In short, the tour program must include variety of literature, unity of planning, a well-paced arrangement of works, appropriate length, and appeal to the audience for which the choir will sing. The latter point is very important because a tour program for a sophisticated concert audience in Boston, New York, Philadelphia, or Washington may not be appropriate for a concert audience in a small town in the Midwest. In this case, careful planning and a lot of good plain common sense will go a long way toward insuring an effective audience response to the tour program.

The repertoire for a concert series on campus or in a church should be selected with the overall purpose of the series in mind. When the series occurs during the anniversary year of a major composer of choral works, it might be appropriate to include one of that composer's works on each program. Or, the series might be organized around different choral forms: motets, madrigals, chansons, cantatas, passions, etc. Another approach might be to emphasize the choral works of a given period in each concert of a series, i.e., Renaissance, Baroque, Classical, Romantic, Twentieth Century. The possibilities are limitless, but imagination and careful planning are obvious and necessary ingredients in the planning of programs for a series of concerts.

The one-composer concert is very difficult to plan unless that composer has written a variety of works and styles from which to choose. In cases where the contrast of choral works is limited, it might be advisable to add piano, voice, or chamber works to round out the program. An effective program that includes a variety of works is nearly always preferable to one that includes poor or questionable choral works. This variety program might also better represent the composer's total creative accomplishments.

Choral programs built around special topics, such as "Twentieth-Century American Choral Music" or "The Choral Music of Moravian Composers," are usually well received if they are planned carefully. Again the key concepts of variety, unity, arrangement, length, and appeal must be kept in mind when planning programs that concentrate on a specific subject.

The type of program that is perhaps the most difficult to plan is one that might be called the critic's program. This program must satisfy the professional critic (or in the case of the convention or university program, the professionals and students in the audience) but it must also, in most cases, appeal to the public-at-large as well. Because the critic's program demands such careful planning, a few guidelines can be used in its preparation:

1. The program should include works ideally suited for the vocal abilities of the singers. It would be poor planning to select a group of works for musical reasons and discover that the range and technical demands were beyond the capabilities of the vocal ensemble.

2. It should begin with a number or a group of numbers that are relatively easy but also sound well.

3. It should include works from various style periods to show off the choir's understanding of and sensitivity to style.

4. It should contain pieces in at least two languages besides English (preferably French and German).

5. It should present some new works; either some unknown or rarely performed compositions, or even a first performance of a piece commissioned especially for the concert.

6. Since the concert will probably be reviewed, the most interesting part of the program should be placed just before or right after the intermission. This will give the critic time to make a copy deadline for a morning paper and also give the choir time to warm up and shed its nervousness.

Planning for Encores and Substitutions

One phase of program building often neglected, because the director feels the pressure of time that must be devoted to the program itself, is the provision for encores and substitutions. The extra numbers the conductor has available can often make the difference between a concert that is politely received by the audience or one that receives a standing ovation. There is a wealth of effective encore material from which the conductor may choose: folksong arrangements, spirituals, excerpts from Broadway musicals, etc. However, the conductor should avoid the overperformed or hackneyed encores that every choir sings. The time and effort spent on this phase of program building will yield rich dividends—the appreciation of the audience and the respect of the singers.

The Conductor's Preparation

The very special relationship the conductor enjoys with the composer makes it imperative that he begin his preparation early. His role as coauthor in the public performance requires careful study geared to the discovery of the central idea of a given work.

Every choral work has a central idea or purpose to which all of its musical elements contribute. Another way of phrasing it is to say that every composer strives for a distinctive variety within the unity of the composition. One of the reasons so many choral performances lack excitement and direction is that the conductor has failed to spend the time and to exert the effort necessary to discover the central purpose or the subject of a piece of music. The result is a performance that is enigmatic and fragmented.

In determining the central idea of a work the conductor should begin by asking a series of questions: What is the basic character of the piece? (Is it a folksong? A lullaby? A patriotic work?) Did the composer have a program in mind? (Was the composition composed for a worship service? A public concert? A festive occasion?) What is the form? (Is it in sonata form? Ternary song form? Through-composed?) These are but a few of the questions the conductor must ask himself as he prepares for the rehearsal and eventual performance of a choral work.

Since choral music is usually composed with some kind of text, it is here that the conductor must begin in his search for the central idea of the work. The text will usually provide the basic clue as to the nature of the work: sacred or secular, folksong or lullaby, love song or concert piece. If the text is in a foreign language, it is imperative that a translation be available for the singers. It is impossible to teach a work to a choir when its message is not known or its text understood.

The next step in discovering the central purpose of a choral work is to determine what characteristics of formal structure give the piece unity. This is necessary so that the choir and the audience will be able to perform the work in their imaginations. The clearly defined structural organization must become apparent, especially when thematic material returns as in a three-part sonata-allegro, or rondo form.

When the formal structure is readily apparent, the conductor should turn his attention to the melodic, harmonic, and rhythmic elements that give the work unity. Here a critical balance is necessary. When a work is in three-part sonata form as opposed to one that is organized on the basis of the text alone, the relation between the melodic, harmonic, and rhythmic elements of the two different sections are normally easily discernible. In the choral music of the late nineteenth century, in which composers tend to ramble and not present musical material in concise classical form, the conductor must work harder to determine the central purpose. The central purpose is always discernible, and careful study by the conductor can bring it out.

In summary, the conductor's preparation must be so thorough that he will be convinced he has found the way to make all the elements in a work appropriate to one another: form, melody, rhythm, harmony, texture, etc. In the final analysis, the performance is successful when the listener is also convinced.

Performance Practice

There is another aspect of the conductor's preparation that is so important we have devoted all of Part Four of this book to it. This aspect is performance practice, the study of conventions of performance of music literature of various periods. The conscientious conductor will always consider the available evidence relating to the expectations of composers and the customs of performers from various eras.

Performing Arrangements and Seating Plans

One of the more fascinating studies in the field of choral performance is the manner in which individual conductors have arranged their singers for public performances. To enhance this study, we have chosen performance plans devised by six American choral conductors (F. Melius Christiansen, John Finley Williamson, Robert Shaw, Roger Wagner, Norman Luboff, and William Hall), and then presented more specialized and unusual performance situations.

F. Melius Christiansen and the St. Olaf Choir

When performing under its founder, F. Melius Christiansen, the St. Olaf Choir usually consisted of 58 voices: 18 sopranos, 15 altos, 11 tenors, and 14 basses. The final size depended on the size of the smallest section. For example, if there were 11 capable tenors available during a given tour season, the number of singers in the other sections would be chosen to balance the tenor section. A choir of 58 voices would include 11 first sopranos, 7 second sopranos, 7 first altos, 8 second altos, 5 first tenors, 6 second tenors, 5 baritones and 9 basses. A smaller choir of 46 voices might include a similar balance: 8 first sopranos, 6 second sopranos, 5 first altos, 7 second altos, 4 first tenors, 4 second tenors, 4 baritones and 8 basses. Notice that there were more second altos and second basses than tenors, which is consistent with the acoustical principles of the overtone system.

Because of the priority placed upon blend in the St. Olaf choirs, Christiansen further classified the singers according to vocal color: bright and dark voices. The ideal performance arrangement thus mixed the bright and dark qualities in such a manner that the listener would hear an ideal choral blend in any section of the hall.

Basses	2nd Tenors
Baritones	1st Tenors
2nd Sopranos	2nd Altos
1st Sopranos	1st Altos

Conductor

This particular arrangement is especially effective in the performance of Renaissance and Baroque choral literature. It allows the sections to maintain their identity in polyphonic music, while at the same time preserving the important soprano-bass orientation that is so necessary in the choral works of J. S. Bach, Handel, and their contemporaries.

John Finley Williamson and the Westminster Choir

The touring Westminster Choir, as distinguished from the larger choral ensemble of the same name which sings and records with the major orchestras of the United States, usually consists of 40 voices: 5 first sopranos, 5 second sopranos, 5 first altos, 6 second altos, 4 first tenors, 4 second tenors, 5 baritones, and 6 basses. This choral ensemble is smaller in number than most comparable college groups because each singer is considered a soloist and the resultant tonal sound is one that is vital and fully resonant.

The most important consideration underlying the arrangement of the voices of the Westminster Choir in public performance was the strong foundation of the bass section. John Finley Williamson, its founder and conductor (1919–1958), believed that a choral ensemble should be as solidly constructed as a New England church. He often compared the first sopranos to the glistening point of the spire. The second sopranos were the base of the tower that supported the tapering top. The first and second altos, the first and second tenors, and the baritones made up the body of the church. The entire structure was then supported by an alive, vital, and responsive bass section, upon which the rest of the choir depended for pitch and rhythmic vitality.

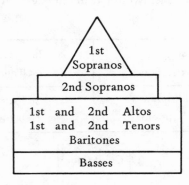

This approach to ensemble singing is especially effective with literature of the Classical and Romantic periods and in music in which there is an homophonic texture and orchestral accompaniment.

To achieve the proper blend and balance the choir performs in an arrangement that is basically sectional in orientation.

2nd Tenors	1st Tenors	2nd Basses	Baritones
2nd Tenors	1st Tenors	2nd Basses	Baritones
1st Altos	2nd Altos	1st Sopranos	2nd Sopranos
1st Altos	2nd Altos	1st Sopranos	2nd Sopranos

Conductor

The preceding diagram is a classic example of a block performing formation; basses behind sopranos and tenors in back of altos. Williamson chose this arrangement for aural purposes. The bass section was the foundation of the sound. The voices between the basses and the first sopranos provided a rich tonal texture to the ensemble, while the first sopranos brought the entire structure to a focus through the clarity of a pure, crystal-clear thread of tone. Williamson believed that a great choral ensemble could not exist unless the soprano section restrained its sound and by doing so allowed the basses to emerge as the solid foundation of the choral sound.

The Robert Shaw Chorale

The touring Robert Shaw Chorale, which was perhaps the finest choral group in the world during the eighteen-year period of its existence (1947–1965), consisted of thirty singers: 8 sopranos, 7 altos, 7 tenors and 8 basses. The actual division of voices by section depended on the individual vocal quality and strength of the voices and varied from year to year as the personnel and repertoire changed. A typical breakdown by section would include 4 first sopranos, 4 second sopranos, 3 first altos, 4 second altos, 4 first tenors, 3 second tenors, 4 baritones, and 4 basses. Shaw preferred sections that were equal in number. One might speculate that the reason for this was that he auditioned his voices carefully and was able to select those voices which gave him the ideal in terms of balance and quality.

Robert Shaw's performing plan normally consisted of seven quartets plus two extra singers, with voices arranged in mirror fashion:

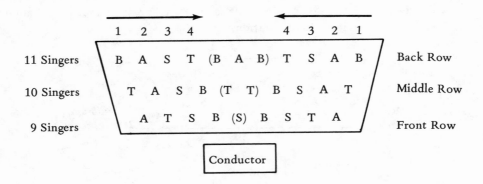

	1 2 3 4	4 3 2 1	
11 Singers	B A S T	(B A B)	T S A B	Back Row
10 Singers	T A S B	(T T)	B S A T	Middle Row
9 Singers	A T S B	(S)	B S T A	Front Row

Conductor

There were also other interesting aspects in this plan. Each singer had a four foot area between himself and the singers on the right and left, and four feet between himself and the singers in front and back. The ensemble was usually arranged with the strongest voices in the rear, although even this varied from year to year depending on the voices. A closer study of the plan will reveal that the back row consisted of a quartet on either end in mirror (B, A, S, T) with two basses and an alto in the center. The middle row was similarly arranged with a quartet on either end in mirror (T, A, S, B) with two tenors in the center, while the front row had two quartets in mirror (A, T, S, B) and a soprano in the center. The arrangement of the quartets in each row differed from the arrangement in the two other rows.

The soloists in the Robert Shaw Chorale were members of the chorus. If a singer who normally stood in one of the two rear rows was the soloist for the evening, he or she moved to the front of the chorus, and a member of the same voice category moved from the front row to the vacated place.

Robert Shaw achieved maximum tonal flexibility by selecting two baritones who could also sing second tenor, two altos who could sing second soprano, two basses whose range allowed them to sing baritone, and two second tenors who were able to sing baritone.

When working with a large amateur chorus, Shaw tends to group the men together in the center of the group.

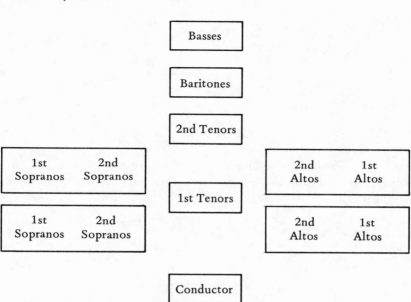

In addition to this performing arrangement, Shaw will borrow voices from one section to strengthen another section. For example, he will use some second sopranos to help the altos when the altos are singing in their lower register against the tenors in their higher tessitura. In like manner, he will use some tenors to assist the altos when they are singing in the lower part of their range.

The Roger Wagner Chorale

The Roger Wagner Chorale, the most recorded of all American choral groups (with more than sixty professional albums to its credit), consists of twenty-four singers: 6 sopranos, 6 altos, 6 tenors and 6 basses. Where the stage size allows sufficient space, Wagner prefers a distance of one and one-half feet between each singer. This allows maximum freedom of movement in expressive music like the *Liebeslieder Waltzes* of Brahms.

In music that is characterized by a vertical chord structure or homophonic orientation, the ensemble performs in a quartet arrangement with the low voices on the outside. Whenever possible Wagner prefers that the Chorale perform in two rows.

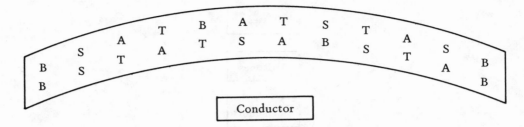

If a stage is too narrow for the Chorale to perform comfortably in two rows, Wagner arranges the singers in three rows with a distance of approximately two feet between singers.

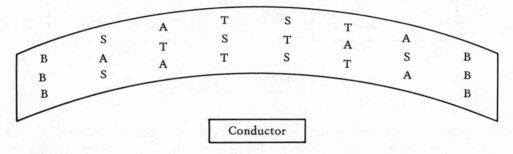

In the polyphonic literature of the Renaissance, a repertoire which Wagner interprets and performs without peer, the Chorale usually stands in a block formation with the basses behind the sopranos and the tenors behind the altos. This arrangement facilitates sectional blend and tonal balance consistent with the performance practices of the period.

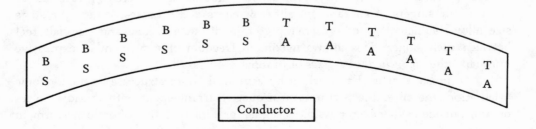

The Norman Luboff Choir

The Norman Luboff Choirs perform both in sections and in quartets, on either three or four levels, depending on the individual height of the singers involved. Sometimes the ensemble will sing in a block formation—basses behind the sopranos—for the purpose of improving the pitch in those sections.

Luboff believes that the block formation is the optimum performing arrangement for a concert choir. On rare occasions he has performed with the men in the middle, sopranos stage right, altos stage left, and the tenors between the basses and sopranos.

When the touring group consists of 30 singers—16 men and 14 women—the following performing arrangement is used:

Basses	Tenors
Sopranos	Altos

Conductor

The William Hall Chorale

The William Hall Chorale changes formation three or four times during

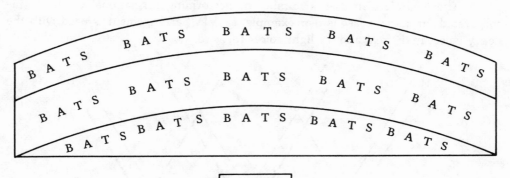

Conductor

each performance. The reasons given for these changes are twofold: musical style considerations and visual variety.

An informal quartet arrangement—or in the words of Hall, a "salt and pepper" formation—is used to enhance the sound of nineteenth-century choral literature.

Most polyphonic literature of the sixteenth and eighteenth centuries is performed in a block formation for the purposes of blend and sectional equality.

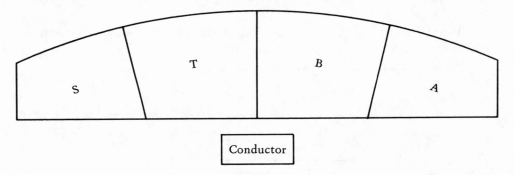

If the concert hall in which the Chorale is singing lends itself to a stereophonic, "group-in-the-round" formation, an attempt is made to make use of this opportunity for a certain variety in the interpretation of works which lend themselves to such an arrangement.

The Chorale also uses a number of performing formations which are incorporated for visual reasons. For example, a "VW" arrangement is used with the heavy voices in the rear and the light voices forward.

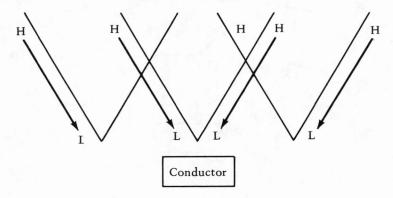

William Hall also uses a "V" arrangement for similar reasons, with the men on the outside and women in the inside, and a curved "half moon" arrangement with the men and women in the same positions.

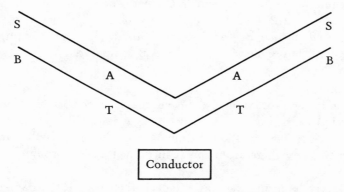

The Chorale also performs in a "separation of the sexes" formation for reasons of looks more than anything else. The stylistic value of a plan of this type is that it creates a "light-heavy" aural awareness in the listener.

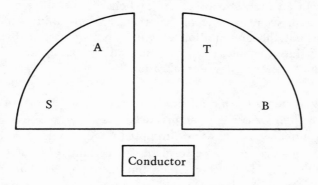

Unusual Performing Arrangements

Often the performing arrangement of a choral group will be determined by the nature of a particular work, the acoustics of a concert hall, the demands of radio or television broadcasting, or the request of the composer. In recent years choreography has become almost a sine qua non for school groups, a practice of many college choruses, and a virtual necessity for popular music ensembles and television groups.

Some of the more interesting examples of unusual performing formations are the Gregg Smith Singers, the King's College Choir, John Nelson and the Pro Arte Double Chorale, the Fred Waring Glee Club, and a special performing arrangement devised by conductor Leopold Stokowski and composer Andresz Panufnik for the world premier of a work by that composer.

The Gregg Smith Singers

Conductors will occasionally devise unusual performing formations for specific musical reasons. For example, the Gregg Smith Singers feature a section in their programs called "multidimensional" performance, a plan in which the singers are spread anywhere from ten to fifty feet apart throughout the concert hall.

Charles Ives, pointing the way to such practices, wrote in an essay entitled "Music and Its Future":

> Experiments, even on a limited scale, as when a conductor separates a chorus from an orchestra or places a choir off the stage or in a remote part of the hall, seem to indicate that there are possibilities in this matter that may benefit the presentation of music, not only from the standpoint of clarifying the harmonic, rhythmic, thematic material, etc., but of bringing the inner content to a deeper realization.[4]

In this article Ives suggested that musical performance in the future will have many more dimensions than are currently in practice.

It is the influence of Ives that prompted Gregg Smith to spread his singers throughout the audience in the performance of certain types of choral literature. The most important guide for the Gregg Smith Singers is that the performance formation utilized should follow the structure of each piece of music. Very often music that does not seem to lend itself to antiphonal or multidimensional spacing can, upon further study, have intriguing possibilities. For example, *Nymhpes des bois*, a five-part funeral madrigal with the Latin *cantus firmus* in the tenor, can be performed with the tenors spread throughout the hall while the other parts sing their lines on stage in French. The effect is stunning!

The King's College Choir

One of the most challenging choral works in the entire repertoire is the little-performed sixteenth-century motet *Spem in alium* by Thomas Tallis. Composed as a canon for forty parts, this work makes some interesting acoustical and musical demands on the performers. It also creates the need for a distinctive performing arrangement.

Conductor David Willcocks devised a unique plan for a performance of this work in the chapel of King's College (Cambridge). Each of the eight choirs —five parts to a choir—was separated from the other by approximately thirty feet and placed in horeshoe formation with the audience and conductor inside the circle. This kind of separation of the choirs insured that the full impact of the work was felt by the entire audience.

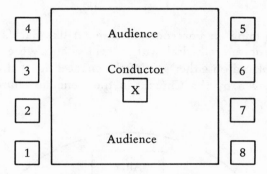

John Nelson and the Pro Arte Chorale

Some of the richest repertoire for chorus is found among the polychoral literature of the sixteenth, seventeenth, and eighteenth centuries. John Nelson and the Pro Arte Chorale have specialized in the performance of this literature. Some of their concerts have been presented in very interesting settings.

For a work like Johann Sebastian Bach's *St. Matthew Passion*, which would be sung in a concert hall like Carnegie Hall (New York), Nelson will perform in a simple double-choir setting like the one shown on the following page.

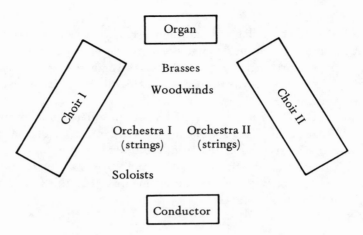

When performing an unaccompanied motet like Bach's *Singet dem Herrn*, in a church or European cathedral with a split chancel, the choir would be divided equally and placed on either side of the chancel in front of the altar. Such a performance was given by the Chorale in the Venetian church S.S. Giovanni e Paolo during a European tour.

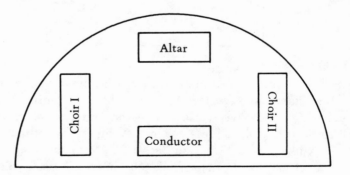

In the same Venetian church, Nelson achieved a very effective result by opening the concert with a four-choir work by Heinrich Schütz (1585–1672), *Warum toben die Heiden?* By placing the four choirs in a formation which surrounded the audience on all four sides, the individuality of the choirs was preserved and heard with utmost clarity.

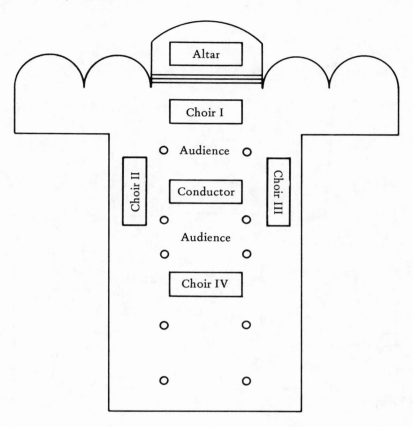

The polychoral music of Giovanni Gabrieli (1557–1612) lends itself to many exciting possibilities, depending upon the type of church or concert facility in which the performance is taking place and on the acoustical properties of the hall. In a spacious basilica like St. Mark's in Venice (the original setting of many of Gabrieli's polychoral works), the methods of performance are almost limitless. (See the floor plan that follows.) With its twin lofts elevated on either side of the chancel (1), its choir behind the altar (2), its elevated steps on the ground floor in front of the altar (3), and its rear balcony containing a second organ (4) (the other organ is in the left front chancel loft), the imaginative conductor can place his singers and instrumentalists in many different locations for a stimulating effect.

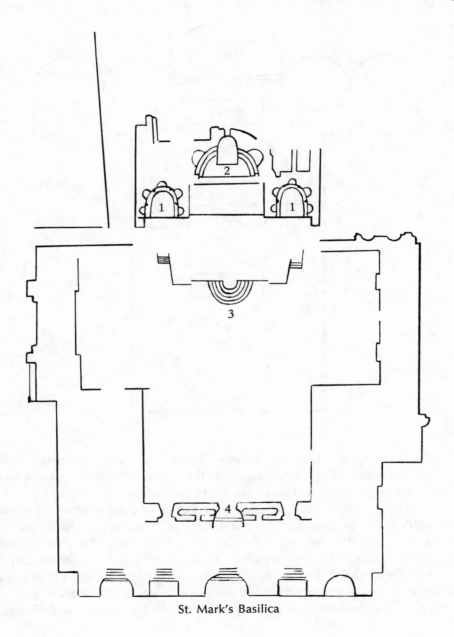

St. Mark's Basilica

The Fred Waring Glee Club

The personnel of the Fred Waring Glee Club normally included 22 singers, 14 men and 8 women divided into the following sections: 3 first tenors, 3 second tenors, 3 baritones, 2 bass-baritones, 3 low basses, 4 first sopranos, and 4 second sopranos (sometimes 3 second sopranos and 1 alto).

For rehearsal purposes Waring used a seating plan that separated the sections in the following manner:

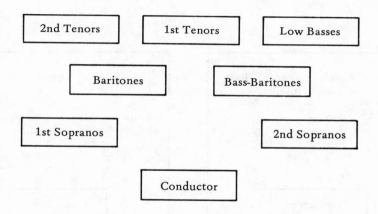

In performance the tallest men were in the center or at the end; the women in front. The type of voice determined where a particular singer would stand. The heavier voices, and those which projected best, would be placed furthest from the microphone. They would move from one position to another according to Waring's demands for vocal and orchestral blend, or for the predominance of one over the other, or of one section over another, or of a soloist over the entire group. All efforts to achieve a distinctive choral sound were built around the demands of the microphone, the television camera, or the nature of the choreography.

Leopold Stokowski—Panufnik's Universal Prayer

An unusual performing arrangement for a contemporary work was devised by conductor Leopold Stokowski for the first performance of Andresz Panufnik's *Universal Prayer* in the Cathedral of St. John the Divine in New York City. Conceived stereophonically by Panufnik, the work involved two groups of performers:

Group I—4 solo voices and 3 harps performing with precise indications of rhythm and tempo
Group II—Organ and 100 voices interpreting the music aleatorically with approximate note and time values

Stokowski experimented with two different performing arrangements in rehearsal. Because of the immense physical size of the cathedral, the first plan was chosen for the performance.

Plan I

Plan II

Soprano soloist Alto soloist Tenor soloist Bass soloist

1st Harp 2nd Harp 3rd Harp

Conductor

Audience

Women's voices Men's voices

Women's voices Organ Men's voices

Soprano soloist Alto soloist Tenor soloist Bass soloist

1st Harp 2nd Harp 3rd Harp

Conductor

Audience

CONDUCTING THE PERFORMANCE

The choral conductor has five important responsibilities in a public performance:

1. He must prepare the singers for the first entrance and subsequent entrances and changes of tempo.

2. He must provide those gestures that will establish the correct pace (tempo), dynamic level, articulation, style, and tone quality.

3. He must evoke an empathic response that will inspire and sustain the choir throughout the entire performance.

4. He must create a feeling of involvement in and commitment to the music that will communicate the inner essence of the work to the audience.

5. He must bring the movement or work to an effective and appropriate conclusion.

The Preparatory Gesture

A clear, precise preparatory motion is the most important of all the conductor's physical gestures. A performance may be crippled beyond repair (and thus the overall effect of the concert ruined) because of a poor preparatory motion on the part of the conductor. In the correct preparatory position the hand will begin high and proceed on the pattern, in front of the body at approximately eye level, and at the moment of attack will continue through the pattern.

The preparatory motion can be defined as the silent beat immediately preceding the first written note of the work. For example, when a composition begins on a beat, the preparatory gesture takes place on the preceding beat:

Example 1

Bach, *Cantata 214*

Tö - net ihr   Pau - ken

When a piece begins on a note or notes that are one-half or less the beat value, the preparatory motion is the beat itself.

Example 2

Handel, *Messiah*, "Thus saith the Lord"

Because this one gesture is so critical to the successful start of the piece and to every new entrance as well, it must communicate important information to the choral ensemble: the pulse (the basic beat value), the pace (the speed), the dynamic plan (the loudness), the style (the texture), the articulation (the legato, staccato, or marcato nature of the work). This motion should be considered as the model for the beginning sounds and should start on the same plane and follow the same basic pattern as that in which the normal beat will be given.

Example 3

Bach, *Jesu, meine Freude*

Preparatory motion for a piece that starts on the first beat of the measure.

Example 4

Pachelbel, *Christ lag in Todesbanden*, Vs. 7

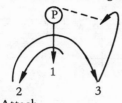

Preparatory motion for a piece that starts on the second beat of the measure in 4/4 meter. It is important here to make an abbreviated downbeat motion so that the choir will not make a false start.

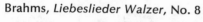

Example 5

Brahms, *Liebeslieder Walzer*, No. 8

Preparatory motion for a piece that starts on the second beat of a 3/4 measure.

Example 6

Killmayer, *Villanela*

Chi la ga-gliar-da, _____ chi

Chi la ga-gliar-da, _____ chi

(8) Chi la ga-gliar-da, _____ chi

Preparatory motion for a piece that starts on the third beat of a 4/4 measure.

Example 7

Bruckner, *Te Deum*

In te Do - mi-ne spe - ra - vi

Preparatory motion for a piece that begins on the fourth beat of a 4/4 measure.

The preparatory motion in other systems of metric organization is similar: a special attempt must always be made to keep the gestures high, in front of the body, and on the general plane of the beat pattern.

Continuing Conducting Gestures

When conducting a work in performance it should be understood that all conducting gestures derive their size and character from the nature of the music. As a general rule the motions of the conductor should not get in the way of the music but should allow the singers the freedom to express the intentions of the composer.

The size of the conducting gesture is usually dependent upon two primary factors: the tempo of the piece and the volume of sound desired. In all cases the conductor should maintain the feeling of bringing the singers to him rather than reaching to the choral ensemble. This is to say that there should be an economy of physical gesture so that the choir will feel the intensity and control of the conductor's activity. Within the context of this controlled conducting technique, it might be said that the slower the tempo, the larger the beat, and the louder the sound desired, the larger the beat pattern.

The character of the conductor's gestures is obviously determined by the nature of the music itself. The motions must reflect the musical style and type of tone quality desired, from short, vigorous, even jerky motions in staccato, marcato, and dotted rhythm to smooth, intense, and controlled hand, arm, and upper body motions for legato and cantabile expression. As a general rule, the more intense the nature of the musical line that is desired, the smaller the gesture that is needed to evoke this response from the group.

In the final analysis it should be noted that all beats derive their speed, size, and character from the nature of the music that is being performed. All gestures must be modified and adapted to suit the demands of the music if they are to evoke a correct response from the choral ensemble.

One of the many pitfalls that the conductor must avoid is a performance in which the music of different style periods is performed with a certain sameness. A concert in which the music of Palestrina and Brahms sound the same is deadly to an audience that expects a variety of style in the choral performance. Robert Shaw emphasizes this point in the following quote:

> The qualities which make a choir successful and unique are, to my mind, clarity of enunciation, vitality of rhythm, and variety of tone color. Many choirs, I find, make the mistake of trying to develop a single, fixed

color of their own, as a sort of hallmark. I think it is better to avoid any fixed norm and to try for as great a variety of color as possible. Color is improved by regarding the works to be performed as *dramatic* expressions which must impart a story, mood and thoughtful significance in addition to the sensation of tone. The director can draw out this dramatic quality by insisting on absolutely clear enunciation, by stressing the poetic value of the lyrics, and by adapting the color of each musical phrase to the mood of the words it accompanies.[5]

The final five chapters of this book, which are devoted to the topic of musical style as it relates to the performing practice of the different periods of music literature, should be consulted for a further clarification of this important topic.

Empathic Conducting

Choral conducting differs from orchestral conducting in one important way: in orchestral conducting the performance is controlled by the tip of the baton or the hand whereas in choral conducing the eyes, the gestures of the body, and the manner in which the conductor breathes with the ensemble are all critical to the response of the choir. The choral conductor must possess the technical skills of the orchestral conductor and must also serve as a model—physically and spiritually—of the response that he is seeking to evoke from the choral ensemble. Especially important is a dramatic ability, communicated through the eyes and facial expression, that assists the individual singer vocally through a very special empathic relationship.

This empathic relationship is established when the conductor first steps to the podium and faces the choir. Eye contact, communicating a seriousness of intent and yet at the same time a warmth of understanding, must be maintained from the first note of the work to the final release.

Because the first beat of every measure is a downbeat, it is this gesture, along with the preparatory beat, that gives the choir its feeling of rhythmic stability in any tempo or style.

To establish the pulse of the downbeat with a clear and consistent conducting motion, the following exercise should be practiced until it becomes natural:

1. Place your forearm on a table or desk in front of you in a relaxed position.

2. Lift the hand and forearm to a 45° angle above the table while allowing your elbow to rest naturally on the table.

3. Then let the arm drop and allow the dead weight of the forearm to establish the feeling of the pulse.

4. Do this four times or more to establish the feeling of pulse.

5. After this feeling has been established, allow your wrist to rebound in rhythm by tapping your fingers on the table.

6. Do this exercise until you can feel a solid pulse in both the downward and upward motions.

7. Practice this gesture in large patterns, small patterns, and intense legato patterns until a variety of conducting gestures has been developed that can be applied to choral music of varying styles, articulation, and tempo. In all cases, however, take care to insure that there is a clearly defined bounce (*ictus*) to every beat and a wrist motion that leads each beat throughout the pattern in a free and flexible —though not limp—manner.

Creating a Feeling of Involvement and Commitment

Once the performance of a work has begun, it is the conductor who is generally responsible for the impact of that performance upon the audience. We have all heard performances that are technically adequate yet dull and lifeless. There are obviously many reasons why the reading of a work does not reach the audience, even when all the notes are in their proper place. We will examine four of these reasons: poor diction, blank facial expression, lack of rhythmic vitality, and indefinite conducting gestures.

Because choral music is almost always sung with a text of some kind, it is necessary that the choral ensemble communicate the message of the work to the audience. This is basic to exciting choral singing. Pure vowels and clearly enunciated consonants rarely happen by chance. It is thus the responsibility of the conductor to insist on this aspect of choral technique. (For further information refer to chapter five.)

Next to clear choral diction, the facial expressions of the individual choral singers are an important ingredient for an exciting choral performance. Expressive choral singing begins with the conductor, since his face must communicate the mood and style of the work to the choir. This important aspect of choral technique does not come naturally to every conductor. Yet this empathic relationship between conductor and singer is absolutely necessary if a performance is to excite an audience. As the face of the conductor comes alive, the mood as well as the central idea of the work will become evident to the listener.

Following closely on the facial expression of the conductor is the need for rhythmic vitality if a performance is to excite the audience. A work comes alive rhythmically because the conductor exudes and projects this vitality in every gesture. It is not the size of the beat pattern but its controlled intensity that quickens the musical result. A conducting posture that is erect, flexible, and expansively vital will bring rhythmic excitement to the performance.

A final ingredient in an exciting performance is the podium style of the conductor himself. This is obviously something that is ultimately dictated by good taste and self-control, but the manner of the conductor can become the difference between an acceptable and an exciting choral performance. Often a conductor can add "electricity" to the reading of a choral work by the manner in which he walks on stage, acknowledges the applause of the audience, and prepares the choir for their first entrance. The thin line between exciting conducting and overt showmanship must be kept in mind at all times, and the sensitive conductor will be careful not to cross that line.

Etiquette in Choral Performance

It is often the little things in a performance that tend to dim its overall impact upon the audience. For example, the way a group walks on stage, the manner in which they leave the stage, the way a conductor acknowledges the applause of the audience, these all seem like relatively unimportant details when considered in the light of the technical demands of the music. Yet they are the very reasons that a conductor must give attention to every phase of the choral art if his group is to be successful in public performance.

COMMON PROBLEMS IN CHORAL PERFORMANCE

The conductor will often recognize certain musical deficiencies in a performance but not realize that the cause of these problems can be traced directly to that conductor's technique. This section will identify some of these common conduct-ing problems and prescribe a simple solution for them.

Indecisive Attack by the Chorus

This very common problem in choral groups is caused by the lack of a clear pre-paratory gesture on the part of the conductor. Every preparatory gesture—whether at the beginning of a work or following a pause or fermata—must be in the exact tempo of the composition and must begin with a definite impulse or "ictus," and must be high enough in the pattern to be clearly visible to all the singers. This preparatory gesture must be absolutely clear rhythmically, as well as in the style and dynamic level of the passage that follows.

Lack of Control of the Group

Eye contact is very important for control, especially with amateur singers, but the surest method of controlling the ensemble is for the conductor to employ a con-ducting gesture that will bring the singers to him. Reaching toward the group with conducting gestures, or with the left hand in making cues, will often result in an unusually large beat pattern that tends to diffuse control. The posture of the conductor is also a factor in control. If the conductor's posture is vital and alive, and the singers are taught to model this good posture, the result will be a finely controlled performance.

Ragged Entrance by the Chorus

Ragged entrances by the entire choir or an individual section can usually be traced to an unrhythmic preparatory beat or a lack of eye contact with the singers at the moment of their entrance. In choral conducting the eye is nearly as important as the clear and rhythmically precise preparatory beat.

Unmusical Accents in the Melodic Line

Excessive accents of this type are caused by a conducting technique that overem-phasizes the rhythmic pulse. This can be overcome by a conducting pattern that lies closer to a horizontal plane and by greater use of a tense yet flexible wrist in legato passages.

Lack of Dynamic Control

The general tendency to make gestures in soft passages much too large can result in a performance that lacks intensity or dynamic control in the soft passages. These large gestures also tend to produce a sameness or monotony in the dynamic span of control.

A Performance Lacking Vitality

Indecision, poor posture, and a flabby wrist (or conducting pattern) on the part of the conductor are deficiencies that tend to create this kind of performance. A conductor must have confidence in himself and his knowledge of the score, and transmit this to his singers through a technically correct and physically vital conducting posture. It is this model that the amateur choral singer will imitate and the result will be a vital and fully resonant choral sound.

BEYOND THE MECHANICAL ASPECTS

The most important fact a conductor must recognize in performance is that none of the mechanical aspects of choral art—clear conducting gestures, correct tempi, logical phrasing, accuracy of pitch, fully resonant tone quality, elegant diction, sense of style, and knowledge of the musical tradition—can in themselves insure an exciting musical experience for the singer and the audience. Each is important and necessary and must become an essential part of the conductor's rehearsal technique, but just being correct or accurate is not enough. The capstone of artistic choral singing must be found elsewhere. Transmitting the intentions of the composer from the choral ensemble to the audience involves emotion, love, dedication, and mutual respect.

In short, this is what communication is all about. When the conductor can fuse the mechanical elements of rehearsal with an indefinable emotional content in performance that brings something special to the listener, and this is all balanced with intelligence and imagination, the result is choral singing that comes alive. This is the ultimate challenge of the choral experience.

NOTES

1. Herbert Witherspoon, *Singing* (New York: G. Schirmer, 1925), p. v.

2. Wilhelm Ehmann, *Choral Directing* (Minneapolis: Augsburg Publishing House, 1968), p. 7.

3. Ibid., p. 7.

4. Charles Ives, "Music and Its Future," *American Composers on American Music* (Palo Alto, California: Stanford University Press, 1933), p. 197.

5. Robert Shaw, "Choral Art for America," *Etude* (Vol. 63, October, 1945), p. 564.

Chapter Six

RECOMMENDED READING LIST

Ehmann, Wilhelm. *Choral Directing.* Translated by George D. Wiebe. Minneapolis: Augsburg Publishing House, 1968. A sound pedagogical and artistic basis for choral singing presented by one of Germany's leading authorities on church music and choral singing.

Garretson, Robert L. *Conducting Choral Music.* 3rd edition. Boston: Allyn and Bacon, Inc., 1970. As one of the most popular works in the field of choral techniques, this book deals with tone and diction, rehearsal techniques, conducting techniques, and organization and management of choral groups.

Green, Elizabeth A. H. *The Modern Conductor.* 2nd edition. Englewood Cliffs: Prentice-Hall, Inc., 1969. This important work contains information on all phases of the conducting process including basic elements of choral tone and conducting technique.

Lamb, Gordon G. *Choral Techniques.* Dubuque, Iowa: Wm. C. Brown Company Publishers, 1974. A valuable book on rehearsal procedures, conducting techniques, and choral department management.

National Association of Teachers of Singing Committee. "The Solo Voice and Choral Singing." *The Choral Journal,* December, 1970, pp. 11–12. This article represents a successful attempt to establish a common ground of understanding between the voice teacher and the choral conductor regarding vocal techniques.

Swan, Howard. "Style, Performance, Practice, and Choral Tone." *The Choral Journal,* July–August, 1960, pp. 12–13. A classic article on choral technique and interpretation by one of the leading authorities in the field.

Weingartner, Felix. *Weingartner on Music and Conducting.* Translated by Ernest Newman, Jessie Crosland, and H. M. Schott. New York: Dover Publications, Inc., 1969. Three important literary works are included in this volume which contains valuable insights for the conductor.

BASIC MUSICIANSHIP

Introduction to Part Three

IN RECENT YEARS there have been increasing demands for the incorporation of basic musicianship training into the choral rehearsal. However, the choral conductor, faced with a busy performance schedule and limited rehearsal time, may justly question the feasibility of devoting time to this endeavor.

The usual justification for basic musicianship training is that the time devoted to it is more than compensated for by the fact that singers learn to sight read better and require less time to learn new works, and by the fact that they sing with better understanding of the musical structure and meaning. As valid as these justifications may be, and there is strong evidence to support them, they may not be as convincing as the contention that basic musicianship training can in itself be an interesting, exciting, and intrinsically valuable activity. The material provided in this unit should assist the conductor in integrating a meaningful program of basic musicianship training into the choral experience.

Basic musicianship for the choral singer should include a knowledge of the common symbols of music notation, an ability to translate these symbols into musical sounds through vocal performance, and an understanding of general principles of structure and organization in rhythm, pitch, harmony, texture, timbre, and form. In the following chapters choral conductors are given specific practical suggestions on how to present aspects of basic musicianship to their chorus members. In most cases alternate approaches are given, allowing the conductor to choose an approach he considers most effective and meaningful.

The exercises cited in these chapters will all be contained in the *Singer's Manual*. Conductors are encouraged to adapt these exercises to the special needs of their singers. The material for basic musicianship training should not be regarded as something totally separate from the rest of the rehearsal program. Whenever possible, concepts should be drawn from or related to passages in the music being studied. It will also frequently be effective to combine some aspects of basic musicianship training with aspects of vocal training.

Obvious limitations of space make it impossible to present a full-fledged introduction to all aspects of music theory, nor is it considered necessary for each chorus member to have such detailed knowledge. Instead our purpose has been to select those aspects that have the most immediate reference to choral performance. For this reason material on such subjects as orchestration or counterpoint has been limited to allow more extensive treatment of the two basic aspects that will have most relevance to the choral singer—rhythm and pitch. The two chapters covering these elements form the core of this unit. The final two chapters covering harmony, texture, and form have somewhat less direct bearing on the singer's performance. However, some work in these areas may help the singer develop a musical understanding and sensitivity, making his contribution not just that of mechanical production of his choral part, but rather a vital participation in the total experience of music-making.

Chapter Seven

Rhythm

Underneath the rhythm of every art and every work of art
there lies as a substratum in the depths of the subconsciousness,
the basic pattern of the relations of the live creature to his
environment.—JOHN DEWEY[1]

TEACHING RHYTHM is a challenging and complex task, involving not only the development of a valid intellectual understanding of rhythmic structure but also the development of a vital physical response to rhythmic stimuli. For the choral conductor working with high school students, college students, or adults, the task may be complicated by the fact that he must not only teach new ideas and techniques, but often must counteract and correct wrong ideas and techniques learned earlier.

For example, one of the most pernicious, wrong ideas is that the individual symbols of rhythmic notation have a direct, absolute relationship to duration or speed. This idea is usually suggested by such statements as "the quarter note is a walking note, eighth notes are running notes, sixteenth notes are very fast, half and whole notes are very slow, etc." With such unfortunate generalizations appearing in elementary school music and beginning instruction books for piano and other instruments, it is no wonder that students develop an incorrect concept of the nature of rhythmic notations.

The obvious problem with this misconception is that students find it difficult to perform music in which, for example, eighth notes are slow or half notes are fast. An even more serious problem, however, is that they tend to see just individual notes and to hear and perform isolated individual durations rather than developing the ability to project *foreground durational patterns* against *background metric structure.*

As a first step in counteracting such incorrect ideas, review the symbols of rhythmic notation (Ex. 1) with your singers, stressing the fact that the individual symbols themselves tell us nothing about the *absolute* duration of the sounds they represent; rather they give information only about the relative duration of these sounds. Each symbol is twice as long as the next symbol below it.

Example 1
Rhythmic Notation

NOTES		RESTS
▮◗▮	Breve (rarely used)	⊢⊣
𝅝	Whole	▬
𝅗𝅥	Half	▬
𝅘𝅥	Quarter	𝄽 or 𝄾
𝅘𝅥𝅮	Eighth	𝄿
𝅘𝅥𝅯	Sixteenth	𝅀
𝅘𝅥𝅰	Thirty-second	𝅁

Flags may be replaced by beams for groups of notes:

(𝅘𝅥𝅮𝅘𝅥𝅮 , 𝅘𝅥𝅯𝅘𝅥𝅯𝅘𝅥𝅯𝅘𝅥𝅯 , 𝅘𝅥𝅰𝅘𝅥𝅰𝅘𝅥𝅰𝅘𝅥𝅰 , etc.).

Note values smaller than the thirty-second notes are created by adding additional flags or beams.

A dot following a note or rest adds one-half of the value of the note or rest. For purposes of developing a viable performance conception of dotted notes, it is advisable to think of them as representing (as shown in Ex. 2) the combined duration of *three* of the next smaller note value.

Example 2
Dotted Notes and Rests

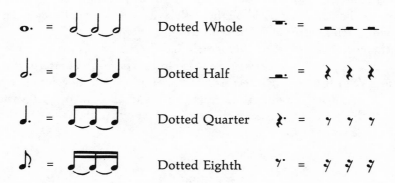

The *tie* (⌣ or ⌢) is used between two notes of the same pitch to indicate that they are to be sung as one united duration without intervening pause
or articulation. The use of the tie in Example 2 is purely for theoretical or ex-
planatory purposes, but in music it is used for durations that extend beyond a
measure, or in some cases half a measure, and for durations that cannot be expressed otherwise.

Example 3
Uses of the Tie

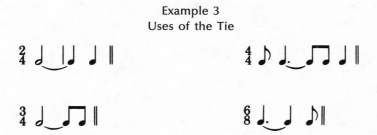

Another common mistake with regard to rhythm is overemphasizing the
intellectual or theoretical aspects at the expense of the physical and emotional.
Rhythm, if it is to be vital and meaningful, must be experienced physically.
Though some choral conductors may be reluctant to incorporate physical movement into their rehearsal programs, those conductors who make judicious use of
movement may find that it contributes greatly not only to the singer's sense of

rhythm but, perhaps of equal importance, to his sense of physical well-being and his enjoyment of the rehearsal. At the very least the rehearsal should involve both sitting and standing, and the conductor should always insist upon a good, upright, and vitally expansive posture. Throughout this chapter we shall make suggestions for movement, such as clapping and conducting.

With these basic considerations in mind, let us now proceed to an examination of the three primary aspects of rhythm—pulse, pace, and pattern.

Our task in teaching the performance of rhythm is to develop an awareness of a network of *pulses* moving at various *paces* and then to project various *patterns* against these in an artistic *performance*. Just what this implies should become clear in the sections that follow.

PULSE

Pulses are regularly recurring stimuli: they may be felt, as in the case of the pulses of the heart; they may be seen, as in the case of a flashing light at a crossroad; they may be heard, as in the case of music; or they may simply be imagined. Pulses in music are sometimes called beats, but we shall reserve the word *beat* for a more specific usage.

Begin by having the chorus members clap a series of pulses as represented by vertical lines. They should clap the exact number they see in each line and should try to keep them *steady* and *equal*.

Example 4

(a) | | | | | | | |

(b) | | | | | | | | | | | |

As they clap, you should point out that though it is possible to keep the pulses steady, it is almost impossible to keep them equal in importance. Psychologists tell us that whenever we experience a series of pulses like this, we will always tend to put them into groups of twos or threes; in other words, every second or every third pulse will seem somehow marked for more importance. No matter how hard we try to make the pulses of equal weight or importance, we will tend to stress some more than others, at least in our mind. The act of emphasizing some pulses more than others can be called *accentuation*. We can mark the accentuated or strong pulses with this symbol (—) and the unaccented or weak pulses with this symbol (◡). (The same symbols are used in poetry to indicate stressed and unstressed syllables.) Now have the choir clap the following lines and make the accentuation obvious by clapping the strong pulses slightly louder (dynamic accent) than the weak ones.

Example 5

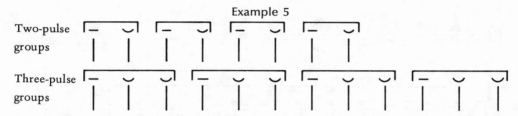

This grouping of pulses into groups of twos or threes by means of accentuation may be accomplished in other ways than by simply sounding one pulse louder than others. Sing the following examples and point out how change of duration (Ex. 6, *a* and *b*), change of pitch (*c* and *d*), or change of harmony (*e* and *f*), may also serve to accentuate pulses and thereby organize them into groups. Other factors such as texture, instrumentation, textual consideration, etc., may also affect accentuation.

Example 6

In music, pulses may be heard or imagined on several different levels of activity, that is, at several different rates of speed. Using groups of twos or threes on two different levels, there are four basic combinations. Have the chorus members practice Example 7 until they can perform it with ease in any of the following arrangements.

1. Have half of the chorus sing or clap the top part, the other half the bottom part, then reverse.

2. Have them tap the bottom line with the right hand, tap the top line with the left hand, then reverse hands.

3. Have them clap the bottom line, sing the top line on a neutral pitch and syllable ("dah" is a good syllable to use), then reverse the lines.

4. Have them conduct the top line with one hand, tap the bottom line with the other hand. Have them then use simplified conducting gestures.

Example 7

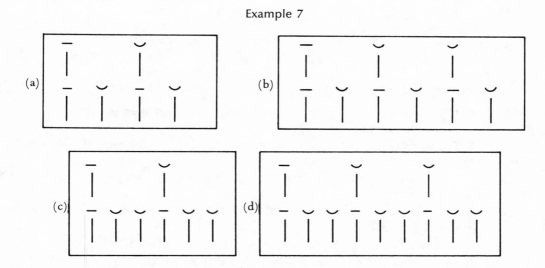

Repeat each pattern several times.

We may call the top level of pulses the *beat level*, implying that this is normally the level that a conductor will beat. We may call the bottom level the *division level*, indicating that the pulses heard on this level are parts or divisions of pulses on the beat level. In Example 8 these basic combinations are represented with notes instead of lines and they are presented in terms of meters.

Example 8

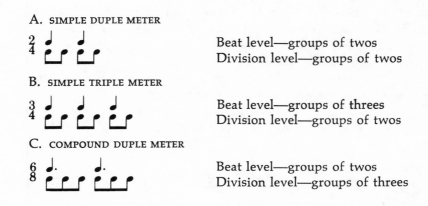

A. SIMPLE DUPLE METER

Beat level—groups of twos
Division level—groups of twos

B. SIMPLE TRIPLE METER

Beat level—groups of threes
Division level—groups of twos

C. COMPOUND DUPLE METER

Beat level—groups of twos
Division level—groups of threes

D. COMPOUND TRIPLE METER

Beat level—groups of threes
Division level—groups of threes

You can point out the following aspects to your chorus members.

1. Combinations A and B are called *simple* meters because the division levels are in groups of twos.

2. Combinations C and D are called *compound* meters because the division levels are in groups of threes.

3. Combinations A and C are called *duple* meters because the division levels are in groups of twos.

4. Combinations B and D are called *triple* meters because the beat levels are in groups of threes.

5. The double figure ($\frac{2}{4}$, $\frac{3}{4}$, etc.) at the beginning of each combination is a *meter signature* or *time signature*. The bottom figure indicates the note value (4 = quarter note, 8 = eighth note, etc.). The top figure indicates how many notes are in a measure of music in this particular meter. Notice that the signature for simple meters ($\frac{2}{4}$ and $\frac{3}{4}$) provides information on the beat level; the signatures for compound meters provide information on the division level.

6. The note values shown here indicate nothing about the absolute speed, pace, or *tempo* of the music. Although it is true that the quarter note often has a moderate rate of speed (about the rate of walking), it by no means has this moderate rate in every piece of music. This whole question of pace will be considered in the next section of this chapter, and it will be an important aspect to be considered in the performance practice chapters in Part Four. All that we are demonstrating here is the relation of one note to another in a given meter.

7. Other notes may be used for the beat and division levels. Although it is true that quarter notes and dotted quarter notes are frequently used for beats, they are by no means the only notes that can represent beats. Example 9 shows the beat level and division level of other meters.

Example 9
SIMPLE DUPLE METERS

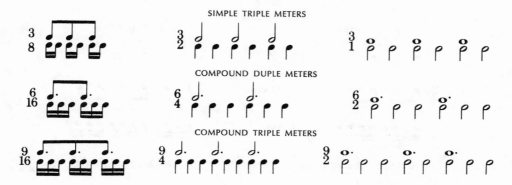

Have the chorus members perform various segments of Examples 8 and 9 using the techniques suggested for Example 7. You should also refer to similar musical examples in the literature you are rehearsing and ask the chorus members to discover the basic metric structure.

Up to this point we have been considering pulses on two levels only; the beat level and the division level. We can also consider them on a third level, namely the *subdivision level*. In most music, pulses on the subdivision level are regularly in groups of twos, that is, there are two subdivision pulses for every one division pulse. Example 10 illustrates four meters with subdivision levels. Practice them by (1) conducting the beat level, (2) tapping the division level, and (3) singing the subdivision level on "tah" or "dah." You can also practice them by dividing the chorus into three groups of singers and having one group sing beats on one pitch, a second group singing divisions on another pitch, and a third singing subdivisions on a third pitch. For example, you might use the pitches F, C', and A'. Although some singers may find it difficult at first to conduct, tap, and sing all at the same time, it is worth the time and effort because it will give them a clear and vital picture of meters "in action" rather than just "on paper."

Example 10

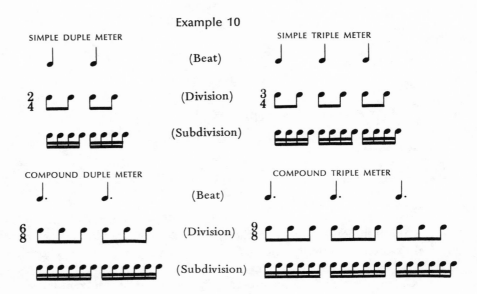

In addition to duple and triple meters, that is, two and three beats per measure, we can also have meters with more beats per measure. The most common of these is quadruple meter which represents, in effect, two duple meters combined. The accentuation in quadruple meter is usually as follows:

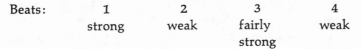

Beats:	1	2	3	4
	strong	weak	fairly strong	weak

Practice the quadruple meters in Example 11 using the techniques previously discussed.

Example 11
SIMPLE QUADRUPLE METER

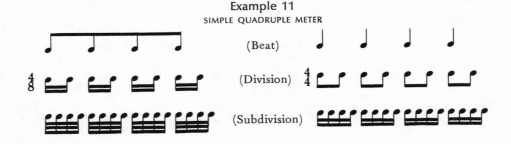

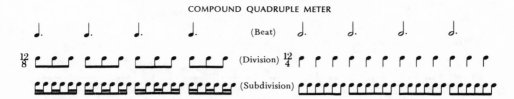

COMPOUND QUADRUPLE METER

Sextuple meter is really similar to compound duple meter, but at a slower rate of speed, so that now the division level becomes the beat level. For example, in fast $\frac{6}{8}$ there are 2 beats in a measure; in slow $\frac{6}{8}$ there are 6.

Example 12

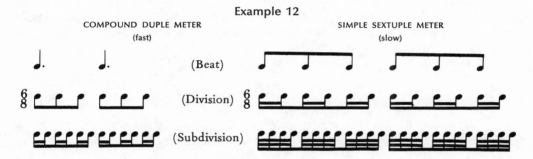

COMPOUND DUPLE METER   SIMPLE SEXTUPLE METER
(fast)   (slow)

Quintuple and sextuple meters—five- and seven-beat meters—really represent various alternations of groups of two and three beats. Though not as common as the previous meters, they are used effectively in some modern compositions, and are usually very interesting and enjoyable to perform.

Example 13
QUINTUPLE METER

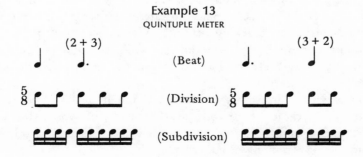

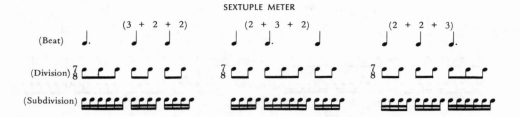

You should explain to the chorus that sometimes the meter signature does not actually indicate the true metric organization. A typical example would be fast waltzes in which the meter signature indicates that there are three quarter-note beats to a measure, but in actual practice the conductor beats one dotted half-note beat per measure.

PACE

As we indicated earlier, the kind of note value used really gives us no idea as to the tempo or length of a note. This point is worth emphasizing again because all too often musicians will look at passages with eighth or sixteenth notes and automatically assume that they are fast, when actually the passage may be moderate or even slow.

We need to know the pace or speed or pulse on a given level and then we can relate other pulse levels to these. The commonly used word for this idea of pace in music is *tempo*. Sometimes the composer indicates pace, speed, or tempo very precisely by showing the metronome marking of a particular note. A metronome marking of 60 (M.M. 60) would indicate 60 pulses per minute or one pulse per second. A metronome marking of 120 would indicate 120 pulses per minute or two pulses per second. Even if you do not have a metronome you can find these two markings by using a second hand of a watch; other tempo markings can be roughly estimated from these.

In many works, however, the tempo is not indicated precisely by metronome markings but rather more generally by means of words. Italian terms are used most frequently but occasionally tempi will be indicated in other languages. Here are some of the commonly used terms:

ENGLISH	ITALIAN	GERMAN	FRENCH
Slow Tempi			
broad	largo	breit	large
slow	lento	langsam	lent
slow	adagio (literally, at ease)	getragen	lent
heavy	grave	schwer	lourd
Moderate Tempi			
moderate	andante (literally, walking)	gehend	allant
	moderato	mässig	modéré
Fast Tempi			
fast	allegro (literally, cheerful)	schnell	vite
lively	vivace	lebhaft	vif
very fast	presto	eilig	rapide

Slight adaptations or modifications in these tempi can be indicated thus.

ENGLISH	ITALIAN	GERMAN	FRENCH
very	molto	sehr	très
somewhat	poco (or) un poco	ein wenig (or) etwas	un peu
more	più	-er	plus
even more	-issimo	noch -er	encore plus
not too	non troppo	nicht zu	pas trop
less	meno, -ino, (or) -etto	weniger	moins

Sometimes a composer wishes to change or modify his original tempo. He then uses terms such as those that follow:

ENGLISH	ITALIAN	GERMAN	FRENCH
accelerate	accelerando	schneller werden	accélérer

becoming faster	stringendo (literally, tightening)	drängend	en pressant
faster	più mosso	bewegter	plus animé
retard	ritardando,	langsamer werden,	ralentissant,
(gradually)	rallentando	zurückhalten	ralentir
held back	ritenuto	zurückge- halten	retenu
(immediately)			
broaden	allargando	verbreitern	élargissant
less fast	meno mosso	weniger bewegt	moins vite
freely	rubato (literally, robbed)	frei	libéré
gradually	poco a poco	allmählich	peu à peu
suddenly	subito	plötzlich	tout à coup
decrease in tempo and loudness	calando	nachlassen	en diminuant
decrease in tempo and loudness, dying away	smorzando	verlöschen	en s'effaçant
decrease in tempo and loudness, dying down	morendo	esterben	en mourant
return to original tempo	tempo primo, a tempo	erstes Zeitmass	premier (l[er]) tempo

In some music, such as operatic recitative, there may be no clear, regular sense of pulse. Often the composer will place a great emphasis on the use of rubato or freedom in rhythmic interpretation.

It should be remembered that tempo or pace refers to the speed of the beat and not to the speed of the rhythm patterns projected against this beat. Thus a composition in a slow tempo may have sections where patterns of fast notes are projected against the basic slow beat. This does not change the tempo. The tempo is only changed when the speed of the beat is changed.

PATTERN

Pulse and pace (or meter and tempo) give us a background of metric structure against which the performer must project the particular rhythmic patterns the composer has written. Sometimes these patterns will be identical with the pulses on a given level. Then the task is relatively simple. All that the performer must do is be sure that he is on the right level and sing pulses on that level. Let us imagine that the composer has written the following passage:

Example 14

Before reading, the chorus members should establish all levels of the metric framework.

Example 15

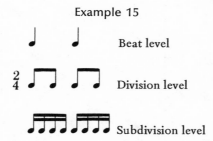

Now have them perform Example 14 in the following manner: For the first two measures they should sing pulses on the division level; for the second two measures they should sing pulses on the subdivision level; and for the last four measures they should sing pulses on the beat level.

Rhythmic patterns that duplicate pulse groupings of a meter may be called "basic" or "even-note" patterns. In addition there are other patterns that the performer must master.

The following patterns occur so frequently in music that they should be thoroughly learned.

Example 16

TWO-PULSE PATTERNS

1. [musical notation]
2. [musical notation]

THREE-PULSE PATTERNS

3. [musical notation]
4. [musical notation]
5. [musical notation]
6. [musical notation]

FOUR-PULSE PATTERNS

7. [musical notation]
8. [musical notation]
9. [musical notation]
10. [musical notation]
11. [musical notation]
12. [musical notation]
13. [musical notation]
14. [musical notation]

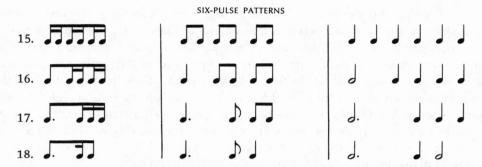

SIX-PULSE PATTERNS

In practicing these patterns it is important that the pulse note (indicated above each column in Example 16) be performed in some manner simultaneously with the patterns. The pulses may be clapped, conducted, or sung; the patterns may be clapped or sung. Divide the choir into two sections and have one perform the pulses while the other sings the patterns, or have each student perform both pulses (clapping or conducting) and patterns (singing) simultaneously.

You may go through the patterns in order or you may perform them in random order by calling out the appropriate numbers. Be sure to work with all three columns at various times so the chorus members get accustomed to seeing the patterns in various notations. You should also vary the tempi in performing the patterns.

After the chorus members have developed a degree of familiarity and proficiency in working with these patterns they should learn to apply them on various levels of a given metric structure as indicated in Example 17. The top line shows the given patterns, the bottom lines indicate which level of the metric structure would be involved.

Example 17

Perform this example by first sounding all three levels of the metric structure simultaneously. Then perform the individual lines of the metric structure in the order given above (i.e., first measure—beat level, second level—division level, etc.). Then repeat this and, against it, sing the patterns of the top line. Then repeat it in various ways, for example clap only beat level pulses throughout while you sing the patterns against this. Do the same with division level pulse and then with subdivision pulse. Finally have the chorus just sing the pattern line above but ask them to be aware of the metric background of pulses moving at various paces on different levels. When this "mental metric background" is established, it can do wonders in making the singing rhythmically accurate and alive.

Examples 18 to 21 provide additional practice for developing this skill. Perform them using the techniques mentioned above.

Example 18

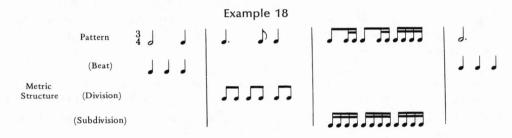

Example 19

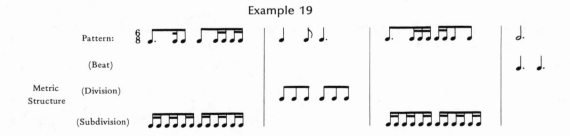

Example 20

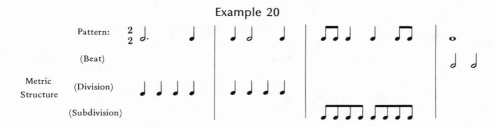

Example 21

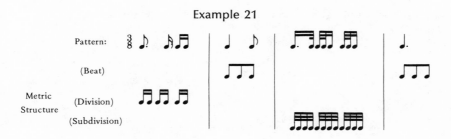

Two further problems in working with rhythmic patterns remain to be discussed—the use of rests within patterns, and the use of ties between patterns.

In working with rests the cardinal principle is to treat the rest actively, not passively. A rest should always be a signal for increased attention and effort, not inattentiveness and relaxation. To make this concept meaningful, the following approach to patterns with rests is recommended:

Example 22

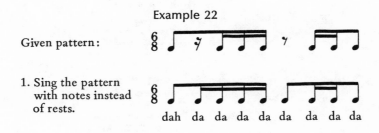

2. Sing the pattern but say the word "rest" on each rest.

dah rest da da da rest da da da

3. Sing the pattern but think actively and in tempo, the word "rest" on each rest.

dah __ da da da __ da da da

It is important to do something *active* during the rest.

In working with ties between patterns, it may prove helpful to practice first without ties. Avoid giving an extra accent during the tied note.

Example 23

Given Pattern:

Perform without ties, then as written above.

We might mention, in conjunction with this pattern, that in some jazz- or Latin American-influenced works the pattern would actually be more effectively performed with an irregular underlying pulse as indicated.

Example 24

Instead of:

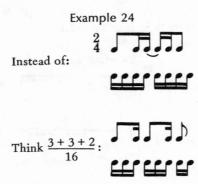

Think $\frac{3+3+2}{16}$:

COMMON RHYTHMIC ERRORS

Before concluding this section we should mention some common errors in rhythmic performance and suggest ways of avoiding them. Making chorus members aware of the possibility of these errors should do much to eliminate them from their performance.

1. Inaccurate endings of long notes. Too often the ending long note of a phrase is not held for its full value. To avoid this, think not only of the pulses in the note but of one final pulse at the end of the note. Stop the tone the instant before this final pulse.

Example 25

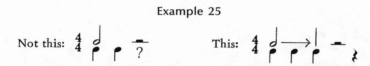

2. Unfortunately this suggested solution can bring its own problem, namely an uncalled for accent at the end of the note. Chorus members should carefully avoid this.

Example 26

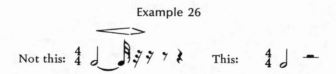

. **3.** Coming in late after a rest at the beginning of a rhythmic pattern can be avoided by making the rest active, by anticipating rather than delaying, and by leading to the accented note within the pattern.

Example 27

Anticipate rather than delay

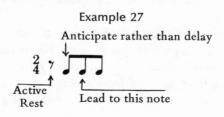

4. Avoid coming in too soon after a rest ending a pattern; make the rest active and think of the underlying pulse.

Example 28

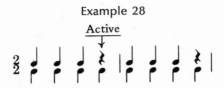

5. Inaccurate performance of the 3 : 1 ratio

as a 2 : 1 ratio

In jazz this is actually correct, but in other music it is usually the mark of an unconcerned amateur. Have the chorus members think of the underlying pulse, and also think of the short note at the end of the pattern leading to the next long note. Sometimes thinking in words may clarify the situation.

Example 29

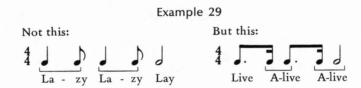

6. Rushing on black notes, dragging on white notes. Remind the chorus members that the note value itself tells us nothing; they should consider the pace of the underlying pulse.

7. Making accelerandos and ritardandos too soon and too suddenly. Again this is the mark of the amateur, but this time of the *over*concerned amateur. He is too anxious to show that he knows what these terms mean. Chorus members should be aware of this tendency and learn to look ahead and gauge these changes of tempi. It is helpful in accelerando to think in terms of larger note levels.

Example 30

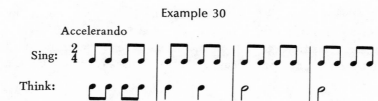

For *ritardando* reverse the process and think in smaller note levels.

Example 31

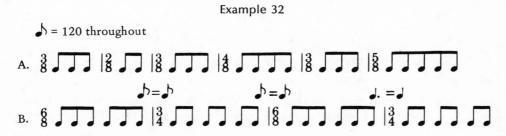

CHANGE OF METRIC ORGANIZATION

We have thus far considered music that retains one basic metric organization throughout. Now we must consider music in which the metric organization may change. In any change of meter it is important to consider the relationship between a specific note value in the old meter to a note value in the new meter. Sometimes this is clearly indicated as in Example 32. Sometimes it is not clearly indicated but rather subject to various traditions, such as those discussed in the chapter on performance practce in the Baroque period.

Performing music with changes of meter is not difficult, but it does require the performer to be willing to make rapid, decisive changes in metric organization. The following exercise may be helpful in developing this ability.

Example 32

Notice that in Example 32A all eighths are equal in length, whereas in Example 32B the eighths in the last measure are longer or slower.

Changes in metric organization may also be effected momentarily by the use of triplets, duplets, or other unusual divisions. These are illustrated below.

Example 33

To perform these, it is usually best to focus upon the pulses that remain constant and to relate the unusual division to these.

Example 34

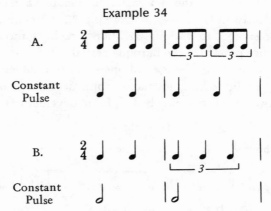

Another approach is to think in terms of a common denominator pulse. In mathematics we use sixths as a common denominator for dealing with halves and thirds (e.g., 1/2 + 1/3 = 3/6 + 2/6 = 5/6). So, in music we can use sixth notes as a common denominator when working with notes in the ratio of 2 to 3.

Though this mathematical explanation may sound somewhat complex, the application as illustrated below is relatively easy to apply.

Example 35

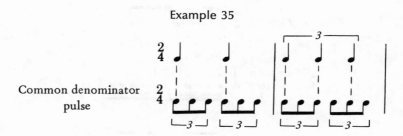

Common denominator
pulse

Similarly, in 3 : 4 ratios the following situation would apply:

Example 36

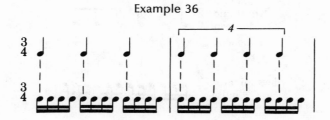

The technique illustrated above may also be applied to performing passages in which two different metric organizations or two different rhythmic patterns are superimposed.

Example 37

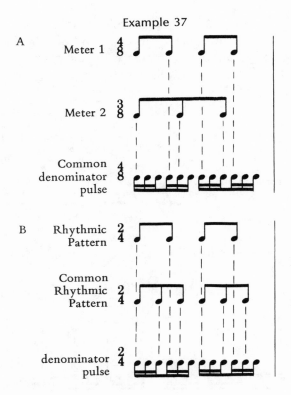

To begin to "get the feel" of a simple 2 against 3 (Example 37B), have chorus members practice the following by tapping the left hand as they say "left," the right hand as they say "right," both hands together as they say "both," and neither hand as they say "rest."

Example 38

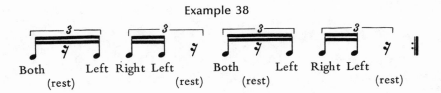

Both   Left Right Left   Both   Left Right Left
(rest)   (rest)   (rest)   (rest)

The result will be as follows:

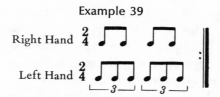

Example 39

By now you should have a clearer idea of what we meant in the beginning of this chapter when we said that our task in the teaching and performance of rhythm was to develop an awareness of a background of metric structure consisting of several levels of pulses moving at various paces; and then to project against this a foreground of durational patterns in an artistic performance. We have discussed some of the technical factors that are involved in rhythm. Now we must turn our attention to aspects of rhythm that go beyond these fundamental considerations.

ARTISTIC PERFORMANCE OF RHYTHM

It is difficult, if not impossible, to communicate in words meaningful concepts of artistic rhythmic performance. Ultimately, your chorus members must learn this through personal experience and observation in the chorus rehearsal and elsewhere. You can, however, give some general ideas which may lead the chorus members beyond the basic concepts we have discussed.

The first is to emphasize the idea of flow in rhythm; indeed the Greek root of the word *rhythm* means flow, as in the flow of a river. Music should flow from a point of origin to a point of arrival. We might compare this idea of directed motion in music to the shooting of a bow and arrow. There is the initial impulse when the arrow leaves the bow, the arched flight of the arrow through the air, and finally, the arrival of the arrow at the target or goal. The image of the bow and arrow is also apt in another sense. Before we can shoot the arrow, we must pull back on the bow string and build up tension, then we have to sight and take aim. Similarly, before we begin a piece or a section, we also need to build up preparation, or tension, and look and listen ahead to where we are going and how we are going to get there. Sometimes the first notes of the composition are in a sense part of this preparation, as is the case when a work begins with one or more upbeats, that is, notes before the initial downbeat.

More specifically, the sense of flow in rhythm should mean that though we work with patterns in rhythm, we do not perform them as separate isolated entities, but rather, that we always lead from one pattern to the next. This is especially true when one pattern ends with a short note and the next begins with a longer note. We should think of the short note at the end of the first pattern as leading into the next note, in a sense, as though it belonged to the following note rather than to the preceeding note. Example 40 should clarify this point.

Example 40

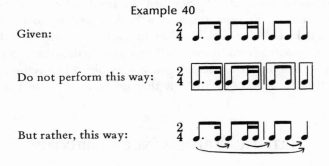

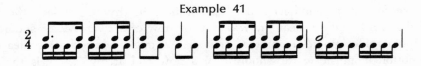

There is another more subtle approach to rhythm that can aid in achieving the sense of rhythmic flow and directed motion. This is to move to ever larger (i.e., slower) levels of rhythm. In the preceding example we treated rhythmic patterns on the same level as the fastest note in the pattern.

Example 41

Thinking on these small (i.e., faster) levels will help in developing accuracy, but they will not help, indeed, they may *hinder* developing flow and musical phrasing. As soon as chorus members can perform the patterns accurately, they should move toward hearing them in the context of larger (i.e., slower) levels.

Example 42

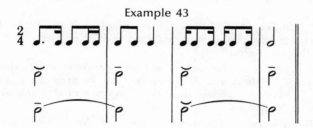

Ultimately, you should consider them in terms of larger levels where the pulse is a measure or even longer.

Example 43

Decisions as to which beats, measures, or groups of measures are to be heard as strong or weak must be based upon many factors beyond simple matters of duration, such as pitch contour, harmony, texture, text, etc. The important thing is not the correctness of the final result, but rather the process of considering rhythm on these larger levels (which helps the choral singer to focus his attention on the larger shape or structure of the music he is performing).

A rather quick grasp of the rhythmic element can be achieved by clapping each note of a new piece of music. Sometimes it is helpful to go through this exercise even before attempting to sing the number for the first time. In other cases, it is better to do so while learning the notes. By clapping the rhythms vigorously, understanding of pulse and pattern develops, which allows the singer to perform the music with confidence and attention to the other musical considerations (vocal tone, phrasing, text, etc.).

This chapter has sought to explore some of the basic concepts of rhythms and to follow them through considerations of artistic performance. No single chapter on rhythm could hope to give sufficient material to insure complete mastery of these concepts, but it is hoped that this discussion has laid a foundation for continued development and exploration of this all-important musical element.

NOTES

1. John Dewey, *Art as Experience* (New York: G. P. Putnam's Sons, 1934), p. 150.

Chapter Seven

RECOMMENDED READING LIST

Cone, Edward. *Musical Form and Musical Performance.* New York: W. W. Norton, 1968. Provides refreshing insight into both general and specific problems in the interpretation of rhythm as well as other aspects.

Cooper, Grosvenor and Meyer, Leonard. *The Rhythmic Structure of Music.* Chicago: University of Chicago, 1960. A stimulating analysis of the problems of perception and performance of rhythm, with special attention to questions of rhythmic grouping and accent on various hierarchical levels.

Hindemith, Paul. *Elementary Training for Musicians.* New York: Associated Music Publishers, Inc., 1949. Concise explanations of basic elements of music with rigorous exercises in sight reading and ear training.

Winold, Allen and Rehm, John. *Introduction to Music Theory.* Englewood Cliffs: Prentice-Hall, Inc., 1971. An integrated approach to notation, music reading, and ear training with special attention to melody.

Chapter Eight

Pitch

Melody . . . belongs to the noblest gifts which an invisible
godhead has made to humanity.—RICHARD STRAUSS[1]

THE PITCH ASPECT of music presents some obvious and difficult problems for the
conductor, the singer, and the listener. In the initial stages of learning a choral
work, finding the correct pitches often presents the most formidable challenge;
in performance, singing the pitches with proper intonation often presents the
greatest pitfall. It is unfortunately true that audiences and critics are likely not to
notice subtle mistakes in rhythm or in dynamics, but they are usually quick to
criticize even small errors in intonation.

   We must recognize that the pitch aspect of musical performance presents
two separate but related problems: the discrimination of different pitches, or the
development of sight singing skill in pitch; and the fine tuning of an individual
pitch in relation to others, or the development of intonation. Interestingly enough
there are many singers who find one of these aspects easy to master and the other
difficult. Some individuals with perfect pitch recognition, for example, may be
able to sight sing without any problem, but may have great difficulty singing with
true intonation. On the other hand, there are many singers who have difficulty
finding their way from one pitch to another, but once they have found the pitch,
they will sing it with good intonation. In the following discussion we shall treat
these problems separately, beginning with the problem of sight singing of pitches.

SIGHT SINGING

In approaching the problem of pitch discrimination there are probably as many solutions and methods as there are choral directors, theory teachers, or music educators. However, it is possible to group the various methods of pitch discrimination under five general headings:

pitch imitation
pitch location
pitch function
pitch distance
pitch pattern

We shall discuss each of these in turn and then present an eclectic program that seeks to combine the best features of all these approaches.

Pitch imitation refers to the so-called pound out the notes approach, which is all too prevalent in the choral rehearsal, the voice lesson, and the vocal coaching session. The choral conductor or the accompanist simply sounds the notes of one of the parts on the piano and the members of that section sing the notes by imitation. This rote process is repeated often enough for the singers to learn their parts. Although this approach does have the advantages of speed and simplicity, the obvious disadvantage is that it must be repeated each time the chorus learns a new work. The singers do not develop any skill in sight singing which they can use to approach new works, and they do not experience any sense of musical growth. If the choral experience is to be truly meaningful to the singer, this method has obvious limitations.

The *pitch location* approach tries to develop some sense of the absolute location of pitches in the singer's voice and memory. Although this approach is common on the European continent—particularly in the French solfège system— it is not widely used in this country. The various methods used to train pitch location or pitch memory include the use of note names and the use of syllables.

Example 1 shows how the chromatic scale would be expressed in six systems. The first system uses English or American note names which has the advantage of relating directly to the common names used to identify notes in America and England; but has, nevertheless, the disadvantage of requiring unsingable sounds and the use of two-syllable sounds for some of the notes. The German

Example 1
The Chromatic Scale in Six Systems

	English Note Names	German Note Names	Adapted English Note Names	Traditional Fixed-Do Syllables	Revised Fixed-Do Syllables	Donarego
	C	C	C	Do (or Ut)	Do	Do
	C♯ (C sharp)	Cis	Cees	Do	Di	Na
	D♭ (D flat)	Des	Deef	Re	Ra	Na
	D	D	D	Re	Re	Re
	D♯ (D sharp)	Dis	Dees	Re	Ri	Go
	E♭ (E flat)	Es	Eef	Mi	Me	Go
	E	E	E	Mi	Mi	Mi
	F	F	F	Fa	Fa	Fa
	F♯ (F sharp)	Fis	Fees	Fa	Fi	Ke
	G♭ (G flat)	Ges	Geef	So (or Sol)	Sa	Ke
	G	G	G	So	So	So
	G♯ (G sharp)	Gis	Gees	So	Si	Vi
	A♭ (A flat)	As	Aeef	La	Le	Vi
	A	A	A	La	La	La
	A♯ (A sharp)	Ais	Aees	La	Li	Be
	B♭ (B flat)	B	Beef	Ti (or Si)	Te	Be
	B	H	B	Ti	Ti	Ti

system in the second column also uses an alphabetic system, but the Germans have developed a method of designating their notes with a single syllable sound that is, in most cases, fairly singable. Column three represents one possible attempt to adapt this principle to English note names.

The traditional "fixed" *do* system used in France, Italy, Spain, and other countries is indicated in column four. Only seven syllables are used in this system. To express sharp or flat notes the singer uses the same syllables but adjusts the pitch. The success that many foreign-trained singers have with this system tempts many Americans to advocate its use in the United States. It should be remembered, however, that for the singer in France or Italy, the syllables are not *substitutes* for note names as they would be in America—they *are* the note names. For a Frenchman the two Beethoven masses are not in C and D; they are in *do* and *re*. Thus, in the truest sense, if we wanted to adopt the essence of the French system for American use, we would sing letter names.

The revised fixed *do* system introduces special names for sharp and flat notes. As shown in column five this system has one name for C♯ (di) and another for D♭ (ra).

The Donarego system listed in column six was devised by Allen Winold and Lee Humphries and has been used with some success in advanced training, especially for work with twelve-tone compositions. This system adds five syllables to the traditional seven syllables of fixed *do*, so that each note of the tempered chromatic scale has its own syllable regardless of the spelling chosen.

Example 2 illustrates the application of these systems to a short passage from a Schubert mass.

Though it might be tempting to believe that extensive work with one of these systems might lead to the development of absolute pitch, psychological research has shown that this is usually not possible unless it is undertaken at a critical age, usually sometime between ages four and eight. However, "short term" pitch memory can be a useful tool, and this skill can be developed at any age.

Most singers are not aware of the fact that they already have some degree of ability for *pitch memory*. It is the task of the conductor to make this ability conscious in the choral singer and to develop it as far as possible. It is important in all exercises of this type that the choral conductor insist on quality vocal production. Vital choral singing is dependent upon regular and careful vocalization which also promotes a group awareness.

Begin by asking the entire chorus to sing the pitch "a," have them sustain

Example 2

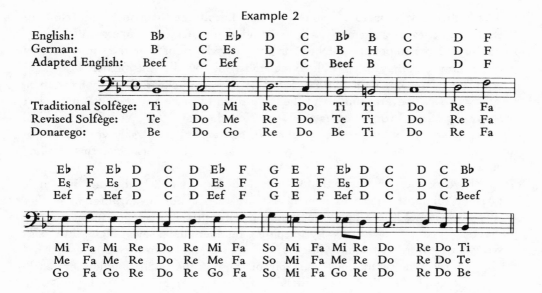

English:	Bb	C	Eb	D	C	Bb	B	C	D	F
German:	B	C	Es	D	C	B	H	C	D	F
Adapted English:	Beef	C	Eef	D	C	Beef	B	C	D	F

Traditional Solfège:	Ti	Do	Mi	Re	Do	Ti	Ti	Do	Re	Fa
Revised Solfège:	Te	Do	Me	Re	Do	Te	Ti	Do	Re	Fa
Donarego:	Be	Do	Go	Re	Do	Be	Ti	Do	Re	Fa

Eb	F	Eb	D	C	D	Eb	F	G	E	F	Eb	D	C	D	C	Bb
Es	F	Es	D	C	D	Es	F	G	E	F	Es	D	C	D	C	B
Eef	F	Eef	D	C	D	Eef	F	G	E	F	Eef	D	C	D	C	Beef

Mi	Fa	Mi	Re	Do	Re	Mi	Fa	So	Mi	Fa	Mi	Re	Do	Re	Do	Ti
Me	Fa	Me	Re	Do	Re	Me	Fa	So	Mi	Fa	Me	Re	Do	Re	Do	Te
Go	Fa	Go	Re	Do	Re	Go	Fa	So	Mi	Fa	Go	Re	Do	Re	Do	Be

it and listen to it. Pause for approximately ten seconds and ask them to hear the "a" in their heads and then sing it again. Repeat this procedure, lengthening the interval of silence in between. Change the procedure by having them shout, converse, or vocalize for a short time in lieu of the silent interval, then returning to the "a." Once more have them sing the note, then play a musical passage on the piano which stays basically in the key of A or the key of D, and then have the group sing "a." As a final test, change the intervening passage to one that modulates to distant keys and see if they can still remember the "a." Write "a" on the board in both treble and bass clefs and mention that this is the note that orchestras tune to, and that A-440 cps (cycles per second) has been established by our Bureau of Standards as the standard pitch. You might also mention that there are tuning forks available for this pitch.

Repeat the same procedure on "d," writing it on the board and drilling on it as explained previously. Finally, have the group alternate between singing "d" and "a" with intervening silence or interrupting sounds. Call upon a few individual singers to test their pitch memory on these pitches.

Give a short speech, such as a discussion of the work you plan to rehearse. After about a minute of talking, ask the members if they can still hear the "d" and "a"; then ask them to sing one of them. Encourage them to be conscious of these two pitches as a memory skill. Remind them that few singers will develop the ability to remember the pitches for an entire day, but that they may be surprised at how long they will be able to remember the sound of the pitches.

The next step, perhaps introduced at the next rehearsal, is to have them sing "d" and "a" several times and then ask them to place a note in the middle of these two pitches. In most cases they will sing the note "f♯." You can then drill on pitch memory for these three pitches. In subsequent rehearsals you can introduce other sets of between two and five notes and drill on them in terms of pitch memory.

Psychological experimentation has tended to establish the fact that it is impossible for most people to remember more than about seven different pitches at any given time. Interestingly enough, the same principle applies to memory of numbers, which is one reason why telephone numbers have seven digits. In music, if we wish to work with more pitches, we need to find other techniques besides pitch memory. One of the most valuable of these is the pitch function approach.

The *pitch function* approach is useful for tonal music, that is, music in which there is a definite hierarchy of pitches with the tonic as the most important or central pitch, the dominant as the second most important or pivotal pitch, and other pitches heard in functional relation to these. To develop the singer's skill in hearing and performing pitches according to their functions within a tonality, several systems using either numbers or syllables have been developed, and these are shown in Example 3.

The traditional scale number system, shown in column one of Example 3, has the advantage of simplicity and direct relationship to the scale degrees. For chromatic notes in the scale the singer simply sings the same number but makes an adjustment up or down according to the accidental. The disadvantage of this system is that some of the numbers, like seven, require two syllables and some of them, like five, are rather unsingable. Another disadvantage is that the chromatic alterations are not specified.

The inflected number system in column two does specify the chromatic alteration of the scale degree, but this presents even more unsingable and multisyllabic sounds.

The Mod 12 system shown in column three was developed originally by theorists dealing with the twelve-note system but has since been adapted for use in traditional tonality. This system is based upon the simple concept of number-

Example 3
Notes in Tonality of G

	Simple Scale Numbers	Inflected Scale Numbers	Mod 12	Traditional Solfège	Revised Solfège	Scale Degree Names
𝄞	1	1	0	Do	Do	Tonic
𝄞	1	1♯	1	Do	Di	Raised Tonic
𝄞	2	2♭	1	Re	Ra	Lowered Supertonic (Neapolitan)
𝄞	2	2	2	Re	Re	Supertonic
𝄞	2	2♯	3	Re	Ri	Raised Supertonic
𝄞	3	3♭	3	Mi	Me	Minor Mediant
𝄞	3	3	4	Mi	Mi	Major Mediant
𝄞	4	4	5	Fa	Fa	Subdominant
𝄞	4	4♯	6	Fa	Fi	Raised Subdominant
𝄞	5	5♭	6	So	Sa	Lowered Dominant
𝄞	5	5	7	So	So	Dominant
𝄞	5	5♯	8	So	Si	Raised Dominant
𝄞	6	6♭	8	La	Le	Lowered or Minor Submediant
𝄞	6	6	9	La	La	Submediant
𝄞	6	6♯	10	La	Li	Raised Submediant
𝄞	7	7	10	Ti	Te	Lowered Leading Tone or Subtonic
𝄞	7	7♯	11	Ti	Ti	Leading Tone

ing the halfsteps of a chromatic scale from 0 through 11. The advantages of the system are that it can be used with equal facility for both tonal and atonal or twelve-tone music, and that it employs a limited number of names as compared to some of the other systems. There is also an advantage in the treatment of intervals according to this system, as we shall see in the next section. Its chief disadvantage would be the conflict with the original scale numbers shown in the first column. This is especially true for singers who have had some experience in singing the traditional number names. For other singers who have not had such experience, and for those who are willing to work for even a short time with the Mod 12 system, its logical consistency and efficiency soon become apparent. With a reasonable amount of practice it is just as easy to sing a major scale with the numbers 0 2 4 5 7 9 11 0, as it is with the numbers 1 2 3 4 5 6 7. In particular, it is easy to sing various minor or modal scales and various chromatic inflections with this system. The harmonic minor scale, for example, would be 0 2 3 5 7 8 11 0. The change in numbers from the major scale to the harmonic minor scale makes the different locations of the halfsteps readily apparent.

The traditional movable *do* syllables and the revised movable *do* syllables in columns four and five are the same as the fixed *do* syllables in Example 1, but now *do* is always used for the tonic of major tonalities rather than the note "c." In minor tonalities the tonic may be represented "la," or, in some systems, by "do." These systems have the advantage of using only very singable, monosyllabic sounds and also the advantage of familiarity for many singers. Under the name of "tonic sol-fa," the revised movable *do* system was used with great success in training amateur singers in England at the beginning of this century, and it has continued in widespread use at all levels.

The traditional scale degree names in the sixth column are given only to complete the list of possibilities; they are rarely used as mnemonic (memory aiding) sounds in pitch training. Example 4 illustrates the application of the various pitch function systems to the same Schubert passage written in the treble clef.

Neutral syllables, such as "lah," "loo," "dah," "doo" or others, may be used both in training for *pitch location* or *pitch memory* and in training for *pitch function* or tonality. As they sing, the members should think about the names of the notes for pitch location training, or the scale degrees or functions of the notes for pitch function training. The advantage of using a neutral syllable is that it allows the singing to be more legato and expressive; the disadvantage is that the conductor can never be sure if the members are actually thinking of the purpose of

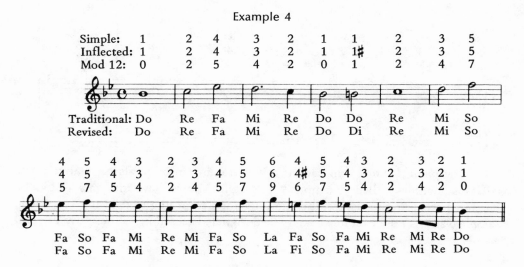

Example 4

the exercise or if they are just "singing along." One solution to this problem is to alternate singing neutral syllables with "sol-fa" syllables or numbers.

Whatever system is used, there are a number of techniques that may be selected to help reinforce a sense of pitch function or tonality. One of the most effective is to combine training in pitch memory with training in pitch function. After you have trained the majority of the singers to the point where they can remember the two pitches of "d" and "a," tell them that these pitches are regarded as tonic and dominant and are represented with syllables or scale numbers. If the singers can hold tonic and dominant in mind, they can find other pitches by relating them to these two important "axis" pitches.

To help the singers remember the two tonic and dominant pitches, keep playing them on the piano, or, more effectively, have these pitches sustained by the men's voices while you drill on various pitches with the women's voices and then vice versa, as illustrated in Example 5. To continue with this type of training, write a scale on the board and point to the various notes one at a time.

Example 5

Sol-fa	So	Do	Mi	Fi	So	Ra	Do	Te	Le	So
Number	5	1	3	4♯	5	2♭	1	7♭	6♭	5
Mod 12	7	0	4	6	7	1	0	10	8	7

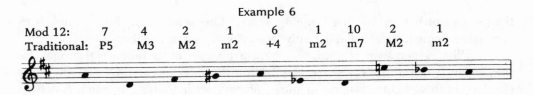

The *pitch distance* approach involves training in intervals or relative pitch, as it is sometimes called. Example 7 (at right) shows how intervals would be designated according to the traditional system and according to the Mod 12 system. Example 6 shows how Example 5 could be designated according to these two interval schemes.

Example 6

Mod 12:	7	4	2	1	6	1	10	2	1
Traditional:	P5	M3	M2	m2	+4	m2	m7	M2	m2

In actual practice it is rare to use either the traditional or the Mod 12 names of intervals as mnemonic devices. One common method for developing interval sense is to associate the interval with a well-known melody. The perfect fourth (0–5) interval, for example, may be associated with "Here Comes the Bride" or the tritone (0–6) with the opening measure of Leonard Bernstein's "Maria." The problem with this is that having learned an interval in one particular melodic context, one sometimes finds the same interval occurring in a different functional context and it sounds quite different. The perfect fourth used in "Here Comes the Bride" is actually a dominant-to-tonic relationship. The same perfect fourth occurring as a mediant-to-submediant relationship would have a different character.

There is a long-standing controversy as to whether or not interval singing is more effective than functional singing or singing based upon tonality. Many singers claim that they are singing by interval, but often close listening reveals

Example 7

	Notes	Traditional Interval Names	Mod 12 Interval Names
	A - A	Prime or Unison	0
	A - A♯	Augmented Prime or Chromatic Half-Step	1
	A - B♭	Minor Second or Diatonic Half-Step	1
	A - B	Major Second	2
	A - B♯	Augmented Second	3
	A - C	Minor Third	3
	A - C♯	Major Third	4
	A - D	Perfect Fourth	5
	A - D♯	Augmented Fourth or Tritone	6
	A - E♭	Diminished Fifth or Tritone	6
	A - E	Perfect Fifth	7
	A - E♯	Augmented Fifth	8
	A - F	Minor Sixth	8
	A - F♯	Major Sixth	9
	A - F𝄪	Augmented Sixth	10
	A - G	Minor Seventh	10
	A - G♯	Major Seventh	11

that they are singing by a kind of "musical geography." When the notes go up, they go up; when the notes go down, they go down. But they are not actually going through any process of strictly measuring interval distance. Advocates of the interval approach point out that once a singer masters the intervals he is equipped to sing any music, tonal or atonal, at sight. Others point out that too much drill on intervals leads to a note-by-note approach that is counter to the flow and sense of the music.

The *pitch pattern* approach is based upon the idea of mastering a limited number of commonly used pitch patterns and then developing the ability to adapt these patterns in various ways. It is difficult to select a limited number of patterns from among the almost infinite number of pitch patterns appearing in the literature of music. We have organized these patterns in a manner somewhat similar to that proposed by Deryck Cooke in his book *The Language of Music*.[2]

Cooke suggests that each type of pitch pattern has its own particular emotional character or association. This thesis is similar to a degree to ideas proposed by Albert Schweitzer in his fascinating study of the music of Johann Sebastian Bach. Both authors can be said to refer back to the "Doctrine of Affections" and to other theoretical ideas of the Renaissance and Baroque periods, when certain types of pitch patterns were associated with certain types of affections or emotional states. Without denying the possibility of such associations, we are presenting pitch patterns here simply as objective phenomena which can, it is hoped, assist the singer in developing skill in reading and singing. If individual singers or conductors wish to make their own associations of specific patterns with specific emotions, they are certainly free to do so.

One of the fundamental patterns in all music is the ascending triad. Variants of this pattern may be achieved by filling in the thirds with stepwise motion as shown in Example 8. To remember the four patterns shown here, one can associate them with the opening of such songs as "The Marine's Hymn," "When I Grow Too Old to Dream," "Tennessee Waltz," and "When the Saints Go Marching In." Individual singers and conductors will find their own memory-aiding literature for these patterns. In some cases patterns will not be common as open-

Example 8

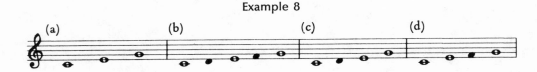

ing patterns of a song, but rather as patterns normally found in the middle or at the end of songs.

Instead of decorating the notes of the triad with passing notes—that is, stepwise notes that pass from one note of the triad to another—it is also possible to decorate the notes of the triad with neighbor tones—that is, notes lying immediately above or below the triad tones. Some of the many possible patterns are illustrated in Example 9. These patterns may be taught by rote and, if desired, at least some of them could be associated with known melodies. After they have been thoroughly learned, the conductor may move from one pattern to another by calling out the appropriate letter.

Example 9

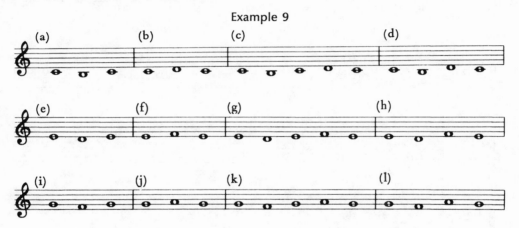

Example 10 shows how the triad could be extended to a full octave and also sung beginning on the dominant. Some of the more common passing patterns are also included.

Example 10

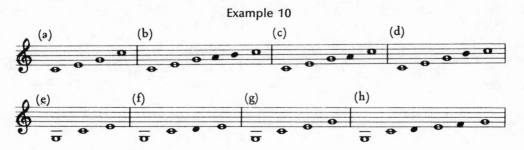

All of the patterns, to this point, have only involved leaps between the members of the triad. It is also possible to have leaps involving other tones as shown in Example 11. It is sometimes helpful with these patterns to think of the nontriad note as an incomplete neighbor note. Thus the pattern C-F-E could be regarded as C-E-F-E with the first E omitted. Ultimately, any such crutches must be discarded and the pattern simply learned as a pattern.

Example 11

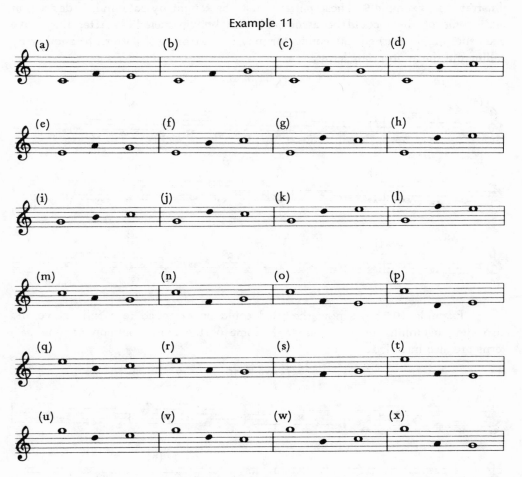

We have presented 48 basic patterns that singers should learn thoroughly. Once they have learned them, the patterns should be adapted using the following techniques—retrograde, rearrangement, repetition, change of mode, and transposition. Retrograde simply means that one sings the notes of the pattern in reverse order from right to left. Example 12 shows how the patterns of Example 8 would be sung in reverse order. Once the singers grasp this principle they should be able to sing other patterns in retrograde.

Example 12

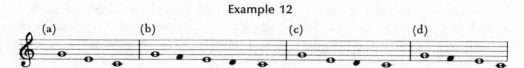

Rearrangement means singing the notes of the pattern in an order other than the original or retrograde. Example 13 shows some of the rearrangements possible with a simple triad figure, in addition to the patterns given in Examples 8 and 12.

Example 13

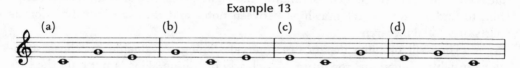

Repetition simply means that any note of a pattern may be repeated, or the whole pattern may be repeated. Change of mode means that the patterns that are presented here in major may also be sung in minor or in any of the church modes. Finally transposition means that the patterns that were presented here in C may be transposed to any other pitch level. Example 14 represents various applications of these techniques.

Example 14

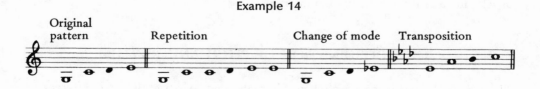

Pitch patterns can be used effectively in several ways. They may be applied directly to sight-reading problems, especially when the passage is reasonably close to the original form of the pattern. They may also be used to promote the development of other pitch skills. For example, they may be related very effectively to the development of pitch function or tonality, and to the development of pitch distance or intervals. The approach to pitch patterns given here is one that could be used with adult groups. An approach to pitch patterns suitable for use with children's choruses may be found in the *Open Court Music Program*.[3]

Dealing successfully with the complex and difficult problems of pitch in choral singing will ultimately depend upon a combination of all the methods described in this section. The singer should develop some sense of pitch memory and should use it when the occasion demands. If, for example, he sings E-B and is then required to return to the first E, pitch memory is obviously the most efficient tool to use. Pitch memory can also serve as a cornerstone for the development of pitch function.

Pitch function is probably the single most important skill to develop for the singing of music with a clear tonality basis. Pitch function not only helps the singer in the mechanical task of finding the right notes but also ultimately helps him to understand the relationships between notes and the way they function as parts of a tonal hierarchy.

The skill of pitch distance or interval singing is valuable for those situations in which functional tonality is not clearly operating. This is not only the case with contemporary atonal or twelve-tone music but also with modulatory or transitional passages in more traditional music. Sometimes there is simply nothing else that will help the singer except the ability to produce, upon demand, certain specific intervals. We would urge, however, that training in intervals evolve out of and be based on training in pitch function or pitch patterns.

Skill in using pitch patterns can help a singer move from note-by-note reading to the reading of a larger gestalt. The technique may also be effective in developing a sense of tonality and intervals.

THE COORDINATION OF PITCH AND RHYTHM

Though we have presented pitches, intervals, and exercises without reference to rhythm, in actual context the pitch aspect is always strongly influenced by rhythmic factors. Some pitches—usually those with a long duration or strong metric position—will be heard as the basic pitches or structural pitches of a melodic line, with other pitches related to them as decorative or embellishing pitches. We might compare this to an English sentence in which some words, usually important nouns or verbs, are the essential structural elements of the sentence, while prepositions, adjectives, or adverbs stand in a dependent or modifying relationship to them. Likewise, when learning a new piece of music it is helpful to begin by emphasizing the basic or structural melodic tones for each part. Example 15 presents a melody with the structurally important pitches marked with an asterisk (*). It is possible to approach this passage by first singing aloud only the structural or basic pitches in their appropriate metric locations with the other pitches sung silently as shown in Example 15. When the structurally important pitches are well established, singers may then sing aloud the other pitches as connecting links to the structural pitches.

Example 15

Bach, *St. John Passion*, "Herr unser Herrscher"

The technique of using the metrically strong or durationally long pitches as structural guides for the performance of a melodic passage is especially appropriate and effective when the pitches form a *step progression*, that is, when they move in ascending or descending stepwise or scalar motion. This motion is illustrated in Example 16. Notice how the step progression serves as a strong organizing force in this melody, making it easy to perform if the singer focuses on the step progression formed by the structural pitches.

Example 16

Bach, *B Minor Mass,* "Kyrie"

The combination of the pitch pattern approach described earlier and the structural pitch approach described above can improve the choral singer's ability to read music at sight, deepen his insight into the structural significance of a melody, and enrich his or her skill as a performer.

INTONATION

Intonation is properly an aspect of artistic interpretation, and, as such, is more subject to the individual preferences of conductors and singers than to universally accepted, scientifically verifiable criteria. Therefore we will not prescribe what system of intonation should be used but rather will describe what systems of intonation could be used. Neither shall we enter into the controversy as to whether the "a" on the second space of the treble staff should be 440 cps, or higher or lower. Rather, intonation will be considered in terms of the relationship of two or more successive or simultaneous pitches to each other. This will be presented by various systems of tuning and temperament, and then their advantages and disadvantages will be considered as well as some pedagogical approaches to problems in intonation.

Unison and Octaves

We shall begin with the study of two intervals which, in a sense, lie outside the considerations of the systems we shall discuss subsequently. In almost all systems of tuning or temperament, the unison is understood to have a ratio of 1 : 1, the octave, a ratio of 2 : 1.[4] We shall study these first since they provide an excellent opportunity to observe a phenomenon that is of fundamental importance in other aspects of intonation, namely beats. Beats are produced when two singers, or other sound sources, produce pitches whose frequencies are close together but not identical. Beats are heard as "thumps" or intensifications of loudness, and are produced by alternating reinforcements and interferences of the sound waves from the separate sound sources. The number of beats per second is equal to the difference in frequency between the two pitches. Thus, if a pitch of 442 cps is sounded simultaneously with a pitch of 440 cps, there will be 2 beats per second. Slow beats like this are generally not heard as unpleasant; they become unpleasant gradually as they approach 30 beats per second and return to pleasantness gradually if they increase in speed beyond this point.

It is possible to train singers to listen for beats in unison and octaves and other intervals. Singers who have difficulty in hearing beats may be helped if the conductor moves his hand in time with the beats, so as to direct the singer's attention to their periodic recurrence. Once the singers have learned to detect beats, they may use them as an aid in tuning simultaneous intervals or chords. A well-tuned unison or octave is simply one in which no beats, or at any rate extremely slow beats, are heard. It is doubtful if it would be possible or even artistically satisfying to sing an extended passage of unisons or octaves without any beats at all. However, practice devoted by trying to sing sustained unisons or octaves without beats can do much toward developing the sensitivity of the singer's ear. The Johnson Intonation Trainer may be used to aid this training.

Just Intonation

Turning now to tuning systems that involve the other intervals, we shall begin with the system known as just intonation. To consider the complete mathematical operations involved in this or any other system would be beyond the scope of this text. Instead we shall briefly note that all the intervals are derived from the perfect fifth with a ratio of 3 : 2 and the major third with the ratio 5 : 4. Since these are the ratios of these intervals as they appear in the natural overtone series, they are called natural or pure fifths or thirds.

The just intonation ratios for the C major scale are shown in Example 17.

Example 17

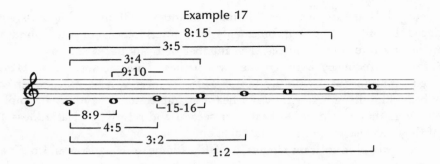

These ratios reveal some of the advantages and disadvantages of this system. Its chief advantages are the pure or natural triads on C, F, and G, that is, triads whose ratios correspond to the ratios of the overtone series.

Its disadvantages outnumber its advantages. One fifth (D-A) has a ratio 40 : 27, which is almost ¼ of a half-step flat in comparison with the pure fifth.[5] Any progression involving these notes will always end up about ¼ of a half-step flat. Thus if the following simple progression were sung four times in perfect just intonation, the choir would end almost a half-step below where it started.

Example 18

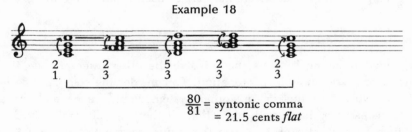

If the progression of Example 19 were sung twice in just intonation, the passage would also end almost a half-step below where it began.

Example 19

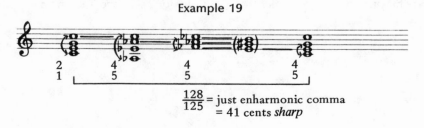

Another disadvantage is the presence of two different-sized whole steps (9 : 8 and 10 : 9) which virtually make modulation impossible within the system. Note, for example, that even to make a modulation from C major to G major would require an alteration of A so that G-A-B would have the same interval ratios as C-D-E (i.e., 9 : 8–10 : 9).

A common misunderstanding in connection with just intonation is that it provides the theoretical justification for playing sharp notes higher than their equivalent enharmonic flat notes. Actually the reverse is true: C-D♭ = 16 : 15 or 112 cents, while C-C♯ = 135 : 128 or 92 cents.

Pythagorean and Mean-Tone Tuning

Two other historical systems, Pythagorean tuning and mean-tone tuning, may be mentioned briefly. Pythagorean tuning is based exclusively on the pure fifth 3 : 2. The resulting scalar ratios are as follows:

Example 20

From C:	9:8	81:64	4:3	3:2	27:16	243:128	2:1
	C	D	E	F	G	A	B	C

Between each pair:	9:8	9:8	256:243	9:8	9:8	9:8	256:243

This system naturally results in all pure fifths, and it also has equal-sized whole tones. The special features of the system are the major third which is considerably larger or sharper than a pure third, and the half-step which is smaller than that of just intonation. String players, perhaps influenced by the tuning in fifths of their instruments, are frequently reported in research studies as favoring the sharper Pythagorean thirds.

The mean-tone system, based upon pure major thirds and slightly flat fifths, represents a compromise system which has primarily historical and theoretical interest. There is some debate as to whether it was ever systematically applied in practice and it finds as advocates only the performers of pretempered music.

Equal Temperament

Equal temperament is a system based on the principle of dividing the octave into

12 equal half-steps. This results in all equal-sized intervals, but, with the exception of the octave, none of them conform to the pure or natural ratios. The fifths are all very slightly flat, the major thirds are sharper than just intonation but not as sharp as the Pythagorean thirds. The obvious advantage of the system, and the one for which Johann Sebastian Bach's *Well-Tempered Clavier*[6] was perhaps a propaganda effort, is the fact that one can play in any key with equal effectiveness and can modulate with ease between any keys.

Practical Implications

Having explored the characteristics of these systems, we should now move from the precision of mathematics to the practicalities of performance. Obviously no one can think about, much less accurately perform, choral music in terms of strict mathematical ratios. It should also be obvious that no single system of intonation can claim only advantages and no disadvantages. With this in mind what should the practicing choral conductor strive for in terms of intonation?

As mentioned earlier he can certainly work toward the goal of beat-free unisons and octaves. In singing major thirds, perfect fifths, and the combination of these two intervals, the major triad, he may also choose to strive for beat-free sonorities, which means that he will be singing fifths imperceptibly sharper than those of an equal-tempered keyboard instrument and thirds which are considerably flatter. He can extend this use of just intonation principles to simple progressions like I-V-I or I-IV-I. However, if he attempts to carry this use of just intonation any further to chords that involve relations between the second and sixth scale degree, he would certainly be asking for intonation problems, and if he tried to extend this practice to chromatic harmony, he would be guaranteeing problems. One only need experiment by tuning any keyboard instrument in just intonation in the key of C and then proceeding to play chords I-III-IV-V-I in every key.

One possible solution in tonal music is to fix the tonic and dominant pitches and their associated triads in just intonation but to compromise on other intervallic relations both successively and simultaneously. Some conductors and listeners, however, find the major triad in just intonation somewhat dull in sonority and prefer the triad with the higher third of equal temperament or even Pythagorean tuning. Especially in the case of the dominant triad, the sharper third may serve to accentuate the leading tone tendency of the seventh scale degree.

And so we return to the point where we began, regarding intonation as essentially an aspect of artistic interpretation like slight *rubati* in rhythm and tempo. And yet, some knowledge of intonation systems can be of value. Knowing, for example, that a progression like that of Examples 18 and 19 will inevitably end up flat if sung in perfectly pure intonation can alert the conductor to the necessity of compromise. Knowing that keyboard instruments are usually close to equal temperament[7], and knowing the preference of some string players for the sharper thirds of Pythagorean tuning, can prepare the conductor for possible problems when the chorus is singing with these instruments.

Beyond this there is, of course, the interesting interaction of science and art that manifests itself so vividly in the whole subject of intonation. This would be a fascinating subject to explore with singers in an academic institution, so they could see the relationship of their studies in choral music to their studies in other areas.

NOTES

1. Richard Strauss, *Betrachtungen und Erinnerungen* (Zurich: Atlantis, 1949), p. 134.

2. Deryck Cooke, *The Language of Music* (London: Oxford Paperbacks, 1962).

3. Allen Winold, *Open Court Music Program* (La Salle: Open Court Publishing Company, 1974).

4. Exceptions to this are the Neubarger system of tuning and others which have slightly sharp octaves.

5. $3/2 - 40/27 = 81/80 = 22$ cents. This is called the syntonic comma.

6. Some authorities maintain that Bach's tuning was actually closer to mean tone. The issue has not been clearly resolved.

7. In actual practice, piano tuners often introduce personal variants of equal temperament in their tuning.

Chapter Eight

RECOMMENDED READING LIST

Berkowitz, Sol; Frontrie, Gabriel; and Kraft, Leo. *A New Approach to Sight Singing.* New York: W. W. Norton, 1960. Melodies, duets, variations, and improvisation exercises specifically composed for the study of sight singing.

Christ, William, et al. *Materials and Structure of Music.* 2nd edition. Englewood Cliffs: Prentice-Hall, 1972. 2 vols. A comprehensive study of all aspects of music beginning with a detailed study of melody.

DeLone, R. P. and Winold, Allen. *Music Reading: An Ensemble Approach.* Reading, Massachusetts: Addison-Wesley Publishing Co., 1971. An eclectic study of music reading including work in rhythm, tonality, intervals, and coordinated approaches, all written for ensemble performance.

Edlund, Lars. *Modus Novus.* Stockholm: Nordeska Musikforlaget, 1963. Studies in reading atonal melodies, based primarily on an intervallic approach.

Kliewer, Vernon L. *Music Reading: A Comprehensive Approach.* Englewood Cliffs: Prentice-Hall, 1973. 2 vols. A systematic study of music reading from the simplest materials to the highly complex, including specially composed exercises and excerpts from music literature.

Chapter Nine

Harmony and Texture

Harmony alone can stir the emotions.—JEAN PHILLIPE RAMEAU[1]

THE HUMAN VOICE is a single-line instrument, capable of producing only the successive pitches and rhythms of a melody. However, as soon as the voice is incorporated into a choral ensemble, it participates in the production of simultaneous pitches of harmony and the coordinated lines and other elements that make up texture in music. As Paul Hindemith has so graphically put it, music moves in space and time. Our study of rhythm and pitch has given us some insight into the narrower aspects of these two dimensions. We must now move to larger considerations of musical space in our discussion of texture and harmony and later to larger considerations of musical time in our discussion of form. The complete choral musician must be as aware of these larger dimensions as he is of the smaller. It is not enough for him merely to sing the right pitches at the right time; he must also be aware of the role his line plays in both the overall texture and the overall form of the work.

HARMONY

The choral conductor who has spent many semesters mastering the intricacies of harmony might wonder if it is necessary or possible to bring this knowledge to chorus members. Should the typical choral singer be able to spell a German sixth chord, take harmonic dictation of a chromatic progression, write a modulation to the relative major, or be able to improvise at the keyboard a progression involv-

263

ing secondary dominants? The answer can only be that such detailed knowledge of harmony is not to be expected of the typical choral singer. What can be reasonably expected is that he will develop a curiosity about and a sensitivity toward harmony as a vital shaping force in the musical experience, and that he will develop an understanding of such basic aspects of harmony as the way chords are constructed and connected and the relationship of melody to harmony.

Chord Construction

Probably the first thing a singer notices about chords is the aspect of consonance and dissonance—the fact that some chords sound more euphonious than others or that tones seem to blend well together in some chords and not in others. As singers, they may find it easier to locate or hold their pitch in consonant chords than in more dissonant harmonies. This general aspect of consonance and dissonance provides probably the most effective introduction to the study of harmony, especially if approached from the aural rather than the visual aspect.

Simply play pairs of chords such as those shown in Example 1, or have them sung, and ask the chorus members to decide which chord of each pair sounds more consonant. Notice that these pairs are arranged in progressively finer discriminations. The opening pairs represent extremes of consonance and dissonance, the later pairs are much closer; indeed, it would be difficult, even for the trained ear, to establish which is more consonant.

Example 1

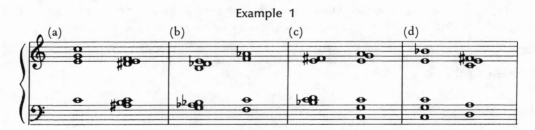

When the singers have demonstrated their ability to discriminate at least obvious differences in consonance and dissonance of single chords, proceed to playing passages from the literature to see if they can discriminate between short sections of music in terms of consonance and dissonance. This training of the musical ear is important not only for its practical value to the singer, but, perhaps even more importantly, for its value to the singer as a listener.

The exploration of larger, more general aspects of harmony can serve to arouse the singer's curiosity and to motivate him to delve into more specific aspects of harmony. From now on the study of harmony may be approached simultaneously in terms of its aural and visual aspects, but the aural must always be given precedence. Probably the simplest aspect of harmony to discuss is the number of individual pitches in a chord. In terms of number of pitches we shall consider two-pitch chords (diads or harmonic intervals), three-pitch chords (triads), four-pitch chords (tetrads or seventh chords) and other miscellaneous chords.

The study of harmonic intervals provides an opportunity to review both the traditional and Mod 12 names of the intervals introduced in chapter eight, considering them now as simultaneous pitches rather than successive pitches. One possible order of presentation for these intervals suggested by Hindemith is illustrated in Example 2 and the intervals are identified in both traditional and Mod 12 terms.[2]

Example 2

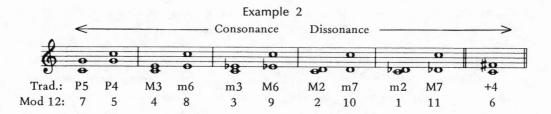

		←		Consonance		Dissonance				→
Trad.:	P5	P4	M3	m6	m3	M6	M2	m7	m2	M7	+4
Mod 12:	7	5	4	8	3	9	2	10	1	11	6

There are two intervals in each measure and one is the inversion or compliment of the other in traditional terms. In Mod 12 we would say that both intervals belong to the same *interval class*. For the mathematically inclined members of a chorus, you could explain that there are six interval classes, numbered 1, 2, 3, 4, 5, 6. Intervals larger than six are subtracted from 12 to determine their interval class—interval 9 (major sixth) would be in interval class 3 (12−9=3). The important thing, however, is not the name but rather the fact that an interval and its inversion, or two intervals in the same interval class, have similar qualities when played simultaneously as harmonic intervals. The major sixth (C-A) and the minor third (A-C) sound similar when played harmonically, though they differ markedly from each other when played melodically.

Not only does Example 2 show which pairs of intervals sound similar, it also shows what Hindemith believed to be the order of relative consonance and dissonance or, as he expressed it, the relative harmonic strength of the intervals, moving from the strongest and most consonant intervals on the left to the most dissonant on the right. The *tritone,* that old "devil in music" of the medieval theorist, stands outside the classification as an interval of such strongly marked tension and piquancy that Hindemith and other theorists believed it determined the character or flavor of any chord in which it appeared. We could almost compare the tritone in this respect to a strong dose of garlic that tends to dominate the flavor of any dish in which it is used.

To a certain extent all the harmonic intervals have a characteristic flavor. It is also possible to group them into traditional categories as perfect consonances (P1, P4, P5, P8, or interval classes 0 and 5); imperfect consonances (m3, M3, m6, M6, or interval classes 3 and 4); and dissonances (m2, M2, tritone, m7, M7, or interval classes 1, 2, and 6). Though it is probably too much to expect amateur singers to be able to identify intervals exactly, most can learn to distinguish different categories. Sometimes it helps to associate interval categories with specific characteristics. Most listeners would characterize the perfect consonances as hollow, pure, or perhaps oriental; the imperfect consonances as euphonious, sweet, or pleasant; and the dissonant intervals as harsh, jarring, or not blending. These characteristics are, however, not nearly as universal as some maintain. Chorus members should be encouraged to find their own associations rather than merely accepting standard descriptions. Furthermore, consonance and dissonance are always subject to context, to the influence of surrounding musical material. Major seconds played in a middle register, pianissimo, and legato following a series of loud, accented, minor seconds might sound consonant. Major thirds played fortissimo, staccato, in the lowest possible register, might sound dissonant.

Individual intervals might be played for identification, or pairs of intervals played for comparison. More important, however, is to alert the singers to harmonic intervals as they appear in the course of actual examples from the literature. Particular attention should be given to the difference in sound and the relative difficulty of singing passages in parallel imperfect consonances (thirds and sixths) as opposed to passages in perfect consonances or dissonances. This can be accomplished by comparing the effects of the following passage in its original versions, in parallel thirds, and in two alternate versions, in fifths and sevenths.

Example 3

Beethoven, *Mass in C*, "Kyrie"

(a) Original form

(b) With parallel perfect fifths

(c) With parallel sevenths

Once the chorus members have learned to hear the different effects, they may use this as a guide in singing—if they are called upon to perform a passage in parallel sevenths, they should not expect it to have the sweet, harmonious effect of thirds, or the hollow sound of fifths, but rather the more pungent characteristics of dissonant intervals. Training of this sort may not only help the singers in their performance but also in their appreciation and understanding of the music. To return to our culinary comparison, one would hardly enjoy the taste of a sour delicacy if he expected all food to be sweet. So, too, one can hardly expect to enjoy the fascination of music using dissonances if he expects all music to sound consonant. One of the responsibilities of the choral conductor is to open up for the singers new worlds of sound experiences, and not to limit their musical horizon. Work with intervals and chords can be one practical way to accomplish this.

Since most choral music will be in more than two parts, triads and other chords should be studied even more than harmonic intervals. Indeed it is also possible to begin study of harmonic intervals after the study of chords and to derive intervals, such as the major and minor thirds and perfect fifth, from the major triad.

It is a time-honored tradition to begin the study of harmony by deriving the major chord from the overtone series. By holding the notes C', E', and G' down silently on the piano and then striking C loudly, it is possible to demonstrate the derivation of the major triad from the overtone series in a vivid way. This is certainly effective and helpful, however, any attempt to follow this by deriving other chords from natural phenomena seems doomed to failure despite a long history of attempts in this direction. It is more in accordance with the modern view simply to explain the major and minor triads in terms of their interval structure as shown in Example 4. The Mod 12 numbering of the chord may be used for an effective drill as shown below. The conductor plays a major or minor triad and the singers respond by singing 0–4–7 or 0–3–7 respectively. This may also be done using the syllables do-mi-so and do-me-so (or la-do-mi).

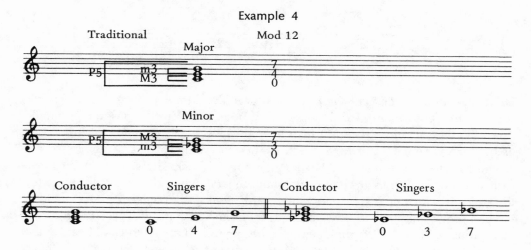

One of the most important aspects of harmony for singers to learn is the difference in function and character of the three constituent notes of the triad—the root, third, and fifth. This is especially crucial for the basses and sopranos, but it is also important for the other voices. Example 5 shows a B-flat major triad in three different inversions (i.e., with three different bass notes), each one with three different soprano notes. Sing these chords with your chorus and play them on the piano in random order and discuss the difference in sound and function of each arrangement. Different people may hear these chords in different ways but the following represents typical descriptions of the chords:

INVERSIONS	SOPRANO POSITIONS
Root position—strong, solid	Root in soprano—solid
First inversion—less stable (third in bass)	Third in soprano—softer
Second inversion—quasi-dissonant (fifth in bass, needs resolution, often regarded as a double suspension)	Fifth in soprano—energetic

Example 5

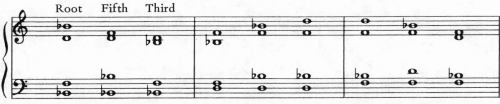

Root Position   First Inversion   Second Inversion

A simple exercise that may be used to strengthen singers' understanding of the members of a triad is to sound a triad and then call on various sections in turn to sing the root, third, or fifth. Include this exercise as a normal part of rehearsal procedure. At the beginning of a piece or section, instead of sounding the notes one at a time, simply sound the full chord and have the singers find their notes. As in so many other instances in basic musicianship training, we never know what singers are capable of until we present them with a challenge.

In most choral literature the major-minor seventh chord or dominant seventh chord is the most frequently used chord after the major and minor triads; it therefore deserves considerable attention. The double term "major-minor" indicates the type of triad and the type of seventh. Major-minor denotes a seventh chord formed from a major triad with an additional tone a minor seventh above the root. The most typical usage of this triad is, of course, as a dominant seventh chord leading to the tonic triad. Example 6 shows several versions of the dominant seventh chord moving to the tonic triad. Practice these chords with a chorus, pointing out the typical resolution tendencies of the various tones of the dominant seventh chord, especially the tendency of the third of the dominant seventh to move *up* to the root of the tonic triad and the tendency of the seventh of the dominant seventh to move *down* to the third of the tonic triad.

Example 6

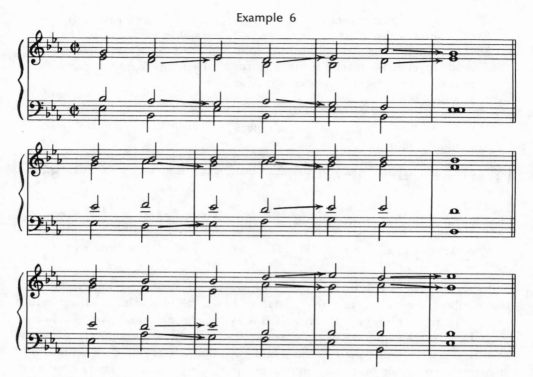

The singer who is aware of such harmonic aspects, is able to sing with more assurance, understanding, and sensitivity. To be sure that singers are thinking about such matters as they practice Example 6, have one section at a time sing the name of the chord member they are singing while the rest of the chorus hums their parts. Naturally, the chords must be sung slowly. A similar approach may be taken with brief excerpts from the choral literature.

In addition to the major and minor triads, traditional theory recognizes at least two other types of triads. The diminished triad (0–3–6 in Mod 12) can be regarded as the top three notes of a major-minor seventh chord; indeed, it often functions like a dominant chord leading to the tonic. It usually appears in first inversion in common practice harmony. The augmented triad (0–4–8) may be regarded as a major triad with the fifth expanded or augmented.

It is usually more difficult to learn to discriminate aurally between augmented and diminished triads than between major and minor. Example 7, which gives an opportunity for singers to gain some experience in singing and hearing the different triads, should be sung on a neutral syllable with careful attention to good tone production and vocal quality. The chords may be sung simultaneously in six parts, separately in three-part male or female voices, or arpeggiated (broken) and sung in unison or octaves. When sung without the assistance of a piano or other instrument, the exercise not only provides an introduction to the sound of the triads but also can be a challenging study in intonation.

Example 7

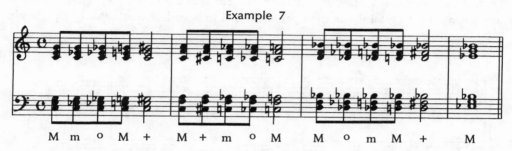

Seventh chords other than the dominant seventh are introduced in Example 8 along with some extended tertian sonorities (ninths, elevenths, and thirteenths). The sheer number of these makes it impossible to drill on them in any systematic way; however, the examples provide an introduction to the look and sound of these chords.

Example 8

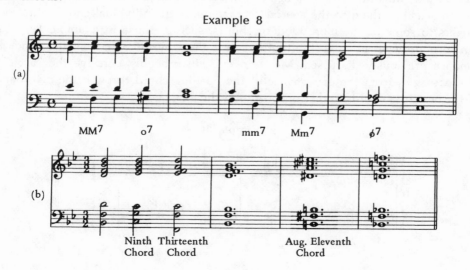

You might point out some of the characteristics of these chords, such as the construction of the diminished seventh chord in nothing but minor thirds. More effective and interesting for singers making their first acquaintance with these sonorities is to relate them to famous examples from the literature. The vividly characteristic use of the diminished seventh chord in tremolo is a cliché in almost every old-fashioned melodrama. One can almost hear the villain saying "You must pay the rent" as this chord is struck. Similarly, the half-diminished chord should be familiar to most people, if not from the famous passage in Wagner's *Tristan und Isolde,* then certainly as the opening chord in Mendelssohn's *Wedding March.*

Example 9

etc.

In introducing these chords the point is not to develop extensive writing or recognition skills but rather to make singers aware of the vertical aspect of music and to sensitize them to the special characteristics of individual chords. Introduce singers to some of the more modern chords, such as those in Example 10, which can also provide an opportunity to review the concept of consonance and dissonance previously discussed. Most singers will probably perceive the "arch" of this passage—from the consonance of the opening chord through the dissonances of the next four chords to the consonance of the final chord.

Example 10

Having discussed some of the construction characteristics of single chords in these examples, you may then point out similar aspects in chords appearing in the literature you are rehearsing. More important, however, than the individual chords is the way they are connected, for music does not consist of a string of isolated individual chords but rather of patterns of chord connections or progressions.

Chord Connection

The way one chord moves to another is a characteristic aspect of music of many different styles. This movement is usually described in terms of the relationships between the roots of successive chords. As Example 11 shows, there are three basic types of movement—by fifth or fourth, by third or sixth, and by second or seventh. Movement by fifth is generally heard as the strongest, most convincing type of movement. In the form of an authentic or a plagal cadence it provides the most effective close of a section or a movement in music of the common practice period. Movement by third is the weakest and least convincing harmonic progression, because it usually involves the least amount of motion. In diatonic progressions by thirds, there are two common tones between the two chords and only one tone changes. Movement by second has a special characteristic of its own which is almost more contrapuntal than harmonic. Since there are no common tones and all voices must change, it has a maximum of contrapuntal motion. No verbal description of these types of progression can hope to capture the essential aural characteristics involved. However, by having the chorus sing the progressions given in Example 11, their ears should become sensitive to the different "dynamics" (in the sense of activity, not loudness) that are associated with each type of progression.

Example 11

⟶ = Common Tone

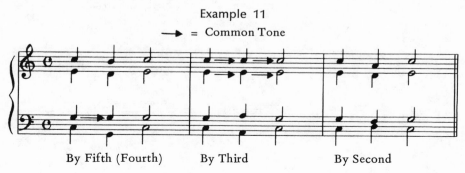

By Fifth (Fourth)   By Third   By Second

Moving from the consideration of root movement between two chords to longer progressions, it is possible to classify these into five general types, which, for want of better terminology, we might describe in terms of physical motion as *zigzag, arch, circle, parallel line,* and *other.*

By *zigzag* progressions we mean those that alternate between two different chords. Though these are usually the tonic triad and the dominant triad or seventh chord, they can be any two chords as illustrated in Example 12. The effect is of an abrupt, reiterated motion. Handel is one composer who often used progressions of this type to achieve the effect of solidity and strength.

In Example 12, the roman numerals refer to the scale degree of the chord root. In D major, a IV chord is a chord built on the fourth scale degree, G. Large roman numerals indicate major triads (I, IV, V, etc.); small roman numerals indicate minor triads (ii, iii, vi, etc.); diminished and augmented triads are indicated with the signs ^{0} and $^+$ respectively (vii^0, III$^+$, etc.).

Example 12

(a) Handel, *Messiah,* "Hallelujah"

(b) Monteverdi, *Orfeo,* "Chorus of Shepherds"

The *arch* progression usually involves a series of four chords—an initial tonic chord as a point of establishment, a predominant chord as a chord of preparation, a dominant chord as a point of greatest tension, and a tonic chord as a point of resolution and return. In its simplest terms this progression may involve the so-called primary triads I–IV–V–I. However, it is by no means limited to these. Example 13 shows a movement from a mass by Mozart that uses the arch progression in a typical form.

Example 13

Mozart, *Mass in C, K. 257*

Example 14

Mozart, *Requiem Mass*, "Rex tremendae"

The *circle* progression consists of a series of chords related by the interval of a fifth. Indeed, it was the traditional name given to this type of progression—the "circle of fifths"—that suggested the possibility of describing other basic types of harmonic progressions with particular types of actions. The original designation of circle of fifths for this progression came from the fact that it was based on a special way of representing the notes of the chromatic scale in theory treatises of the Baroque period, rather than from a description of a type of motion. Nevertheless, the term "circle" or "circular" does describe very aptly the smooth, inevitable effect of this progression. Some writers have described the "roller coaster" effect of the progression—once you get on it you are irresistibly propelled forward, and it is difficult to get off until you are back to the point of departure. This effect is particularly strong if a series of seventh chords, rather than simple triads, is used for all members of the progression except for triads on the first and last chords, as illustrated on the opposite page.

A series of *parallel* chords moving by major or minor seconds may be represented appropriately enough as a series of parallel lines. In traditional music this progression is almost exclusively limited to parallel sixth chords—under the title *fauxbourdon*, the progression was a standard device used both in improvised and written music of the Renaissance period. In more recent music, especially since the Impressionist period, composers have used root-position triads, extended tertian, and nontertian chords for this type of progression, and it is often identified with the term "planing." Whatever type of chords are used, this progression usually has a less definite sense of harmonic action and sounds more melodically or contrapuntally generated.

Example 15

(a) fauxbourdon   (b) planing

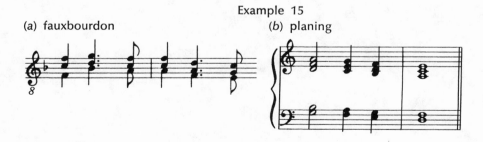

Although the four types of harmonic progressions listed above may be used to describe a large percentage of harmonically oriented music, there are still many passages that represent variants, combinations, or departures from these categories. For example, a progression based on a series of third-related chords as illustrated in Example 16a does not clearly fall into any of the categories listed above, nor would seemingly random progressions such as Example 16b.

Example 16

(a) Beethoven, *Mass in C*, Op. 86, "Gloria"

(*b*) Benjamin Britten, *War Requiem*, Op. 66, I, p. 6–7. © Boosey and Hawkes, 1962.

Many chord progressions such as those in Examples 14 and 15 begin and end on the tonic chord; they are complete progressions starting from tonic, moving away, and returning. Allen Forte[3] has called our attention to the fact that there may also be incomplete progressions which are either *opening* progressions, starting from the tonic and moving away, or *closing* progressions, starting away from tonic and moving to the tonic. It should be obvious that an opening progression, such as Example 17a, has a sense of departure and a closing progression, such as Example 17b, has more of a sense of arrival.

Example 17

(a) Beethoven, *Missa Solemnis*, "Agnus Dei"

(b) Beethoven, *Missa Solemnis*, "Credo"

With some progressions it is possible to reverse the normal order. This is particularly effective with the arch (tonic-predominant-dominant-tonic) progression and the circle-of-fifths progressions. In reverse order they have much less of a sense of forward motion or goal direction. Another factor that can affect harmonic progressions is whether or not they are made up of chromatic chords. Progressions with only diatonic chords will sound more solid and conventional than those with extensive chromaticism.

Chorus members will find it helpful to go through various types of harmonic progressions and then try to find them in operation in the literature they are singing. The important thing is certainly not the names given the progressions (you and your singers should feel free to find other descriptive terms for them), but rather the ability to recognize that harmonic progressions do have certain very definite musical and emotional characteristics. An understanding of these may enable singers to move from an aimless chord-by-chord approach to a broader and more meaningful conception of the music they are singing.

Harmonic Rhythm: Structural and Embellishing Chords

We have been discussing harmonic progressions as though all the chords in them moved at the same rate of speed and had the same degree of importance or weight, but in actual music literature this is not the case. The rate of speed at which chords change has been given the name *harmonic rhythm* by such theorists as Walter Piston.[4] It may range from extremely slow harmonic rhythm of one chord for several measures, through the more usual type of harmonic rhythm of one chord per measure, to the extremely fast harmonic rhythm of several chords per beat.

Being aware of harmonic rhythm may contribute to the singer's general appreciation of the music he performs and hears. In more practical terms, it is an aspect that should be considered in the choice of music; works with extremely fast harmonic rhythm are usually more difficult to sing, especially if they involve a high degree of chromaticism as in the works of Max Reger, Cesar Franck, and Charles Ives.

Turning to the way chords differ in terms of importance or weight, we find that this may be regarded as an extension of the principles we discussed in the section on pitch function in chapter eight. Just as individual pitches may be classified as structural and embellishing, so chords may be classified as structural and embellishing. The *structural chords* are the pillars or the steel girders of the musical edifice; the *embellishing chords* are ornamental, extra material. In architecture as well as in music it is important to have a clear understanding of the structural components for they are responsible for the general shape of the work. Embellishing components are important for the aesthetic look or sound and must be worked out with care. However, they should not be mistaken for structural components or else the shape of the work may be distorted.

The relation between structural and embellishing components is not always obvious. If we stay with our architectural analogy, we could point out that size does not always determine importance: sometimes an important structural piece of material will be much smaller than the embellishing material surrounding it. Its essential nature may best be realized by trying to imagine the building without it. So too in music, structural chords may sometimes be shorter than embellishing chords; the essential nature of the structural chords may only be realized if one tries to image the work without them. The most obvious example of this would be the dominant chord preceding the final tonic in a movement or section. Though this chord may in some cases be extremely short, it plays a structural role that is much more important than other chords preceding it that may be several times longer. Structural and embellishing chords may be analyzed on several levels as shown in Example 18.

Example 18

Beethoven, *Mass in C*, Op. 86.

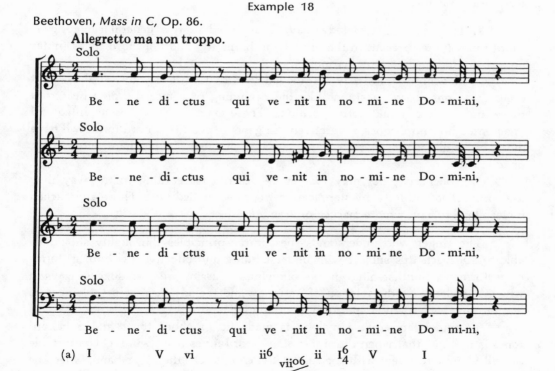

Harmony and Melody: Chord Tones and Nonchord Tones

Having examined the way chords are constructed and connected, we will now turn to the relation of harmony and melody. To introduce this fascinating subject, it is not necessary to give extensive lists of terms and rules governing the use of nonchord tones. The value of these "rules" is questionable at any rate in view of the fact that so many composers write what often seems to contradict them. The important aspects of the relation of harmony and melody may be summarized in three brief statements.

1. The notes of a melody may be analyzed in two general categories—chord tones (notes present in the underlying harmony) and nonchord tones (notes not present in the underlying harmony).

2. Nonchord tones may be divided into two basic categories: those that occur on strong metric positions like the beginning of a measure or a beat, and those that occur in weak metric positions. These may also be called accented and unaccented nonchord tones, respectively. In general, accented chord tones will have more of a dissonant character and a more pungent or poignant effect than unaccented.

3. Nonchord tones may further be described according to the way they are approached and left—by step, leap, or repeated or tied note. Those approached by leap tend to have a more marked or dramatic effect.

The singer who understands these three principles thoroughly should be able to approach this subject with understanding and effectiveness both in terms of performance and listening. In the following discussion we shall suggest ways in which knowledge of the relation of harmony and melody may help the singer to learn to sing his part and to perform it with understanding.

To understand that a melody is made up of chord tones and nonchord tones is to know that when the singer sings chord tones these will feel comfortable or will blend effectively with the rest of the chorus. On the other hand, when the singer sings nonchord tones these will not be as comfortable nor blend as well with the other notes of the chorus. To perform nonchord tones means to overcome a certain built-in musical resistance. Example 19 provides an opportunity to compare the effect of singing chord tones and nonchord tones. We have taken the chords from Example 8 and have used them as the underlying harmony for four melodies. The first, Example 19a, uses only chord tones; the second, Example 19b, introduces various types of nonchord tones. It is important that the singers experience the difference in performance difficulty and emotional character between a melody based only on chord tones and one involving nonchord tones.

Example 19

The nonchord tones in Example 19b are unaccented. Example 19c consists of the same chord progression, this time with a melody that emphasizes accented nonchord tones. The difference between the accented and unaccented nonchord tones should be obvious to the singers. Example 19d introduces nonchord tones at various times in all voices.

The important thing is not the identification of the nonchord tones; indeed, there is considerable disagreement among theorists as to the proper terminology. Some theorists use the term *appoggiatura* (Italian—leaning) for all accented nonchord tones except suspensions; other theorists reserve the term appoggiatura for nonchord tones approached by leap and left by step. The important thing is for singers to become sensitive to the characteristic effects of nonchord tones. The following examples from choral literature illustrate some of the many possible uses of nonchord tones. Notice the striking use of suspensions in John Ward's madrigal "Hope of My Heart" to accompany the words "to my eternal pain," or the use of accented appoggiaturas in the "Lacrymosa" from Berlioz's *Requiem*.

Example 20

(a) John Ward, madrigal, "Hope of My Heart"

* Suspension

(b) Berlioz, *Requiem*, "Lacrymosa"

* accented appoggiatura

A highly effective example of an accented nonchord tone may be found in the opening of the popular songs "Yesterday" by John Lennon and Paul McCartney of the Beatles, and "Maria" from *West Side Story* by Leonard Bernstein. The nonchord tone in "Maria" is the raised fourth degree of the scale and it is possible to find a very similar nonchord tone use in the opening of the "love theme" from Tchaikovsky's *Romeo and Juliet*. The similarity is especially interesting in view of the fact that *West Side Story* is a modern adaptation of Shakespeare's romantic tragedy. This surface similarity is cited not as evidence of plagiarism but rather to emphasize the fact that the use of accented nonharmonic tones is an effective part of the musical vocabulary which not only these two composers, but many others have used for poignant expression. It is not possible to give a lengthy and specific glossary of musical expressions, but the singer should be aware of the possibilities of emotional expression inherent in various types of nonchord tones as well as in various types of chords and chord progressions. It is this kind of sensitivity and understanding that can help to change the choral experience from a routine chore to a perceptive encounter with the essence of music.

TEXTURE

Texture in music refers to the relationship of simultaneously sounding elements. Harmony, the study of simultaneously sounding pitches or chords, is thus one aspect of the larger study of texture. Other aspects would be counterpoint, the study of simultaneously sounding lines, and orchestration, the study of both single and simultaneously sounding instrumental timbres.

In general terms, it is customary to speak of three principal types of musical texture—monophonic, one melody alone; homophonic, melody with accompaniment; and polyphonic, two or more relatively independent melodies sounded simultaneously. The singer should be aware of the type of texture in the music and the implications this has for performance.

In monophonic choral music the single melodic line will usually be doubled in one or more octaves because of the difference of ranges of the voice parts (male voices sounding an octave lower than their female counterparts). When this is the case it is a general rule that the lower octave should be the loudest in volume and the singers of the higher octaves should adjust their intonation to that of the lower octave. There may be two general approaches to monophonic or unison singing: one in which an attempt is made to have the voices blend as perfectly as possible so that the effect is almost that of a single amplified voice, and another in which an attempt is made to preserve some sense of individuality in the various parts and still have them close enough in interpretation that the sense of line is not destroyed.

In Western music the tradition of monophonic texture is limited almost entirely to Gregorian chant, the liturgical music of the early Catholic church. Since there is no problem of coordinating different melodic lines in chant, it is possible to achieve in this music a sense of rhythmic subtlety that would be impossible in more complex polyphonic music. This is probably best achieved by demonstration and by the use of free *chironomic* conducting gestures—that is, gestures that do not show the metric structure but rather illustrate the shape of the melodic line. You might experiment with your chorus in a performance of the following "alleluia." Notice the long *melisma* or *jubilus* on the concluding syllable, which should be sung with a feeling of exultation and controlled freedom. The chant is given in modern notation and in the older neumatic notation. A comparison of the two versions will give your singers an idea of some aspects of the older notation system, such as the use of the clef sign to indicate where the pitch C is, the use of the dot to indicate notes approximately twice as long, and the use of ligatures or connected groups of notes.

Example 21

(a) Alleluia: Angelus Domini (Easter Monday) (neumatic notation)

(b) Same chant (modern notation)

Polyphonic texture involves a variety of considerations for the singer who should be aware of how the rhythms of his line relate to the rhythms of other lines, as in Example 22a. The rhythms may be identical in all parts, or one part may be more active rhythmically than another, as in Example 22b. One of the most effective rhythmic relations is a reciprocal or "give and take" relation in which rhythmic activity alternates between two lines as shown in Example 22c. While one part has an active and interesting rhythm, the other part has a sustained note, and then the rhythmic interest reverses. Here the singers must be careful to lose no time coming off the half notes. They should perform the measures of active, interesting rhythm with more volume and importance, and then sing the sustained notes with a softer tone, yielding to the rhythmic interest in the other parts. Instead, amateur singers may sing the active notes softly because they present more performance problems, and then sing loudly when they finally reach the security of the long note. Example 22 may be used to introduce and explain these rhythmic aspects to the singers.

Example 22

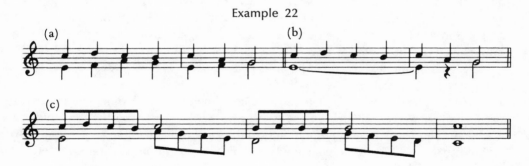

The singer should also be aware of the pitch relations between polyphonic lines. As indicated in Example 23 these may be classified as parallel, similar, oblique, and contrary.

Example 23

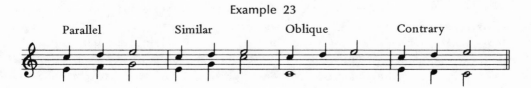

Of more importance to the singer is the awareness of the melodic relations between lines. Sometimes one voice imitates another, that is, it repeats a melody introduced in another voice part at a later time and sometimes at a different pitch level. When this is the case, there are generally two performance aspects that the singer must observe. The first is that the imitating voice should sing the melody with the same inflection and interpretation as the first voice. Nothing marks a poor performance of polyphonic imitative music more clearly than an "every man for himself" approach to the imitated material. To hear the same melody or figure chirped by the sopranos, caressed by the altos, crowed by the tenors, and croaked by the basses rarely accords with the composer's intentions.

The second point that should be observed in the performance of imitative music is that the first voice should yield slightly in volume and importance at the time the second voice enters with the imitation. This should, however, not be over-done. A performance in which the voices begin fortissimo and then drop to pianissimo when the imitation enters will only sound ridiculous and will tend to lose the sense of seamlessness that should mark the effective performance of polyphonic imitative music. Not all polyphonic music is imitative. Sometimes two or more different melodies will be heard in counterpoint, and in this case the emphasis should be on the individuality of each melodic line.

Homophonic textures may be classified into two general types. In one type, sometimes called familiar style, the accompanying parts move in the same rhythm as the melodic line. This type of texture—commonly found in hymns—presents no special performance problems except for the surprising fact that the inner voices of amateur choruses, especially in young children's choirs, may find it more difficult to "hold their part" in this type of texture than they would in textures where their part is disinguished in rhythm from the melody line. In the other type of homophonic texture the accompanying parts move in different rhythms from the melodic line. They may sustain chords while the melody moves in faster notes, or they may repeat chords or even imitate the "oompah," or "oompahpah" of instrumental march and waltz accompaniments. Obviously in such textures the accompanying parts must be sung softly enough for the melodic line to be heard clearly. At the same time, accompanying parts must never be sung with a lifeless, disinterested tone. Fortunately choral singers are not as prone to sing inner parts with the dullness that some instrumentalists bring to their performance. There is a famous story of a violist who was dreaming he was playing the *Messiah* only to wake and find that he was. It is unlikely that choral singers would ever relax to that extreme, but still even the best singers must occasionally be reminded that even though they are singing a soft accompanying part, they must still sing with life and intensity.

SUMMARY

In this brief chapter we have suggested many facets of harmony and texture that you might introduce to the members of your chorus. This can be done through the exercises provided, but it is always most effective if these aspects emerge directly from the study of a work of the choral literature. We would emphasize again that the goal is not to give the singers a long list of terms and theoretical procedures, but rather to make them more aware of harmony and texture as shaping forces in a piece of music. Success should be measured not in terms of how many singers can identify a half-diminished chord or oblique motion, but rather how many singers are able to balance and relate their part to others in a polyphonic composition and, above all, how many find their participation as performers or listeners enriched by an understanding of the way harmony and texture contribute to the structure and significance of a work.

NOTES

1. Jean Phillipe Rameau, *Observations sur notre instinct pour la musique et sur son principe* (Paris, 1734), p. 3.

2. Paul Hindemith, *The Craft of Musical Composition*, trans. Arthur Mendel and Otto Ortmann (New York: Associated Music Publishers, 1942), p. 87.

3. Allen Forte, *Tonal Harmony in Concept and Practice* (New York: Holt, Rinehart and Winston, 1962), pp. 102–106.

4. Walter Piston, *Harmony* (New York: W. W. Norton and Company, Inc., 1941), p. 124.

Chapter Nine
RECOMMENDED READING LIST

Forte, Allen. *Tonal Harmony in Concept and Practice.* 2d ed. New York: Holt, Rinehart and Winston, Inc., 1974. A brilliantly organized and insightful study of harmony.

McHose, Allen Irvine. *The Contrapuntal Harmonic Technique of the 18th Century.* New York: F. S. Crofts and Company, 1947. A detailed study focusing on the harmonic practice of J. S. Bach, his predecessors, and his contemporaries.

Piston, Walter. *Harmony.* Rev. ed. New York: W. W. Norton and Company, Inc., 1948. The classic text on common practice harmony.

Chapter Ten

Form

Form in the arts, and especially in music, aims primarily at
comprehensibility.—ARNOLD SCHOENBERG[1]

THIS FINAL CHAPTER on basic musicianship differs from the other chapters in that it
contains fewer specific practical suggestions and exercises for the singers. Instead
it introduces some of the basic concepts and terms used in the study of form in
music and then presents analyses of some specific works from the choral literature.
We leave it to the discretion of the individual conductor to decide how much of
this material will be introduced in the course of the choral rehearsal.

Form in music may be defined as everything pertaining to the relationship
of one temporal unit in a composition to others, or to the composition as a whole.
Consideration of form takes two main directions—one is concerned with general
principles, the other with specific schemes. In this chapter we shall be concerned
mainly with general principles, such as the length and delineation of formal units;
the operations of presentation, repetition, variation, contrast, and return; and the
concepts of unity and variety, symmetry and balance, continuity and discontinuity,
and function and content. We will, however, devote some attention to specific
schemes, such as binary form and rondo form, and then present representative
analyses of two choral works.

FORMAL UNITS

One of the most vexing problems in the analysis of instrumental music is deciding where formal units, such as motives, phrases, or periods really have their

beginning and ending. To a large extent this problem is obviated in vocal music by the presence of a text that can usually be taken to indicate the delineation of formal units. Without text, the following melodies could be broken up in several different ways.

Example 1

(a) Liszt, *Stabat Mater*

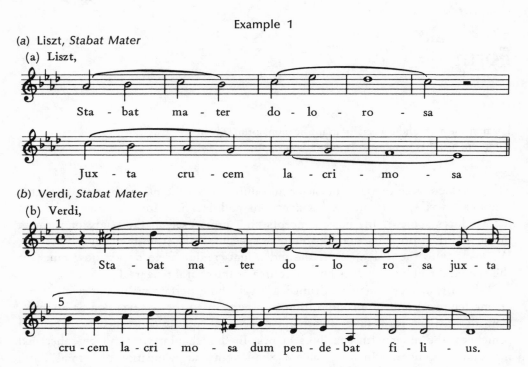

When the text is added, it strongly shapes the division into units. In Example 1a, the way Liszt has placed the text to the music leads to a division that would have been suggested by the music alone. On the other hand, Verdi's setting in Example 1b will strike many musicians as going against the division suggested by the music alone. It is especially problematic to regard the two notes in measure two as belonging to the same formal unit because of the long-short rhythm and because of the leap between them. This is even more true in measure six where the leap is larger and where the leading tone F♯ has a strong tendency to belong to the following tonic G, rather than to the preceding E♭. In such cases, singers and conductor will probably allow the division of the words to be heard, but not so strongly as to destroy the natural flow of the music. Incidentally, we should point out that the Verdi excerpt is another example of the poignant effect achieved by the use of the raised fourth degree as an embellishing pitch. We discussed this previously (see page 287) in the major mode in two secular works by Tchaikovsky and Bernstein; here the example is found in the minor mode and in a sacred work.

In addition to the problem of deciding where formal units begin and end, there is another problem of deciding what to call them. For example, most theorists would probably call the units in Example 1 *motives,* but some analysts would call them *subphrases.* We see no point in entering into such hair-splitting debates, and would certainly not recommend that you present such problems to your chorus. Instead, you might wish to use Example 2 as a relatively straightforward example of the various types of formal units that can be found in music.

Example 2

Mozart, *Ave Verum Corpus,* K. 618

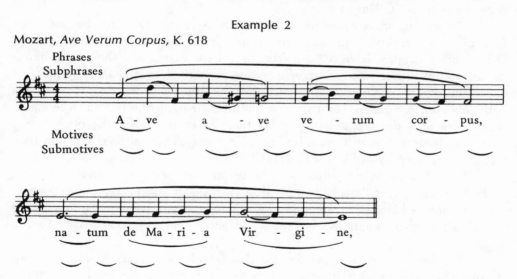

The following definitions of terms for formal units may be presented in connection with Example 2.

Submotives are the smallest constituent units of music, incomplete in themselves, but used to build motives and larger units. They may be compared loosely to syllables in language. It is interesting to note, but merely as a coincidence, that the first syllable of the Mozart example is a single letter just as the first submotive is a single note. Some analysts would argue, however, that even a submotive must contain a minimum of two or even three notes.

Motives are the smallest, relatively complete, self-contained units in music. They may be compared loosely to words in language. It is again an interesting point that most of the motives in the Mozart example coincide with words of the text. This is by no means always the case. Some motives will involve several words, and some motives in highly melismatic music will involve only a single syllable. For some analysts a musical unit must be used as an important building block in the composition, either in original or varied form, to qualify as a motive. If it is used only occasionally, they would refer to it as a figure.

Subphrases may in some cases be identical with motives or, as in the Mozart example, the motives may be made up of several submotives. They are like short, dependent phrases in language.

Phrases are more complete and comprehensive musical units that are often four measures in length in moderate tempi, particularly in classical repertoire. Other phrase lengths, however, are frequently encountered and should not be regarded as unnatural. The ending of a phrase is marked by a *cadence*, a more or less definite point of conclusion. Notice that the cadence in measure four is on a half note and in measure eight on a whole note, making the last cadence somewhat more of a definite stopping place. Both cadences are on the pitch E, the second scale degree, which provides less of a sense of arrival or conclusion than would have been provided by the tonic pitch D.

Periods may be compared to sentences in that they are relatively complete units. They consist regularly of two phrases, as in Example 2. Three or more phrases may be combined into a *phrase group*. Two periods may be combined into a *double period*. Various combinations of phrases and periods may be combined to form a *section*.

Most of the music sung by the chorus will be thematic material. Nonthematic material or quasi-thematic material, such as introductions, transitions, and codas will generally be entrusted to instrumental accompaniments. However, the chorus members should be aware of the difference between sections that clearly present material, and that have a sense of musical stability, and those that have more of a sense of instability or motion. Sometimes such sections will be present, at least to a degree, in the chorus music itself.

MUSICAL OPERATIONS

The masterworks of choral literature can be shown to be organic unities that evolve from the first measure to the last through a process of musical growth and development with a marvelous sense of inevitability. To a degree we can describe and explain this process as involving various operations, such as repetition, variation, contrast, and return. What we can never fully explain is the degree of consummate perfection in structure and expression achieved in works like the cantatas of Bach, the oratorios of Handel, or in more recent works like the *Symphony of Psalms* of Igor Stravinsky or the *Passion according to St. Luke* of Kristoff Penderecki.

If analysis can never fully explain these works, it can nevertheless help to bring us closer to them. It can help us achieve a sense of "psychological ownership," an awareness of the growth processes and structural relations inherent in the works.

The processes of repetition, contrast, and return are relatively easy to understand. In written analysis it is customary to represent repetitions and restatements with the same letter and contrasts with a different letter.

The process of variation is somewhat more complicated and may also be more interesting to study. To qualify as a variation, some clearly identifiable elements of the original unit must be maintained while others are changed. Frequently the rhythm is maintained and the pitch is varied according to such techniques as shown below. To illustrate these we have selected a short phrase from Berlioz's *Damnation of Faust;* the phrase itself was derived by variation techniques from the song "There once was a rat in a basement hole," sung by students in a tavern. The students held a mock funeral when the rat died, and they sang an Amen chorus in fugal style based on a variation of the "rat" song. The opening motive is given in Example 4a. In the following examples we have treated this melodic fragment with several of the common variation techniques.

Example 3

Berlioz, *Damnation of Faust,* "Students' Chorus"

(a) Original version

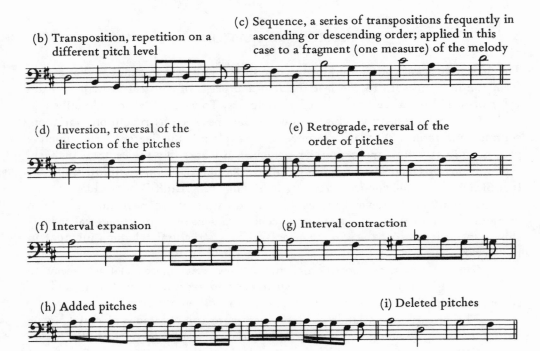

(b) Transposition, repetition on a
different pitch level

(c) Sequence, a series of transpositions frequently in
ascending or descending order; applied in this
case to a fragment (one measure) of the melody

(d) Inversion, reversal of the
direction of the pitches

(e) Retrograde, reversal of the
order of pitches

(f) Interval expansion

(g) Interval contraction

(h) Added pitches

(i) Deleted pitches

Sometimes the pitches are maintained and the rhythms changed according to various techniques as shown in Example 4:

Example 4

Berlioz, *Damnation of Faust,* "Students' Chorus"

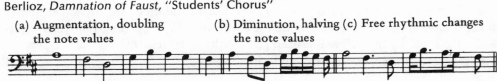

(a) Augmentation, doubling
the note values

(b) Diminution, halving (c) Free rhythmic changes
the note values

When singers recognize these techniques operating in compositions, their sight-reading and performance abilities should then improve, and more importantly, they should begin to gain insight into the underlying structure and rationale of a work. Melodic construction can proceed in several different characteristic ways. Sometimes, a prominent beginning motive, called the head motive (*Kopf-motiv*), will be followed by flowing figures called spinning (*Fortspinnung*). The head motive should be prominent and definite, the spinning figures should flow smoothly and without hesitation.

Example 5

Handel, *Messiah*, "For unto us"

For un-to us a child is born

The lovely "Agnus Dei" from Mozart's *Coronation Mass* shows another typical melodic construction. It begins with a two-measure idea, which is then repeated on a high-pitch level, and followed by a contrasting, more active phrase. It is interesting to note that Mozart uses the same construction and indeed similar melodic ideas in the famous "Dove sono" aria of the duchess in *The Marriage of Figaro*.

Example 6

Mozart, *Mass in C*, "Agnus Dei," K. 317

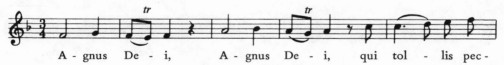

A - gnus De - i, A - gnus De - i, qui tol - lis pec -

ca - ta, pec - ca - ta mun - di.

We have already mentioned briefly one of the most characteristic features of a melody—its cadences or the ways in which phrases of other units are concluded. It is usual to discuss cadences in terms of their melodic, rhythmic, and harmonic aspects. Melodic cadences have been classified by William Christ et al., in *Materials and Structures of Music,* as *terminal* (coming to a definite conclusion on the tonic pitch or on a pitch substituting for it), *progressive* (coming to a momentary conclusion on a pitch other than tonic), and *transient terminal* (coming to a fairly definite conclusion on a pitch other than tonic but with this pitch treated as a temporary tonic, usually with a raised leading tone preceding it). Rhythmic cadences were formerly described as masculine and feminine, but it seems not only more appropriate but also more accurate to describe them as strong-beat and weak-beat cadences, respectively. Harmonic cadences are traditionally classified with such terms as *authentic* (V-I), *plagal* (IV-I), *half* (I-V), *Phrygian* (ii⁶-V in minor), *deceptive* (V-vi), and others.

Rather than put so much attention on the cadence, which is only concerned with the ending of a phrase, it would seem better to consider both the way one phrase ends and the way the next phrase begins. We might call this a musical *seam.* Some seams are quite clear and obvious, like the one in Example 7a. Others are deliberately obscured as in Example 7b. Still others, like Example 7c, lie somewhere between these two extremes. Our point in introducing the concept of a musical seam is to remind singers that they should not merely think about how a phrase ends but should always consider the whole musical area involving the end of one phrase and the beginning of the next.

Example 7

(a) Schubert, *Mass in E♭,* "Credo"

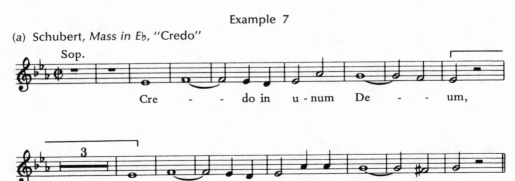

(b) Schubert, *Mass in G*, "Credo"

Cre - do in   u - num De - um, Pa - trem om - ni - po - ten - tem,

(c) Schubert, *Mass in A♭*, "Credo"

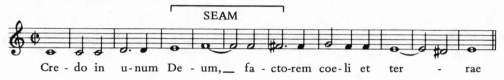

Cre - do in   u - num De - um,__ fa - cto-rem coe-li et   ter - rae

BROADER ASPECTS OF MUSICAL FORM

Musical form, like other aspects we have discussed, may be perceived on several different levels. It is helpful for chorus members not only to be able to see and hear how motives and phrases are constructed on the smaller levels of form, but also to appreciate broader aspects of form—the way large sections of music are related to each other and to the total gestalt of the whole composition.

More general aspects of musical form may also be introduced. It is possible to show how a particular composition exhibits a sense of unity through the use of identical or similar material in various parts of the composition and how it exhibits a sense of variety through the use of contrasting material. The concept of balance between unity and variety may also be used as a criterion of the effectiveness of a composition in many styles or periods. In some styles, however, the sense of unity may be emphasized and in others, the sense of variety. There is no simple rule governing the performance of such works. Some interpreters, for example, might emphasize the unity present in a work, like a monothematic fugal piece, by maintaining the same tempo, dynamic level, and articulation throughout the composition. Others would seek to introduce some variety through interpretive means. The important thing is that such performance decisions be made with a full awareness of the structure of the work concerned and a knowledge of the performance practices of the period.

Another general consideration in the realm of form is that of continuity and discontinuity. We have already discussed this in terms of musical seams between two phrases. Considerations of this nature should also be made in terms of larger formal units in each composition. Which units seem to move forward and which seem to lead to a suspension of motion? How is the whole composition broken into sections and subsections?

Finally, consideration of form should involve some investigation of the function and content of the units of a composition. When we consider function, we are asking what role a particular unit plays in the structure of the composition. We might classify functions as follows:

Introductory—serves as preparation for other musical events.

Presentational—devoted to important musical events such as themes.

Transitional—serves to link one presentational section to another.

Developmental—devoted to the reworking of portions of ideas from other sections.

Concluding—serves to round off the ending of a composition or a section thereof.

Most of the material entrusted to the chorus will be presentational or thematic in nature, but the chorus members should be aware of other possible functions of musical material. Occasionally passages of an introductory, developmental, or concluding nature will be assigned to the chorus, and they must be aware of the role such passages play in the whole composition.

As for content, some analysts would strongly suggest that this should not be discussed in connection with music, except perhaps to say that the content of a musical composition is the music itself, or that content and form in music are essentially the same. Others would see some value in discussing content in music, especially if the term "content" is used in a rather loose sense to mean simply, "What is the music about?" "What does it describe, depict, represent, or suggest?" In the case of choral music this type of question is answered to a great extent by the text, but it is not always answered completely and unequivocally. A Kyrie may be about the mercy of God, but this subject may be handled with completely different emotional expression in a Mass by Obrecht or in a Mass by Beethoven. There is always the possibility in music with a given text that the music is pointing to aspects other than those explicit or implicit in the text. Discussions of this subject may become tricky, maudlin, or cliché-ridden. But it is still a good idea for a conductor to ask his chorus what they think a composer is expressing in a given piece. It can prove valuable to ask them what attitude they think the composer is displaying toward a given text or emotional situation. Such discussions can lead to questions of how musical materials are used in the composition to suggest emotional content and from there to questions of how these materials should be performed if this expression is to be manifested to the listener. If the conductor conceives his responsibility as not just imposing his own interpretation upon the chorus but also helping the performers to find intelligent bases for their own performance judgments, then certainly discussion of formal aspects—incorporating as they necessarily do all aspects of music from pitch and rhythm, to timbre, harmony, and texture—should form a significant part of the choral experience.

SPECIFIC FORMAL SCHEMES

Turning to specific schemes or orders of presentation of materials, we find that it is possible to classify these, as Aaron Copland has done in his excellent book, *What to Listen for in Music*,[2] into five main categories—*sectional, variation, developmental, polyphonic,* and *free.* To these may be added a sixth formal category found mostly in avant garde compositions—*open* form.

A discussion of form should involve not only the way thematic material is handled but also—especially in music of the common practice period—a consideration of the way that tonality is treated. Often tonality will be as crucial in determining the form as thematic material. Other aspects, such as texture, timbre, and tempo may also play an important role in shaping the form of a work. Indeed, in some modern works they may play a more significant and easily perceivable role than either themes or tonality. To consider all of these aspects at length would go far beyond the scope of this chapter. Instead, in the following descriptions of forms, we shall speak simply of sections; bear in mind that these sections may be shaped by any of the factors mentioned—themes, tonality, texture, timbre, or tempo.

Sectional forms, as the name implies, consist of a series of relatively complete, closed sections organized according to a specific scheme or plan, usually involving some repetition or restatement of material. The sections may vary in length from a phrase or a period to a double period or longer unit. Some of the most common sectional forms are presented below:

Binary   A :||: B :|| or A :||: A' :||

Ternary   A B A or A B A' or A B C

Rondo   A B A C A or A B A C A B A (etc.)

"Binary-ternary"   A || B || or A || B ||
                   a a :||: b a :|| a b :||: c a :||
                   I || V I || I || V I ||

The last form cited above, the "binary-ternary," is one of the most common forms in music; it may be found in the choral theme of the last movement of Beethoven's *Ninth Symphony* and in countless other examples. At the same time it is one of the most controversial forms in terms of its theoretical description. It is binary in that it has two sections, each of which is marked by a double bar and a repeat sign. It is ternary in that, at least in terms of tonality, it constitutes a three-fold progression of tonal establishment, digression, and return. In many, but not all, cases this is also paralleled by establishment, digression, and return in thematic material. European theorists tend to call this form "ternary," while American theorists tend to call it "rounded binary." Our designation, binary-ternary, indicates this double possibility.

Variation forms may be divided into two principal types: sectional variations and continuous variations. In sectional variations, or "theme and variations," a theme is first stated and then varied in a series of relatively closed and complete sections, each one usually featuring a specific variation technique. This type of variation is much more frequently encountered in instrumental music than in choral music.

In continuous variations a simple melodic idea or a short harmonic progression is repeated over and over with varied material presented against it. This material is usually written in such a way that the repetitions of the melodic idea or harmonic progression are not obvious, and the piece achieves a continuous flow from beginning to end. Some theorists refer to the continuous variations on a repeated melodic idea as a *passacaglia* or, if the melodic idea stays in the bass part, as a *ground bass* or *basso ostinato*. They refer to the continuous variation based on a repeated harmonic progression as a *chaconne*. However, there is a great deal of confusion over these terms, especially when they appear as titles in pieces from the Baroque period. Continuous variation forms are used in choral as well as instrumental works.

Developmental forms like the sonata-allegro form or the concerto-allegro form are characterized by the presence of a development section, in which motives from previously heard themes are reworked and rearranged. A fuller discussion of the sonata-allegro form is offered in chapter thirteen.

Polyphonic forms like the fugue and canon are probably best not thought of as specific formal schemes but rather as compositional types or procedures. One can expect that these forms will be written in imitative polyphonic texture, but one cannot predict the order in which the constituent units of the composition will appear. This is not to say that a specific fugue will not have a discernible form but rather to say that there is no single formal scheme common to all fugues.

Similarly, in the case of compositions written in a *free* form, one cannot say that they have no form but rather that the order of presentation of units does not conform to any common, predictable scheme. For example, the "Credo" of a mass, with its many varied sections, will often be written as a series of sections arranged in a free sectional form.

Open forms, on the contrary, do move in the direction of formlessness, or at least they move as far away as possible from the sense of organization and closure that marks most other formal types. In some cases open forms are the product of aleatory or chance music procedures, to be discussed in chapter fifteen.

In other cases the tendency toward a lack of organization and closure is written into the music by the composer. Although open forms are usually identified with music of the twentieth-century avant garde, they may be found in earlier music—for example, in some vocal recitatives or instrumental preludes. The distinction between free and open forms is not always easy to make, but in general the free form will be characterized by some repetition, restatement, or varied restatement of material and some sense of completeness or closure, while the open forms will not display these characteristics. Both forms have in common the fact that there is no standardized, predictable pattern in the order of events.

Though it is interesting to consider the types of specific forms discussed in this section, there are also dangers inherent in any such categorization. The first danger is to think that every work must fall into a specific category, when in fact some of the most interesting works will fall on the border between two formal types, or will simply resist categorization. A more pernicious danger is to think that musical forms are like molds into which composers pour their musical material. This goes against the very nature of musical composition as a process of organic growth mentioned at the beginning of this chapter. Composers do not begin with a rigid plan as to how they will divide their compositions any more than dramatists feel bound by a certain layout of scenes and acts. In both arts, form and content are shaped together in a process of mutual interaction.

So too in analysis the first question should never be "In what form is this work written?" Rather the analyst should begin by asking a series of questions. "How is this work divided into sections and subsections or into units of various sizes?" "What factors contribute to a sense of unity or to a sense of variety in the work?" "What factors contribute to a sense of continuity or discontinuity in the work?" "What is the work about?" "What does it express?" "What functions or roles are played by the constitutent units of the composition?" Only after each of these questions has been considered carefully should the analyst ask himself a question about form, and then it should probably be phrased as "What formal type or scheme has characteristics most similar to those displayed by this particular work?"

APPROACHES TO ANALYSIS

There are many different systems or approaches to the analysis of form in music, and among these three basic approaches may be found that account for a substantial portion of the analytical literature. These may be described as a *tonality approach*, a *thematic approach*, and a *linear approach*. To a great extent these systems developed in conjunction with the analysis of music of the Classical period, as well as the late Baroque period and the early Romantic period. The systems can also be applied with some adaptations to music of earlier and later periods. In the following section we shall discuss some general principles of each approach. In chapter thirteen we shall apply some specific aspects of these approaches to the analysis of classical style.

Tonality Approach

Tonality was defined in chapter eight as the relation of a group of pitches to a central pitch—the tonic. For purposes of the classical tonality approach to analysis, we shall adopt a more restricted definition and consider tonality as the relation of a group of chords to a central chord—the tonic triad.

The essentials of the relationships among the chords of a classical tonality were described by Hugo Riemann probably as cogently as by any other writer. Following the lead of Rameau and others, he distinguished three principal triads— tonic (I), dominant (V), and subdominant (IV)—each with a possible "substitute" (in German, *parallel*) triad a third below, and designated them as follows:

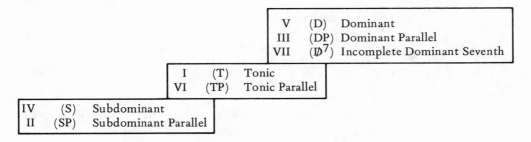

Some modern writers prefer the term predominant for subdominant. The important thing is not the terms used (the Riemann system almost breaks down under the weight of elaborate symbols and terms for various chords), but rather the establishment of three basic chord functions, and the possibility of using a variety of chords to fulfill these functions. For example, the dominant of the dominant (V/V), the Neapolitan sixth, and the augmented sixth chords may all be used for a subdominant or predominant function as well as the supertonic (II) chord.

The functional characteristics of tonic, dominant, and subdominant are suggested by their placement in the chart above. By thinking of a form of "musical gravity" operating, you will see that movement from the tonic to the dominant is an active, tension-creating motion, while movement from the tonic to the subdominant is a passive, tension-releasing motion. The standard harmonic progression of tonic-subdominant-dominant-tonic in any of its varied versions (I-IV-V-I, I-ii $^6_5$-V^7-I, etc.) may be heard as establishment-preparation (or release)-tension-release (or arrival).

You may introduce this concept to your choir members in a vivid manner by having them associate physical motions with the chord categories as suggested below.

CHORDS:	Tonic (I)	Subdominant (IV, II, etc.)	Dominant (V, vii^o, etc.)
GESTURES:	Sit upright.	Lean forward in a relaxed manner with elbows resting on knees.	Stand up.

If you have singers perform these motions as you play a simple harmonic progression or a brief musical excerpt, they should develop a concrete, vital image of the characteristics of the chords.

To describe modulation, we might paraphrase Tovey, who said that form was "melody writ large," and call modulation "harmonic progression writ large." In a typical Mozart *Kyrie,* the movement from the tonality of C major in the opening Kyrie section to G major in the middle Christe section is really the same as the movement from the I chord to the V chord in the opening measures, but only on a larger level. In both cases the movement creates a sense of tension, a need to be resolved. This may be easier to hear on the local level but it is of great importance on the larger structural level.

Modulation, it should be pointed out, is a process that appears in various degrees from a slight allusion to another key by means of a single secondary dominant usage, through such intermediate stages as a tonal region made up of a brief phrase or two in another key, to the full and unmistakable establishment of another key. If tonality is defined as "loyalty to a tonic," then modulation would be "disloyalty to a tonic" and subject to all the gradations from "disaffection" to "treason."

Applied to formal analysis, the tonality approach may be used to define and characterize both small and large units of a composition. It can show how a phrase is organized in terms of harmonic tension and release, or how an entire movement is organized in terms of large-scale tonal areas.

Thematic Approach

The thematic approach to formal analysis emphasizes the melodic element. It offers ways of describing melodies and seeks to discover ways in which motives, phrases, or larger units from one part of a composition are related to or contrasted with similar units from other parts of a composition.

Thematic or motivic analysis presents both opportunities for penetrating deeper into the real meaning and structure of the work and dangers of inaccurate or, at the least, exaggerated interpretation. To avoid these dangers, let us first recognize that some types of motives are so common in a particular style that they may be found in a great many works; their appearance in different parts of the same work is not necessarily a mark of significance or deliberate organic unity but rather a natural consequence of the characteristics of the musical language. (This, incidentally, is one of the problems with statistical analysis. It tells us what is usually about a work or group of works, but what we really want to know, in order to understand the style, are the unusual, striking, or special features.) An analysis of the number of times particular notes or groups of notes occur in the "glorias" of Haydn and those of Mozart would probably not give us very significant information about the essential differences in the styles of the two composers. It would be like counting the occurrences of various letters in the novels of Hemingway and those of Faulkner. We would probably find the frequency of individual letters would be roughly in the order of ETAOIN SHRDLU, but we might be sorely pressed to explain what this contributes to our understanding of the two writers. In defense of the statistical approach, however, we might paraphrase the quote from Talmud with which Willi Apel opens the *Harvard Dictionary of Music*, "If you want to understand the invisible, look carefully at the visible," to read "If you want to understand the unusual, look carefully at the usual." The problem is not with statistical analysis per se, but with its interpretation. Statistical analysis basically helps us to understand the norms of a style; to understand the essence of a style, at least at the present stage of musical analysis, we must rely more on musical intuition and personal observation.

To avoid mistaken or superficial motivic analysis, we must realize that through a combination of pitch and rhythm variation techniques, such as inversion, interval expansion or contraction, retrograde, augmentation, diminution, and others, it is possible to derive almost any motive from another. It is possible to claim that the opening of the "In excelsis" in Mozart's *C Minor Mass*, K. 427, is transformed by the process of inversion and diminution to become the "Osanna" motive as shown below. Such a relationship gains credence especially when one considers that triadic motives play an important role throughout this mass. However, to claim that the opening motives of the "In excelsis" and the "Cum sancto" were related by the process of diminution and by adding extra notes would strain the credulity of the listener more.

Example 8

Mozart, *C Minor Mass*, K. 427

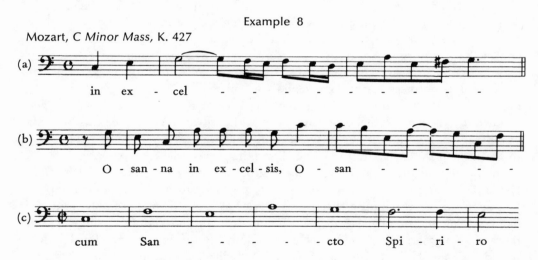

Finally we should be careful not to confuse theories or facts about how a composer went about writing a work with the analysis of the resulting work itself, and we should not confuse visual analysis with aural analysis. An excellent example of both aspects is the occasional use by Bach of figures like the following which he chose not because of their sounding aspects, but because of the fact that they use sharps, and the word for sharp in German (*Kreuz*) has the double meaning of sharp and cross.

Example 9

Bach, *St. Matthew Passion*, No. 54

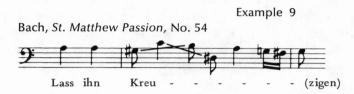

Lass ihn   Kreu - - - - - - (zigen)

Ultimately the best test of a motivic analysis is the trained ear. We should never forget that composers are also listeners. As they write or sound out parts of their works, they listen, and it is only natural that they should remember motives they use earlier in a work and repeat these or transform them, perhaps in seemingly obscure ways, in later parts. If motivic analysis does nothing more than help the conductor to penetrate more deeply into the work, to gain more of a sense of psychological ownership of the work, then perhaps even the most unconventional motivic analysis will prove helpful. Motivic analyses described by writers like Donald F. Tovey, Hermann Abert, and (with a good grain of salt) Rudolph Reti can demonstrate some of the ways this theory may be pursued.

Linear Approach

Linear analysis or structural analysis, as practiced by Heinrich Schenker and his followers, is in many ways the most difficult type of analysis but perhaps the most interesting and insightful. It is difficult because of the obscure, inconsistent, and sometimes contentious manner in which Schenker writes and because of the vast amount of arbitrary, sometimes pseudoscientific, a priori assumptions that Schenker demands his readers make before he presents his idea. Stripped of these features that make it unnecessarily problematic, however, his analyses may be shown to possess an enormous understanding and insight and even now, over forty years after his death, he stands as one of the most powerful influences on contemporary music theory.

Reduced to its simplest terms, Schenker's main theoretical postulate is that music (especially that of the high Baroque, Classical, and early Romantic periods) is the result of a series of diminutions, decorations, or workings out of a basic underlying two-voice formula which is itself, in essence, an unfolding of the chord of nature—the triad. Lest we fall into the same trap of obfuscation that mars Schenker's writing, let us restate this definition as an operative one; that is, in terms of step-by-step operations one must perform to arrive at his system. To do so naturally incurs the risk of oversimplification, but it is our hope that the reader encountering the Schenker system for the first time will be encouraged to investigate it further on his own with such texts as Salzer-Schachter *Counterpoint in Composition*.

We begin with a triad, called the chord of nature because it is actually present as the 4th, 5th, and 6th partials of the overtone series above any given root.

1. We activate, realize, prolong, or "compose out" (*Auskomponieren*) this triad in the simplest possible way by having the bass rise from the root to the fifth and return, and by having the soprano fall in a stepwise motion (*Zug*) from the third to the tonic. The result is a fundamental plan (*Ursatz*) that could be the background (*Hintergrund*) of a number of compositions.

2. We now elaborate, decorate, prolong, or compose out each line of this basic two-voice frame in a series of levels of diminution (*Schichten*) that comprise the middle ground. Each level is more complex and has more notes than the next. Stepwise motion predominates, but some other types may also appear.

3. The final and most complex level is the foreground (*Vordergrund*), the music itself as we see it and hear it. Unlike the background and, to an extent, the middle ground that could be the same for several different pieces, the foreground is unique for each work.

Schenkerian analysis actually proceeds in the reverse direction from the example we have given, beginning with the foreground, and then moving to the middle ground and the background. It is subject to varying interpretations by different analysts, and like motivic analysis has, at the very least, the merit of forcing one to deal intently and thoughtfully with the music itself. It gives a concrete and systematic way of moving from narrow consideration of the surface aspects of a work to a broader consideration of the deeper structural aspects of the work from the individual notes to the long line.

Schenker's motto, *Semper idem sed non eodem modo*, "Always the same, but not in the same way," expresses his conviction that all good music could be reduced to a basic *Ursatz* according to his principles. Music that did not (and this includes not only masterworks of contemporary composers like Stravinsky and Hindemith, but also works by pre-Baroque composers like Dufay and des Prés), were cavalierly dismissed by him as inferior or primitive. These judgments did not contribute to the acceptance of his system, and yet efforts by some of his more recent followers to adapt his principles to the analysis of music other than that for which it was originally intended do not seem helpful. Rather, each significantly different style seems to require a different, though perhaps related, set of tools to explore the style in a penetrating and appropriate manner.

TWO BRIEF ANALYSES

The two brief analyses of works that close this chapter on form cannot answer all possible questions about the particular works, but rather should stimulate conductors and singers to make their own analyses. The essence of formal analysis is always in the dynamic process of questioning and discovering, not in the static report of such investigation.

George Frederick Handel, *Jephtha*, "In glory high"

Jephtha, Handel's last oratorio and one of his last major compositions altogether, was written at a time when increasing blindness made it difficult for him to write. A note in the autograph score at the end of the powerful chorus "How hard, how dark, Oh Lord, is thy decision" reads "until here, the 13th of February, 1751 hindered by the failing of sight in my left eye." Handel finally finished the work in August, 1751 and the first performance took place in London in February, 1752.

Like many of Handel's oratorios, parts of *Jephtha* consist of reworkings or in some cases direct borrowings of music by other composers. The theme of Zebul's opening aria, for example, comes from a mass written by the contemporary Bohemian composer Franz Johann Habermann. A similar theme can be found in the B-flat major fugue from the first book of Bach's *Well-Tempered Clavier*. For the Baroque composer, originality of material was not as important as the effective way in which the material was used. Some critics have charged that *Jephtha* shows a lessening of Handel's dramatic and creative powers as compared to his earlier works. Others cite examples, such as the famous quartet in which each of the four main characters of the oratorio is given distinctive musical expression, as evidence of the fact that Handel was leaving behind in this work a mighty bridge to the future of music.

The story of Jephtha had already been treated by the first great oratorio writer Giacomo Carissimi. In its simplest form, Jephtha makes an oath to God that he will sacrifice the first living thing that comes to his house if God will grant him victory over his enemies. He wins the victory, returns home in triumph, and then is horrified to find that the first living thing to greet him is his daughter Isis. Jephtha is about to carry out his oath when an angel appears and releases him from his vow on the condition that Isis become a priestess of God.

The chorus "In glory high" is sung at the moment of Jephtha's triumphant homecoming.

The chorus opens with a powerful acclamation "In glory high, in might serene," set in four-part harmony for the chorus and orchestra (two oboes, strings, and continuo). The slow tempo (*grave*), the solemn dotted-note rhythms, and the block chord texture effectively underline the solemn confidence of the words. Harmonically, the progression could be described as an open "arch," moving from tonic through predominant and ending on the dominant.

At this point the tempo becomes slightly more moving (*un poco andante*) and the texture changes. Against repeated eighth-note chords in the strings, the chorus sings short two-note motives on the words "he sees, moves all, unmov'd, unseen." Again the music comes to a cadence on the dominant harmony. These two cadences on the dominant provide a sense of punctuation, at the same time they suggest that the music will continue to move forward.

From measure 14 to the end of the piece (measure 58) the music now moves without appreciable break. The text "His mighty arm with sudden blow" is set to an ascending eighth-note scale that is heard in the soprano, then imitated in the tenor, and then imitated in the alto and bass parts moving in parallel tenths. The choice of the ascending scale motive for this text was one of the masterstrokes of simple effectiveness so typical of Handel. Even when writing music for texts in English, a language he never fully mastered despite his years in England, Handel almost always chose a musical setting that was so appropriate, one can hardly imagine the words being sung to another melody. Notice also how Handel planned his rhythm so that the word "blow" comes with the powerful attack of the downbeat. When this would not be the case, as in the tenor part that begins in measure 14, he stopped the text and music before they reached the word "blow."

In measure 16 the strings sound impetuous sixteenth-note figures that prepare the mood of the next line of text, "dispers'd, and quell'd the haughty foe." This is set in two-note motives that recall the two-note motives heard earlier. Now, however, the first note is reduced to an eighth note, giving it a more vigorous character. In measure 20, in a highly literal setting of the words, Handel "dis-perses" the word "dispers'd" among pairs of voices, alternating tenor and bass with soprano and alto. In measures 27–28 and 40–41 he also created the same effect of dispersion, this time with single voice parts. In measure 23 the last important motivic material is introduced, an ascending scale in sixteenth notes on the word "foe." This could be regarded as a diminution of the eighth-note scale material. A further variant of this motive, a descending (i.e., inverted) sixteenth-note scale is used in measures 30, 43, 53, and 56.

The analysis reveals that Handel used a limited amount of musical material, but used it with telling effectiveness and variety. We also see that he achieved both articulation and continuity in his overall design, but that the emphasis in this chorus was upon the sense of continuity. From measure 14 to the end there was a sense of basically uninterrupted forward motion that was achieved by such devices as the overlap of voice parts, the avoidance of a harmonic cadence on the tonic, and the use of harmonic and melodic sequence. At the same time, the recurrence of certain musical ideas, such as the "dispers'd" figure we discussed earlier, gives a sense of structure to this passage and keeps it from being just an undifferentiated stream of music.

The singer who is aware of these aspects will probably be able to learn his part more efficiently and effectively. More important, he should gain a sense of participation and even of shared responsibility in the recreation of a work that is a marvelous example of musical craftsmanship and poetic expression.

Johannes Brahms, *Geistliches Lied*, Op. 30

Brahm's first choral work, the *Geistliches Lied*, Op. 30, for four-part chorus and organ shows a marvelous union of the old and the new that characterizes most of his great works. Its construction as a strict double canon looks back to the art of the Renaissance; its melodies and harmonies are more typical of those of the Romantic period.

The work may be regarded as a large three-part form with organ introduction and interludes and with an extended "Amen" coda for chorus and organ. In each of these sections the order of entry of the canonic sections is slightly different, as will be explained in the following analysis.

The work is written in ¢¢ or $\frac{4}{2}$ meter, a meter that Brahms no doubt chose because it had the appearance and character of the meter used in Renaissance editions. At the time Brahms wrote this chorus, he was pursuing intensive studies of Renaissance choral music. The influence of this study can be felt not only in choral works like this and in *A German Requiem*, published four years after Op. 30 in 1868, but also in many of his instrumental compositions. The tonality of E-flat was frequently chosen by Brahms for compositions of a comforting character, as "Wie lieblich sind deine Wohnungen" (How lovely is thy dwelling place) from the *Requiem*.

The organ introduction moves primarily in ascending quarter-note arpeggio figures, but at the same time, in the inner voices, it hints at the motives that will be used in the coming choral parts. The introduction begins on the dominant and emphasizes this degree throughout. It ends on a predominant chord based on the second scale degree that prepares the entrance of the voices.

In the first choral section the soprano begins with a stepwise motive that is imitated one measure later and one step lower by the tenor. In the following measure the alto begins with a different motive that is imitated one measure later and one step lower by the bass. In measure 15 the mood of the text changes to the imperative "sei stille" (be still), and this is reflected in the melody that now moves in quarter notes with a vigorous leap of a fifth. This is answered half a measure later and a perfect fourth lower in the alto which sings the inversion of the fifth, i.e., a perfect fourth. In the following measure the tenor enters with an imitation of the soprano a step lower, and the bass enters a half measure later with an imitation of the alto that is also one step below. In other words, throughout this first section we have a strict canon between the soprano and tenor and another strict canon between the alto and bass. What changes is the time relation between the two canons. The first section ends with a cadence on the tonic.

The organ interlude actually overlaps with the final measure of the first section, thus avoiding an overemphasis on the cadence at this point that would have tended to end the work prematurely. The organ interlude is similar to the introduction, but it lasts for only three measures. Then the soprano begins the second part with a motive that is actually the inversion of the opening motive of the first choral section. The use of techniques like inversion and canon is not a matter of technical display with Brahms but rather an effective means for achieving unity in the work without resorting to overly obvious repetition. In the following half-measure intervals we hear the alto with a different melodic line, then the tenor with the imitation of the soprano a step lower, and finally the bass with an imitation of the alto a step lower. This arrangement continues throughout the second section which comes to a cadence in measure 36 on the relative minor (C minor). All of the cadences in this work are written so that the final chord comes not on the downbeat but on the third beat of the measure, thus giving them a somewhat lighter character.

In the first section the organ part was confined mostly to chordal support of the voice parts. It begins this way in the second part, but in measure 27 the quarter-note arpeggio figures return in the organ part for the next six measures. As the voices cadence in measure 36, the organ part returns to these figures to lead into the interlude preceding the third part. This interlude is five measures long and uses the same material as the last five measures of the organ introduction, thus preparing effectively for the return of the original melodic material in the chorus in measure 42. This material is identical with the first section except for the change of text.

The "Amen" coda begins with the bass voice which is imitated two measures later and one step lower by the altos. In measure 57 the imitation changes to a time distance of one measure between these two voices, and then soprano and tenor enter with a new motive in imitation. The strictness that has characterized the imitation to an amazingly high degree in this work is broken for one small moment as the tenor part has an added note in the upbeat to measure 59. The whole coda is characterized by an emphasis on the subdominant that adds a calming effect to the coda. From measure 61 to 65 the quarter-note arpeggio figures return in a descending sequence in the organ as an accompaniment to the double suspension figures in the voices. The concluding plagal cadence reaffirms the subdominant emphasis of the coda.

In summary, this work is marked by a clear three-part division but the seams are hidden by the overlapping of the organ interludes. The voice parts are always in a double canon, with soprano and tenor in imitation at the second (or ninth) and alto and bass in imitation at the second (or ninth). The time relation between the soprano and alto voices varies in different sections. Except for a few places, like cadential endings or measure 59 in the tenor, the imitation is strict. A sense of unity is achieved through such specific devices as the recurrence of the quarter-note arpeggio figures in the organ part and the use of inversion of motives, and also through general similarities in the contour and character of the melodic material and the type of harmonic material used. The harmonic progressions on a smaller scale are a fascinating mixture of traditional progressions and some more modal or archaic progressions. On a larger scale we could point to the emphasis on the dominant at the beginning organ introduction, on the tonic and relative minor during the body of the work, and on the subdominant in the "Amen" coda.

It is possible that chorus members could sing this work without any knowledge of the way that harmony, imitative texture, and formal techniques contribute to its sense of shape and to its emotional expression. Certainly one should not overemphasize these theoretical matters at the expense of a vivid aural experience of the work. But even a small amount of time spent in discussing them should enable the singers to appreciate the marvelous blend of craft and expression that constitutes the core of this work and others like it.

Specifically, we would urge that the chorus read through the work several times before any discussion of its structure and materials be undertaken. And we would further urge that, as far as possible, singers be led by questions and suggestions on the part of the conductor to discover for themselves the techniques and structure that we have presented here in a straight expository manner.

NOTES

1. Arnold Schoenberg, *The Composition with Twelve Tones* (1950), translated by Dika Newlin in *Style and Idea* (New York: Philosophical Library, 1950), p. 103.

2. Aaron Copland, *What to Listen for in Music* (New York: McGraw-Hill Book Company, 1939).

Chapter Ten
RECOMMENDED READING LIST

Christ, William, et al. *Materials and Structures of Music.* 2 vols. Englewood Cliffs: Prentice-Hall, 1966. A conceptual approach to the understanding of music theory.

Cone, Edward. *Musical Form and Musical Performance.* New York: W. W. Norton and Company, Inc., 1968. This work is a must for every conductor who wishes to achieve a thorough understanding of musical form in performance.

Copland, Aaron. *What to Listen for in Music.* New York: McGraw-Hill Book Co., 1939. A classic introduction to musical processes written for the musical layman but containing valuable insights for the professional musician.

Fontaine, Paul Hendricks. *Basic Formal Structures in Music.* New York: Appleton-Century-Crofts, 1967. A clear, concise, and comprehensive description of traditional forms.

Levarie, Siegmund. *Mozart's Le Nozze di Figaro, A Critical Analysis.* Chicago: University of Chicago Press, 1952. Provides not only a concentrated introduction to the theories of Riemann and Lorenz but also an interesting application of them to Mozart's opera.

Reti, Rudolph. *The Thematic Process in Music.* New York: Macmillan, 1951. A fascinating though somewhat controversial study of the thematic process.

Salzer, Felix. *Structural Hearing.* 2 vols. New York: C. Boni, 1952.

Salzer, Felix, and Schacter, Carl. *Counterpoint in Composition.* New York: McGraw-Hill Book Co., 1969. Both Salzer works provide an excellent introduction to the theories of Schenker, the first emphasizing vertical aspects and the second emphasizing linear aspects.

PERFORMANCE PRACTICES

Introduction to Part Four

THE CHORAL CONDUCTOR of today is confronted with problems that were largely unknown to his counterpart in previous centuries. If we compare a typical choral performance of the 1970s with a choral performance from the 1670s, we would probably find first that the contemporary performance would be devoted to a number of works from different chronological periods and national styles, assembled for a program that would have no special function beyond that of providing a meaningful listening experience for the audience. The earlier performance, on the other hand, would be devoted to a single work or a group of closely related works written expressly for a specific sacred or secular function. Second, we would probably find that the twentieth-century performance would be led by the silent gestures of a conductor's baton or hands; the seventeenth-century performance, in contrast, would be led by the sounding impetus of a harpsichord, organ, or violin, played by the composer himself or by a musician with firsthand acquaintance with the style and conventions of the work.

It is easy to understand how difficult it is for a present-day conductor to match the immediacy and authenticity in performance practice of his predecessor from three hundred years ago. He must be familiar with a chronological range of music literature that embraces centuries rather than decades, and with a geographical range that embraces continents rather than countries.

Faced with this problem there are several options open to the contemporary choral conductor. He can, for example, deliberately limit his repertoire to Broadway show tunes or to Renaissance madrigals, and develop an expertise in his chosen area. Though we can be grateful to many specialists in our own time who have chosen this path and have provided us with exemplary performances of works in their special areas, many conductors would probably find this too confining and would be reluctant to deny themselves, their chorus members, and their audience the experience of masterworks from other periods of music literature.

Another solution would be to perform works from a wide variety of music literature, but to perform all of them with a single set of performance practices, drawn in many instances from the nineteenth century, rather than attempting to perform them in the style intended by the composer. Until the beginning of solid scholarship in performance practice in the twentieth century, this was the usual approach to the performance of earlier music. However, the fact that good musicians of the nineteenth century followed this practice is poor justification for the continuation of the trend.

The most satisfactory option would be to perform as wide a variety of music literature as possible with as much authenticity of performance practice as possible. This places great demands upon the conductor but it may bring great rewards. Performance practice is not something apart from or added to the music; it is part of the very essence of the musical experience. Knowledge of performance practice does not provide rigid, unequivocal solutions to interpretive problems; rather it establishes acceptable limits, often quite broad and flexible, within which the performer may interpret the music according to his own individual judgment and artistic personality.

The study of performance practice does not begin and end with the complex interpretation of mysterious musical hieroglyphics. It is concerned first and foremost with the expressive character and the structural nature of the music of a particular period or style and the sound ideal through which these are realized. Furthermore it must always be considered within the framework of the sociocultural conditions at the time the work was written. Specific problems relating to these general concerns may be organized under the following general headings.

1. *Choice of Voices and Instruments.* This would include not only the types and numbers of voices and instruments but would also include such questions as vibrato, tone quality, bowing, and other instrumental problems.

2. *Problems of Notation.* These are problems relating to the interpretation of pitch, rhythm, and other symbols. Included in this category would be such matters as *musica ficta* in the Renaissance, over-dotting in the Baroque, or the interpretation of signs for quarter tones in twentieth-century music.

3. *Ornamentation and Improvisation.* This would cover such problems as the interpretation of specific written signs for ornamentation, the conventions and traditions applying to ornamentation that are not specifically indicated, improvisations, figured bass realization, and the performance of aleatory music.

4. *Interpretation of Tempo.* This involves such problems as establishing a correct basic tempo, the possibilities of tempo modification, and the performance of rhythmic figures in various tempi.

5. *Phrasing, Articulation, and Dynamics.* This includes not only such specific questions as whether to play loudly or softly or whether to play smoothly or in a detached manner, but also, in some cases, more general questions relating to the basic structure of the music.

Some of these problems are more critical in certain periods than in others. Problems in the interpretation of pitch notation, such as the *musica ficta* of the Renaissance and early Baroque periods, are virtually absent in the music of the Classic and Romantic periods, only to reappear in some avant garde music. Solutions to problems of performance practice may be found in a variety of sources, four of which are listed below.

1. Probably the most valuable source would be written directions or suggestions from the composer himself, or, in the case of more recent music, performances or recordings of the music made by the composer himself or under his direct supervision. There may be some instances where a composer is not necessarily the best interpreter of his own music, sometimes by his own admission. Still, one should be very hesitant to reject the composer's interpretive ideas.

2. It is not always necessary to have direct information from the composer. Sometimes it will be possible to clarify a questionable passage by comparing it to similar passages in the same work or in other works. In some cases it is valuable to consult transcriptions or altered versions of a work when these are by the composer himself or by other musicians versed in the style and conventions of the period.

3. Other significant sources of information, especially for earlier music, are the writings of theorists and other commentators of the time. Though sometimes contradictory or even downright inaccurate, these can provide indispensable insight on both general character and specific details.

4. Finally there are valuable secondary sources, especially for earlier music, in the scholarly writing of Arnold Dolmetsch, Thurston Dart, Robert Donington, and other writers. These works are based on a thorough study of both the music and the theoretical writings of earlier periods of music history. The most compre-hensive study of performance practice, *The Interpretation of Early Music* by Robert Donington, devotes more than half of its six hundred pages to direct quotations from writers of the Baroque period. A more recent book by the same author, *A Performer's Guide to Baroque Music,* deals exclusively with the Baroque period.

Obvious limitations of space in this book make it impossible to quote so extensively from primary sources. Instead, in the chapters that follow, we have attempted to distill their essence into a set of definitions, rules, explanations, and principles stated tersely in modern language. To do so is to lose much of the flavor of the earlier sources, and we would recommend that whenever possible conductors should consult the original material as listed in the bibliography at the end of the chapter. Space limitations have also necessitated foregoing lengthy discussions of debatable issues in which evidence from primary and secondary sources might be cited for more than one interpretation. In such cases we have concentrated on the interpretation that seems best supported by the evidence available.

One final point concerning the relationship of the study of performance practice to the actual rehearsal and performance of a work needs to be discussed. This is the possible necessity of compromise between the ideals of authentic per-formance practice and the limitations imposed by acoustical conditions, availability of instruments, length of rehearsal time, and the technical skill and artistic per-sonality of the performers. From the point of view of the purist, it might be better to refrain from performing a work in any but ideal and authentic conditions. The other extreme would be blithely to ignore aspects of performance practice and to present works in a manner that would sometimes be totally out of style and character.

We would urge a middle ground between these two positions. Certainly whenever possible a stylistically authentic performance should be preferred. The increasing availability of older instruments and the increased skill and under-standing of performance practices make such authentic performances of earlier music far more possible today than they would have been several decades ago. When, however, circumstances dictate the need for minor alterations that do not change the fundamental structure and character of the music, it would seem to be possible to make them. To eliminate the performance of works merely because of the necessity of such compromises would seem a needless impoverishment of the musical experience. Furthermore, to make such compromises within the limitations of good taste and fidelity to the essential aspects of the music can frequently be justified by the fact that similar compromises or adjustments may have been made in the performance of the work in its own time.

The essential thing is that, as far as possible, decisions on performance practice be based upon knowledge and understanding as well as sensitivity and intuition. It is our hope that the chapters that follow will provide an effective introduction to this fascinating study.

Chapter Eleven

The Renaissance Period

Music is both an art and a science; like every art and every
science it has no enemy save ignorance.—THURSTON DART[1]

THE PERIOD of the musical Renaissance (c. 1450–1600) is extremely important to
the present-day choral conductor. Music reached an incredible height of accomplishment during this period and the focus of this achievement is revealed in the
choral art. Because the composers of the Renaissance were no longer willing to be
bound by the strictures of the Middle Ages (strict liturgical texts, tonal limitations
of chant, and rhythmic modes), a body of new forms, new styles, new texts, new
instruments, and new compositional techniques appear in the music of the fifteenth
and sixteenth centuries. Choral music emerged in a new idiom as composers brought
harmonic and polyphonic techniques together in a new synthesis of musical
texture.

As a result musical composition developed from the desire of the Renaissance artist to conceive of his work as a well-planned and carefully organized
whole, rather than as a structure of several successively erected layers. New
timbres began to appear as voices and instruments were combined in planned, as
well as extemporaneous, performances. The text also served a new function, and
in the process became a primary source of musical inspiration. A wedding developed between the syllable and the note, and the seeds for the modern relationship between music and literature were planted, a new direction that eventually
led to word painting and primitive forms of musical drama.

It is this spirit of freedom and curiosity that serves as the point of departure for the present-day choral conductor as he approaches the study and per-

formance of Renaissance music. Edward Lowinsky provides an important insight for the modern performer when he writes: "every musical enterprise is characterized by an endless curiosity, a firm—if at times concealed—refusal to abide by authority for authority's sake, an intrepid pioneering spirit and an inexhaustible joy in theoretical speculation, personal and literary controversy and debate, and practical experimentation."[2]

GENERAL CHARACTER AND STRUCTURE

The development of choral music as a form of musical composition and performance coincided with the flowering of the musical Renaissance. The clearest picture of musical life in the Renaissance can be gleaned from two sources: the Church and the court. Throughout this period the finest composers and the best singers were to be found in these institutions that served as the cultural focus for a given geographical area. In the great urban cathedrals of the North the composers learned their trade as choirboys, and as they matured and their voices changed, they served as choristers, conductors, and composers. The music that they wrote often found a place in the court chapel—an essential area for courtly life on which the dukes of the period spent vast sums of money. The chapel, which was part of the cultural life of the court, always included a choirmaster and a choir of men and boys, in addition to the priest, vestments, furnishings, and of course the building necessary for the religious life of the court.

One interesting aspect of choral music during the Renaissance is that it developed under the mutual influence of the cultures of both northern and southern Europe. Geographically, the Netherlands—which then included northern France, Belgium, and Holland—and Italy were the leading centers of musical development. Many of the most important composers of the period came from a surprisingly small area near the Franco-Belgian border. Limited contributions were made by France, Germany, England, and Spain, but these countries did not take key roles in the emerging synthesis of northern and southern styles into the musical practice of the period.

From the north came the polyphonic style of Jean de Ockeghem, Josquin des Prés, Nicolas Gombert and their contemporaries. Emerging from the south was a new harmonic language that found its cultivation in the secular forms of the late fifteenth and the sixteenth centuries: frottola, villanesca, madrigal, balletto, and the

Ockeghem and His Singers. Fifteenth-century miniature.
(The Bettmann Archive)

vernacular lauda. Thus a simultaneous conception of harmony and of polyphony emerged that became the key factor in the compositional style of the period.

One important factor that contributed to the success of choral music during this period was the invention about 1450 of the printing press. In the late fifteenth century there was a gradual increase in the availability of books, especially the Lutheran Bible, as well as religious pamphlets and musical scores. Prior to this practically all copying was done by the slow manual process. Now mechanical reproduction allowed fast circulation of printed material. This was of ultimate benefit in the education of common people and was partly responsible for the success of the Reformation under Luther. In music it meant that more people were brought in contact with the newest compositions written by the prominent Church and court composers.

While it is difficult to make broad generalizations that apply universally in a period as dynamic as the Renaissance, there are certain characteristics that can serve as guidelines to our study of performance practice:

The Singing and Playing Angels (1420). Hubert and Jan van Eyck. (The Bettmann Archive)

1. Renaissance music allows the performer substantial freedom in interpretation. We only need to consult the writings and paintings of the period to discover that the purity and sacredness that we tend to associate with Renaissance performance today was true only of performances in certain religious settings, such as the Papal chapel in Rome where instrumental accompaniment was not allowed.

2. Renaissance music includes no distinction between instrumental and vocal style. There was only one musical idiom during this period. Voices and instruments were interchangeable.

3. Renaissance music demands that the performer also be an interpreter who brings considerable knowledge of the style of the period to each performance.

4. Renaissance music brings new forms and timbres to musical performance that need to be handled with the utmost care. Works composed for the cathedral should be performed in a different manner from the intimate solo compositions that were written for the drawing room. Outdoor music or tower music must be approached differently from the vernacular pieces that were used in lay congregations. These distinctions demand careful study by the conductor to insure stylistic authenticity and tasteful performance.

THE USE OF VOICES AND INSTRUMENTS

The recent revival of Renaissance and pre-Renaissance music as a regular part of programs of church, school, and community choral groups has created a desire on the part of conductors to perform this music "correctly." This ideal has raised many questions concerning the nature of Renaissance performances. Most of the music that has come down to us from this period brings with it little evidence regarding the manner in which it is to be performed. Thus performance guidelines must be reconstructed from the writings of contemporary composers and authors and nonmusical sources, such as paintings, poetry, sculpture, etc. In the sections that follow we will first consider the concept of vocal quality and nature of choral singing in Renaissance music, then the question of the use of instruments in the present-day performance of Renaissance music.

Vocal Quality and the Nature of Choral Singing

The present-day choral conductor faces three basic problems in the interpretation of Renaissance choral music: recreating vocal sounds that have disappeared; recreating tone colors that have changed; and recreating the performing environment of a bygone era.

Many vocal colors of the sixteenth century have completely disappeared in the four hundred years since most of this music was written, among them the male soprano and the male alto. The male castrato was perhaps the most important single contributor to the distinctive timbre of Renaissance choral music, and male castrati simply do not exist today. The closest comparable quality is heard in the countertenor, yet countertenors are extremely rare. Thus any conductor who attempts authentic Renaissance interpretation must accept the fact that these vocal colors are extinct and simply cannot be reproduced in present-day performances.

A second factor that must be considered in the interpretation of this music is the choral sound itself. While most present-day performances of Renaissance music use female voices for the soprano and alto parts, sixteenth-century performances used choir boys for the soprano part and often used male altos for the alto part. Choir boys were paid to sing and received a musical and humanistic education as part of their training. The use of male altos was only one of the differences that existed between the vocal sound of the Renaissance and that of today; the method of vocal production was also quite different. This must be taken into consideration when performances use mixed voices.

From evidence that we observe in viewing the paintings and sculpture of the period, the vocal production of the individual choral singer was characterized by tenseness, rigidity, and a relatively closed mouth. These visual symptoms normally lead to a vocal sound that is nasal, reedy, and strident. There is also evidence that little or no vibrato was used in the ensemble singing of the Renaissance. When vibrato is discussed by writers of the period, it is condemned as an undesirable musical trait. Dart recommends little vibrato in the performance of complex polyphonic choral works so that the individual lines can be heard with the utmost clarity. Care must be taken however, in present-day choral performances to insure that there is a certain tonal vitality in the choral sound. We believe that it is possible to perform without vibrato and still maintain a fully coordinated and vital vocal production. The performances and recordings of the Roger Wagner Chorale are wonderful examples of a clear, vital choral sound in Renaissance music.

The number of voices to be used in the performance of this music is also a factor that must be carefully considered if a performance is to approach authenticity. Perhaps the most important thing to keep in mind here is that there are essentially two streams of vocal development in the period between 1450 and 1600. One is the development of choral music from its beginnings as an idiomatic vocal form (about 1430) to the liturgical and chorus-conscious music of Ockeghem, Obrecht, and Josquin, the polychoral extension of the choral idiom with Willaert and the Venetian School, and the ultimate synthesis in Palestrina and di Lasso. The other is the solo music, which is particularly strong in the secular literature of the chanson and madrigal. Each makes different demands upon stylistic interpretation.

The number of voices that appeared in accounts of performances of liturgical choral music in the fifteenth and sixteenth centuries fluctuated, but the totals were generally less than we find in present-day concerts and worship services. For example, in 1436 the Papal choir included only nine singers; this number gradually increased to ten in 1442, to twelve and sixteen in following years, and finally to twenty-four by 1483. During the sixteenth century the size of the choir increased to about thirty singers, but generally was held to around twenty-four, a number that soon came to be regarded as the ideal size for the Papal choir. These performances were also sung without accompaniment, since instruments were forbidden in the Sistine Chapel.

It is assumed that two or three singers would perform on a part, except for the soprano, where a few more boys helped to achieve better balance. Choral groups with more than thirty singers were rare during this period. Bukofzer writes of performances of Palestrina's works by soloists with strong voices, but most of the liturgical choral works composed after 1450 are intended for chorus and should be performed by a choral ensemble.

Outside the confines of the Papal chapel greater freedom in performance practice was exhibited by those responsible for liturgical choral performances. Lowinsky informs us that in the Capella Giulia—which functioned in the Basilica of St. Peter—the organ was used in the sacred service. This was in contrast to the policy in the Papal court's Sistine Chapel where no instruments were allowed to "intrude upon the sacred services." At the Cathedral of Our Lady in Antwerp the choir was open to lay singers, a practice that marked the advent of the lay professional musician into the service of the church. The number of singers who performed in the liturgical services was more than twice that of the Papal choir: fifty-one singers in 1443, sixty-three in 1480, and sixty-nine in 1549.

Developing side by side with the polyphonic choral music of the Church was the secular music of the court. While there are examples of choral singing in the court during this period, the solo song with accompaniment of a viol is definitely preferred. This room music, or chamber music, which was performed with intimate subtlety and soft tone, in contrast to the massive sonority of the cathedral or open air music, will be discussed in greater detail in the next section.

The existence of this type of performance environment is confirmed by paintings that have come down to us of fifteenth- and sixteenth-century performances of chansons and madrigals: they show very small groups of solo performers in contrast to large choral groups. Dart supports this view by pointing out the distinction between choirbooks and partbooks.[3] The choirbooks for sacred music are large and written with very large notes and have only one part to a page. The partbook is much smaller and includes all parts on the page. Many pictures exist showing a group of men and boys—perhaps a dozen—grouped around a lectern holding a single book of this kind. The secular partbooks are smaller and are limited to no more than three or four performers at a time. This is without doubt the most convincing evidence that the vast repertory of fifteenth- and sixteenth-century secular music was designed as chamber music to be performed by one or possibly two musicians to a part.

The Use of Instruments

Two main schools of thought have developed concerning the appropriate use of instruments and voices in fifteenth- and sixteenth-century music. One group has attempted to adhere faithfully to findings of recent scholarship in this field, including the use of "old" (authentic) instruments, old forms of tuning, and the old manner of singing, while another has sought to adapt Renaissance music to the "modern" taste, resulting in either exclusive a cappella performances or the use of vast resources of singers and instrumentalists.

The influence of Palestrina's a cappella performances in the Sistine Chapel remains with us four hundred years later. This is evidenced by the lead Pope Pius X took by joining Gregory and Marcellus II in the tradition of great music-loving popes who stand out in the history of Church music. The conservation of the so-called "Palestrina style" as set forth in the *Motu proprio* (1903) was one of the primary reasons for the continuance of the a cappella ideal of polyphonic sacred choral performance in our century. The following quotation from this landmark document discloses the reason for present-day practices:

> With the exception of the melodies proper to the celebrant at the altar and to the ministers, which must always be sung in Gregorian chant and without accompaniment of the organ, all the rest of the liturgical chant belongs to the choir of levites, and therefore, singers in church, even when they are laymen, are really taking the place of the ecclesiastical choir. Hence the music rendered by them must, at least for the greatest part, retain the character of choral music.[4]

Perhaps the soundest approach in the use of instruments in choral performances is one that takes a middle ground between these two extremes: one that accepts the fact that a completely faithful and accurate reproduction of the original sound is simply not possible. In most cases the instruments are not available and the style of singing has changed so dramatically that exact reproductions are virtually impossible.

A second factor must also be considered: a distinction between vocal and instrumental music simply did not exist in the Renaissance. The present-day performer is trained to recognize a difference between the instrumental idiom and the vocal idiom, but this distinction is not valid in the music of the fifteenth and sixteenth centuries. Bukofzer reminds us that "the Renaissance knew only *music* . . . ; in this respect the Renaissance continued the medieval tradition, which spoke of '*musica instrumentalis*,' meaning all music made by a natural instrument (voice) or by an artificial instrument (instrument)."[5] The distinction between instrumental and vocal music was first clearly defined in polyphonic music in the late sixteenth and early seventeenth centuries with the introduction of the term *concerto*. It is in these later concerto compositions that a conscious and deliberate idiomatic vocal and instrumental style was first realized. The present-day performer of music from this period must recognize the fact that most Renaissance music can be performed as well by instruments as by voices.

A third consideration in the use of instruments in the performance of Renaissance music is acoustical. What circumstances surrounded the performance of this music in its original setting? Dart identifies three types of acoustical settings: *resonant, room,* and *outdoor*. Music composed for the cathedral or court chapel—plainsong, motets of the Notre Dame school, and the music of St. Mark's in Venice—might be considered resonant. The intricate rhythms and often dissonant harmonies in fourteenth-century music, the madrigals and chansons of the fifteenth and sixteenth centuries, and the Elizabethan music of the fourteenth to sixteenth centuries, can be thought of as room or chamber music. The music for brass instruments by composers such as Hassler and Locke, and the festive outdoor music that emanated from sixteenth-century Florence, can be considered outdoor music. Evidence that composers in early times were sensitive to the nuances of writing for special sonorities can be found in the records that have survived of musical festivities associated with the Medici family in Florence.

The festival associated with the wedding of Duke Cosimo I and Leonora of Toledo in 1539 included a variety of instrumental and vocal performances. The use of voices and instruments in sixteenth-century Florence can serve as a useful guide to us today. Notice the effective combinations that were used during this wedding celebration:

1. *Motet Ingredere*

The opening work of the festival, written for outdoor performance, was scored for outdoor instruments in the style of a large ceremonial motet. In eight parts, it was sung by twenty-four singers, acompanied by four *cornetti* and four *tromboni*. Doubling of this type (there were no separate instrumental parts) was a normal practice of the time. The range of the parts indicates two soprano cornetti, two tenor cornetti, two tenor trombones, and two bass trombones.

2. *Eight Madrigals*

The banquet included eight madrigals, with various instrumental accompaniments. The opening madrigal was scored for nine voices, each of which carried an instrument: *trombone* (small trombone), *dolzaina* (wind-capped instrument), *violone* (viol), *piffero* (treble shawm), *flauto* (recorder), *leuto* (lute), *storta* (krumhorn), *cornetto* (zink), or *ribechino* (violin-type instrument). There is a good chance that these instruments doubled the voice parts. The other seven madrigals, each of which represented a city or river under the possession of Cosimo I, were for four or five voices and were probably performed without accompaniment.

3. *Seven Intermedii*

Composed as incidental works for use at the wedding, the seven intermedii were written in the Italian madrigal style of the time. They are in four to six parts. While there are homophonic sections, the style is essentially contrapuntal. One of their most unusual features is the instrumental scoring:

Prologue—four-part madrigal (Dawn); soprano, harpsichord, and positive organ.

Intermedio I—six-part madrigal (Morning, Pastoral Scene); six male voices accompanied by krumhorns.

Intermedio II—six-part madrigal (Midmorning); six voices accompanied by three transverse flutes and three lutes.

Intermedio III—four-part madrigal (Noon); tenor accompanying himself on a gamba.

Intermedio IV—four-part madrigal; eight voices.

Intermedio V—five-part madrigal (Night); voice accompanied by four-trombones.

Finale—four-part madrigal sung and danced by eight characters accompanied by various instruments.

The wedding of Costanzo Sforza and Camilla of Aragon in 1475 was celebrated with a triumphal Mass with organs, flutes, trumpets, numerous tambourines, and two sixteen-voice choirs that performed in an antiphonal style.

It is from these contemporary accounts that we learn of the interesting combinations of instruments and voices that were a part of the musical performances of the time. Lowinsky writes of mass celebrations that include two alternating choirs, wood and brass instruments, and tambourines. Such sonorities indicate a "secular gaiety" in the Church and shed light on the bitter complaints about the profanation of Church music throughout the sixteenth century, which of course culminated in the strictures and regulations of the Council of Trent.

In the secular music of the time the viol was considered the ideal instrument for chamber music. The quartet of viols and the keyboard instruments of the day were considered standard equipment for every nobleman's entertainment program. The mixture of voices and instruments was appealing when the soloists were accompanied by the viol.

The size of a group and its layout on the concert stage or in the chancel are also important considerations in modern performances of Renaissance music. When polychoral music is performed—or music that uses both instrumental and vocal forces—the singers and instrumentalists must be separated sufficiently to insure the integrity of the separate lines. The best example of this type of performance setting is the chancel area in St. Mark's Basilica, Venice (see diagram of St. Mark's on page 190). The two or more groups of voices or instruments that performed the works of Willaert and the Gabrielis were placed in separate galleries that insured a clarity of the double chorus polyphony. Each group had its own conductor who also served as the continuo player in most cases. This distance between the two choirs enhanced the effect and produced a distinctive timbre in this extremely reverberant building.

Some of the best advice for the combined use of voices and instruments in sixteenth-century music is found in Praetorius's *Syntagma Musicum*. In this important treatise Praetorius offers some practical suggestions for anyone who wishes to add vitality to the performance of this music:

Orlando di Lasso (at spinet) and Bavarian court orchestra. (The Bettmann Archive)

1. Reinforce the bass line with a double bass or a contrabassoon. This will give body to the tone.

2. For the same reason, the inner parts may be doubled at the unison or upper octave by an instrument.

3. Try performing a madrigal once on voices, once on instruments, and finally on both in combination.

4. In a long choral work, let there be an extemporized organ prelude and postlude, and perhaps some interludes as well, or perhaps a pavanne or solemn madrigal played on the keyboard will do instead.

5. Experiment with sonorities in works that at first glance appear to be a cappella; thus for di Lasso's *Laudate pueri à 7*, try a combination of two flutes, violins or cornets, two altos, and three trombones. For his *In convertendo à 8:* three flutes (or three mute cornets; or a violin, a mute cornet, and flute or recorder; or a boy may sing the top line of all), and a tenor (doubled or replaced by a bassoon or a trombone) for one choir; and voices, viols, violins and cellos, or recorders (with a bassoon) for the other. For his *Quo properas à 10*, let each choir be composed of one of the following possibilities:

Cornet (or two flutes in unison), four trombones;

Voices;

Two violins, two violas, and a cello;

Two recorders, two trombones, and a bassoon.

6. Any of the top instrumental parts can be replaced by a voice. "Wert's *Egressus Jesus à 7* was once performed in my hearing by seven viols, two flutes, two boys, an alto, a violine, two theorbos, three lutes, four harpsichords and spinets, and two citterns, and it sounded very beautiful."[6]

These examples demonstrate the potential that exists for exciting and meaningful performances combining instruments and voices. Because this experimentation is possible without destroying the authenticity of this music, it is advisable that every choral conductor make an effort to secure those instruments that will enhance the experience of the choral singers. We would suggest the following:

1. Recorders—a set of four recorders (SATB)
2. Krumhorns—a set of four krumhorns (SATB)
3. Percussion instruments—finger cymbals, small tambourine, and tabor
4. Handbells—a set on these pitches: C G F A E D
5. Keyboard instruments—a harpsichord and a portative organ
6. Stringed instruments—include a viola da gamba if possible
7. Brass instruments—trumpets (cornets) and trombones for outdoor music
8. Wind instruments—include a flute for certain effects
9. Miscellaneous instruments—psalteries, rebecs, hurdy-gurdys

Such an assortment of instruments as this will lend excitement and interest to the study and performance of Renaissance music.

With these instruments to vitalize the performance of Renaissance choral music, we would suggest a few simple guidelines that can be applied when instruments and voices are used together in this music.

1. Because of their distinctive and soft timbre, recorders can be used effectively to double voice parts or to perform the vocal lines as an instrumental SATB quartet. For shorter works it is always effective to have the solo quartet play through the piece once, the choral group sing it a cappella, then double the voices with recorders on the third hearing. This use of the recorders adds a bright quality that sounds one octave higher than scored.

2. Krumhorns can be used in the same way, but they are much more difficult to play, especially for the inexperienced player. Doubling with krumhorns adds a solid unison support to the vocal sound. Do not, however, combine recorders and krumhorns in performance; they are incompatible. Krumhorns are more effective in homophonic textures—chorales, part songs, etc.—and when doubling the "cantus firmus" tenor in masses and motets.

3. Percussion instruments are effective in works containing a strong and predominant rhythmic character. The tabor, for instance, is a good basic pulse indicator; the tambourine should be used when light off-beats and accents are desired; and the finger cymbals are best used to highlight sections or longer phrases.

4. Handbells should be used sparingly in Renaissance music. They are most effective in highlighting cadences and phrases by playing the tonic and dominant scale degrees of the mode. They also are a fine harmonic pedal point for short pieces or sections that center around one tonality.

5. The harpsichord is almost essential for the authentic performance of music before 1600. The piano should be avoided as an accompaniment instrument if at all possible.

6. The portative organ is also an effective accompaniment instrument to be used with voices, because it can double the voice parts, replace a missing voice part, and serve the function of a recorder or krumhorn in completing an ensemble of these instruments.

For the conductor who has not previously experimented with the combined use of instruments and voices in music before 1600, we would suggest the following combinations as a starting point:

1. A relatively simple way of combining voices and instruments is to contrast choral sections with instrumental sections, or to contrast choral sections with vocal solo or instrumental sections. There is considerable latitude in this practice in the performance of Renaissance music.

2. Alternate a cappella sections in a polyphonic mass with sections sung by a solo quartet, or with sections with one solo voice and the other parts taken by instruments, or with one section of the choir taking one part and instruments performing the other parts.

3. Perform a double chorus work with the choral group singing as one choir with brass, recorders or strings as the other.

4. Substitute one movement of a polyphonic mass with an appropriate section from a monophonic plainchant mass.

5. Double the cantus firmus in a cantus firmus mass with different instruments. This produces the wonderful effect of reinforcing the formal structure of the work.

PROBLEMS OF NOTATION

The modern shape of notes appears to have been generally established about 1600. Yet the survival of earlier systems, such as tablatures, extends well into the seventeenth century. The scored page of the late sixteenth century contained little more than the notes proper. Tempo marks were rare; the tempo was still suggested to some degree by the time signatures.

The desired dynamic level in Renaissance music was very rarely prescribed; phrasing never. This is not surprising, for even more important things were left to the discretion of the performer, such as free improvisatory elaboration of the melody and the execution of ornaments. However, the performer was by no means left entirely on his own. Composer and performer were very closely related; music, as a rule, was written for special occasions or on local demand, and therefore for performers whose capacities and temperaments were well-known to the composer. More often than not the composer participated in the performance or conducted from the keyboard. Under such circumstances problems of interpretation could hardly arise. Moreover, at that time, and even well into the eighteenth century, only a small percentage of the music composed was printed, and the writing of copies was too slow and expensive a procedure to carry a work to a large number of performers outside the local circle of the composer.

The notational principles that prevailed in the Renaissance can be traced to the early fourteenth century. The primary difference between the notation of the *Ars Nova* and that of the period 1450–1600 was the change to white notation. This change occurred when scribes began to write notes that should have been red by using hollow black notes, thus saving themselves the trouble of looking for and using different inks and pens. When paper became cheaper, and subsequently of a poorer quality, less ink was used so that the paper would last longer. Thus to use hollow notation was the norm and filled-in notes for coloration was a more sensible procedure. The essential feature of coloration was that notes of the same shape but of different colors would have different values. This principle still survives to some extent in present day notation: the half note and quarter note have the same shape, but one is white and the other is black, and thus their time values are different.

This is obviously only one aspect of the interpretation of notation that must be considered in the interpretation of Renaissance choral music. The conductor must also be able to investigate the original score and determine the composer's intentions. This is a very complicated matter and must be approached with the greatest care. We would thus suggest the following basic principles in the interpretation of sixteenth-century notation:

1. The conductor must attempt to discover the exact symbols the composer used. One complex problem in this study is that different notational principles were used in different countries. For example, French music of the *Ars Nova* developed under the influence of Philippe de Vitry, who codified the rhythmic organization of the music of his time. Italian music of this period was influenced by the reforms of Petrus de Cruce. Over the years a highly complex system of rules and signs was evolved by the leading theorists, but space does not allow a full discussion of this subject here.

2. The conductor must determine the exact meaning of the symbols that were used. When duration is the problem in question, the context within which the symbol appears must be examined. The duration may be affected by the kind of note that precedes or follows it, or by a dot placed before or after it. This problem is discussed in the next section.

3. The conductor must make his determinations in relation to the time in which he lives. We are making music in the twentieth century, not the sixteenth; thus we must edit and interpret music in a manner that will make sense in present-day performance.

While it is sometimes difficult to determine which aspects of notation should be the responsibility of the conductor, all of them are important. Thus the careful choral conductor must become knowledgeable about notation. The performer of the sixteenth century was required to interpret the music from the manuscript. Dart reminds us that the "further we go back in musical history, the rarer such markings become and the more trust was evidently placed in a performer's training, his sense of tradition, and his innate musicianship."[7]

The Interpretation of Pitch Notation

Another important consideration in Renaissance notation involves chromatic tones —those that are not contained in the diatonic gamut prescribed by the so-called Guidonian hand.[8] The use of B flat was adopted very early in the performance of Gregorian chant, and in theory as well, through Guido's hexachords. The introduction of additional chromatic tones became necessary for two reasons: first, the church modes became modified melodically, and secondly, they were transposed. Thus a C sharp could occur as an artificial leading tone in the Dorian mode, or as the normal third degree of the Mixolydian scale beginning on A rather than G. References to this *musica falsa* are found in the writings of Odo of Cluny (d. 942), a predecessor of Guido, and later (c. 1325) in a statement by Philippe de Vitry. De Vitry wrote that *musica falsa* is "not false, but true and necessary for musical instruments, and especially in *organa*," which refers, according to Johannes de

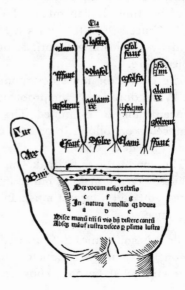

Guidonian hand (The New York Public Library Picture Collection)

Garlandia (middle or late 13th century), *"ad omnem mensurabilem musicam"*—to all rhythmic polyphonic music. It was during this period that the term *musica ficta* supplanted the older term, which was objectionable because of its implied falseness.

Problems for modern performers arise because of the very scarce indications of chromatic tones in music sources prior to 1600. There is a striking incongruity between the theoretical and the musical sources of the Medieval and Renaissance periods. For example, there are numerous long and important compositions throughout the sixteenth century without any indications for accidentals whatsoever.

Prior to 1450 the manuscripts contain sufficient indications of accidentals. Because of the limited tonal resources of this polyphonic music (the harmonies are clearly modal), few accidentals were needed except for a B flat which frequently occurs as a signature in one of the lower parts. Manuscripts of the fourteenth century begin to show a marked increase of notated accidentals, in accordance with the development system of harmonies and "keys." Still, modern editors are obliged to aid the performer where such indications were thought too obvious by the early composers. There are a few relatively simple rules that can be applied to the addition of accidentals in Renaissance choral music. Those which require the editor to raise the note one-half step are listed below.

1. When the seventh degree of the scale is moving to the tonic, it must be raised one half-step to establish the interval of the major sixth with the second degree of the scale below.

2. When the rising sixth is involved, it must be raised one half-step to avoid the interval of the diminishing fifth.

3. When the shape of the melodic line creates the possibility of an augmented fourth, the note must be raised to avoid a tritone.

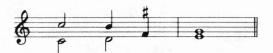

There are also occasions when a note must be lowered one half-step. Two such examples are shown below.

1. When the melodic line establishes the possibility of an augmented fourth, the note must be lowered one half-step to avoid the tritone.

2. When the vertical structure of the harmony creates a diminished fifth chord in the melodic note, the note below must be lowered one half-step to create the interval of a perfect fifth.

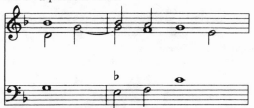

With the rise of the Flemish school of composers (c. 1450) comes a striking change in that accidentals now disappear almost completely from the sources. This may suggest a return to the church modes as the basis of polyphonic writing, since it may be noticed that there is a decided return to sacred forms in this period. As late as 1550, Glareanus discusses the tonality of numerous compositions by Josquin, Isaac, and others, without ever mentioning the possibility of raised sevenths.

In general, composers of this period did in fact favor diatonic progressions, and their music contains few accidentals. However, it is quite evident that numerous pitch alterations are necessary to prevent the occurrence of forbidden inter-

vals. A motet by Clemens non Papa, *Fremuit spiritu Jhesu,* has been used by some
writers to support the claim that the elaborate chromaticism, which was produced
by the application of *musica ficta* to music seemingly lacking accidentals, had to be
kept secret for religio-political reasons. Lowinsky has presented this viewpoint at
some length in his book *Secret Chromatic Art in the Netherlands Motet* (New York:
Columbia University Press, 1946). Some other writers disagree with this explanation, but regardless of whether secrecy was involved, it does seem that chromati-

Clemens non Papa, "Fremuit spiritu Jhesu." Part I, meas. 62–74

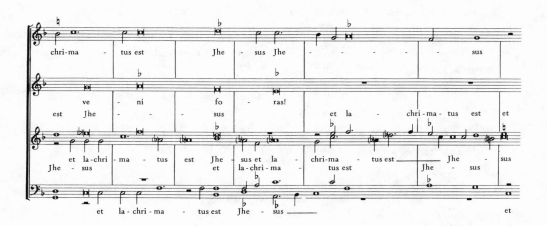

cism was implied in many works of this period. A possible solution for one section of the Clemens motet appears on page 347. The editorial accidentals appear above the affected notes, as the general practice for distinguishing the composer's manuscript suggests. If such interpretations were the intention of the Flemish composers of the Renaissance, then the implicit chromaticism in these compositions would make the once supposed progressive chromaticism of works such as the *Prophetiae Sibyllarum* of Orlando di Lasso seem commonplace.

Pitch Levels in the Renaissance

The relationship of pitch notation in the fifteenth and sixteenth centuries to pitch standards of our day is another performance problem that the conductor of Renaissance music must consider. Contemporary writings on this subject are confusing. Pietro Aaron states early in the sixteenth century in his *Toscanello in Musica:* "You must first consider the string or degree called C, giving it whatever pitch you please."[9] Praetorius adds to the confusion by describing two standards of pitch in the late sixteenth century. He called these two types of pitch "choir" and "chamber":

> Choir Pitch. At the beginning of the seventeenth century the choir pitch customary in church use was a whole tone lower than chamber pitch.
> Chamber Pitch. In the sixteenth and seventeenth centuries [pitch] seems to have been very high in Germany, as appears from the pitch of old organs, which are about a whole tone higher than our chamber pitch.[10]

A little over one hundred years later (1713) Mattheson, the important German Baroque composer, records that there is still not a standard of pitch upon which musicians of the day can agree:

> Now whether or why this or that tone is called *a* or *b*, chamber, choir, or opera pitch—this is a matter of no basic importance.[11]

The lack of consistency regarding the tuning of organs also contributed to this confusion. Writing in 1783 Jacob Adlung points out the problem:

> Whence do we take the beginning of our tuning, or how do we determine the depth of C? It is well known that organs do not agree, so that the musician must always carry with him, in addition to his trumpet, several crooks or inserts if he is to play in various churches. One wishes not

without reason that organ builders were agreed in this matter, and that they would have a certain rule which would enable them to arrive at the same depth and height. But this is lacking, up to now.[12]

These references establish rather conclusively that the pitch that the present-day performer finds on the printed page may or may not be the same as it was in an earlier period. To the performer before 1750, the notes of the staff, and the names by which they were known, represented degrees in a gamut that had no permanent anchor at a standard pitch level. They were moved quite freely up and down according to the nature of the voices or instruments that performed on any given occasion.

Praetorius writes extensively about pitch in his treatise *Syntagma Musicum*. He discusses many pitches and defines them mostly in terms of the pitch that prevailed in the North German church organs of the late sixteenth and early seventeenth centuries. He calls this pitch "chamber pitch," and although this pitch was commonly referred to in his time as "choir pitch," he prefers to reserve that term for the pitch a tone lower.

Arthur Mendel has summarized the existing writings on the subject in the following table.[13] Note that these approximate pitches are listed in relation to A = 440.

SOURCE	PRESENT-DAY "A"	APPROXIMATE DIFFERENCE FROM A = 440
Schlick (recommended pitch)	C – C♯	+ 3.4
Schlick (alternative pitch)	F – F♯	– 3.4
Praetorius (chamber pitch)	C – C♯	+ 3.4
Praetorius (pitch recommended for church organs); actual pitch of Frederiksborg organ, built 1610	B – B	+ 1.2
Pitch in use in Praetorius's time in the Netherlands, Italy, and many Catholic courts of Germany; and earlier in England; used by the Flemish harpsichord maker Bossus	A – B	+ 0.1
Pitch used in Prague and some other Catholic choirs, there being called "choir pitch"	B – B	+ 1.2

Pitch said by Praetorius to have been used in old organs for plainsong	F — F or F — F♯	— 3.4 or + 8.9
Pitch of Halberstadt organ, according to Praetorius	D — E	+ 5.7
Pitch of St. Blasius in Nordhausen, according to Praetorius	D — E	+ 5.6

In summary then, there are certain generalizations that can be made about Renaissance pitch:

1. The exact pitch of music composed before the second half of the nineteenth century cannot be determined with any accuracy because pitch varied greatly from town to town, and even from church to church.

2. The pitch of secular music probably was even less consistent than church music because it did not have the organ to serve as the basis for establishing a constant pitch.

3. The precise pitch of any individual church cannot be determined from the available data. Because the tuning fork was not invented until 1711, all vibration frequencies cited for periods before 1700 are at best rough approximations and should be labeled "plus or minus a semitone or more."

4. The pitch that any individual composer had in mind when he composed choral music can be determined by a careful study of the range of his compositions. However, there is evidence to show that a composer's secular music may have been intended at a different pitch from his sacred music.

5. When transcribing or editing choral music written during this period, the editor can be flexible and should feel free to place the music in the tonal center that sounds the best for voices.

6. The conductor should experiment with the pitch of a given composition and not feel "duty-bound" to adhere rigidly to the advice of the editor.

The Interpretation of Rhythmic Notation

Three standard notational systems existed between the ninth and sixteenth centuries:

9th – 13th Century	14th Century	c. 1450–1600*
Double long (‖ooo‖)	Maxima (‖ooo‖)	Maxima (‖oo‖)
Long (‖oo‖)	Long (‖oo‖)	Longa (‖o‖)
Breve (‖o‖)	Breve (‖o‖)	Breve (o or o·)
Semi-breve (o)	Semi-breve (o)	Semi-breve (o or o·)
---	Minima ( )	Minima ( )
---	Semi-minima ( )	Semi-minima ( )
---	Fusa ( )	Fusa ( )
---	Semi-fusa ( ) ; perfect prolation	Semi-fusa ( )

* Depends on Mensuration

The system of rhythmic notation that we use today originated in the Renaissance as a means of indicating the duration allotted to each note value in proportion to the others within a given work. The name given to this system was proportional notation. A system was necessary because the proportions were variable. Today we enjoy a consistent notational proportion of one to two between each successive note value: one whole note equals two half notes (○ = ♩ ♩), one half equals two quarters (♩ = ♩ ♩), and so on. In the notation of the Renaissance, one *longa* could equal two or three *breves*: ⊓ = ■ ■ or ■ ■ ■ one *breve* could equal either two or three *semibreves*: ■ = ◆ ◆ or ◆ ◆ ◆ or one *semibreve* could equal either two or three *minims*: ◆ = ◆ ◆ or ◆ ◆ ◆ However, one similarity did exist between sixteenth-century and present-day rhythmic notation: all values smaller than the minim were in double proportion.

Proportional notation had its roots in the system of rhythmic notation codified by Philippe de Vitry in the treatise *Ars Nova* (c. 1320). As the first musician to describe duple meter as of equal rank with triple meter, de Vitry presented a thorough explanation of both binary and ternary mensuration and introduced a system of time signatures that provided the basis for our modern-day rhythmic notation. The principles of this system, based on what came to be called "the four prolations" (equivalent in a way, to our $\frac{9}{8}$, $\frac{6}{8}$, $\frac{3}{4}$, $\frac{2}{4}$), remained in use well into the Renaissance. One of his time signatures, the C, has survived to the present day, although its meaning has changed over the years.

What is actually new in the rhythm of the *Ars Nova* is a recognition of the *modus imperfectum* (longa equals two breves) and the *tempus imperfectum* (brevis equals two semibreves) and the idea of the four prolations: *Modus* (major), *Modus* (minor), *Tempus*, and *Prolatio*. The relationship of the *maxima* to the *longa* was known as *Modus* (major), a term also used for "time-signature" itself. This relationship was either perfect (a triple metric scheme) or imperfect (duple). The same principles apply to the *Modus* (minor)—*longa* to *brevis*; *Tempus*—*brevis* to *semibrevis*; and *Prolatio*—*semibrevis* to *minima*. During the period 1450–1600 the modus gradually disappeared from use as time values became smaller. The essence of de Vitry's system is illustrated below:

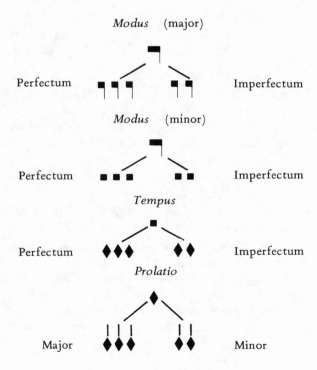

By 1600 the signs and symbols of proportional notation were somewhat standardized into a system as shown below:

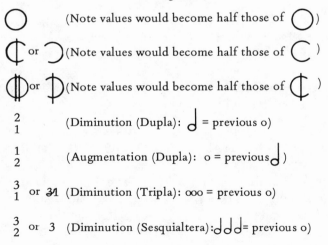

Time Signature	Term	Perfect	Imperfect	Symbol
☉ or ⊡	=Modus (maj.)	╗╗╗ (ooo)	╗╗ (oo)	= ╗ Maxima
ℭ or ⊡	=Modus (min.)	■■■ (o·)	■■ (o)	= ▌ Longa
○	=Tempus	♦♦♦ (𝅗𝅥·)	♦♦ (𝅗𝅥)	= ▢ Brevis
ℭ	=Prolatio	♦♦♦ (♩·)	♦♦ (♩)	= ◇ Semibrevis

There were, of course, variations to this practice, especially where diminution and augmentation were required, but the system included these elements.

Time Signature

○   (Note values would become half those of ○)

₵ or ⊃ (Note values would become half those of ℭ)

⦶ or ⊅ (Note values would become half those of ₵)

$\frac{2}{1}$ (Diminution (Dupla): 𝅗𝅥 = previous o)

$\frac{1}{2}$ (Augmentation (Dupla): o = previous 𝅗𝅥)

$\frac{3}{1}$ or 3ᴵ (Diminution (Tripla): ooo = previous o)

$\frac{3}{2}$ or 3 (Diminution (Sesquialtera): 𝅗𝅥𝅗𝅥𝅗𝅥= previous o)

For the purpose of transcribing or editing music into modern notation, it is probably advisable not to use the exact equivalents but smaller note values that more properly conform with the actual temporal duration of the old symbols. A reduction in value of 1:4 is suggested, so that the semibrevis is actually transcribed as a quarter note.

	Brevis	Semibrevis	Minima	Semi-minima
Renaissance Symbol:	☐ (∞)	◊ (○)	◊ (♩)	♦
Suggested Transcription:	𝅗𝅥	♩	♪	♫

Thus it was the theorists of the fourteenth century who freed the composer from the bondage of the five rhythmic modes in ternary meter. Not only is a new metric scheme admitted—duple meter—but a rhythmic notation is introduced that is based on the principle of the repeated mathematic multiplication of 2 or of 3 by itself. This simple yet ingenious mathematical mensuration of rhythm opens the way for the vast development of rhythmic and polyrhythmic figurations and suddenly allows the possibility for a whole array of smaller note values and an entirely unprecedented variety and contrast of rhythmic figures.

Although these almost limitless mathematical possibilities existed, their full potential was not realized until much later. The medieval theorist imposed severe restrictions on rhythmic creativity. The result was an organization of the rhythmic element called *isorhythm*, in which an entirely arbitrary sequence of rhythms would return again and again throughout the composition. It was not until the first half of the fifteenth century that isorhythmic organization was finally replaced by an entirely free rhythmic invention based on proportions.

ORNAMENTATION AND IMPROVISATION

The practice of ornamenting or improvising during a performance is as old as the art of music itself. Praetorius believed that the Psalms of David were originally sung in an improvised manner. The "spiritual songs" of the first-century church were probably sung extemporaneously. In plainchant, the *jubilus*, an extravagant vocalise sung on the last syllable of Alleluia, was referred to by St. Augustine as a "free pouring forth, on the spur of the moment." This spontaneous element in musical performance is evident in all phases of music history, but its use in the Renaissance was so widespread and so much a part of the performance tradition of the period that its practice in present-day readings of this music is essential if there is to be any attempt at authenticity.

The sixteenth-century quartet—vocal or instrumental, professional or amateur—prided themselves on the skill with which they could elaborate a madrigal, motet, or fantasy. For example, a performance of Palestrina's music in an important church or chapel in the sixteenth century probably bore very little resemblance to the score as it is printed today. The existing treatises of the period suggest that we obtain a false impression of sixteenth-century polyphony if we merely reproduce this music as the symbols on the score seem to demand. As we have noted, these early manuscripts present little, if any, information regarding tempo, phrasing, articulation, and performing forces. But further, and more importantly, they do not indicate the notes which a skilled performer of the time would have employed to fill in the structural outlines given by the composer.

The processes of such elaboration were called by various names. In Italy the changing of a simple contrapuntal original to a highly ornate version was called *diminutio*. The Germans used the term *sortisatio* (counterpoint), taken from the Latin *sortitio* (the casting of lots), thus "music by chance," or improvised music. Morley used the term *descant* to differentiate this practice from *pricksong* (written composition). Thus ornamentation in the choral music of the fifteenth and sixteenth centuries occurred in two manners, either by a prearranged plan or by extemporaneous performance.

It is thus the responsibility of the present-day choral conductor to try to re-create Renaissance music through the use of both written and improvisatory ornamentation. Since the art of ornamentation is not natural to modern performers, the conductor must write in passing tones and ornaments according to rules such as those presented below. Even in the Renaissance, composers wrote out ornaments to their own works, or for the works of contemporaries. The madrigal *Signor mio caro* by Cipriano de Rore, for example, is a work to which later composers (Nicolo Dalla Casa, Giovanni Battista Bassano, and Giovanni Bassani) have added diminutions for the *cantus* part. Bassani has added a special part for the *viola bastarda,* a viol between the size of the bass and tenor viols.

Improvisatory ornamentation takes place when the performers simply agree, before the performance, to add passing tones or other ornaments at specified points in the composition. Training in extemporaneous ornamentation was an integral part of the schooling of choral singers of the sixteenth century. Since this training is not available today, the conductor or singer who wishes to become fluent in the art of ornamentation must first become acquainted with the many practices and suggestions described and offered by musicians of the period, and then experiment, always seeking the solutions that make the best sense musically.

Our knowledge of the ornamental adaptation of vocal music is found in a great number of books on improvised and written embellishment. Among these are treatises by Giovanni Baptiste Ganassi, Diego Ortiz, Hermann Finck, Giovanni Bassano, and Lodovico Zacconi.[14] A summary of the instructions or rules found in these works of the sixteenth century follows.

1. The emphasis should rest almost entirely on the contrapuntal behavior of each melodic line and scarcely at all on the idiomatic behavior of the medium chosen to convey it. Ganassi states that the "diminution is nothing but an ornament of the counterpoint." This is a significant statement because it implies that the chief places for ornaments were the cadences and sustained notes.

More explicit for the singer are the suggestions offered in the introduction to Ortiz' *Tratado de glosas sobre clausulas* (1553),[15] where he gives the following advice to viol players:

> The first and most perfect way is that after having made the diminution or variation on a given note, before passing on to the following note, the last note of the embellishment should be the same given note that was varied, as these examples show—

Ortiz believed this was the best way because it began and ended the improvisation on the note that was being embellished, and proceeded by a diatonic step, which was the practice in the performance of chant.

> The second way is a little more ambitious and freer for the performer. Here the last note is not the same as the note which is being ornamented . . . because at the time of the change from one note to another, it does not progress as in the plain notes, but on the contrary as these examples show—

This type of improvisation was preferred by Ortiz in situations where a little variety was desired.

There was still another manner of improvisation that Ortiz recommended for the more gifted performer:

> The third way is to depart from the composition and play by ear, or with little difference, without any certainty of what one is doing. Some use this, for since they have a little ability they wish to practice.

Indeed when more experience is gained, the performer becomes more adept at locating those passages where freer spontaneous embellishment may occur. The following de Rore madrigal is an example of a work to which various composers have added improvisations which are representative of all three types mentioned above.

Besides ornamentation occurring between two scale steps or melodic leaps, the cadences received the most extended elaborate embellishment. Ortiz provided a series of possible solutions for ornamenting a typical cadential pattern:

In the de Rore madrigal, one may see that each composer has heavily ornamented the cadential points that occur at textual breaks as well as where all four voice parts are performing.

2. Ornaments should be vocal or instrumental. Although the earliest books on ornamentation were written for instruments (recorders and viols), the authors believe that ornaments are also suitable for the voice. As we know, much of this music was suitable for either instruments or voices, or both, and the choice of medium was characteristically left by Renaissance composers to their performer's tastes. Obviously, diminutions involving very small notes (sixteenth or thirty-second notes) are more appropriate for instruments that can articulate them at the proper speed.

3. Ornaments should not occur in two parts at the same time. A single part was allowed to perform in ornamentation against other, unornamenting parts. Several parts were allowed to perform in ornamentation by prearranged order, this often was prescribed by the fact that individual voices (in imitative compositions) cadence alternately, seldom all at once. On rare occasions, more than one part would ornament at a time, but care was taken by the individual performer to prevent dissonances from coinciding with the tactus. However, dissonances occasioned by quick-passing notes between pulses were allowed.

Ornamented passages were alternated with unornamented passages, thus leaving enough room for brilliant improvisatory elaborations. Such a plan is illustrated on page 359 in the de Rore madrigal *A la dolc' ombra*.

4. While the soprano seems the most likely part for ornamentation, one finds many compositions, such as the de Rore piece, in which diminution is appropriate in all parts. The bass is probably the least often ornamented part since it must remain the foundation of the composition and the support of the harmonic structure.

5. Ornaments should be performed expressively, so as to be natural and unforced within the context of the piece. They should be used sparingly and in good taste. If a suggested ornamentation does not sound right, it should be replaced by one of the singer's own making.

6. Ornaments were to be avoided at the beginning of a piece. The place of greatest usage would be near the end of the composition.

7. Ornamentation should not be restricted exclusively to chamber groups where each part is entrusted to a soloist, but should also be cultivated in choral groups as well. The most common feature of sixteenth-century ornamentation is

A la dolc' ombra

Cipriano de Rore (1516–1565)

that it affects the individual linear progressions but not the harmony, with the result that it can be performed simultaneously with the original. A section-leader can often perform the ornamented version while the other singers maintain the unornamented version. Of course, some dissonance is to be expected with this procedure.

8. While chansons and madrigals are the most popular type of music for embellishment, the practice occurs in sacred music as well. The sacred polyphonic masses and motets of the Renaissance are as appropriate for ornamentation as the eighteenth-century opera aria.

The ornaments commonly associated with the Baroque era—the trill, mordent, turn, and appoggiatura—can be observed in the above examples. All received their impetus from this "experimental" Renaissance music. By recognizing certain melodic indicators that are evident both in Baroque as well as Renaissance music, the modern performer is aided in deciding the appropriate places for ornamentation.

INTERPRETATION OF TEMPO

The solution to the problem of determining the right tempo in choral music of the fifteenth and sixteenth centuries is complicated by the lack of clear direction in the score. Since few tempo markings are found in this music,[16] it must be assumed that the performers knew the tradition of the time and thus sang accordingly. The importance that the sixteenth-century composer attached to the selection of correct tempi can hardly be overrated. There are repeated attempts at fixing a basic tempo, many of which make conflicting statements concerning the establishment of tempi for various musical forms.

Later writers like Praetorius and Quantz are also vague in their attempts to clarify this elusive topic.

C is slow and C is fast, but look at the music to discover exactly how slow or how fast it should be. Choral music should be much slower than other music; if a song or an anthem is hurried it becomes confused and meaningless. Let there be a gentle rallentando at the end of a piece. Quarter note = 80 is a good average sort of speed; *Piano* may mean slow as well as soft. If trumpets are being used in the piece, let the tempo slacken slightly when they are playing and gather a little speed when they are silent.— PRAETORIUS, *Syntagma Musicum* (1615–1619)

The sense of the words should be taken into account, the movement of the notes, especially the fastest, and in quick arias the skill and the voice of the singer. A singer who pushes his quick passages with his chest can scarcely take them as fast as one who only sings them from his throat, though the first will always excel the second in clarity. . . . It is the same with church music as it is with arias, except that both expression and tempo should be more restrained than in opera, to show respect for the sacredness of the place.—QUANTZ, *Versuch einer Anweisung die Flöte traversiere zu spielen* (1752)

While these accounts are interesting they hardly give us the specific help we need in present-day performances. Even Quantz, writing in the middle of the eighteenth century, presents only generalities not specific directions. It is obvious, therefore, that we will need to search more deeply to find the solution to our problem.

There is considerable evidence to support the theory that the notational signs in music prior to 1600 indicated not only relative values—as do the notes of modern notation—but also signified absolute temporal durations. This fact illustrates a basic difference between this system and the modern system, in which the duration of a given note may vary in tempo from several seconds in a very slow work to fractions of a second in a fast piece. The assumption that the modern principle of unlimited variability of tempo is a recent phenomenon can be supported by a study of the practice of the seventeenth and eighteenth centuries in which the spread of tempo variation is considerably narrower, and in which the rather rare use of tempo marks points strongly to the existence of normal tempi from which only moderate deviations were permitted. We may conclude from this that in the period before 1600 extensive variability of tempo was practically unknown.

Further evidence in support of the principle of tempo stability is found in the fifteenth- and sixteenth-century theory of proportions, which is essentially based upon the idea of a fundamental and unchangeable unit of time, the *tactus*. To the singer of this period the time signature ☉ (*proportia tripla*) meant a definite and fixed tempo, derived from the *integer valor* (the normal value of the note—

brevis, semibrevis—as distinguished from the reduced or enlarged values caused by the proportion), and familiar through long training in a normal tempo that represented the natural pulse of the music.

Another source of evidence is the body of theoretical treatises of the sixteenth century. Nearly every theorist who writes about the musical practices of the period deals with the tactus as the basic unit of musical time; and, while the problem of tempo is not completely solved in these treatises, the writings are consistent in that nowhere is evidence to be found which would support the assumption that the duration of a note could be varied according to the text, the character or feeling of the piece, or the emotions of the performer.

In the sixteenth century the means of varying the tempo of a piece was done simply by changing the temporal duration of a given note, or in other words, by proportions. Thus the time signature, the proportional sign, became the tempo mark, or in present-day language, the metronomic marking of the music of the fifteenth and sixteenth centuries. The fundamental conception of the tactus as the basic pulse of music of this period helps to explain why the conductor did not become an essential force in musical performance until the nineteenth century. It is now generally agreed by writers on Renaissance music that the simple motions used by the time-beater in this period were vertical. Based on the idea of a mathematically controlled tempo, the term *tactus* (Eng. *time* or *stroke*) first appeared in Ramis de Pareia's treatise *De Musica* (1482), and was used to mean a unit consisting of a downbeat and an upbeat.

Another detailed description of the tactus dates from 1565 and may be found in the *Libro llamado de tenor fantasia* by the Spanish organist and Dominican monk Fray Tomas de Santa Maria (d. 1580). The keypoints are as follows:

1. The tactus was divided into two parts.

2. His advice to the student to "mark the beat with the foot" would appear to indicate that audibility of the beat was a desired characteristic in sixteenth-century performance.

3. Both the downbeat and the upbeat were beaten alike, and the agogic accent on the downbeat that developed later was unknown. "Both beats should be made evenly."[17]

The following table illustrates the principle by which the semibrevis was chosen to receive the time value designated by the tactus.

	M	L	B	SB	M	SM four to one stroke	F eight to one stroke	SF sixteen to one stroke
⊙ 3	21	9	3	1				
3	21	9	3	1	½			
3	12	6	3	1	½			
	12	6	2	1				
	12	6	2	1				
	8	4	2	1				
	12	6	3	1	½			
	8	4	2	1	½			

—Ornithoparcus, *Micrologus* (1517)[18]

The indications concerning the duration of the tactus as they appear in various treatises of the period are not especially clear. On the basis of evidence which is presented in the chart on page 364, the speed of the tactus has been estimated by such modern authorities as Reese and Sachs at approximately 60 to 80 semibreves per minute; Willi Apel has described a slower tactus, one with a speed of 48 to 60 semibreves per minute. The performer will find that this slower tempo is appropriate for the major portion of the choral music of the Renaissance, which is practically always written in brevis, semibrevis, minima, semiminima, and fusa, the latter used only in groups of two as a quick cadential mordent. The conductor should also do some experimentation in this area.

One other factor should be mentioned in passing: the effect of ornamentation on the tempo of a Renaissance choral work. The extent of ornamentation used in a composition will obviously slow the performance. This may be one of the factors that have led musicologists in recent years to conclude that fifteenth- and sixteenth-century tempos were much slower than modern-day performances without ornamentation.

PHRASING, ARTICULATION, AND DYNAMICS

In most choral music of the Renaissance the phrasing and articulation are left almost completely to the performer. This does not mean that the composer considered distinctive phrasing of less importance. On the contrary, the breaking up of a

	Apel	Bessler	Sachs	Dart
c. 1200 Perotin	♩. = 80	♩· = 80	♩· = 80	
c. 1250 Franco	♩· = 40 ■ = 120	♩· = 44 ■ = 132	♩· = 44	■ = 120
c. 1280 Cruce	♩ = 27 ■· = 80 ♦ = 240	■· = 54 ♦ = 162	■· = 54	■· = 80
c. 1315 early De Vitry	■· = 40 ■ = 80 ♦ = 120	■· = 40 ■ = 60 ♦ = 120		
c. 1325 De Vitry	■ = 40 ♦ = 120 ♦ = 360	■ = 42 ♦· = 84	♦· = 84	♦ = 120
c. 1350 Machaut	■· = 27 ♦ = 80 ♦ = 240	■ = 40 ♦· = 80	♦ = 60	♦ = 80
c. 1400 Tapissier	♦· = 48–60	♦· = 50 ♦ = 150	♦· = 66	♦·= 50 (O or C) = 100 ($\varnothing$ or $\mathbb{C}$) = 70(C_2^3) = 140 (C3 or C_2^3)

melodic line by articulation and punctuation is even more necessary than in music of later styles, though probably less emphatic, because of the demand for clarity of texture. The absence of markings to guide the performer in phrasing is merely one other aspect of a policy of entrusting as much of the interpretation as possible to the individual singer.

The composers of the period often supervised their own performances and the singers were expected to interpret their parts according to their knowledge of the performance practices of the time. It was a rare occasion when a composer was not present to rehearse the singers and instrumentalists prior to a performance. Consequently, the fewer the markings, the greater is the performer's responsibility for an intuitive understanding of the style and for a singing approach that emphasizes clarity and distinctiveness.

There are also very few directions given that can guide the conductor in the interpretation of the dynamic contour of fifteenth- and sixteenth-century music. Composers gradually began to indicate specific instructions in their music, but rarely do these indications appear before 1600. For example, Giovanni Gabrieli provides explicit indications for dynamics in the famous *Sonata pian' e forte*, where the echo effects are clearly prescribed. This is one of the earliest instances of dynamic markings in the history of music. Giulio Caccini, in the preface to his *Nuove musiche* (1602), presents a comprehensive terminology for dynamic shadings of the voice. His *esclamazione viva, esclamazione languida, messe di voce*, and combinations of these correspond to the modern symbols $<$, $<$ $>$, $<$, or $<$ $>$. Praetorius, writing in *Syntagma musicum*, mentions the indications *forte* and *piano* as customary terms for the music of his time. In English choral music around 1600, directions such as *loud, soft, louder, softer by degrees* were used by the composers of the time.

Since these indications do not appear in the choral music prior to 1600, the present-day conductor will need to consider other factors in his interpretation of this music: (1) the purpose of the performance (church music, room music, or outdoor music); (2) the dynamic possibilities of the instruments that are used; (3) the density of the musical texture; and (4) the mood of the text.

SUMMARY

The two striking characteristics of the music of the Renaissance were freedom and curiosity. No longer willing to be bound by strict liturgical texts, by the tonal limitations of chant, or by the rhythmic modes, the composer during the period 1450–1600 exhibited a new curiosity that resulted in new forms, new styles, new texts, new instruments, and new compositional techniques. This new freedom paved the way for performances combining voices and instruments and eventually led to the emancipation of instrumental music from its dependence upon the choral art. The implication for the modern day performer is an approach to this music that is characterized by lively performances and continuous experimentation.

NOTES

1. Thurston Dart, *The Interpretation of Music* (New York: Harper Colophon Books, 1963), p. 168.

2. Edward E. Lowinsky, "Music in the Culture of the Renaissance," *Journal of the History of Ideas*, 15 (1954), p. 553.

3. Dart, op. cit., p. 52.

4. *Motu Proprio* (Rome, 1903).

5. Manfred Bukofzer, "On the Performance of Renaissance Music," *MTNA Proceedings*, 36 (1941), p. 227.

6. Michael Praetorius, *Syntagma Musicum III*, translated by Hans Lampl (Unpublished D.M.A. dissertation, University of Southern California, 1957), pp. 260–270.

7. Dart, op. cit., p. 14.

8. The "Guidonian hand" was essentially a teaching device to transmit a correct understanding of the hexachord and to aid in solminization.

9. Pietro Aaron, *Libro Secondo* (Venice, 1539).

10. Praetorius, op. cit.

11. Johann Mattheson, *Das Neu-eröffnete Orchestre* (Hamburg, 1713), p. 74.

12. Jacob Adlung, *Anleitung zur musikalischen Gelahrtheit* (Dresden and Leipzig, 1783), p. 373.

13. Arthur Mendel, "Pitch in the 16th and Early 17th Centuries," Part II, *Musical Quarterly*, 34 (1948), p. 221.

14. The writings of Ganassi, Ortiz, and Bassano refer primarily to instrumental ornamentation; while those of Finck and Zacconi are directed substantially to vocal ornamentation.

15. Diego Ortiz, *Tratado de glosas sobre clausulas y ostros generos du puntos en la musica do diolones*, Book I, translated by Max Schneider (Basel: Barenreiter, 1936), pp. 8–9.

16. It is believed that the earliest tempo markings appear in the lute pieces of Luis de Milan (*El maestro*, 1536).

17. Fray Tomas de Santa Maria, *Libro llamado de tenor fantasia* (Valladolid: Impresso por F. Fernandez de Cordova, 1565).

18. Andreas Ornithoparcus, *His Micrologus of Introduction: Containing the Art of Singing*, translated by John Dowland (London: Thomas Adams, 1609).

Chapter Eleven
RECOMMENDED READING LIST

Bukofzer, Manfred. *Studies in Medieval and Renaissance Music.* New York: W. W. Norton and Co., Inc. 1950. A scholarly study of medieval and Renaissance music, composers, and social factors which shaped the art of the period.

Crocker, Richard L. *A History of Musical Style.* New York: McGraw-Hill Book Company, 1966. An insightful study emphasizing musical style rather than historical facts and emphasizing those periods, schools, composers that contributed significantly to stylistic changes rather than concentrating on the well-known masterpieces.

Dart, Thurston. *The Interpretation of Music.* New York: Harper & Row, 1963. Probably the most concise and respected performance guide to music before 1800.

Donington, Robert. *The Interpretation of Early Music.* London: Faber and Faber, 1963. The most thorough study in performance practice available.

Reese, Gustav. *Music in the Renaissance.* New York: W. W. Norton and Co., Inc., 1954. A scholarly study of Renaissance composers, compositions, styles, and sources.

Chapter Twelve

The Baroque Period

. . . baroque music has ceased to be merely a historical issue.
It has become a living force in the music of our day.
—MANFRED F. BUKOFZER[1]

OF THE MANY CHARACTERISTICS that could be identified with the Baroque period, perhaps the most significant would be variety or contrast. These characteristics are manifested not only in the strong sense of contrast between movements of individual works, but on the larger scale of differences in national styles, functional purposes, and chronological periods within the boundaries of the Baroque era. These differences contribute to the fascination and vitality of Baroque music, but at the same time they compound enormously the difficulty of determining authentic performance practices.

GENERAL CHARACTER AND STRUCTURE

Although there were characteristic national schools in Germany, England, Spain and other countries during the Baroque era, the most vividly differentiated and stylistically influential national schools were in Italy and France. Italian music is described in Baroque sources in such terms as passionate, impetuous, affecting, unrestrained, harsh, and eccentric; French music, in contrast, is described as smooth, easy, soft, flowing, restrained, and coherent. Quantz contrasts the clarity of the French manner of performance with the chiaroscuro (emphasis on light and shade) of the Italian manner, and states that "French [music] depends more on the com-

Johann Sebastian Bach, 1685–1750
(*The New York Public Library
Picture Collection*)

position than on the performance, the Italian almost as much, and in some pieces almost more, on the performance than on the composition." This is reflected in the fact that ornaments, dynamics, articulation, and figured bass symbols are more apt to be clearly specified in French music, whereas in Italian music they are left more to the discretion, taste, and imagination of the performer.

These stylistic differences are found in music by composers from other countries: Italian and French influences are, for example, very significant in the works of Johann Sebastian Bach. Thurston Dart has suggested that clues to national stylistic characteristics may be found in the language chosen for movement titles or indications of tempo and character.

In addition to differences of national styles, writers of the Baroque period recognized three distinct functional styles—church music, theater music, and chamber music; and two compositional practices—*prima prattica* (first practice) which emphasized restrained word setting, modality (i.e., the use of the "church" modes), evenly flowing rhythm, and polyphonic texture; and *seconda prattica* (second practice) which emphasized more affective word setting, a tendency toward major-minor tonality, extremes of strict and free rhythm, and homophonic texture.

For a time in the early seventeenth century the two practices existed concurrently: the prima prattica, based on models from the previous century, was preferred for sacred music, the seconda prattica for secular music, especially opera.

The characteristic textures of these two practices are shown in Examples 1a and 1b. The first is a balanced texture of several equal voices based upon intervallic counterpoint, with restrained dissonance treatment; the second is an unbalanced texture with an affective melody moving against a block chord accompaniment and with a somewhat less restrained treatment of dissonance (unprepared sevenths, for example). Example 1c represents the characteristic texture of the later Baroque. The relatively static bass is replaced by a more active bass line which assumes equal importance to the soprano line and must be performed with equal weight. Middle voices are considerably less important, though occasionally the upper line will in effect be divided into two complimentary lines as in a trio sonata or a vocal duet. All voices are governed by harmonic counterpoint, and the harmonies themselves are governed by the strong directional force of functional tonal harmony as manifested, for example, in a progression such as I $\longrightarrow$ $^{ii}6$ $\longrightarrow$ $^{V}7$ $\longrightarrow$ I.

Example 1

(a) *Prima prattica*
(Renaissance)
(b) *Seconda prattica*
(Early Baroque monody)
(c) Late Baroque

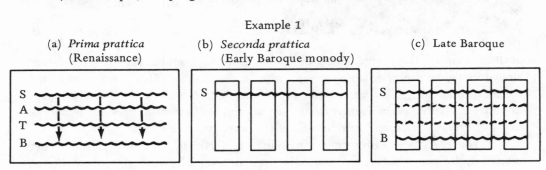

Turning to differences in chronological periods within the Baroque era, one will find that the changes in texture and tonality mentioned above are probably the most significant. Other changes included the development of specific forms, styles, and vocal and instrumental idioms. In view of this great variety, it is difficult to make general statements that would be equally valid for all aspects of Baroque music. The following may, however, serve at least to correct some established misconceptions regarding Baroque music.

1. Baroque music is not meant to be performed in a pale, prim, and passionless manner. We have only to read descriptions of performers' behavior and audience reaction of the time to know that this music was meant to touch the heart and soul of man in a direct and immediate way. Granted that passion is meant to be kept within the limits of good taste and the artistic and social conventions of the time, it is nevertheless present. Ideally, performances of Baroque music should reflect elements of both passionate subjectivity and calm objectivity in such a manner that the two are integrated and yet still exert their characteristic forces.

2. Baroque music, like Baroque psychology, is not dynamically dualistic like the music and psychology of later periods. Baroque psychology tended to view man at a given period of time under the influence of a single affect, emotion, or mood—melancholic, sanguine, bilious, or choleric. So too, a given single movement of Baroque music is usually governed by a single, unvarying affect or mood. To introduce the kind of mood contrast present in a Beethoven sonata into the performance of a Bach suite is inappropriate and would dilute the strength of both. Notice, for example, how the varying moods of the Credo of Bach's *B-minor Mass* are each set in separate movements. In general, Baroque music should be performed with contrasts *between* movements rather than *within* movements. This is naturally subject to some exceptions in specific works.

3. To a far greater degree than is true in later music, Baroque music demands that the performer be an active, spontaneous collaborator rather than merely a passive, restricted reproducer. It would be highly unfortunate if the search for "correct" tempi, ornamentation, and other aspects were done in such a manner that this sense of validity and participation were destroyed. Ideally the details of performance practice should be so thoroughly integrated into the performer's approach and technique that they become natural and effortless.

4. Finally, it can be said in general that one should avoid distorting Baroque music with stylistic traits from later periods, such as the sweet sentimentality of some early nineteenth-century music, the massive pomposity of some late-nineteenth-century music, the blurred vagueness of some Impressionist music, or the calculated objectivity of some twentieth-century music—to take only the most blatant examples.

But what we really should not tolerate are those semi-historical performances that show this music through the powerful spectacles of another historical period—the Romantic age. This dual historicism, the performing of a work of art of the 18th century in the spirit and with the resources of the 19th century in the 20th century, is untrue in itself, and we can probably only bear it, because the greatness of Bach's music easily overshadows all these stylistic and intellectual deficiencies.—NIKOLAUS HARNONCOURT[2]

The lines of Baroque music should be sharply etched and expressive; the rhythms should be incisive and vital, or supple and free in the case of recitative; the textures should be transparent and lucid with generally equal weight on the important bass and soprano lines; the timbre should be clean and yet resonant; and the form should be clear, convincing, and balanced.

THE USE OF VOICES AND INSTRUMENTS

A Baroque writer describes the ideal singing voice as follows:

> A perfect voice should be sonorous, extensive, sweet, neat, lively, flexible. These six qualities which nature assembles but once in a century, are usually found bestowed by halves.[3]

Among other points admired by writers of the time were the ability to execute ornaments (especially trills) cleanly and effectively, and the ability to bring out words clearly and expressively in singing. Though most writers of the time are describing solo voices, it is likely that the same techniques were expected of choral singers. The question of vibrato will be discussed later in this chapter; we may anticipate somewhat by noting that in general an "intensity vibrato" (actually tremolo) was considered appropriate, but a pitch vibrato, especially a wide one, was not. In any case, however, a pure, white, lifeless tone is nowhere cited as a sound ideal by Baroque writers.

The seventeenth century marked the beginning of a practice of vitalizing choral music by the use of rich registration comparable to that available to the organist. This was accomplished by setting up several separated choirs, by using choral groups of varied size, and by developing comparable orchestral forces when performance with instruments was demanded. These variations in choral strength were sometimes clearly stated by the composer, or they were left—as was so often the case in the Baroque period—to the discretion of the performers. In time definite musical styles developed for the various choral and solo forces, so that in later music most choral registrations arose automatically from the musical structure

Baroque double chorus with two organs, Munich.

(The Bettmann Archive)

and were defined in the musical score, according to patterns suggested by such writers and composers as Praetorius (*Syntagma Musicum*, 1615–1619) and Schütz (prefaces to his collections).

Turning to the problem of instruments, space does not permit more than a cursory examination of this involved subject. For more details, readers are referred to the works of Carse, Boyden, and others in the Bibliography. The following general suggestions may be of some assistance to choral conductors in working with instruments in Baroque music.

Baroque instrumentation, especially in the earlier periods, need not be treated with the same absolute fidelity as later music. Availability of instruments, technique of players, acoustics of the performance location, and other factors sometimes dictated substitutions of instruments in Baroque performances. The modern performer may find such adjustments necessary also. Some substitutions, however, are more appropriate than others. The substitution of cello for gamba on continuo parts is certainly possible, especially if the player does not try to make the part sound like the Dvořak concerto, but rather seeks to recreate somewhat the quieter and more pointed sound of the gamba, as discussed below. On the other hand, substituting oboes for high trumpet parts in a cantata of Bach would rob the music of the brilliant, festive character which is associated with the trumpet.

The substitution of piano for harpsichord is a debatable point which is fortunately becoming less critical with the increasing availability of good modern harpsichords. If a substitution must be made, it is usually better to use a small portative organ, or equivalent stops on a large organ. When only a piano is available, it is probably better not to attempt to play it in imitation of a harpsichord but rather let it speak discretely and quietly in its own natural timbre.

It was apparently quite common to double written instrumental and vocal parts with other instruments. This possibility applies to seemingly unaccompanied works such as the Bach motets. Sometimes musicologists have confused modern performers by the introduction of conflicting viewpoints.

> . . . the German motet arrived at its peak in the six motets by Bach, four of which are written for unaccompanied double-chorus of eight voices, while one ("Jesu, meine Freude") is for five voices and one ("Lobet den Herrn") for four voices with organ.[4]

> For one or two choirs, the motets are impressive though as a rule short compositions, akin to the cantatas but for the fact that they have no solo passages and no independent accompaniments—if we infer from the single accompaniment which has been preserved, the one for *Der Geist hilft unsrer Schwachheit auf*, that the other motets were intended to be backed by instruments doubling the voices.

> Historical and musical reasons bear out the inference. Sir Donald Tovey had this to say on the subject: "Only five 'unaccompanied' choral works of Bach are extant. . . . Of his choral works with organ and orchestra we possess at least two hundred and fifty. . . . These facts alone would prove that the very notion of an unaccompanied chorus had become unfamiliar in Bach's day, even if we had not the still more striking fact that . . . Handel never wrote a line of unaccompanied choral music." Tovey goes on, "There are hardly two consecutive pages in all these five motets

without some passage which proves that Bach had imagined the basses to be supported by some instrument an octave below them."[5]

The idea that such music is to be performed without accompaniment probably stems from the same misconception that has caused most Renaissance music to be sung a cappella until recently.[6] The latest scholarship suggests that each voice of such compositions should be doubled by an instrument and the whole texture supported by keyboard and string (double-bass or violone) continuo. Bach himself illustrates such a procedure in *Der Geist hilft* (BWV 226). A related practice was to add some instruments for an entire movement and then to withdraw or exchange them for other instruments in a manner comparable to a change of registration on the organ.

From a modern-day point of view we might describe bowing on string instruments in the Baroque period as colorful but conservative. A variety of strokes and articulations from pure legato to a lightly brushed spiccato may be appropriately used, but specific nineteenth-century virtuoso strokes like down bow staccato or ricochet are not recommended. As a general rule the norm of bowing, for example in passage work of an allegro movement, should be somewhat more clear and separate or lightly detached than the norm of modern playing, which tends toward extremes of absolute legato even in notes taken with alternating up and down bows and, on the other hand, strongly marked hammered strokes, or crisp, bounced, spiccato strokes. In general, the modern French or Franco-Belgian school of bowing with its emphasis on bow speed is more similar to Baroque bowing than the modern Russian school with its emphasis on a lusher sonority produced with more bow pressure.

Whenever available, Baroque wind instruments should be used; in particular the distinction between the recorder and the transverse flute should be observed. Baroque brass instruments had a narrower bore than their modern descendants, and this tended to favor the high harmonics producing a more brilliant and more focused sound than modern instruments. If modern instruments are used, the players may attempt to come as close to this type of sound as possible in order to contribute to the clarity of texture essential for Baroque music. There is some evidence to indicate that Baroque wind players favored a softer articulation than modern players, using the consonants T and R as in "territory" rather than the T and K in 'Too-koo-too-koo," which is used today.

The relative numbers of players and singers in a Baroque ensemble may be

Georg Friedrich Händel, 1685–1759
(*The New York Public Library Picture Collection*)

Nineteenth-century performance of *Messiah*
(*The New York Public Library Picture Collection*)

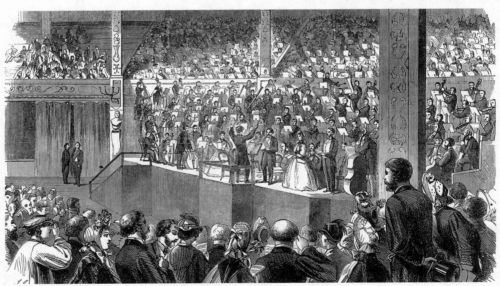

suggested by the following lists, drawn from (*a*) a memorandum written by Johann Sebastian Bach in 1730 at Leipzig; (*b*) a performance of Handel's *Messiah* at the Foundling Hospital in 1754; (*c*) a list of the musicians at the court of the King of Prussia, also in 1754; and (*d*) the strings recommended by Quantz in 1752.

Except for the Bach list, the distribution of singers is estimated since only the total number was given. It will be noticed that forces that would be regarded as large today were only found at that time in open air performances, and not at the indoor performances described here.

	(a) Bach	(b) Handel	(c) King of Prussia	(d) Quantz
Violin I	2–3	7	6	–
				6–8
Violin II	2–3	7	6	–
Viola	I–2	6	3	1–2
	II–2			
Cello	2	3	4 (plus 1 gamba)	1–2
Double Bass	1	3	2	1–2
Flute	2		5, including the King as soloist	
Oboe	2–3	4	3	
Bassoon	1–2	4	4	1
Horns		2	2	
Trumpet	3	2		
Kettledrum	1	1		
Harpsichord	1*	1*	2	
Organ	1*	1*		
Theorbo (Bass lute)			1	
Soprano	2–4	7 (2 women, 5 boys)	2	
Alto	2–4	6 (1 woman, 3 boys, 2 men)	2	
Tenor	2–4	7	2	–
Bass	2–4	7	2	–

* Not specified because the composer himself or his assistant would play those instruments.

From these and other lists, certain general conclusions may be reached. Instrumentalists generally equalled or outnumbered singers, and the ratio of strings to winds tended to be much closer than in a modern orchestra, about 60 percent strings and 40 percent winds. These guidelines and other general principles, such as the preference for equally strong bass and soprano lines, with weaker middle voices, the tendency toward preserving one orchestral timbre rather than the more staggered type of entries of different parts in later music, and the general desire for clarity and transparency in texture, may guide the conductor in choosing instruments for works in which the instrumentation is unspecified, incomplete, or requires some alteration.

PROBLEMS OF NOTATION

Most musicians of today would probably be able to read the manuscript or an early edition of a work by Bach or Handel, and yet there are sufficient differences between late Baroque notation and present day conventions to justify a discussion of these problems. This is even more true of the notation of the early and middle Baroque.

The Interpretation of Pitch Notation

Parallel to the gradual establishment of functional, major-minor tonality during the Baroque era was the gradual establishment of modern conventions of pitch notation. At the beginning of the seventeenth century many remnants of the old Renaissance modal notation system were still in evidence.

Key signatures in early Baroque are often used, not to indicate a key in the modern sense, but rather to indicate transposition of mode. The basic modes and their finals or tonics were Dorian on D, Phrygian on E, Lydian on F, and Mixolydian on G. Although modern treatment of modes often stresses the intervallic structure, especially the presence of such "color notes" as the raised Dorian sixth, or the lowered Mixolydian seventh scale degrees, earlier treatment placed emphasis on the pitch location as much or more than upon intervallic relations. Indeed, through the practice of either written or unwritten accidentals, the color notes were often changed; the Dorian sixth, for example, is frequently lowered to a flat sixth similar to that of diatonic natural or harmonic minor. However, as long as the final or tonic was on D, the mode was regarded as Dorian.

A key signature of one flat was used to indicate a transposition down a perfect fifth; D Dorian would thus become G Dorian. A key signature of two flats indicated a transposition down two perfect fifths, in effect, down a major ninth or a major second. This type of signature is sometimes called a "modal signature" and may be found even in some works of Bach, even though most works would show the modern full signature. The use of sharps in a key signature to indicate transposition up a fifth is less frequent but still may occasionally be seen. Another peculiarity of Baroque signatures is the occasional doubling of an accidental at the octave; for example, F sharp may be indicated on both the fifth line and the first space.

Accidentals added during the course of a piece in early Baroque music were not subject to the modern convention that an accidental is understood to apply throughout the bar. This explains the necessity for the repeated sharp in Example 2a, and justifies the editorial emendations in Example 2b. This general rule applies to sharps more generally than to flats: indeed, in some early Baroque music a flat is understood to apply until cancelled by a natural sign, even if this involves several measures. These problems are no longer acute in late Baroque music where modern conventions apply.

Example 2

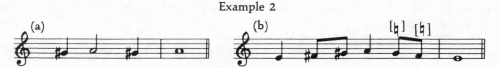

In addition to the problem of interpreting written accidentals, there is also the question of if and when to add accidentals to the music. The following general rules apply primarily to the interpretation of earlier Baroque music.

1. The leading tone should be raised, if it is not already, for all final cadences and for important internal cadences so that the strong cadential pull of the half-step approach to the tonic may be realized (Example 3a). The one exception to this is the Phrygian cadence, where, in effect, the half-step approach is taken over by the bass (Example 3b).

Example 3

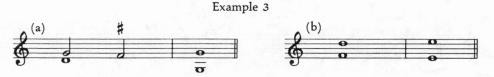

2. By extension this half-step principle may also be applied to certain neighbor tone figures at the summit of phrases. This is the justification for the editorial emendations in Example 4. Notice that the use of B flat in Example 4a and E flat in Example 4b contribute to a smooth line at the high turning point of the phrases. On the other hand, no editorial emendation is necessary in Example 4c because E-F is already a half-step, and none is required in Example 4d because the neighbor tone figure is not at the summit of a phrase.

Example 4

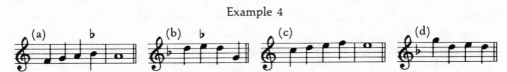

3. The tritone was the *diabolus in musica* (devil in music) for early theorists. When it occurs either as an augmented fourth or in inversion as a diminished fifth, it should be corrected by altering the second note of the interval as shown in Example 5. The ban against tritones could also be extended to notes occurring some distance apart at significant points in a phrase. This provides an additional justification for the B flat in Example 4a, since F and B, the bottom and top notes of the phrase, form a tritone.

Example 5

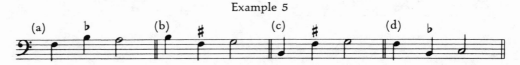

4. On the other hand, the melodic or harmonic cross-relation (i.e., the successive or simultaneous appearance of two different versions of the same note such as F natural and F sharp) is a typical, piquant feature of early Baroque music and should not be avoided. Indeed, it may need to be introduced in some instances as in Example 6b. The harmonic dissonance of the diminished octave is justified by the motion of the melodic lines.

Example 6

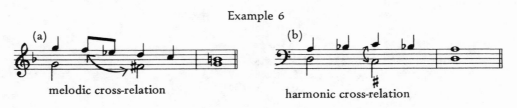

melodic cross-relation   harmonic cross-relation

5. There is some evidence to support the contention that final cadences in early Baroque music should always end on a major tonic chord, even when the composition is in minor (Picardy third). Sources are not clear on this point and the principle may well have been limited to the realization of the figured bass.

6. In addition to these specific cases, Baroque theorists also recognized that accidentals could be justified on the general basis of the performer's taste. Modern performers and editors, however, should exercise extreme care in going beyond the rules stated above. They should have little hesitancy in applying the specific rules in early music and, to a lesser extent, in later music, where the absence of accidentals would more likely be a result of copying error than of a notational convention. Any reluctance to use accidentals in such instances as a raised leading tone in a final authentic cadence on the basis that it is going against the composer's wishes, or that the lowered leading tone sounds "authentically antique," is reluctance to join in collaboration with the composer in the realization of the piece, and is evidence of timidity or misunderstanding.

The Interpretation of Rhythmic Notation

In matters of rhythmic notation, just as in matters of pitch notation, the Baroque era, especially the early part, was a period of transition between Renaissance practice and modern practice. Other problems in rhythmic interpretation stem from the fact that the Baroque composer did not always regard rhythmic notation as fixing mathematically exact durations as later composers more or less did. The degree of freedom or strictness in the interpretation of rhythm varied with different countries, periods, and types of composition, and, in many if not most instances, the modern performer should at least begin by assuming that the rhythm should be interpreted strictly and only move to a varied interpretation if he can clearly justify it on the basis of clear evidence in the music itself or in other sources.

At the beginning of the Baroque era there was still some use of Renaissance time signatures. These indicated proportional relations, showing *tempus* (time), i.e., how the breve was divided into two or three semibreves, and *prolationis* (prolation), i.e., how the semibreve was divided into two or three minims. In either case triple relations were called perfect, and duple relations were imperfect. We can gain some understanding of this if we think of tempus as being similar to the division of the measure into two or three beats, and prolationis as being similar to the divsion of the beat into two or three subdivisions. The four standard signatures are shown below with their modern equivalents. Note that the modern time signatures are based upon note values twice as short as those of the older notation. This is a common practice in the transcription of older notation.

Tempus			Prolationis		Modern	
⊙ Perfect ♮	= ooo	Perfect o	= ♩ ♩ ♩	Compound Triple $\frac{9}{4}$
○ Perfect ♮	= ooo	Imperfect o	= ♩ ♩	Simple Triple $\frac{3}{2}$
⊂˙ Imperfect ♮	= oo	Perfect o	= ♩ ♩ ♩	Compound Duple $\frac{6}{4}$
C Imperfect ♮	= oo	Imperfect o	= ♩ ♩	Simple Duple $\frac{2}{2}$

A single vertical line through a signature was used to indicate diminution, i.e., the note values were halved; a double line indicated double diminution (C ¢ ₵). Occasionally Ɔ was used in place of ¢, and ♭ in place of ₵.

Sometimes fractional signatures were used, but not in our modern sense indicating unit note value and number of units per bar. Instead the older fractional signatures are to be interpreted as follows: the numerator indicates the number of notes in the new section that are to be played in the same space of time as the number of notes from the previous section indicated by the denominator. Thus $\frac{3}{2}$ indicates "play three notes in the new section in the same space of time occupied by two notes in the previous section," $\frac{9}{6}$ means "play nine notes in the new section in the same amount of time as six notes in the previous section." Gradually during the seventeenth century this older type of signature yielded to the modern meter signature. Fortunately the context usually makes it clear which type of signature is intended.

Occasionally we find the use of double signatures such as C$\frac{24}{16}$, which means that the music will sometimes move in regular quarters, eighths, and sixteenths, etc., but at other times it will move in six sixteenths per quarter note beat.

Note values used in the Baroque period were generally the same as or similar to modern notation. The "white notes" with single and double flags were rarely used, but when used indicated a note value twice as long as the same black note.

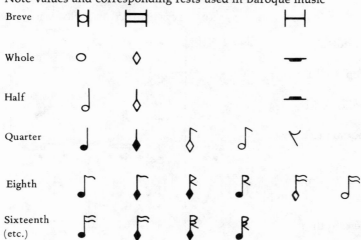

Example 7

Note values and corresponding rests used in Baroque music

Two other values, the large and the long were caried over from the Renaissance but were soon dropped from practice. The breve was normally the longest value used. Occasionally at the end of pieces or sections a breve would be used to signify a note of indeterminate length, somewhat like our modern use of the corona (⌒). Beaming was used beginning in the seventeenth century but was not always subject to such modern conventions as grouping by beat or bar.

If the note values are relatively easy to interpret, the dot in Baroque music presents one of the most challenging problems. In many instances it is true it will have the modern meaning of making a two-pulse note into a three-pulse note, or adding half of the value of the note to the principal value. In other cases it may have any of the following meanings:

Example 8

	BAROQUE NOTATION	INTERPRETATION	BAROQUE NOTATION	INTERPRETATION
A. Double dotting				
B. Double dotting, partially indicated				

Example 8 *Continued*

	BAROQUE NOTATION	INTERPRETATION	BAROQUE NOTATION	INTERPRETATION
C. Triple dotting	♩. ♪	♩... ♬	[dotted eighth–sixteenth]	[triple-dotted figure]
D. Dot replaced by rest	♩. ♪	♩ 𝄾 ♪	[dotted eighth–sixteenth]	[figure with rest]
E. Dot followed by rest	♩. ♪	♩ 𝄾 ♪	[dotted eighth–sixteenth]	[figure with rest]
F. Dot equals tied-over note	♩. ♬	♩‿♬♬	[dotted figure]	[tied figure]
G. Double dotting in reverse (Scotch Snap)	♪ ♩.	♪ ♩..	[figure]	[figure]
H. Triplet rhythm	♩. ♪	♩ ♩ (3)	[dotted eighth–sixteenth]	♩ ♪ (3)

How is the performer to know which interpretation to apply? The general principle, as is so often the case in Baroque music, is to base the decision on the character of the music. More specifically the following conventions may apply:

1. If dotted notes are not used prominently or frequently, it is likely that a "modern" interpretation (a 3:1 ratio) would be appropriate. However, we should note that even in later music there is a natural tendency to think of the short note following the dot as leading to the following note and to make it subtly shorter. This tendency should definitely be followed in Baroque music. Also there is a tendency in later music to regard the dot as, in effect, a rest, especially in music of a brisk or energetic character (see D in Example 8 above). This tendency should also be followed in Baroque music.

2. When dotted notes are used frequently or as the characteristic rhythmic motives of a piece, then it is appropriate to apply the principle of "overdotting," that is, to lengthen the dotted note and shorten the following note (see A,B,C,E in Example 8 above). The choice of double dotting or triple dotting would depend on tempo and character. The combination of double dotting and a rest (see E in Example 8 above) is probably the best solution for pieces in French Overture style, since it brings out the intended majesty and verve of such pieces. On the other hand, when the dotted note figures are under a slur, it is possible, but not required, that they be performed without the rest, according to A,B, or C.

3. The solutions involving tied-over notes shown at F in Example 8 should always be played as indicated. These figures are evidence of the occasional lack of mathematical accuracy in the rhythmic notation of the Baroque period.

4. The application of overdotting to the Scotch Snap or reverse dotted note figure is debatable. Some authorities like Quantz recommend it; others like Carl Philippe Emmanuel Bach do not (see G in Example 8 above).

5. When dotted note figures are used in successive or simultaneous combination with triplet figures, they should be played as triplet figures in 2:1 ratio (see H in Example 8 above, and also Example 12).

A related rhythmic problem is the treatment of rapid runs in the French Overture style. In general they are to be played faster than indicated, which requires lengthening the rest or note that precedes them.

Example 9

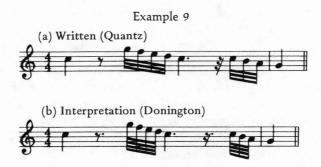

(a) Written (Quantz)

(b) Interpretation (Donington)

Not only was it the custom to lengthen dotted notes, it was also an accepted convention, especially in French Baroque music and to a degree in other music, to change pairs of equal notes to unequal notes (*notes inégales*), as shown in Example 10. The two problems confronting the performer here are (1) when to use unequal notes, and (2) what ratios to use between the unequal notes.

Unequal notes are strongly suggested by the following:

1. Paired stepwise melodic motion.
2. Slurs over the note pairs.
3. Rhythms moving in divisions of the beat in simple meters, occasionally also in subdivisions of the beat. This would mean, for example, eighths or occa-

sionally sixteenths in $\frac{2}{4}$, $\frac{3}{4}$, $\frac{4}{4}$; quarters or occasionally eighths in $\frac{2}{2}$, $\frac{3}{2}$, $\frac{4}{2}$.

4. A moderate rate of speed for the notes to be treated with inequality. Generally only the shortest note values in a composition are subjected to inequality.

5. Words such as *inégales, pointer,* or *lourer.*

On the other hand, the application of inequality is strongly discouraged by the following:

1. Extensive use of melodic leaps.

2. Slurs over more than two notes, or the presence of dashes or dots over notes. Dashes (| , ▼, or ▲) were regular Baroque signs for staccato. The dot, on the other hand, was not a sign for staccato, but rather for equality.

3. Rhythms other than paired equal notes; for example, groups of three eighths in $\frac{6}{8}$ or $\frac{9}{8}$.

4. As stated above, inequality was generally reserved for the shortest note values appearing in a piece. If these were either too fast or too slow to be taken effectively and convincingly with inequality, then it would not be applied.

5. Words such as *également, notes égales, notes martelées, détachez, mouvement decidé,* etc.

An indication of the possible choices of ratios between unequal notes is given in Example 10. The 2:1 ratio was frequently applied, especially for pieces marked *lourer.* In such cases it is sometimes effective to rewrite the entire movement in a compound meter, changing ♩♩ to ♩♪ throughout. The 3:1 ratio (or sometimes a 7:1 ratio) was preferred for brisk pieces like marches, the more subtle 3:2 or 7:5 ratios were preferred for gentler, more expressive pieces.

Example 10

Occasionally inequality may be applied in reverse, that is with a shortened first note and a long second note. In French music this was specifically indicated as in Example 11. Note that the ever-problematic dot here means to lengthen the second note.

Example 11

A final problem of Baroque rhythm is the interpretation of seeming conflicts, either successive or simultaneous, between triplet figures and duplet or quadruplet figures. The evidence here would seem to show conclusively that in such cases the duplet or quadruplet figure should be adapted to fit with the triplet figure, leading to solutions such as those shown in Example 12.

Example 12

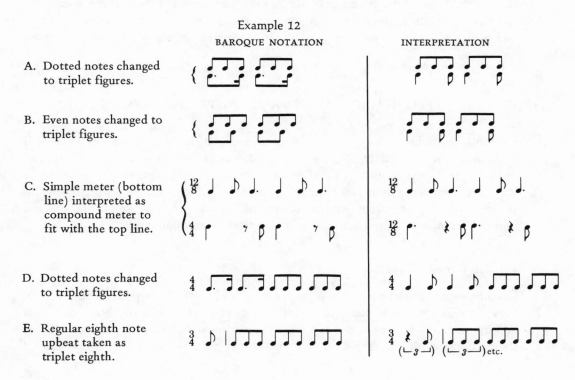

A. Dotted notes changed to triplet figures.

B. Even notes changed to triplet figures.

C. Simple meter (bottom line) interpreted as compound meter to fit with the top line.

D. Dotted notes changed to triplet figures.

E. Regular eighth note upbeat taken as triplet eighth.

Though most authorities and evidence within the music itself would support these interpretations, there is some support (e.g., Quantz) for playing the dotted notes with overdotting rather than adapting them to the triplet rhythm. This would especially be possible in cases like Example 13 which illustrates a combination of inequality and overdotting.

Example 13

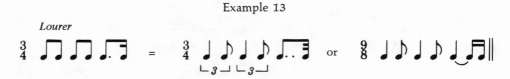

Though great care must be taken in the application of the rhythmic alterations discussed in this section, performers should not hesitate to use them when appropriate. Overdotting can transform a French Overture, like the beginning of Handel's *Messiah*, from sluggish dullness to exhilarating brilliance; inequality can transform a movement of Lully from routine simplicity to persuasive elegance; and triplet adaptation can change passages of ambiguous complexity to convincing naturalness.

ORNAMENTATION AND IMPROVISATION

For musicians who have dealt primarily with music of the nineteenth and twentieth centuries, where virtually all notes to be played are written out completely and precisely, it may be difficult to realize how intrinsic, important, even indispensable the use of ornamentation and improvisation is for Baroque music. In the following sections we shall consider written ornamentation, unwritten ornamentation and improvisation, and the performance of figured bass accompaniments.

Written Ornamentation

Ornaments make the music more expressive, elaborate, and elegant. Specifically, they provide smooth melodic connections between notes, add rhythmic emphasis and interest, and bring out the expression of the music, often by means of coloring the harmony with expressive nonharmonic tones such as the appoggiatura. Before discussing specific types of ornaments, we may make the following general observations:

1. Some ornaments, especially the cadential trill and the long appoggiatura, are obligatory and should *always* be performed when indicated. Indeed, even when they are not indicated, they should be added if clearly implied by the musical context. Other ornaments are more or less optional; though they should generally be performed, they may on occasion be omitted or altered.

2. The treatment of ornaments may vary according to national school, musical context, and performance medium. While it is not possible to summarize all of these differences, it can be said in general that French ornaments may be treated with more exactness than Italian, and slow movements or long notes may be provided with more ornamentation than fast movements or short notes. Some music, intended to express simplicity or sadness, may best be performed with little or no ornamentation. Certain instruments, especially the harpsichord, may allow for more ornamentation than others. Usually high instruments will have more ornamentation than low instruments.

3. When ornaments are repeated successively as in fugal entries or when they are used simultaneously in an ensemble, they should be played consistently and uniformly. In sequential passages, however, they may be played in an increasingly elaborate manner to create a cumulative effect.

4. With very few exceptions all Baroque ornaments are played on the beat, or stated more accurately, all ornaments take their time away from the main note to which they are attached rather than from the preceding note. Failure to observe this general rule is one of the most glaring errors made by uninformed modern performers.

Turning to a discussion of specific ornaments, we shall begin with the appoggiatura. The term actually means "to lean" and this leaning character is to be found in the movement of an expressively emphasized ornamental note on the beat to the slightly less emphasized main note which follows. The ornamental note is usually an upper or lower neighbor located a half or whole step away from the main note, and it is usually dissonant to the underlying harmony. However, exceptions to these two characteristics may occasionally be found.

The characteristic appoggiatura of the late Baroque period is the so-called long appoggiatura. It may be indicated in a number of ways such as shown in Example 14.

Example 14

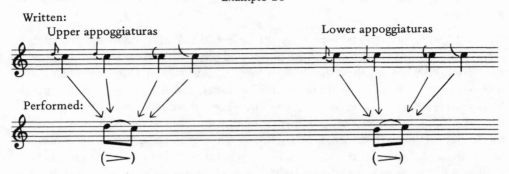

The choice of notation for the ornamental note does not tell us anything about its duration, instead this is subject to the following rules:

1. If the main note is undotted, the appoggiatura lasts one half the value of the main note (see Example 15a).

2. If the main note is dotted, the appoggiatura lasts two thirds of the main note (see Example 15b).

Example 15

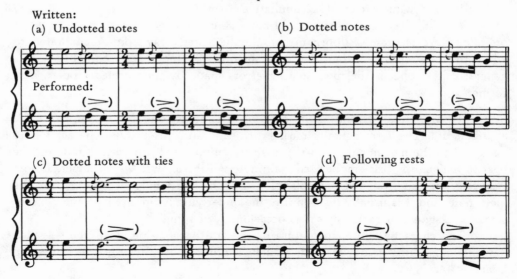

3. If the main note is a dotted note tied to another note in a compound meter, the appoggiatura lasts for the full length of the dotted note (see Example 15c).

4. If the main note is followed by a rest, the appoggiatura lasts for the full length of the main note and the main note itself is played in place of the rest (see Example 15d).

Notice that in every instance the appoggiatura begins at the time indicated by the main note and not before. Notice also that it is separate in articulation from the preceding note, but slurred to the main note, whether or not this slur is indicated.

The shortest duration for a long appoggiatura is one half of the main note. Any appoggiatura with a duration shorter than this, down to the shortest possible, is called a short appoggiatura. Short appoggiaturas still take their value from the main note and are still played with more emphasis than the main note. It is not always clear in Baroque music whether the long or short appoggiatura is intended, but as a general rule the long appoggiatura should be preferred. Some possible indications of short appoggiaturas are the use of appoggiaturas with repeated notes, syncopated notes, quick notes, or notes separated by a third. They may also possibly be suggested by the use of small sixteenth or thirty-second notes for the appoggiatura notation; however, none of these are conclusive and there is inconsistency in various sources in the treatment of the subject. In early Baroque music the short appoggiatura was more frequently encountered.

Example 16

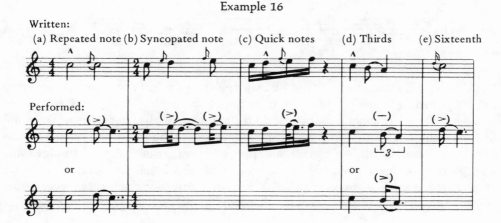

There are several other variants of the appoggiatura. The double appoggiatura (or double disjunct appoggiatura) differs from the regular appoggiatura in that it has two ornamental notes, usually the upper and lower neighbors of the main note, and in that the ornamental notes are to be played softer than the main note. The ornamental notes are to be played quickly, and their value is taken from the following main note (see Example 17a). The slide (or double conjunct appoggiatura) consists of two stepwise ornamental notes leading to the main note. Although some early sources suggested that the slide may be played with the ornamental notes, taking their value away from the preceding note (an exception to the general rule), most reliable primary and secondary sources indicated that it should be played with the value of the ornamental notes taken from the main note (see Example 17b). One of the most pungent Baroque ornaments, the acciaccatura, may also be regarded as an appoggiatura type. The term acciaccatura means "crushed stroke" and indicates that the ornamental note is to be sounded simultaneously with the main note and then quickly released. The ornament was primarily used on keyboard instruments (see Example 17c).

Example 17

The trill is an essential and obligatory ornament in Baroque music and may be performed in a number of ways in terms of its beginning, its ending, and the number of notes it contains. The standard Baroque trill always begins at the point of time indicated by the main note and always begins on the note above the main note. In effect, the trill begins with an appoggiatura that is typically sustained and emphasized (see Example 18a). In Baroque terms this beginning with a sustained, emphasized upper neighbor is called a *prepared* trill. Sometimes, however, especially when the trill is short or when it occurs at the beginning of a passage, this appoggiatura upper neighbor is played at the same rate of speed as the other notes of the trill (see Example 18b). In Baroque terms this is an *unprepared* trill.

Example 18
Trills with turn endings

Trills with anticipation endings

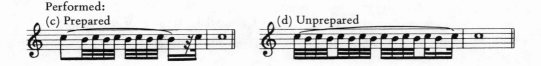

There are also two typical endings for Baroque trills, the turn ending shown in Example 18a and b, and the anticipation ending shown in Example 18c and d. When there is no written ending given, the performer chooses between the two types shown. When written endings are given, they signify the type of ending (i.e., turn or anticipation) but not necessarily the rhythm of the ending. As a general rule the notes of the ending should be played at the same rate of speed as the notes of the trill itself. Applied to the so-called Corelli clash, these principles result in a mitigation of the "harshness" that some modern writers mistakenly attribute to this progression (see Example 19).

Example 19

Corelli Clash

Written: Performed:

The half trill usually implies that the trill lasts for half of the value of the main note. It typically begins unprepared, i.e., without a long appoggiatura, and ends directly on the main note with neither a turn nor an anticipation. It was used for trills in fairly fast-moving music, especially in passages involving descending stepwise motion. Note that Example 20b has the minimum number of notes for a trill. At very rapid rates of speed where this is not possible, the trill may become, in effect, an inverted mordent (see Example 20c and page 395).

Example 20

Written: Performed as half trill: Performed as inverted mordent:
(a) *tr*   *tr*   (b)   (c)

The speed of the trill depends on the length of the note and the character of the music. Quantz's words on this subject are characteristic of the importance that musicians of the eighteenth century placed on practical performing conditions as opposed to arbitrary dogma.

> There is no need to make all trills with the same speed. It is necessary to adapt yourself not only to the place where you play, but also to the piece itself which you have to play. If the place where you play is large, and if it reverberates, a rather slow trill will make a better effect than a quick trill (and vice versa). . . . In addition you must know how to distinguish what sort of piece you are playing, so as not to confuse one thing with another, which is what happens with a lot of people. In sad pieces the trills are made slowly; but in gay pieces they ought to be made more quickly.[7]

Though most trills should probably be performed at a regular even rate of speed, there are some indications that they could be played with acceleration (i.e., starting slowly and gradually increasing in speed) or with dotted rhythms (the so-called *ribattuta*).

The term "trillo" is used in early seventeenth-century Italian music for an entirely different ornament, namely the rapid repetition of a single pitch, in other words, a type of tremolo. Typically this was performed with acceleration as shown in Example 21.

Example 21

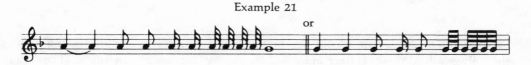

The *mordent* is in the same general category of ornaments as the trill, but whereas the trill involves the upper neighbor, the regular mordent involves a rapid alternation of a main note and its lower neighbor. The term mordent means "biting" and the mordent should be played with a fast, biting rhythm. The single mordent (Example 22a) is the preferred type of the main Baroque period. The inverted mordent (Example 22b) was used in pre-Baroque music and then dropped out of practice during the main Baroque period until about the middle of the eighteenth century, when writers like C. P. E. Bach recommended its usage but only in specific instances, such as descending stepwise passages where the normal mordent would be heard as a weak anticipation of the succeeding main note. The double mordent (Example 22c) and the continued mordent (actually a lower neighbor trill) (Example 22d) were also used in the Baroque period.

Example 22

(a) Single mordent

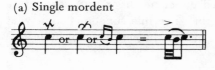

(b) Inverted mordent

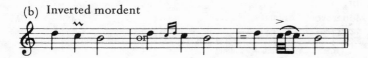

(c) Double mordent

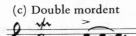

(d) Continued mordent

(e) Added accidental

Notice that all mordents are played rapidly and with emphasis and that they always begin at the time indicated by the main note, not before it. They all conclude on the main note without any special ending. Though some writers recommend the use of a half-step in all mordents, most authorities recommend using a diatonic note. In cases like Example 22e where the music has clearly modulated, an accidental may have to be added even when not indicated.

In contrast to the biting character of the mordent, the *turn*, which involves the decoration of a main note with both upper and lower neighbors, was a gentler, more graceful ornament. As shown in Example 23, turns may begin on the upper neighbor, lower neighbor, or main note, but the upper neighbor is more common. They may begin at the time of the main note or they could be played somewhere in the middle of the main note (i.e., unaccented). Sometimes, but by no means always, the placement of the turn sign may indicate whether the turn is to be accented or unaccented. Unaccented turns on a dotted figure may result in a shortening of the note following the dot. In the interpretation of questionable passages in Baroque music, the accented, upper neighbor turn with diatonic upper and lower neighbors is probably to be preferred, but the musical context may suggest one of the other equally appropriate solutions. Accented upper neighbor turns should be played with some emphasis on the upper neighbor since this functions somewhat like an appoggiatura. All turns should be played in one slur, even if not indicated.

Example 23

(a) Accented upper neighbor

(b) Unaccented upper neighbor

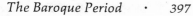

(c) Accented lower neighbor

(d) Unaccented lower neighbor

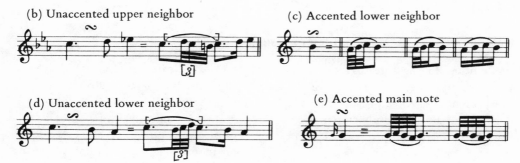

(e) Accented main note

A selection of other ornaments used in the Baroque period is given in Example 24. For full information on this subject consult the recommended works in the Bibliography.

Example 24

(a) Anticipation **(b) Changing note** **(c) Passing acciaccatura** **(d) Broken chords**

Written:

Performed:

(e) Doppelt cadence

Written:

Performed:

Unwritten Ornamentation and Improvisation

In addition to the interpretation of ornamentation indicated by special signs or notes, there is also the problem of introducing ornamentation where no indications are present. Whether or not one does this, and if so, when and to what extent all depend on the skill and temperament of the performer and on other factors. Improvised ornamentation would seem to be more appropriate in early Baroque music than later Baroque music, in Italian than in French music, in solo than in ensemble music, in slow music than in fast movements, and in repeats of passages than in original presentations.

It is probably demanding too much of modern performers to expect them to reach the degree of proficiency in improvised ornamentation attained by the best players of the Baroque period, especially considering the fact that these players usually created new embellishments for each performance of a work. Some idea of how to develop this ability, at least in terms of being able to write out an embellished version of a Baroque piece, may be gained by taking a typically elaborate adagio movement by Johann Sebastian Bach and reducing it to a series of main notes and ornamental notes as shown in Example 25a and b. This may give a good idea of appropriate procedures to be used when writing out decorated versions of passages where only the main notes are given, as shown in Example 25c and d.

Example 25
Bach, *Cantata 120,* "Gott, man lobet dich in der Stille"

Perhaps even more importantly, the procedure shown in Example 25a and b will give a clear idea of the structure of the original Bach melody. Even in his own time Bach was criticized because he expressed "all embellishments, all little graces, and all that is understood by the method of playing . . . in actual notes, and not only deprives his pieces of beauty and harmony but makes the melodic line unclear."[8] If this could be said in the eighteenth century by a writer familiar with Baroque conventions of ornamentation, then it is easy to see how a twentieth-century musician without this familiarity might need some help in understanding the structure of such movements. Reducing this music to main notes and ornamental notes cannot only reveal this structure, but it can help the performer to achieve a sense of spontaneity and freshness in his performance if he is careful to bring out the subtle differences in emphasis and duration between main notes and ornamental notes (see also chapter nine).

More specifically, it is possible to venture the discrete introduction of relatively simple ornamentation, such as appoggiaturas and trills, in places where their use is justified by the fact that similar places in the same piece or other pieces are actually marked with these ornaments. Appoggiaturas, for example, are often implied by passages, such as those shown in Example 26a, b, and c. The use of a trill on a long penultimate note of a cadence may be taken as a virtual rule in Baroque music, whether written or not (see Example 26d). Mordents may be effectively used on ascending stepwise passages, and passing tones may be added to passages ascending by thirds (see Example 26e and f).

Example 26

In vocal recitative, in particular, the addition of appoggiaturas is clearly sanctioned by such sources as the preface to the Telemann cantatas (see Example 27a,b,c,d). Conductors who refrain from this type of interpretation on the grounds that they want to perform the music "as the composer wrote it," are inappropriately applying twentieth-century attitudes to eighteenth-century practices. The important thing is not what the composer wrote but rather what he expected to hear.

Example 27

In a sense, the use of vibrato may be regarded as ornamentation and was sometimes treated as such by Baroque writers. The subject of vibrato in Baroque music is one of the most controversial issues in performance practice, and support may be found for several positions.

1. No vibrato should be used.

2. Vibrato should be used only when specifically indicated or only on long notes.

3. Continuous vibrato may be used in the sense of a moderate intensity vibrato for singers or a narrow pitch vibrato for strings, but the vibrato should never be so intense or wide that it "muddies" the sound.

4. Continuous wide vibrato, such as one might employ for a Romantic composition, may be used with equal effectiveness for Baroque music.

We would reject the first position not only because a complete lack of vibrato sounds sterile to modern ears, but also because there is ample evidence in sources from the Baroque period to indicate that vibrato was indeed used. We would reject the last position because a continuous wide vibrato would destroy the requisite clarity of Baroque music and because there is no evidence in early sources to indicate approval of it. Indeed Leopold Mozart complains about some performers who "tremble (i.e., vibrate) on every note without exception as if they had the palsy."

We would suggest a combination of the second and third positions, that is, the discrete use of a light or narrow continuous vibrato, coupled with a wider, more intense, or more expressive vibrato on some longer notes or in some slower passages. Support for this may be found in the following quotations:

A singer must have a fine, pleasing, trembling and shaking voice, yet not used as in some schools, but with especial moderation.[9]

The tone of the violin is the most ravishing when the players sweeten it . . . by certain tremblings which delight the mind.[10]

A long, expressive note (on the clavichord) may be performed with vibrato. The finger holds down the key and rocks it, so to speak.[11]

FIGURED BASS ACCOMPANIMENTS

The importance of the active, spontaneous participation of the performer in Baroque music has frequently been mentioned. Perhaps nowhere is this principle so obvious and important as in accompaniments for keyboard instruments (or occasionally plucked string instruments such as the lute) based upon the realization of a figured bass. Unlike the carefully and completely written out accompaniments of later periods, the typical Baroque accompaniment consisted only of a bass line provided with various figures and signs to suggest the proper harmonies.

The realization of these harmonies in terms of texture and voice leading was left to the taste and ability of the performer. The basic principles of figured bass realization are summarized below and illustrated in Example 28.

A. *Diatonic figuration.* The general rule is that the notes above the bass are to be drawn from the diatonic set of notes indicated by the key signature. Figures used do not usually indicate specific octave location, except in some early Baroque music. Usually 3, for example, may be interpreted as 10 or 17, i.e., one or more octaves higher.

1. A bass note with no figures or signs usually indicates a triad in root position with the given bass note as root, as in Example 28a. The type of triad would be determined by the diatonic context. In some special instances the figures 3 or $\frac{5}{3}$ may be used to insure that a root position triad is played (see Example 28b, measure 2).

2. Triad inversions are indicated with 6 or $\frac{6}{3}$ for first inversion and $\frac{6}{4}$ for second inversion (Example 28b).

3. Seventh chords are indicated as follows (Example 28c):

7 or (rarely) $\frac{7}{5}{}_{3}$, $\frac{8}{7}{}_{5}{}_{3}$, or $\frac{7}{3}$ for root position seventh chords;

$\frac{6}{5}$ or occasionally $\frac{6}{5}{}_{3}$ for first inversion seventh chords;

$\frac{4}{3}$ or occasionally $\frac{6}{4}{}_{3}$ for second inversion seventh chords;

$\frac{4}{2}$ or 2 or occasionally $\frac{6}{4}{}_{2}$ for third inversion seventh chords.

4. Suspensions are indicated with figures such as 4–3, 7–6, 9–8, or 6–5 (Example 28d).

5. A line following a figuration indicates that this particular harmony is to be maintained even though the bass moves to other notes (Example 28e).

6. A series of figures may be used to indicate changing harmonies over a static bass note (Example 28f).

B. *Chromatic figuration.*

1. Any note of a triad or seventh chord may be altered by placing an accidental before (or sometimes after) the figure referring to the note to be altered, as shown in Example 28g. An accidental appearing alone is always understood to indicate an alteration of the note a third above the bass.

Example 28

2. In the top row of numbers (Example 28g and h), the accidentals refer to the actual pitch to be sounded. Sometimes as in the second row, accidentals refer instead to the act of chromatically raising or lowering a particular pitch; ♯ indicates raising a pitch one half step, ♭ indicates lowering a pitch one half step, and ♮ indicates a return to the original (diatonic) pitch.

3. Chromatic alterations may also be indicated by special signs added to the figures themselves; usually these refer to the act of chromatically raising or lowering the designated pitches.

Raising (♯)	~~1~~	2 4	4+	5⁺	6́	7	8̸	9̸

Lowering (♭)   4♭   5̸   3̸   5♭   6♪   ~~7~~   ♭7   ~~9~~

Return to diatonic   5♮
pitch (♮)

4. Occasionally in early Baroque music the raised third is indicated by an accidental placed on the proper line or space of the staff itself. Care should be taken not to confuse this with an accidental applying to the bass note (Example 28i).

C. *Exceptions to the General Rules.* Though the preceding rules will be valid for most Baroque music, exceptions will be encountered more or less frequently depending on period, nationality, and other factors. Problematic passages may often be solved by studying the harmonies implied by the written melodic lines at that given moment. When this is not helpful or possible, the solution must be based upon a familiarity with the harmonic conventions of the period. The following exceptions occur with enough frequency to warrant special mention.

1. Exceptions to the rule that an unfigured note indicates a root position triad are frequently seen, especially in early Italian figured basses. In almost every case where a bass note has been chromatically raised and thereby functions like a leading tone moving by half-step to the following note, it should be harmonized with a sixth chord rather than a root position chord. Even without chromatic alteration, most instances of an ascending half-step in the bass imply a first inversion chord moving to a root position chord.

2. Not every instance involving a sustained harmony against a moving bass is clearly indicated with lines as in Example 28e. As a rule of thumb, notes with durations shorter than the basic duration (i.e., usually the value indicated in the lower figure of the time signature) should be treated as decorative or nonchord pitches; in other words they should not all receive fresh harmonies.

3. All authentic cadences (i.e., with root movement down a perfect fifth) should have a major triad or a major-minor seventh on the penultimate chord. If this is not indicated the player must make the necessary chromatic alterations.

4. Some evidence suggests that the final chord in a minor composition should be changed to a major chord (Picardy third), if this does not contradict a minor third in other written parts. This principle should, however, be applied with discretion. One solution, justified by written out cadences in other music, is to play an open 1–5–8 sonority without any third.

5. Sometimes "unnecessary" figures are added as reminders to the player. In Example 28c, measure 2, the 5♭ in the alternate figuration (enclosed in brackets) simply reminds the player that he should play a diminished fifth; it does not tell him to lower the fifth (i.e., to B♭♭).

6. When long appoggiaturas, prepared trills, or suspensions are present in the upper written parts, the safest and most satisfactory solution will usually be to omit these notes from the figured bass accompaniment, especially in late Baroque music.

7. Occasionally triads may be changed to seventh chords or vice versa, or the entire chord may be changed if there is sufficient justification in the other written parts or in terms of harmonic or stylistic conventions. The bass line itself may occasionally be adapted to the characteristics of the instrument by changing octaves, repeating notes, or with great discretion, adding decorative notes to the line.

8. The words *tasto solo* (single touch) indicate that the bass line is to be played alone without accompanying chords. The term *all' unisono* indicates that the bass line is to be doubled in octaves and the chords omitted. These practices are not always clearly indicated in the music but must sometimes be inferred from the context of the written parts. Fugal sections or pedal point passages, for example, must usually be played tasto solo; unison or octave passages in the written parts would call for all' unisono. Some sections with deliberately thin and simple textures may best be played with no accompaniment (senza cembalo) whether this is indicated in the music or not.

Though a four-part texture with the bass in the left hand and three notes in the right hand may be taken as the norm for realizing Baroque figured basses on the keyboard, there are other appropriate possibilities. The bass may be doubled at the lower octave; other parts may be added in the right hand or the left hand, especially if increased volume is called for by the music. Conversely, a thinner texture of three or even two parts may be used for light or very fast moving sections. In general, the extremely high or low ranges are to be avoided, but sometimes this principle may be abrogated by special characteristics of the music.

The voice leading principles to be followed are in general those of traditional or common practice style—movement by common tone or step whenever possible, a general preference for contrary motion especially between outer voices, avoidance of parallel fifths and octaves, and proper preparation and resolution of dissonance. Bearing in mind the original improvised nature of figured bass realization, however, it is not necessary to search always for antiseptically correct solutions, especially as regards the relation of the upper parts of the accompaniment to the written upper parts. An occasional clash between these two elements is almost unavoidable, and it is often better to have a convincing line in the upper parts of the accompaniment, that momentarily clashes with the written parts, than it is to have an awkward, stilted line merely to avoid such clashes.

As to the choice of instruments for the realization of figured bass, there is some evidence to support a preference for organ for sacred music and harpsichord (occasionally lute) for secular music. This is, however, by no means an absolute principle, and the conductor should feel free to allow factors like acoustic conditions, instrument availability, musical characteristics, and personal taste to influence the choice of instruments. It is both stylistically appropriate and musically effective to double the bass line with gamba, cello, bassoon, double bass, or other instruments, either singly or in combinations such as cello and bass.

In general, the chord progressions of the accompaniment are to be played in a smooth legato manner, but, especially on the harpsichord, various types of broken chords—up, down, or moving both up and down—may be used with great effectiveness. In accompanying recitatives, for example, long chords may be arpeggiated in an effective accompaniment to the singer; more rapidly changing chords may be played without arpeggiation.

In terms of melodic and contrapuntal interest, the general principle is that the accompaniment should not slavishly duplicate the melodic line, nor should it overpower the melody. When the solo line has long sustained notes or rests, however, the accompaniment can and should assume greater importance. Sometimes the bass itself in such instances becomes melodically more interesting, in which case the upper parts of the accompaniment may remain relatively simple. When this is not the case the upper parts should achieve melodic interest, most appropriately by using melodic ideas from the written solo part. It is also possible to introduce imitation of the vocal line in one or more parts of the accompaniment, but this demands a supreme skill and it must be extremely well done to be of any value. Bach was reported to be a master in this respect.

In this brief section it has not been possible to present all of the details of figured bass realization, but it is hoped that enough information has been given to encourage choral conductors to experiment with written realizations or improvised realizations. More typically the conductor will be confronted with published realizations, and it is hoped that sufficient information has been given to enable him to judge the appropriateness and effectiveness of these or to alter and improve them if necessary. As a general rule he should seek a middle ground between a realization that is overblown and studied, as many older nineteenth-century realizations are, and one that is too timid and uninteresting, as some twentieth-century realizations are. Whether the realization is improvised or played from music, it should have the sense of freshness and invention of an improvised realization. Unlike the careful fidelity to the printed scores which characterizes an effective accompaniment of Romantic music, the accompaniment of Baroque music should have a bold sense of adventure and discovery.

INTERPRETATION OF TEMPO

Several writers of the Baroque period sought to give specific information about tempo by measuring it in terms of the human pulse, which for convenience may be represented as MM 80. In the following chart we have combined and interpreted information on tempo words and dance tempi contained in two separate entries in Quantz's *Essay.* The first column lists approximate metronome speeds, the second lists tempo words, and it is understood that the given metronome marking would apply to the quarter note in common time or to the half note in alla breve movements. The third column lists dances, and it is understood that the given metronome marking applies to the quarter note unless otherwise indicated.

METRONOME MARKING	TEMPO WORDS	BAROQUE DANCES
160	Allegro assai (allegro molto, presto, etc.)	Bouree, Chaconne, Furie, Manche, Menuet, Rigaudon, Canarie ♩., Gigue ♩.
120	Allegro (poco allegro, vivace, etc.)	Gavotte
80	Allegretto (allegro ma non tanto, non troppo, non presto, moderato, etc.)	Courante, Entree, Loure, Sarabande, Musette
40	Adagio cantabile (cantabile, arioso, larghetto, soave, dolce, poco andante, affetuoso, pomposo, maestoso, alla siciliana, adagio spiritoso, etc.)	
20	Adagio assai (adagio pesante, lento, largo assai, mesto, grave, etc.)	

As tempting as it would be to take such information as an absolute guide, it must be pointed out that neither modern scholars nor indeed Baroque theorists ever regarded such instructions as universally binding or accurate. These tempo marks did not so much determine the pace of the music but more importantly its expression. Ultimately the choice of tempo in Baroque music must involve such factors as the character of the music, the fastest note values present in the music, the technical abilities and personality of the performer, and the acoustical conditions of the performance location. The enormously wide variety of tempi suggested by the chart above runs counter to statements in both primary and secondary sources recommending against such extremes. On the other hand, at least to some extent, the suggestion of relatively fast tempi contained in these lists is supported by such statements as the following about Johann Sebastian Bach: "In the performance of his own pieces he usually took the tempo very lively, but he knew how to bring in addition to this liveliness so much variety in his performance, that every piece under his direction spoke eloquently."[12]

Once a tempo has been established there is the question of how strictly it should be maintained. There is a tendency in recent years to claim that all Baroque

Claudio Monteverdi, 1567–1643
(*The New York Public Library
Picture Collection*)

Giovanni Pierluigi da Palestrina,
1525–1594
(*The New York Public Library
Picture Collection*)

music, except recitative, must be played with an absolutely unchanging tempo, and there are frequent references in modern writings to the "mechanical regularity" of Baroque rhythm. This position is probably an overreaction to nineteenth-century excesses of freedom in tempo; but as usual the truth is somewhere in between. There is certainly no justification for distorting the music with excessive, arbitrary, and tasteless changes of tempo, but there is also no justification for rigid, mechanical, insensitive maintenance of one unvaried tempo in every piece.

It is obvious that a flexible tempo is demanded not only by recitative but also by unmeasured instrumental preludes and toccatas especially in the early Baroque, by early vocal monody, and in other types of music. In recitative the danger is perhaps in misusing the freedom of tempo. Though the tempo should be flexible, care must be taken to see that the shape of the musical line is discerned, the sense of ensemble between soloist and accompaniment preserved, and the meaning and character of the words recognized.

For other music there is convincing evidence that certain types of discrete tempo changes are stylistically appropriate. C. P. E. Bach suggests that the repetition in minor of a passage originally in major may be played more slowly and expressively. Other writers suggest that changes in tempo between sections of a composition may be appropriate even though not indicated.

Within sections the possibility of tempo changes is also sanctioned by various writers. Cadences, especially at the close of sections, may be played rallentando, even when not indicated, or when indicated by the word *adagio* which in this case may be taken to mean "gradually slower" rather than "suddenly slower." Care must be taken, however, to avoid taking too many ritardandos and thereby destroying the natural flow of the music. In general, fast music should have fewer and less exaggerated changes of tempo than slow music.

There is also some evidence for a judicious use of *tempo rubato* in Baroque music. The term *tempo rubato* means "robbed time" and generally implies that time taken from one note is added to another. Leopold Mozart suggests that a "true virtuoso" may draw out some notes longer than others, but warns that the accompanist must maintain a strict tempo. For a similar recommendation 100 years later see Chopin's words on page 461.

In summary, there were and there are no rigid rules governing the establishment of correct tempo, since pace was also determined by various extramusical factors such as the size of the choral and orchestral forces, the acoustics of the room, and the musical texture of the composition. In general, the writings of the period suggest that the Baroque masters chose considerably faster tempi than one ascribes to them today, particularly in the slow movements. But quick movements too were evidently played with great virtuosity and vitality, as can be substantiated if the pulse (c. MM = 80) and technical possibilities (that the sixteenth notes can still be played wth single bow strokes by the strings and double tonguing by the winds) are used as guides.

PHRASING, ARTICULATION, AND DYNAMICS

The absence of extensive indications for phrasing, articulation, and dynamics in Baroque music should not be taken to indicate that the music should be performed in a colorless, undifferentiated manner. Phrases should be carefully shaped and delineated, articulation varied to suit the character of the music, and dynamics sensitively used.

Signs for holds (⌒) or slight pauses ( ) 𝄓   ) were sometimes used at phrase endings, but more often these are left to the discretion of the performer.

Slurs were used with increasing frequency and explicitness throughout the period but were still often left to the interpretation of the performer. Slurs never represent types of bowing in Baroque music, but are always indications of articulation whose execution is described in the instructional works of the period. The dash (|, ▲, or ▼) was used to indicate staccato. The dot above notes was used for a variety of often contradictory purposes (see also the section on notation), but toward the end of the period sometimes seems to imply a lighter staccato than the dash. Several notes with dots under a slur may be used to suggest a portato articulation, i.e., a slight intensity articulation. In general, slow movements should be more legato and fast movements more detached, but not so sharply detached as to destroy the flow of the melodic line.

There is some tendency to oversimplify the interpretation of dynamics in Baroque music by saying that it was exclusively one of terraced dynamics, i.e.,

Heinrich Schütz, 1585–1672
(*The Bettmann Archive*)

Schütz and his singers, during his conductorship at Dresden
(*The Bettmann Archive*)

abrupt changes of loud and soft. While it is certainly true that terraced dynamics were the rule with certain instruments, such as harpsichord and organ, and in certain instances, such as passages devoted to echo effects, there is ample evidence to indicate that in other instances it was possible to have more gradual changes in volume. This does not give the performer license to introduce overblown late Romantic crescendi and decrescendi but it does justify tasteful, controlled rises or falls in dynamics when they are called for naturally by various factors, such as the melodic line, the rythmic drive, the harmonic force, or the text. Within fugues, for instance, there is a natural and unavoidable crescendo as voices are added in different registers, but the first voices to enter must not then cause further dynamic intensity because they sense the initial buildup.

Occasionally crescendi and decrescendi are clearly indicated by words or (rarely) by "hairpin" signs. More commonly for example in some passages in Vivaldi, a crescendo may be implied by the successive use of $p \ldots f \ldots ff$. Here the dynamics may be interpreted to imply a gradual increase in loudness rather than successive abrupt changes. Indeed, a single dynamic sign may sometimes indicate a gradual change, *p* for example may sometimes mean "becoming softer" rather than "suddenly softer," but in the majority of cases, the abrupt meaning will probably be correct.

The use of different dynamics for repeated sections or change of section is approved by most Baroque authorities. Most Baroque movements are understood to begin forte even if not so marked. Later contrasting sections are frequently marked or they may be interpreted as being softer. However, the change in dynamics does not mean a change in mood. Especially on literal or varied repeats it is appropriate to follow a forte statement with a piano restatement. Similarly, returns of ritornello or rondo sections may be played forte to contrast them with the intermediary sections.

SUMMARY

We have seen that the solution to problems of performance practice in the Baroque period often represents a middle way between excess and timidity, between subjectivity and objectivity, between restraint and freedom, between convention and invention. And yet this middle way is not one of blandness, caution, or pedantry. One possible approach to achieve this would be first to perform a passage in as controlled and colorless a manner as possible, with absolutely regular rhythm, rigid tempo, flat dynamic levels, straight tone and no decoration, and then to perform the same passage with extreme rhythmic rubato, tempo changes, dynamic fluctuations, intense vibrato, and extensive ornamentation. Finally the passage should be repeated with an attempt to reach a natural, convincing middle ground between these two extremes. One can also profitably listen to performances by groups specializing in authentic and effective performance of Baroque music, and then with the style characteristics assimilated in the ear and mind, still have the courage to experiment with introducing appropriate elements of one's own performing personality, so that the spontaneity of the music, which is perhaps its most vital and enduring characteristic, may be fully expressed.

NOTES

1. Manfred F. Bukofzer, *Music in the Baroque Era* (New York: W. W. Norton and Company, Inc., 1947), p. 19.

2. Nikolaus Harnoncourt, the *B Minor Mass* (J. S. Bach), Das Alte Werk (Telefunken), SKN 20, p. 2.

3. Le Cerf de la Vieville, *Historie de la Musique*, Vol. II (Amsterdam, 1725), p. 305; Robert Donington, *The Interpretation of Early Music*, Revised Edition (New York: St. Martin's Press, Inc., 1974), p. 517.

4. Walter E. Buszin, *Foreword* to Edition Peters 6101, J. S. Bach, *Motet I: Singet dem Herrn* (New York: Peters Edition, 1959).

5. Robert Cushman, *Notes* to Recording VUX 2010, J. S. Bach, *Motets* (New York, 1961).

6. This problem is discussed in detail in chapter eleven in the section "Vocal Quality and the Nature of Choral Singing."

7. Joachim Quantz, *Essay* (Berlin, 1752), section 9, p. 2.

8. Johann Adolf Scheibe, *Critische Musicus* (Hamburg, 1737), section 1, p. 12.

9. Michael Praetorius, *Syntagma Musicum*, III (Wolfen-büttell, 1619), p. 231.

10. Marin Mersenne, *Harmonie universelle*, 2 vols. (Paris: S. Cramoisy, 1636–1637). The section on instruments was translated by R. F. Chapman, The Hague, 1957. Book 2, section on Lute Ornaments, p. 24.

11. Carl Philipp Emanuel Bach, *Versuch* (Berlin, 1753), Translated and edited by W. J. Mitchell as *Essay on the True Art of Playing Keyboard Instruments* (New York: W. W. Norton and Company, Inc., 1949), Book 3, p. 20.

12. See note 6 above.

Chapter Twelve
RECOMMENDED READING LIST

Arnold, Frank T. *The Art of Accompaniment from a Thorough-Bass*. New York: Dover Publications, 1965, 2 vols. The standard reference work on this important subject.

Bukofzer, Manfred F. *Music in the Baroque Era*. New York: W. W. Norton and Company, Inc., 1947. Though subsequent scholarship may have found fault with some facts or attitudes, this remains the definitive work on the vast literature of this fascinating period.

Davison, Archibald T. and Willi Apel. *Historical Anthology of Music*. Cambridge, Mass.: Harvard University Press, 1949. Oriental, medieval and Renaissance music, vol. 1; Baroque, rococo and pre-classical music, vol 2. The breadth of examples and the brief but highly informative notes make these volumes a valuable study of these periods.

Landon, H. C. Robbins, ed. *Studies in eighteenth-century music*. New York: Oxford University Press, 1970.

(See also Crocker, Donington, Dorian, and Dart from chapters 11 and 14.)

Palisca, Claude V. *Baroque Music*. Englewood Cliffs: Prentice-Hall, 1968. A brief, valuable introduction to the salient aspects of Baroque music history.

Chapter Thirteen

The Classical Period

What is the point of all this noise about classic and romantic.
The important thing is that a work be well made throughout
and then it will also be a classic.—JOHANN WOLFGANG VON GOETHE[1]

IN THE HISTORY of every art form there are periods that are characterized by stability and restraint, balance and symmetry, clarity and simplicity, objectivity and traditionalism. These are called "classic" periods and are usually best understood in contrast to periods that are called "romantic" and that are characterized by instability and exuberance, imbalance and asymmetry, picturesqueness and fantasy, subjectivity and experimentation. The term "classic" may also be used for periods marked by an extraordinary degree of perfection and achievement. In both senses of the word the period of music history extending roughly from the last third of the eighteenth century into the first third of the nineteenth century and centering on the works of Haydn, Mozart, and Beethoven may be called a classical period. This is true despite the fact that one of the most famous writers on music of the time, E. T. A. Hoffmann, referred to these three composers as the first romantic composers.

This period is also called the Viennese classical period because most of the major works of the period were written or performed in the capital of the Austro-Hungarian empire. It is interesting to note, however, that not one of the famed Viennese triumvirate was a native Viennese. Haydn was born in Rohrau, Mozart in Salzburg, and Beethoven in distant Bonn, Germany.

Between the Baroque and Classical periods, or actually overlapping them, was the Rococo period, extending roughly from 1725 to 1775. This was a period of transition and experimentation that produced some interesting and delightful music but none to rival that of Bach and Handel in the previous period or Haydn and Mozart in the coming period. Three of the most famous sons of Johann Sebastian Bach may be said to personify in their music the main trends of this period. Wilhelm Friedemann Bach continued the basic trends of the Baroque period; Johann Christian Bach represented the elegant and somewhat artificial formality of the *style galant*; and Carl Philipp Emanuel Bach incorporated the brilliant and somewhat violent expressivity of the *empfindsamer Stil.*

In a sense it is difficult to equate the Viennese classical period with its brief span of time, its geographical limitation, and its relatively small number of composers with a period like the Baroque, which stretched over a century and a half, embraced the leading nations of Europe, and involved a large number of significant composers. Our approach to the Classical period will differ from that of previous chapters in that it will focus more on questions of general character and structure than on specific aspects of performance practice.

GENERAL CHARACTER AND STRUCTURE

The Classical period in music is generally associated with the Enlightenment in philosophy. The trend toward secularization that dominated this philosophy could be said to be reflected in the increased importance of instrumental music and secular choral music and the somewhat lessened importance of sacred choral music. To varying degrees, the lives of the three composers also reflected influences of this movement as well as influences from such events as the French Revolution. And yet each in his own way had a strong religious faith and each made a lasting contribution to the literature of sacred choral music.

Our concern will not be to regard their music as the outcome of the social and cultural environment, though that certainly was important, but rather to understand it in intrinsically musical terms, as the result of a process of development that began in the music of the Baroque and Rococo periods and reached a degree of perfection in the Classical period that is one of the unique achievements of mankind.

We could attempt to describe this style by showing its evolution. There is even a quasi-Hegelian explanation according to which the thesis of Baroque polyphony and the antithesis of Rococo homophony resulted in the synthesis of classical style. At the very least this theory suffers from incompleteness, but the concept of the classical style as a synthesis does have a considerable amount of truth to it. A more complete picture can be gained if we consider classical style as a synthesis of expressive content and proportional form, especially if we ascribe the widest possible meaning to these terms and if we are careful to avoid any suggestion that the two are dichotomous.

We could also attempt to describe classical style by comparing it with earlier styles. If we compare the style of Haydn, Mozart, and early Beethoven with that of late Baroque composers like Bach and Handel, we find first of all that both groups represented points of stylistic stability and perfection, and yet they differed from each other in some quite specific ways. Perhaps the most notable differences are in the approaches to the expression of emotion and the articulation of time. We have already cited the Baroque predilection for the full and exclusive expression of a single dominant emotion or mood for a single movement with contrast coming between the moods. This was replaced in the Classical period to a large extent by a more dynamic expression of differing emotions and moods within a movement. We are not speaking here of exaggerated changes of a mood in a sentimental, overly romantic sense, much less of any such nonsense as male and female themes which earlier writers have tried to impute to this music. Rather we are speaking of different approaches to the general expressive character of the music.

The differences in the articulation of time is, in many ways, an outgrowth of the differences in emotional expression. The Baroque treatment of musical time was a continuous flow, interrupted not at all in some works, like fugues, or only momentarily in works like binary dance forms. In contrast, the classical treatment of time was to articulate it into a series of events—motives and phrases on the smaller level, sections on a larger level. In both instances the differences cited above are ones of degree and are not absolute, and in both instances there are works in one period which conform to the characteristics cited for the other. Nevertheless, they stand as generally accepted and significant trends.

Rather than pursue either the historical or the comparative approach we shall focus our study of classical style upon the form which in many ways embodies the essence of the style—the single movement sonata or "sonata-allegro" form. We shall discover that the essence of this form underlies not only the first movements of instrumental works, but rather a whole spectrum of works including the important choral works of the period. Our discussion of this form can lead us, hopefully, to a consideration of all the main aspects of the classical style.

Classical Sonata Form

The sonata form, like the classical style itself, was not recognized and named until long after it had become a part of history. The pianist and Beethoven student Czerny and the German theorist Marx, both lay claim to having "discovered" the form, but they wrote in the second quarter of the nineteenth century after the death of the last of the Viennese classical composers. For the classical composers themselves, the sonata form was not a special form like a *da capo* aria or a French overture—it was simply the way one wrote music.

We shall follow their lead, and rather than attempt to describe sonata form in terms of a rigid pattern or scheme, we shall describe it somewhat like a fugue, as a technique, as a musical "way of doing things." The three main characteristics of classical sonata technique may be described as follows:

1. A balance between continuity and discontinuity is achieved by writing musical material that is organized, to be sure, into articulated phrases, periods, and larger units, but nevertheless has a sure sense of forward, goal-directed motion toward two main cadential points in the movement—one at the end of the first section (often marked with a double bar and a repeat sign) and one at the end of the movement.

2. A balance between unity and variety is achieved not only by repetition, contrast, and restatement, but most especially by reinterpretation of musical material.

3. A symmetrical distribution of stability and instability, tension and release, or establishment and digression is achieved basically by a tri-partite or "arch-like" organization of tonalities, thematic material, and types of expression.

If this description sounds like a prescription for music itself, it should be remembered that this was more or less the view of the classical composer. It is not without significance that he placed titles like *Minuet, Rondo,* or *Variations* on movements that were written in what were by then basically historic, fixed forms, but never put a title on movements in sonata form. To have told Haydn or Mozart that they were writing movements in sonata form would have been almost like telling them they were speaking in German; the form (or technique if you will) was as natural to them as their native language. Furthermore, it should be remembered that sonata principles influenced or were absorbed into almost every other form in the Classical period; they appeared in Kyries of masses, in ensemble numbers of operas, in the Minuets of chamber works, in rondo-finales of symphonies, or in sections of variations and fantasia movements for piano.

Our description avoids most of the time-honored but often fruitless arguments that have grown up around sonata form. Is it a binary or a ternary form? (It has aspects of both.) Is a development section necessary to define the form? (The principle of reinterpretation of material is essential, but this need not be limited to a specific part of the movement.) Is a specified order of themes and tonalities necessary to define the form? (The use of themes and tonalities shape the form, but no single pattern is sacrosanct.)

To penetrate more deeply into the classical style as revealed in sonata movements, we shall apply some aspects of the three analytical approaches discussed in chapter ten—the tonality or harmonic approach of Riemann and others, the motivic or thematic approach of Tovey and others, and the linear or contrapuntal approach of Schenker and others.

Tonality Approach

The essence of the tonality approach of Riemann was the establishment of three basic functional chord categories—the tonic, subdominant, and dominant, together with various possible substitute or alternate chords. Movement toward the dominant was considered to present a sense of tension, movement toward the subdominant or tonic, more of a sense of release.

The tonality approach with its emphasis on harmony is especially appropriate for the analysis of the classical style. Although classical music achieved a unique synthesis of harmony and counterpoint, it is always harmony that led the way. It is not by chance that Mozart began his composition lessons for his student Thomas Atwood with a thorough study of harmony and figured bass.

The use of tonality in classical sonata movements will generally follow the principles we discussed earlier. One of the principal means for creating the sense of stability at the beginning of a movement is the clear establishment of a tonality. The creation of instability or tension in the following sections is created by a modulation "up" to the dominant side (V or III), or by a rapid movement through various keys or regions in the development section.

It is in the nature of the classical sonata with its emphasis on continuity that the precise moment when the establishment of the initial tonality ceases and the

Wolfgang Amadeus Mozart, 1756–1791 (The New York Public Library Picture Collection)

modulation toward the new tonality begins is often difficult to establish. Sometimes, even the point of arrival at the new key may be somewhat ambiguous. The point of return to the original tonality (usually about ⅔ to ¾ of the way through the movement) is, however, almost invariably a clearly established event, especially when preceded by a long dominant preparation; one could almost compare it to the sudden, joyful return of an absent loved one.

Classical composers, especially Mozart, take full advantage of the more relaxed nature of the subdominant function, often writing extended sections in the subdominant tonality that act as a brake on the tension generated by other tonalities. These sections function in a sense like expanded versions of the plagal (IV-I) cadence, used familiarly as the close of hymns.

On the smallest level of harmony, that of the intervallic construction of individual chords, it is certain that classical composers regarded major and minor triads as more stable than other triads or seventh chords, and that they regarded diatonic chords as more stable than chromatic chords. Whether, in addition, they also regarded the major triad as more stable than the minor triad, as some writers maintain, is not clear-cut and seems to vary from composer to composer, or even from piece to piece. Similarly, the stereotyped usage of major chords or tonalities for more positive, pleasant emotional expression and minor for more negative, sad emotions is subject to variance from work to work. Granted, for example, that Mozart will usually choose minor for the expression of sadness, some of his most poignant movements (like the slow movement of the *D Major String Quintet* or the aria "Dove sono" from *Figaro*) are written in major.

The conductor must be aware of the way both small and large scale characteristics of harmony and tonality function in a form. Exactly how these influence his performance is another matter. Knowing that a section near the end of a work is written in the subdominant does not necessarily mean that the conductor should make this section softer and slower; that would almost be like adding salt to a dish that has already been salted. Rather, his function is to be sure that tempo and dynamics do not contradict or interfere with the natural lowering of tension associated with the subdominant, unless of course the composer has specified otherwise.

The effects of tonality may not only apply to relationships within a composition but to the tonalities themselves. Tovey claims that we tend to hear all keys in relation to C major, the tonality most of us first learned. According to this, then, the key of F major has a more relaxed character than the key of A major, because F is to the subdominant side of C, while A is to the dominant side. Though this theory seems to be confirmed in works like Beethoven's F Major *Pastorale* Symphony, it should be pointed out that the characteristics of keys could come as much from instrumental characteristics, such as the open strings of the stringed instruments, or from aspects of tuning as we pointed out earlier.

Thematic Approach

Despite the great importance of tonality in the classical sonata, to concentrate on it to the exclusion of any significant consideration of thematic material would be like studying only the background of a painting and never discussing the foreground figures. On the other hand, to treat the sonata and the classical style as though it were only a certain way of arranging themes would be equally inappropriate.

Although occasionally a harmonic progression, a dynamic change, or even the use of rests may assume thematic importance, for the most part "theme" in classical music means melody. The approach to melody can be centered upon consideration of how the foreground pitch patterns and rhythmic patterns relate to the background of tonality and meter. Do the foreground elements confirm the background elements or do they conflict with it as in the case of dissonant "nonharmonic" tones or syncopated rhythms?

Analysis of this type can bring out the marvelous unity between background and foreground elements that is a hallmark of the classical style. The tempo of a movement, for example, is not some totally mysterious factor that must be derived by intuition or by guesswork, but rather it is based upon a consideration of the way that the various levels of rhythmic activity from the fastest to the slowest relate to one another. A study of the foreground rhythms leads toward an understanding of the proper pace and accentuation of the background tempo and meter. One of the unique features of classical melody is that it often contains rapid but highly effective shifts from one level of rhythmic activity to another. By contrast Baroque melodies usually concentrated on one basic level of rhythmic activity. A movement exclusively in sixteenth notes, like the first two preludes of the *Well-Tempered Clavier*, would be almost unthinkable in the characteristic classic style.

In addition to considering the relationship of melody to the metric and harmonic or tonal background, it is also possible to consider it as an independent phenomenon following its own intrinsically conditioned course of development throughout a piece. As a first step we must recognize that not all classical melodic material is the same. At one extreme are stereotyped formulas, such as scales and arpeggios, which are used as "filler" material almost the same way an artist uses a repetitive design in a painting. These figures fill in musical time much in the same way that the right hand chords of a Baroque continuo part fill in musical space. They are not essential for the basic musical message, and yet the music would sound bare, ungraceful, and incomplete without them. In both cases filler material from one piece could almost be interchangeable with filler material from another, and yet the composition or improvisation of this material can involve a high degree of artistic skill and imagination. Melodic filler material can be used effectively at cadence points where more interesting material would distract the attention from the essential concluding aspects of the passage. It may also be used effectively in transitional passages. With most classical composers there is a subtle difference between the formulas used in transitional passages and those used in cadences or codas. In performance, filler material must be recognized for what it is. To try to sing or play these typical scale and arpeggio passages with exaggerated rubato and emotional expression would be like trying to present mashed potatoes as the main dish of a meal.

At the other extreme is melodic material of strong thematic interest and variety, often made up of musical motives presented in various successive combinations. Classical melodies tend to alternate between these two extremes with not much attention to the type of melodic material that lies between them. This "in between" type of melodic writing, on the other hand, was a staple of Baroque music. A typical Baroque melody begins with a distinctive head motive and then proceeds in a series of figures that may not have the interest, variety, and "catchiness" of the opening head motive, but never descends to the level of mere stereotyped scale and arpeggio figures. Classical melodies will, on the other hand, tend to be made up of a series of motives, with some repeated or varied. "Filler" material may be used at the cadential points or in transitional passages. The difference may be seen in the following examples.

Example 1

Bach, *B-minor Mass*, BWV 232

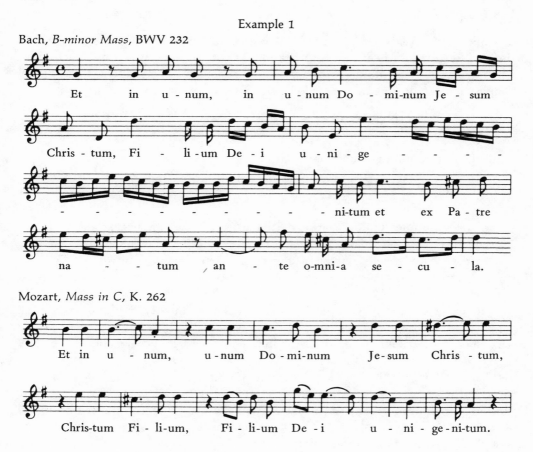

Mozart, *Mass in C*, K. 262

Applied to sonata movements, thematic analysis will usually show well-formed motives used to establish the stability of the opening thematic section and, perhaps to a lesser extent, of subsequent thematic sections. The number and variety of themes may range from the spartan economy of Haydn, who sometimes delights in creating a lengthy movement out of the resources of a single thematic idea, to the sometimes luxuriant profusion of Mozart, who often seems to have such an inexhaustible fund of thematic ideas available that they spill over into transition and development sections.

Linear Approach

Schenker had very specific ideas about basic underlying structure (as opposed to the surface formal scheme) of a sonata movement. He conceived this structure as an "interruption" (*Unterbrechung*) of the fundamental composition (*Ursatz*). In simple compositions the *Ursatz* could be expressed as follows:

Upper voice	$\hat{3}$	$\hat{2}$	$\hat{1}$
Lower voice	I	V	I

With the interruption this became:

Upper voice	$\hat{3}$	$\hat{2}$	//	$\hat{3}$	$\hat{2}$	$\hat{1}$
Lower voice	I	V		I	V	I

It is the interruption that lends the sense of dramatic urgency to a sonata movement. To understand this we can recall Leonard Meyer's theorem that "emotion or affect is aroused when a tendency to respond is arrested or inhibited."[2]

After we hear $\hat{3}$ $\hat{2}$ we have a strong sense of expectancy for a concluding
       I V
$\hat{1}$. This expectancy is heightened by the turbulent instability of the development
I
section. At the beginning of the recapitulation, however, we do not hear $\hat{1}$, but
                                                I
instead $\hat{3}$. When we finally hear $\hat{1}$ at the end of the movement the sense of con-
  I   I
clusion is therefore greatly intensified. The following chart compares the tonal, thematic, and linear analyses of a sonata movement with the traditional formal analytical divisions of a typical sonata movement.

	EXPOSITION				DEVELOPMENT	RECAPITULATION				
	First theme group	Transition	Second theme group	Closing theme group	Several sections	First theme group	Transition	Second theme group	Closing theme group	CODA
Traditional Formal Analysis										
Tonal Analysis	Stability Tonic (I or i)	Instability Modulation	(Partial Stability) Dominant (V or III)		Instability Modulatory (ending on V)	Stability Tonic (I or i)				
Thematic Analysis	Well-formed theme(s)	"Filler" material	Well-formed theme(s)		Fragments of themes and/or "filler material"	Well-formed themes	"Filler material"	Well-formed theme(s)	"Filler material"	
Linear Analysis — Upper voice	$\hat{3}$	$\hat{2}$				$\hat{3}$		$\hat{2}$		$\hat{1}$
Linear Analysis — Lower voice	I	V				I		V		I

An eclectic approach involving aspects of all three approaches will usually be most helpful in revealing the structural dynamics and musical logic of works written in sonata form whether this form is used in the "textbook sense" of the traditional formal scheme or in a freer sense. In most choral music the sonata principle appears in this freer sense, rather than in a traditional sense. Sometimes, indeed, the sonata principle can be seen to operate in such a way that several movements may be drawn together into a single movement in analytical terms.

THE USE OF VOICES AND INSTRUMENTS

The problem of choosing the proper voices and instruments for the performance of works of the Classical period is not as critical as for those of earlier periods because the instruments are more clearly specified and, for the most part, they are instruments which are still in general use. We are part of an unbroken tradition of performances of works like the Haydn *Creation* and, though there have undoubtedly been some questionable accretions to the performance practice of these works, they are not totally strange to present-day interpreters and listeners. The problems that are most important are those of the use of continuo, the relative size of the choral and orchestral forces, and in some cases the choice of instruments.

Church music and opera as the most conservative branches of music were the last to give up the continuo. Most choral works of the Classical period still call for the continuo as can be seen from the presence of figures beneath the bass part in the scores. Its use is not as critical as in the Baroque period, for by now there are written parts for the middle range to fill in the middle of the texture. However, the use of the continuo is still to be recommended, if only for the slight touch of clarity that it can add to the articulation of the sound. In any event, however, an extremely elaborate and highly audible continuo part is not called for. The part, played preferably on a small organ or harpsichord, should be modest in volume and decoration, but played with incisive rhythm.

In contrast to the Baroque period, it is generally more stylistically correct to have larger choral forces than orchestral forces for the performance of classical works, as evidenced by the programs of Classical period performances and by such pictures as the one shown of a performance in Vienna in 1806 of Haydn's *Creation*.

As to the size and makeup of the orchestra there is a general misconception that the classical composers can only be performed with small ensembles. Actually their own ideas on the subject were more liberal and at the same time more practical. Mozart, in a letter to his father dated April 11, 1781, writes with enthusiasm about a performance of one of his symphonies with forty violins, ten violas, eight cellos, ten double basses, all the winds and brass doubled, and six bassoons. Beethoven also writes with approval of performances of his works with large instrumental forces, but, on the other hand, he once refused to conduct a performance with an orchestra of sixty musicians, insisting that the forces be reduced for the performance in the Vienna Musikvereinsaal.

As in so many matters the first concern of the composers themselves was the proper balance between the size of the orchestra, the character of the music, and especially the acoustical conditions of the hall and the nature of the performance. These considerations, rather than any supposed, arbitrary ideal should guide the present-day conductor. Performances of works like the *Creation* or the *Missa Solemnis* of Beethoven may be undertaken with the large resources of the modern chorus and orchestra without fear of violating the spirit of these works for they were conceived essentially as concert works, not as liturgical works. On the other hand it would be totally out of character to inflate the dimensions of an early Salzburg mass of Mozart, a work written essentially for liturgical purposes and not nearly as well suited for the concert hall or for performance by large modern orchestral and choral forces.

Most of the instruments used in the choral-orchestral music of the Classical period are those in present use. Even the trumpet parts, which were originally written for non-keyed instruments,[3] are probably best played on modern keyed trumpets. The possible loss in terms of the sound quality is more than compensated for by the gain in ease of performance and accuracy of intonation.

The question of vibrato is a difficult one. There is little doubt that both singers and instrumentalists of the period used vibrato more as a special effect than as a constant part of tone production, and yet the ears of modern listeners have become so thoroughly accustomed to performances of classical music with constant vibrato, especially in the strings, that a performance without vibrato or with vibrato only on long and expressive notes would probably distress more than it would delight. Obviously, however, the thick wide vibrato and portamento of some Romantic music and performers would be just as inappropriate.

PROBLEMS OF NOTATION

Textual problems in the music of the Classical period are much less severe than in the Baroque. This is true not only because the composers and engravers were more careful and specific, but also because some of the best efforts of musicological scholarship have been devoted to the preparation of definitive editions of this music. The conductor of today has ready access to *Urtext* editions of most of the major works of the period, and in some cases he may also be able to consult a facsimile edition of the composer's manuscript.

The music notation of the scores of the classical period follows essentially the customs of modern notation. The few exceptions, such as the occasional use of treble clef sounding one octave lower in some cello parts, may usually be understood without difficulty from the context of the music. Similarly, those instances where there is some question as to the accuracy of the pitches may be usually solved by referring to the general principles of melody and harmony that are manifest in the music of this period.

Turning to the question of interpretation of rhythm patterns, one main problem is deciding whether or not to continue the Baroque practice of "overdotting," i.e., playing dotted notes as doubly dotted notes. The contemporary sources are unclear on this point, but certainly there would be nothing wrong in following the rather natural tendency of exaggerating, at least to a slight degree, the length of the dotted notes.

ORNAMENTATION AND IMPROVISATION

The classical attitude toward ornamentation and improvisation was quite different from that, for example, of the Middle Baroque. No longer was the compositional process shared between composer and performer as it was in the arias or slow movements of the earlier period. Now the composer wrote out all of the ornamentation either in notes or by using the conventional signs of the Baroque period. Even Mozart's own sister wrote to her brother asking for an ornamented version of a passage in a piano concerto rather than improvise it herself. If someone as familiar with Mozart's style as she would hesitate to add to or change his music, then surely those of us removed so much further in time and temperament must be equally hesitant to add decorations. Even so, Mozart was the closest of the three Viennese masters to the world of opera, where improvised decorations maintained their last bastion, and, therefore, he of all the composers would probably have been the least offended by ornamentation added by the performer. However, even as a seven-year-old, Mozart reportedly criticized a certain Herr Esser who played well but who apparently added too many notes. The genial Haydn would probably also not have objected too strenuously to added ornamentation. But one can almost hear the rage of Beethoven at any singer or instrumentalist who would be so presumptuous as to add ornaments to his music.

Improvisation in classical music was largely confined to such special instances as the cadenzas of concertos; it was no longer the vital ingredient of the art that it was in the Baroque. Granted that all three of the composers we have discussed, as well as other figures like Hummel, were skilled improvisors; they were already recognized as something special. No longer was the average musician expected to master completely the skill of improvisation.

Though the magnitude of the problem of ornamentation is much less, nevertheless there are still some very difficult problems in the interpretation of ornamental signs. Essentially this resolves itself to a decision as to whether one should follow the instructions of writers like Johann Joachim Quantz, C. P. E. Bach, and Leopold Mozart, whose treatises appeared before the birth of Mozart, or whether one should follow the instructions of writers like Johann Nepomuk Hummel, Ludwig Spohr, and Carl Czerny, whose treatises appeared after the death of Beethoven. The treatises of Daniel Turk, Johann Kirnberger, and others that did appear in the middle of the Classical period may be of some assistance, but they are not as extensive and pertinent as the earlier and later treatises.

The trill may be taken as a typical example of the change in performance practice. C. P. E. Bach in 1753 states that every trill must begin on the note above the principal note; Johann Hummel in 1828 states that every trill must begin on the principal note. Whom should we follow when performing Beethoven or Mozart? We know that Beethoven greatly admired Bach's treatise and recommended it to his students; we know that Hummel was not only a pupil of Mozart's, but for a time actually lived in his house and therefore had opportunity to study his method of performance at first hand. Without going into all the details of the problem (the whole issue is complex enough that a recent conference of German musicologists was devoted entirely to it), we shall simply say that the bulk of historical evidence seems to favor applying the ornamentation rules of the late Baroque period for most of the music of the Classical period. Hummel's rule for the performance of of the trill, for example, was not presented as a summary of past practice, but rather it was advocated by him as an *innovation*, one which, of course, was to become the rule in the music of the latter nineteenth century and twentieth century.

On the other hand, the bulk of performance practice tradition since the Classical period, including the performances of some of the most respected recent interpreters, seems to favor a more liberal, progressive interpretation. Support for at least the occasional use of a modern, principal note beginning for the trill can be found in some isolated statements from treatises by Cartier, Adam, and Clementi, all written around the turn of the nineteenth century. Cartier justifies such exceptions in those cases where the melody would otherwise be obscured. This appeal to a sensitive consideration of the music itself, rather than a mechanical reliance on abstract rules, could make a good motto for the whole subject of ornament interpretation.

In the case of the appoggiatura there is general agreement among writers before, during, and immediately after the Classical period that they should be performed according to the principles enunciated in the treatises of the late Baroque, such as the placement of the decorative note at the time of the principal note and not before. The few isolated references in Leopold Mozart and Joachim Quantz to the so-called *durchgehender Vorschlag* (passing "before-stroke") cannot be taken to mean that the placement of the decorative note before the time of the principal note was a regular alternative. It was an exception that appeared only in a few treatises and then only for a few specific musical instances. Most treatises, even those of Hummel, Spohr, and Czerny, written in the 1830s are unequivocal in their prescriptions for the performance of the appoggiatura at the time of the main note, with its length being determined by the principles we have already discussed on page 286.

In view of this unanimity of historical sources, it is difficult to understand how the tradition of performance practice since the Classical period should have departed so strongly from these principles. A modern conductor who would perform the opening of the first chorus from Haydn's *The Seasons* in the historically correct manner as indicated in Example 2a might find himself criticized by singers and listeners used to countless performances as shown in Example 2b. Incidentally, as in Baroque ornamentation, the presence or absence of the slash through the appoggiatura note does not have any special significance as to the manner of performance.

Example 2

Haydn, *The Seasons*, "Komm, holder Lenz"

Turns, mordents, and other ornaments when they appear are also subject to the principles of interpretation discussed in the preceding chapter.

INTERPRETATION OF TEMPO

Edward Cone[4] and others have pointed out that one major change from the Baroque period to the Classical period was a change from music that basically moved by beats to music that basically moved by bars. One of the main reasons for this change is the general slowing down of harmonic rhythm in music of the Classical period. Furthermore, as we have pointed out earlier, rhythm in the Classical period tended to move frequently from one level of pulse to another, and this factor must be taken into account when deciding on the correct tempo. A tempo must be found that fits not only the rhythm of the opening section but also that of later sections with a change in level of rhythmic activity.

How fast should the compositions of the Classical period be performed? We have some specific evidence in letters of the composers. Mozart in a letter to his sister criticizes the charlatanism of the Roman pianist Clementi in designating his works *presto alla breve* and then playing them *allegro* in four. That Mozart himself could and did perform his works in a tempo that was considered very fast by audiences of the time is suggested by an anecdote connected with a concert he gave in Naples. The audience was so struck by his virtuoso speed that they thought it must come from some magic power contained in the ring Mozart wore. Later, when he heard about this, Mozart removed the ring and continued at the same tempo. This same Mozart warned that it was much easier to play a passage quickly because you could make errors without anyone noticing. And yet, he adds, one wonders if this is really beautiful.

In connection with tempo, it is probably not trivial to remark that all three of the classical composers, especially Mozart, were acquainted with Italian, and when they used Italian terms at the beginning of their works, they did not necessarily just think of them as abstract tempo designations as a modern composer might, but rather they were aware of the root meaning of such words as *andante* (walking, not slow), *allegro* (cheerful, not just fast), and *vivace* (lively, not just very fast). The modern interpreter would do well to remind himself of the original meaning of these terms when he encounters them.

Beyond these surface aspects the question of tempo and phrasing ultimately is bound up with the interpreter's understanding of the structure of the music. Once understood, this structure demands a certain tempo if it is to be made manifest, and it demands a sensitive balance between articulation and continuity of phrasing if the relationships between the parts and the whole are to be perceived in their true proportions. An overly slow tempo and exaggerated stops at phrase and period endings can split the living organism of a classical work into a series of dead fragments; an overly fast tempo and blurred cadences can reduce the clarity of the classical form to an inchoate mass.

Most people are convinced that the music of the Classical period should be performed strictly in tempo with no rubato, but that rubato is allowed in music after Beethoven. To put this matter in historical perspective, three quotations are cited:

> If the executant upon the clavier manages matters in such a way that one hand appears to play against time whilst the other hand strictly observes the beat, then the right thing has been done. In such a case the parts rarely move simultaneously, but they fit together all the same.—C. P. E. BACH[5]

> No one seems to understand the *tempo rubato* in an adagio, namely that the left hand does not know anything about it.—W. A. MOZART, letter to his father, 1777[6]

> The singing hand may deviate, the accompanist must keep time. . . . Fancy a tree with its branches swayed by the wind; the stem represents the steady time, the moving leaves are the melodic inflections. This is what is meant by *Tempo* and *Tempo rubato*.—F. CHOPIN[7]

What these three quotations suggest is first of all that rubato was known in the Baroque and Classical periods as well as in the Romantic. Secondly, however, and most importantly, they suggest that the rubato always occurred in the right hand while the left hand kept a steady rhythm. Translating this to choral and instrumental performance this suggests that the melody may be performed with subtle rubato, but the accompaniment should be maintained in a steady tempo.

PHRASING, ARTICULATION, AND DYNAMICS

One of the common faults in the performance of music of the Classical period is that of underphrasing. Daniel Türk in an amusing analogy points out that a change in phrasing in music can be as significant as the following change of phrasing in spoken language:

> He lost his life not, only his property.
> He lost his life, not only his property.

Türk specifically recommended shortening the last note of a phrase when necessary to separate it from the first note of the next phrase. Two other sources may be cited as evidence of the continued importance of this conception of phrasing.

> The caesuras are the commas of the song, which, as in speech, must be made manifest by a moment of relaxation. This is accomplished either by letting the last note of a phrase die away and firmly attacking the following one, or by diminishing the tone somewhat at the end of the phrase and increasing at the beginning of the next.—J. G. SULZER[8]

> Slight separations, such as rests of short duration, are not always indicated by the composer. The player must therefore provide them, when he sees that it is necessary, by letting the last note of the phrase die away. Indeed, in certain cases he must even let it end shortly before the completion of its normal duration.—P. BAILLOT[9]

Articulation in the music of Haydn, Mozart, and Beethoven, at least according to the tradition that is preserved today in the choruses and orchestras of Vienna, is differentiated, but within a more narrow range of possibilities than one would find in music of the late nineteenth century or the twentieth century. An extremely dry, short staccato is simply not to be heard in a performance of Mozart or Haydn

Haydn (at cembalo, left) conducting his opera *The Improvised Meeting*
(The Bettmann Archive)

by musicians steeped in the Viennese tradition. The sound always has a certain body and warmth to it, even when it is marked short as with dots. In particular, it should be remembered that dots under a slur are meant to be played with a portato articulation, rather than with a dry staccato. On the other hand, the unending legato that might be appropriate for some passages of late Romantic music is not appropriate for classical composers. Even a legato line should have a sense of phrasing; it should breathe whether sung or played on an instrument.

Probably the best guide for the proper inflection of music of the Classical period is to listen to the sound of the German language as it is spoken in Vienna. If you cannot hear this from a native Viennese speaker or from a recording, you can get some idea of what it is like by listening to the speech of someone from the southern United States, for the Viennese accent has many of the same gentle, lyrical qualities of the traditional Southern accent. To attempt to capture some of this same quality in the performance of the music may be more helpful than the finicky observance of a multitude of rules.

Dynamics are specified to a large extent in choral works of the Classical period, and one must be careful about adding extra dynamics. On the other hand, the written dynamics must not be timidly observed, for as we noted earlier they are often an integral part of the structure and expression of the music. To neglect or underplay crescendo effects in Haydn's *Creation* or Beethoven's *Missa Solemnis* would be totally against the spirit of the music and of the times. To add quaint little echo effects every time a phrase is repeated, however, would only lend a quality of fussiness and discontinuity that would be just as foreign.

SUMMARY

The masterworks of the Classical period are well known and frequently performed, and there is an unbroken line of tradition in these performances from the composers themselves to the present day. Therein lies the chief performance practice problem, for in the intervening years certain slight or extensive misinterpretations or reinterpretations of these works have acquired such a sense of authority that it would be difficult to contradict them, even if one could prove conclusively that they differed from the original intentions of the composer.

In this chapter we have suggested that the best approach to this music is through an understanding of its basic structure and expression, and we have emphasized this more than specific details. In the interpretation of such details as ornamentation, tempo, dynamics, etc., we have suggested that the Classical period occupies somewhat of a transitional role between the clear prescriptions of the late Baroque and those of the Romantic period.

NOTES

1. Friedrich Blume, *Classic and Romantic Music,* trans. M. D. Herder Norton (New York: W. W. Norton and Co., Inc., 1970), p. 16.

2. Leonard B. Meyer, *Emotion and Meaning in Music* (Chicago: The University of Chicago Press, 1965), p. 14.

3. The valve for use in brass instruments was invented in 1815.

4. Edward T. Cone, *Musical Form and Musical Performance* (New York: W. W. Norton and Co., Inc., 1968).

5. C. P. E. Bach, *Versuch* (Berlin, 1753). Trans. and ed. W. J. Mitchell as *Essay on the True Art of Playing Keyboard Instruments* (New York: W. W. Norton and Co., Inc., 1949), Book III, p. 28.

6. Emily Anderson, *The Letters of Mozart and His Family,* vol. 1 (New York: St. Martin's Press, Inc., 1966), p. 340.

7. E. Dannreuther, *Musical Ornamentation,* vol. II (London: Novello, 1895), p. 161.

8. Johann Georg Sulzer, *Allgemeine Theorie der Schönen Kunste* (Leipzig: in der Weidmannschen Buchhandlung, 1792), p. 125.

9. Pierre Marie Francois de Sales Baillot, *L'Art du Violon* (Paris: au Depot Central de la Musique, 1834), p. 17.

Chapter Thirteen
RECOMMENDED READING LIST

Landon, H. C. Robbins. *Essays on the Viennese Classical Style.* London: Barrie and Rockliff, 1970. A fascinating collection by a leading authority on the period.

Pauly, Reinhard G. *Music in the Classic Period.* 2nd edition. Englewood Cliffs: Prentice-Hall, 1973. A short but thorough introduction to the history of music in the Viennese Classical period.

Rosen, Charles. *The Classical Style.* New York: Viking Press, 1971. This fine book is a model combination of solid scholarship and creative insight from the standpoint of the performer.

Strunk, Oliver. *Source Readings in Music History.* New York: W. W. Norton and Co., Inc., 1950. A valuable collection of writings on all periods of music literature written by composers, theorists, critics, or others from the period.

Chapter Fourteen

The Romantic Period

Leaning, consciously or unconsciously, on the basis of
Beethoven's and Schubert's romanticism, there is a school
which, though not yet fully developed, has the elements of
becoming a notable epoch in the history of art. Its destiny
seems to be to unfetter an age still chained with a thousand
rings to the preceding century.—ROBERT SCHUMANN[1]

THE FIRST THING the interpreter of nineteenth-century music must come to realize
is that romanticism is an eternal factor that must be considered in the performance
of music from all periods. Romanticism was not an isolated phenomenon confined
exclusively to the period between 1800 and 1900. It occurs in all periods of musical
history. The challenge of the nineteenth century to the performer is achieving an
understanding of those characteristics of style that will produce performances which
are in keeping with the intentions of the composer. This is difficult during the Romantic period because the nineteenth century experienced a dramatic change in the
manner in which the artist conceived his work. It is precisely this factor that makes
the study of performance practices during this period so problematic.

When approached in relation to the Viennese classical period, the greatest
single change to emerge in the nineteenth century was that of the individualism and
interpretive subjectivity of the performer. This individuality—in the case of choral
art, the conductor's—gradually emerged in the second half of the century as the
primary driving force of musical interpretation. The performer of the eighteenth
century became the "reproducer" in the nineteenth century. As the period de-

veloped the interpretation of music became more and more subjective. This appeared in the early stages as an appeal to the fantasy of the listener. Finally, in the case of performers like Berlioz, Liszt, Wagner, and Mahler, intellectual understanding in the Age of Reason succumbed to sensuous emotionalism. The individual emerged triumphant.

GENERAL CHARACTER AND STRUCTURE

During the nineteenth century the whole musical life of the Western world underwent an important change. The focus of musical creativity shifted from Austria to Germany. The musical culture was enriched by new national schools of composition in Hungary, Bohemia, Poland, and Russia. The distinctive and highly self-conscious compositional idiom that emerged was, of course, caused by a number of factors: the new sense of national awareness, an eager and increasingly informed interest in the native traditions of folk music, and the premium placed on the expression of subjective convictions and longings by the Romantic composers.

Underlying these general characteristics was the intense desire of the nine-

The Crystal Palace, London (The Granger Collection)

teenth-century musician to use music as the vehicle of personal emotion and for the expression of universal longings. This predilection led to the expansion of musical form and to the utilization of vast vocal and instrumental resources that so characterized the musical style of the period.

The relationship between literary and musical creativity reached new heights during the nineteenth century. The extent to which the Romantic composers drew their inspiration from their literary contemporaries—Byron, Scott, Hugo, Mallarmé —or from the works of Goethe and Shakespeare, is obvious by examining the titles of the musical masterpieces of the period: *Harold in Italy, Fantastic Symphony, Faust Symphony, Song of Destiny,* etc. While there had been examples of descriptive music in earlier periods of music history, the nineteenth century can legitimately claim to have invented program music—that in which composers set about to portray emotional states or national scenes, or to express literary and even philosophical concepts.

To express these personal thoughts, the composer adapted and expanded his material to fit with the resources at his disposal. The parts written for orchestral instruments made full use of each instrument's individual potential. Layers of instrumental and vocal sound were created that enforced the impression of perspective. By the nineteenth century, music, with its subtleties, its treatment of personal and philosophical matter, was far removed from the objective chamber-music style of the preceding century. Romanticism was now in full bloom.

To portray the wide range of ideas and visual sensations that were to become the hallmark of nineteenth-century romanticism, composers turned to instrumental music; choral music served a subordinate role for the first time in musical history. The orchestra became both larger and more flexible than it had been in the eighteenth century. A number of revolutionary technical developments vastly improved the quality and flexibility of woodwind and brass instruments. The piano, modified so as to produce a louder, more resonant tone, emerged as a solo instrument of vast influence. All these developments led composers to give increasing attention to the complex subject of orchestration and to the creative use of the piano in secular choral music.

The public concert grew to maturity during this period and virtually changed the musical life of Europe. There had been various types of public concerts in England, Germany, and France since the late seventeenth century, but the dominant form of public entertainment outside England had been the opera. In Germany the public symphony concert came to rival the opera house. This new accessibility of

Berlioz conducting at mass choral concert in Paris, 1845
(The Granger Collection)

concerts to the masses created a completely new concept of program building. Concert programs now included a variety of works of different composers and periods of composition. Choral music began to develop a secular audience.

As previously noted, Germany became the focal point of musical development in the nineteenth century. With the influence of Beethoven, the lead in Europe's musical life passed irrevocably to Germany, and it was events in Germany and Austria that were ultimately to determine the course of musical development into the twentieth century.

England continued its tradition of choral music, a tradition that has continued unbroken from the time of Tallis and Byrd until the present day. The rapid rise of singing societies in Germany provided yet another outlet not only for the vast and growing popular interest in music, but also for the amateur choral singer.

The nineteenth-century symphony orchestra and opera, with their endless variety of sound colors and novel combinations, created the need for a new figure in the world of music—the conductor. Taking the place of the violinist who had led and disciplined the growing orchestra in the eighteenth and early years of the nineteenth century, the conductor emerged as an interpretative figure because the score markings in the new music now went far beyond the relatively straightforward indications of Haydn and Mozart and acquired a poetry of its own. The conductor thus became a "re-creator" who faced the challenge of grasping with his imagination the fantasy of the orchestral and choral instrument and transmitting it to his players and to the audience. The conductor thus took upon himself the task of "shaping" the performance, a trend that was to reach its height at the end of the century when the conductor was firmly established as the new leading figure in the world of music.

THE USE OF VOICES AND INSTRUMENTS

While most nineteenth-century composers considered symphonic music, opera, and lieder better suited than choral music as the ideal expression of the romantic mind, many did, nevertheless, create spectacular works that combined instrumental and choral forces quite successfully. Some of these works reached colossal proportions. The Beethoven *Ninth Symphony* and *Missa Solemnis*, Schumann *Paradise and Peri*, Berlioz *Damnation of Faust* and *Requiem*, the Liszt *Legend of St. Elizabeth* and *Psalm XIII*, and the Mahler *Eighth Symphony* are but a few of the major choral works that emerged during the century. Even this short list will illustrate the extent to which the voice became the ultimate servant of instrumental music during this period.

The composer left the conductor very little choice in the selection of voices and instruments in the nineteenth century. As the function of the orchestra expanded there was a concomitant increase in the clarity, dependability, and precision of the composer's intentions. While the score tended to be ambiguous in the seventeenth century, offering only vague information as to specific requirements for performance, in the nineteenth century the interpreter was only rarely faced with the question of which instruments or what kinds of voices to use. Rather the conductor's concern now centered almost entirely on the question of the proper utilization of resources: How many singers should be used in a given performance? What size chorus is proper to balance the number of instrumentalists at his disposal?

Perhaps the best way to begin this discussion is by reviewing the resources that were used in combined orchestral and choral performances in the late eighteenth and early nineteenth century. In the Baroque chapter it was noted that, in Bach's Leipzig services, instrumentalists often outnumbered vocalists as much as 3 : 2 (24 to 16). At a London performance of Handel's *Messiah* in 1759— just a few week's following the composer's death—the singers were outnumbered by the orchestra 37 to 24. It was not uncommon in the eighteenth century for singers to be in the minority in combined concerts of this type. This did not create the type of acoustical problem that a similar balance would today however, because the nature and tone quality of instruments at that time was so different. Actually, the relative balance of sound was not dissimilar from what an equal number of singers and instrumentalists would produce under modern conditions.

One of the most famous oratorio performances of all time—the "Grand Commemoration of Handel"—occurred in May, 1784 in Westminster Abbey. On this occasion 535 performers participated, but the singers outnumbered instrumentalists by 275 to 260. There was also a higher ratio of woodwinds to strings, which was typical of Baroque performance practice.

Another Handel festival took place fifty years later (1834), at which the *Creation* and parts of *Samson* were played and sung. This performance used a small chorus of 40 voices for some of the polyphonic choruses and demonstrated a much better overall acoustical balance of 392 singers to 223 instrumentalists. The pianist Moscheles attended the concert and later compared the instrumentation with that of the 1784 performance:[2]

PERFORMERS	1784	1834
Violins I	95	80
Violins II	26	32
Celli	21	18
Double basses	15	18
Flutes	16	10
Oboes	26	12
Clarinets	none	8
Bassoons	27	12
Horns	12	10
Trumpets	12	8
Trombones	6	8
Ophicleides (bugles)	none	2
Serpents (cornets)	none	2
Kettle drums	4	3
TOTAL INSTRUMENTS	260	223

PERFORMERS	1784	1834
Boy sopranos	47	32
Sopranos	11	113
Altos	48	74
Tenors	83	70
Basses	84	103
Soloists	2	5
TOTAL SINGERS	275	397
TOTAL PERFORMERS	535	620

With the growing popularity of the public concert in the nineteenth century, as well as the affinity of the Romantic composer to write works for large forces, a greater number of singers was required simply to produce a satisfactory acoustical effect. Gone was the intimacy of the court chapel and drawing room; in its place was the large concert hall and the expanded orchestra. Consequently, for performances of the large nineteenth-century choral works, it is advisable for the present-day conductor to plan for a ratio of singers to instrumentalists of about three to two. (For groups that include young voices perhaps a 2 to 1 ratio would be more practical.)

It is obvious that forces of this magnitude tend to limit clarity and precision in certain works, and many conductors choose to reduce the number of singers to achieve a more satisfactory musical result. A concomitant reduction of the number of instrumentalists would probably require the elimination of one or two stands of strings in each section.

Of course there are many works for chamber chorus—like the Brahms *Liebeslieder Walzer* and the Schumann *Spanische Liebes-Lieder*—which should be performed with from twenty to twenty-four well-trained voices. (The Brahms *Walzer* were actually composed for mixed quartet and piano four hands.) This is literature that must be sung with utmost subtlety and finesse; a large ensemble would rob this music of its charming lyrical and personal qualities.

TONE QUALITY AND CHORAL SINGING

The nineteenth-century composer and performer had an obsession for tone. "Tone sustained with equal power is the basis for all expression," wrote Wagner in his treatise on conducting which was published in 1869. Even the literary figures of the time expounded on the virtues of tone. Jean Paul stated emphatically that "no color is as Romantic as tone [color]."

The nineteenth century also marked the beginning of the scientific method in vocal training. Nowhere is this fact more apparent than in the writings of certain vocal pedagogues of the period.

> Singing has hitherto been treated too much as an art and too little as a science; it is perhaps for this reason that the simplicity of expression has decayed, while the power of ornament has increased.[3]

This statement by Bacon is typical of the trend away from the *Bel Canto* or natural school of singing that developed in the seventeenth and eighteenth centuries.

An important development resulting from the scientific study of the voice was the invention of the laryngoscope by Garcia in 1855. This device made it possible to observe the physical structure of the voice box and the movements of its component parts in vocalization.

One area of difference in the new vocal methods was the approach to registration. The old Italian school recognized two vocal registers; the nineteenth-century pedagogues insisted that there were three. Caccini wrote of two registers: *voce plena e naturale* (full and natural voice) and *voce finta* (artificial voice). His approach to the interpretation of seventeenth-century music restricted the male singer to the use of the natural voice and rejected the falsetto as ugly and undesirable. Sopranos and altos (male and female), on the other hand, were permitted to use both registers.

The nineteenth-century teacher recognized the middle voice as a third register, bridging the full-bodied chest and the head voice. Each resulted from a varying amount of resonating space present within the three cavities—the chest, larynx, and sinuses. The middle voice consisted, therefore, of a balance between chest and head resonance.

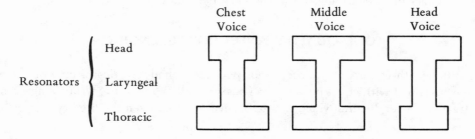

Resonators { Head / Laryngeal / Thoracic

Chest Voice   Middle Voice   Head Voice

Because opera dominated the musical scene in the nineteenth century, the vocal style and tone quality in choral singing tended to be soloistic in nature. Of course the music of these operas was far different texturally from that of the seventeenth-century monodies, and larger orchestras came into being which demanded stronger powers of projection from the singer. This soloistic style, characterized by a fully resonant sound, rhapsodic liberties (rubato, fermatas), and soloistic tendencies (cadenzas, added dynamics, etc.), obviously had an influence on the interpretation of the choral music of the period as well.

The large nineteenth-century orchestra demanded choral forces that were probably not terribly refined in terms of ensemble and precision. The choral works of Berlioz and Mahler were usually performed with as many or more instruments as voices, and a great amount of amplitude was thus required from the singers. For example, Berlioz, for his *Requiem*, recruited 200 singers and instrumental forces that included four brass bands.

In any discussion of choral singing in the nineteenth century, an important distinction must be made between a fully resonant tone, and a "loud" tone, which is little more than noise and which allows neither flexibility nor sensitivity to style. There is a natural tendency for singers to yield to the temptation of forcing the voice to produce a loud tone for large choral works with orchestral accompaniment. Such strained singing is both unmusical and injurious to the voice, and should be avoided at all cost. A correctly produced and fully resonated tone is the very essence of musical quality and is appropriate stylistically to much nineteenth-century choral literature. However, a conductor, recognizing limits in terms of volume, must seldom reach and never exceed those boundaries.

With a fully resonated vocal tone the scale of intensity is always smooth and even throughout the entire range of the voice. Choral singing of this type is characterized by a notable absence of struggle and effort, and the range is usually adequate for the performance of at least moderately difficult music.

For the choral singer who produces only a loud tone, the scale of intensity becomes unbalanced. Most of the volume is concentrated in the upper middle part of the voice and the quality, when forced, tends to sound throaty. The resultant ensemble sound is unpleasant even if only one or two persons are singing in this manner.

In applying any technique of singing to the choral rehearsal, the conductor must take into account textual and musical factors that allow for innumerable variations in the sound of a chorus. If a choir is conscious of musical line and rhythmic qualities (the major characteristics of musical shape), the resultant sound will be vibrant and full-bodied, but never heavy and inflexible. The musical style and the mood of the text should be indications of the appropriate vocal tone. In fact, each phrase within a composition has a stylistically correct tonal color, sometimes soft and subdued, sometimes strong and brilliant, but always exhibiting dynamic (non-static) qualities. The challenge to the vocally sensitive choral conductor is to work with the sound until this proper balance is achieved.

PROBLEMS OF NOTATION

The nineteenth century signaled a new interest in the original manuscript as the sole criterion of authenticity in musical performance. There were two reasons for this change of attitude. The first is fairly obvious. Over the years, copying and editorial errors crept into printed editions of seventeenth- and eighteenth-century music and, in some cases, completely changed the intentions of the composer. The result was, in the words of Schumann, a plethora of "corrupted readings of master-works" which led many of the leading figures to return to the original in self-defense.

The second reason is more obscure. Prior to the first quarter of the nineteenth century few performers were interested in anything but new music—that written during their generation. Older works and printed materials from an earlier era were considered strictly for the musical historian and the musically elite. The idea of including a Renaissance or Baroque work on a concert program around 1800 was virtually unthinkable. The main reason for this attitude was a certain snobbishness about the past; thus many works of major composers of an earlier era fell into oblivion (e.g., the Bach *St. Matthew Passion*).

When the change of attitude did come, partly because of the influence of performers like Mendelssohn and Liszt, the rules and conventions of performance of earlier periods were virtually unknown. As a result, many existing editions of older music ignored the actual intentions of the composer. If the rules and conventions of early music were considered old-fashioned in the eighteenth century, they were almost completely forgotten by the nineteenth century, when the cult of individuality reached its peak and when every artist attempted to personalize each performance. Editors obviously followed suit and cluttered editions with dynamic, expression, and tempo marks in the Romantic style. It is these editions which are largely responsible for the misunderstandings and misconceptions that developed concerning the performance practices of early music.

It is thus essential that the present-day performer apply to his study of the score the same rigorous standard that would be necessary if he were engaged in scholarly research. To insure authenticity Eva Badura-Skoda suggests three questions that the performer should ask concerning each work under study:[4]

1. What did the composer write? This can be determined by consulting the manuscript or a facsimile of the work.

2. What did the composer intend to write? This is a more difficult question because it involves criticism of the text. In most cases this can be cleared up by consulting the definitive edition of the composer's complete works. If not, one of the standard sources on textual problems should be consulted.

3. How would the composer's manuscript appear if it were published today? This is perhaps the easiest problem to solve. Most questions of this type can be answered in the *Urtext* edition of the composer's works.

ORNAMENTATION AND IMPROVISATION

The writings of Carl Philipp Emanuel Bach, Leopold Mozart, Joachim Quantz, and others which served as our primary resource for the interpretation of ornaments in other periods, continue to fulfill this function in the nineteenth century. However, since the problem of ambiguity in notation continues in the works of Romantic composers, and because the circumstances of musical performance change somewhat after 1800, the performer of nineteenth-century music must take a fresh look at the interpretation of certain ornaments to insure that the intentions of the composer are indeed fulfilled.

Since the subject of ornamentation was covered rather thoroughly in the Baroque and Classical chapters, it is our intention in this section to limit our remarks to those ornaments that present specific problems or that need further clarification in the nineteenth century, namely, the *appoggiatura* (including the double appoggiatura and anticipation), the *turn*, the *trill*, and the *pralltriller*. It will be found that these ornaments occur primarily in accompaniments to the choral music of this period, since voice parts are now not conceived instrumentally as they were in the eighteenth century. However, we should bear in mind that passages for solo voices are often ornamented in the nineteenth century.

It is indeed paradoxical that the problem of the proper interpretation of ornaments should arise in the nineteenth century at all. One of the important characteristics of musical composition since 1750 has been a growing clarity of intent on the part of the composer. Using a minimum of signs, composers have attempted to express and even write out complex ornaments in such a manner that there can be little or no doubt as to what notes are intended. All ornaments were not written out, however, because of the necessary labor involved and the clutter which resulted from the printing of trills and other embellishments. The composers probably also felt obliged to keep part of their intentions secret, in order to guard the mysterious aspect of the compositional practice.

Yet, even those ornaments that were written out sometimes raise further questions. Is the ornament to be played or sung on or before the beat? Are all notes of equal importance? If not, which notes are to receive stress? These are just a few of the important questions which must be answered if the execution of ornaments in nineteenth-century choral literature is to be authentic. Conductors who are interested in further study of this subject should consult the important sources on performance practices, such as Daniel Gottlob Türk's *Klavierschule* (1789), Johann Cramer's *Instructions for the Piano* (c. 1810), Johann Nepomuk Hummel's *Anweisung zum Pianofortespiel* (1828), Louis Spohr's *Violinschule* (1832), and Karl Czerny's *Clavierschule* (1839).

Appoggiatura

The intrinsic expressive diminuendo from dissonance to resolution is again proper for the realization of the appoggiatura in the nineteenth century: ♩ ♩. The best authority for the rhythmic duration of the nineteenth-century appoggiatura is Spohr. In his *Violinschule* Spohr reflects the influence of Quantz and C. P. E. Bach when he states:

> If the appoggiatura stands before a note which can be divided into two equal parts, it obtains half of its value. . . . Before a note with a dot it obtains the value of the note, which then begins only at the dot. . . . Where there are two dots the appoggiatura obtains the value of the note and this then begins with the first dot.[5]

Here Spohr is confirming a general rule that dates back to the seventeenth century; namely, that the length of the appoggiatura in relation to the following note is one-half its value, two-thirds if the following note is dotted. This *long* execution is the most common interpretation of the appoggiatura. Often one finds quasi-recitative passages, such as in Example 1 in which the performance is governed by notational practices from earlier periods.

Example 1

Schubert, *Mass in G*, "Agnus Dei"

Although the rule states that the long appoggiatura is to be performed on the beat, the performer will find cases such as in Example 2 where before-the-beat execution is demanded.

Example 2

Schubert, *Mass in G*, "Benedictus"

Since it was the practice of nineteenth-century composers to write more and more appoggiaturas into the melodic line as ordinary notes, another type of appoggiatura appears increasingly as an ornament. This is called the *short appoggiatura, grace note,* or (erroneously) *acciacatura.* (The latter was an ornament for harpsichord music of the period c. 1675–1725.) The short appoggiatura or grace note differs from the long appoggiatura in two important ways:

1. It is distinguished in notation by a stroke across the tail: ♪

2. It is intended—in most cases—to be performed very shortly *before* the beat, in contrast to the long appoggiatura which is usually taken *on* the beat.

Example 3

Schumann, Op. 34, No. 4

The conjunct double appoggiatura, or *slide*, is to be performed in one of two ways in nineteenth-century music:

1. When the notes are not tied to the principal note, the ornament is simply played quickly, on the beat.

Example 4

Brahms, *Liebeslieder*, Op. 52, No. 2

Example 5

Beethoven, Op. 119, No. 5

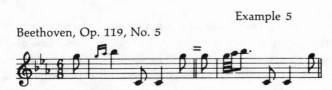

2. When the first note is tied to the principal note, the former is held throughout.

Example 6

Schubert, Op. 94, No. 3

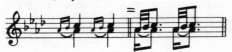

The disjunct double appoggiatura (called *Anschlag* by C. P. E. Bach) consists of two notes, the first of which may be at any distance from the main note, but the second is always only one step from it. This embellishment must be played on the beat:

Example 7

Chopin, Op. 16

When the note following an appoggiatura is identical with the latter, the ornament is called an *anticipation*. As the name suggests, this ornament is performed before the beat. Often the main note is not repeated.

Example 8

Brahms, Op. 52, No. 3

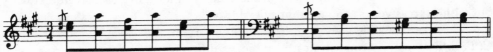

Often chords in the accompaniment which are too widely spaced to be reached by the hand are written with anticipations, so that most of the chord is heard on the beat:

Example 9

The Turn

Prior to the middle of the eighteenth century, the *turn* was regularly performed as four equal notes assuming the entire time value of the written note. And although some composers such as C. P. E. Bach preferred an uneven rhythm where the tempo of the composition allowed it, this practice did not apply to a turn that was placed after the written note or to a turn on a very short note.

During the nineteenth century the turn gradually merged into the ordinary notation of the composition and thus tended to lose ornamental character. A number of Romantic composers adopted this practice, among them Mahler and Wagner.

Example 10

Since the turn ordinarily appears only in the accompaniment of a choral work, the conductor or accompanist should be aware that the turn in this century of music is an extremely important melodic device that must be played distinctly, but with expressiveness and rhythmic flexibility.

There are obviously limitless possibilities in the execution of the turn. C. P. E. Bach alone demonstrates thirty-seven different methods of performance. In the interpretation of nineteenth-century music, five rules should be considered:

1. When a turn is indicated directly over a note, it is taken quickly, on the beat, so as not to rob excessively from the value of the note.

Example 11

2. Turns occurring between notes are to begin on the first note, and are played in the time of that note.

Example 12

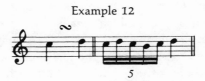

3. Where other rhythmic patterns are not suggested by the context of the piece, the quintolet is probably the most favored solution for between-note turns in moderate tempos. Chopin's written-out turns are usually handled in this way.

4. The symbol for the inverted turn ∾ or ⸴ is seldom if ever found in Romantic music. This melodic figure, which is most always incorporated within the written notes, is occasionally indicated by the normal turn symbol, and leads to a lower pitch than the previous note.

Example 13

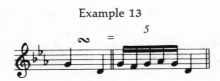

5. The turn's auxilliary tones, when not prescribed by small accidentals found with the symbol, are assumed to be the upper and lower neighbors in the scale involved. Thus:

Example 14

but

The Trill

The Romantic *trill* was first introduced early in the nineteenth century by the Viennese pianists Hummel, Czerny, and Moscheles. Contrary to previous practice, the nineteenth-century trill begins with the main note; it ends, however, with the two-note termination (*Nachschlag*) which has been a common practice since the Baroque. Hummel proposed to standardize the main-note start in 1828, so evidence would lead one to conclude that this practice should be limited to music after the time of Haydn, Mozart, Beethoven, and Schubert. This passage from the "Benedictus" of Beethoven's *Missa Solemnis* illustrates this point; the *trill* should be executed from above:

Example 15

From this discussion it is obvious that the trill no longer has the appoggiatura function it served in the previous two centuries, although some composers often combine the two symbols for this effect:

In the absence of such an indication for an upper-note start, the trill after 1828 should begin on the main note.

The trill usually serves to add brilliance or color to a composition of this period. Often inverted pedal tones in the solo voice are trilled for this purpose:

Example 16

Schumann, Op. 145, No. 15

When a trill has this effect, no suffix should be inserted, unless one is indicated by the composer, as in the following example from the *Missa Solemnis*:

Example 17

Beethoven, *Missa Solemnis*, "Benedictus"

The Mordent

Confusion regarding the execution of the *mordent* has plagued modern performers because nineteenth-century composers like Hummel and Spohr mixed the names, signs, and functions of the *mordent* and the *inverted mordent*. For all practical purposes the *inverted mordent*—the very rapid alternation of the main note with a subsidiary note a step above—passed out of existence during the Baroque period. The only mordent that is known in the Classical period is the so-called *lower mordent*, which consisted of the alternation of the written note with the note immediately below it:

Composers after 1750 often designated the inverted mordent with a short wavy line which was originally the sign for an ornament called *Pralltriller*, a rapid trill of four notes, beginning with the upper note, in the Baroque tradition. The *Schneller*, introduced by C. P. E. Bach after 1750, was a two-note unprepared ornament which occurred on the beat and reached to the step above.

After 1800 the Pralltriller disappeared and in the subsequent period the sign ( ) always indicated the Schneller. At the same time, however, the term Schneller dropped out of use and the ornament designated by this name became known as Pralltriller, which in the nineteenth century is the term used for the English inverted mordent. Around 1830 (due to Hummel and others) the Pralltriller began to be performed *before* the main note, and today this is considered the correct execution.

Example 18

Brahms, Op. 52, No. 7

Example 19

Schumann, Op. 34, No. 1

Example 20

Schumann, Op. 78, No. 1

The former restriction allowing this ornament's occurrence only on the first note of a descending second has also been removed. The inverted mordent may now be frequently found in connection with skips, which adds a certain crispness to the execution.

INTERPRETATION OF TEMPO

Of all the aspects of performance practice in the nineteenth century, tempo is without doubt the most controversial. Wagner pinpoints this issue as central to "correct" musical interpretation when he writes in his important treatise on conducting (1869):

> The essence of all that matters for a correct performance of a composition on the part of the conductor is that he should always give the correct tempo; for his choice of tempo immediately allows us to recognize whether he has understood the composition or not.[6]

Tempo and other expression marks increase in complexity and occurrence during the course of the nineteenth century. Terms such as *presto, adagio, allegro*, which had been recognized as helpful and practical in the eighteenth century, are no longer adequate to express with clarity the demands of the nineteenth-century composer. Yet, the increased controls placed on the performer by the composer were not accepted without occasional doubt and opposition, especially in cases where mechanical methods were introduced to measure and control features of musical performance.

There are many factors that influence the interpretation of tempo in nineteenth-century music. Among those that we will discuss in this section are the metronome and other mechanical methods of tempo determination, the performer's concept of tempo modification (*rubato*), and the change in attitude that evolved during the nineteenth century.

The Metronome

The adaptation of the metronome in 1816 by Johannes Nepomuk Mälzel provided, for the first time, an objective standard of tempo determination. Beethoven and Salieri were the first important musicians to endorse its use in musical performance. In a letter to Ignaz von Mosel in 1817, Beethoven showed his distaste for written terms as a guide to tempo determination, but promised that he would continue to use them to describe the character of a piece:

> We would do well to dispense with headings. The words which describe the character of the piece are a very different matter. These we could not give up; whereas the tempo is really no more than the body, these refer rather to the spirit of the piece. I have often thought of giving up these absurd terms allegro, andante, adagio, presto. Mälzel's metronome gives us an excellent opportunity to do so. I give you my word, in my future composition I shall not use them.[7]

Although Beethoven considered the metronome a decided improvement over verbal tempo indications, there is evidence that he had mixed emotions about this new invention. He was at first enthusiastic, but as time passed Beethoven became increasingly aware of the metronome's limitations. It was obviously incompatible with his innermost thoughts and emotions. On the manuscript of his song *Nord oder Süd* he wrote:

100 according to Mälzel, but this must be held applicable only to the first measures, for feeling also has its own tempo and this cannot entirely be expressed in this figure.[8]

In spite of his early interest in the metronome, which went so far that he added metronome markings to his first eight symphonies and recommended it to his contemporaries, Beethoven was reluctant to use it for the works of his last period, 1816–1827.

Beethoven's attitude toward the metronome certainly does not make it any easier for the interpreter to solve the problem of tempo in his scores. Most scholars would agree that his metronomic markings are generally too fast for careful performance. Explanations of his rapid tempi have centered on the argument that he lacked the requisite patience and inner tranquillity for a careful study of the relationship between Mälzel's figures and his feelings about the tempo of the music. In general, however, it is probably safe to assume that Beethoven disregarded any consideration for the mechanisms of performance, which probably helps to explain his predilection for quick tempi.

Similar doubts about the value of the metronome were expressed by Carl Maria von Weber:

> For all this we have no correct measurements in music. They only exist in the feeling heart and if they cannot be found there, the metronome will not help, which anyhow serves only to prevent gross errors, nor the very vague tempo marks.[9]

Weber constantly fought against what he called "tyrannically restraining . . . mill-hammer" tempos.

Brahms expressed reservations about mechanical tempo markings on the occasion of the performance of *Ein deutches Requiem* in 1871:

> As far as my experience goes, everybody who has given metronomic numbers has renounced them later. The numbers found in my compositions have been talked into me by friends, for I myself never believed that my blood and an instrument can agree so well. The so-called 'elastische Tempo' is certainly no recent invention. 'Con discrezione' should be added to this and to how many other things. . . .[10]

Johannes Brahms, 1833–1897 (The New York Public Library Picture Collection)

Claude Debussy, 1862–1918 (The New York Public Library Picture Collection)

It is obvious that Brahms favored verbal rather than numerical tempo directions, and this fact should be considered when studying and interpreting his works.

Wagner considered the metronome of little use in determining the true tempo of a work:

> The way the conductor sets and maintains the tempo is as eloquent as his grasp of the content of the composition. Performers are guided to a correct rendition of the tempo, which, at the same time, reveals the extent of the conductor's knowledge of the composition. But the difficulty of finding the right tempo becomes manifest when we realize that only thorough and detailed acquaintance with the work will yield this vital knowledge.[11]

Debussy summed up the attitude of a number of nineteenth-century composers in a letter written to his publisher, Jacques Durand, on October 9, 1915:

You want my opinion about the metronomic indications: they are true for just one measure.[12]

When examining representative scores from this period we find that the composers who did use metronomic markings were careful to place the customary Italian terms next to them. Composers like Schumann, MacDowell, and Debussy who wished for nationalistic reasons to use their own languages, translated the Italian terms instead of relying solely on the metronome. Bartok and Stravinsky, however, usually indicated the proper tempo by metronomic marks alone. But they did so for structural reasons, not instructional reasons. They desired not so much a particular tempo as an unyielding beat during the course of a composition. It is an interesting yet puzzling fact that no two conductors perform the same work in the same tempo whether an exact metronomic figure is given or not.

Tempo Modification as a Guide to Performance

The definitive authority on tempo interpretation in the first half of the nineteenth century was Beethoven's pupil Czerny (1791–1857). Writing on the subject in his *Clavierschule*, Czerny has this to say about tempo modification:

> Every composition must be played in the tempo prescribed by the composer and adhered to by the executant, notwithstanding, however, that in almost every line there are certain notes and passages where a little ritardando or accelerando is necessary, to beautify the reading and to augment the interest.[13]

Czerny's references to tempo modification within a phrase or period signals a middle ground between the two extremes of rigid objectivity (the Mendelssohn school) and unwarranted liberty (the Wagner school).

The term *tempo rubato* was another step in the evolution and was introduced by Chopin later in the century:

> While the singing hand, either irresolutely lingering or as in passionate speech eagerly anticipating . . . , the other, the accompanying hand, continued to play strictly in time.[14]

These facts lead the present-day performer to ask: When is it correct to use rubato? *Groves Dictionary* offers this suggestion:

In music everything is relative: no element enters in without modifying, however slightly, other elements. A note held for a certain length at one pitch does not affect us in the same way as when held at another, and this difference of affection is expressed by altering slightly the note. This alteration is a matter of nice judgement, and the act of *rubato* is a golden opportunity for the exercise of economy, without which it is apt to defeat its own end.[15]

Since tempo modification is an important factor in the interpretation of nineteenth-century music, it is necessary to know how the Romantic composer and performer approached this problem. According to Dorian, Czerny's *ritardando* or *rallantando* is allowed under the following circumstances:

1. At the return of the principal subject.
2. When a phrase is to be separated from the melody.
3. On long notes strongly accented.
4. At the transition to a different tempo.
5. After a pause.
6. On the diminuendo of a quick, lively passage.
7. Where the ornamental note cannot be played *a tempo guisto*.
8. In a well-marked crescendo serving to introduce or to terminate an important passage.
9. In passages where the composer or the performer gives free play to his fancy.
10. When the composer marks the passage *espressivo*.
11. At the end of a shake or cadence.[16]

Rubato likewise becomes an important element in the interpretation of nineteenth-century choral music. The late-romantic performer considered rubato the very heart of expressiveness in tempo; he recognized two kinds of rubato: *classical* (melodic rubato) and *expressive*. In classical rubato only the melody is affected by the change of tempo while the accompaniment is played strictly in time. Expressive rubato affects the entire musical fabric, both the melody and the accompaniment. This distinction is especially critical in the performance of choral music because the voice is by nature an expressive medium which totally defies the mechanical limitations of the metronome.

Though the late Romantics argued heatedly about the proper method of performing rubato, they did agree on its purpose—to color expressive passages—and its importance—music would be machine-like without it.

They were also in agreement as to the importance of tempo modification for expressive purposes. Their attitudes on this subject, however, were not new ideas but older ones long in practice. The point is significant because it identified their ideas on tempo as the culmination of an entire century's thought on the topic. This is a terribly important factor that must be considered whenever one is performing a choral work from the late nineteenth century.

The Evolution of the Romantic Concept of Tempo

The present-day choral conductor must recognize that there was a vast difference in the way the early- and late-nineteenth-century performers conceived of tempo. In the early years of the century the performer took certain liberty, but always within well-defined limits: its extent was to be almost imperceptible, the sections carefully determined, and these confined to so-called "cantabile," or song-like, passages.

The next step in the process, a development still very much under the influence of the conservatives, was in essence a "plan of compensation." The basic outline in the tempo was maintained with extra time given to certain notes and taken away from others.

With the influence of performers like Liszt and Wagner, a cleavage developed between conservative and radical interpreters of tempo in the 1850's which threatened to destroy the fragile balance that existed between classical and romantic points of view. Czerny spoke out for the conservative tempo interpretation, complaining that "the principle of maintaining a uniform tempo has almost been unlearned. Arbitrary slackening or accelerating of the pace is now [1847] being applied to caricature." Liszt, who represented a more radical point of view, vehemently rejected mechanical time-beating as "clashing with the sense and expression" of music. In kindred spirit, Wagner called those performers who favored uniformity of tempo "eunuchs of classical chastity," an obvious reference to Mendelssohn and later, Brahms.

For Wagner the primary obligation of the conductor was to understand the will and intention of the composer and to respect his instructions. In order to achieve this, his first consideration was to discover the "true" tempo of the composition.

Richard Wagner, 1813–1883 (The New York Public Library Picture Collection)

Giuseppe Verdi, 1813–1901 (The New York Public Library Picture Collection)

The whole duty of a conductor is comprised in his ability always to indicate the right tempo. . . . The true tempo induces correct phrasing and expression, and conversely, with a conductor, the idea of appropriate phrasing and expression will induce one conception of the true tempo.[17]

How does one discover this tempo? Wagner wrote that the conductor could arrive at the true tempo only if (1) he had a thorough and detailed knowledge of the complete work; and (2) he had an understanding and a feeling for the melody. He explained that when he conducted the Overture to *Der Freischutz:*

I simply took the tempo of the introduction to the *Overture* as I *felt* it; whereupon a veteran member of the orchestra, the old violoncellist Dotzauer turned toward me and said seriously: "Yes, this is the way Weber himself took it. I now hear it correctly again for the first time."[18]

Wagner subsequently enunciated several principles of tempo—not new in themselves—which were destined to influence the interpretation of tempo in the latter part of the century. Among these, four seem to represent the essence of his thinking on the matter: (1) that tempo modification finally be accepted as a *sine qua non* in musical interpretation; (2) that sections of sharply contrasting tempi be linked "unobtrusively"; (3) that singing be regarded as the essential way of selecting the correct tempo; and (4) that the true adagio tempo could not be taken too slowly.

The third principle, by which tempo is tied to singing, was a key element in the interpretation of the music of the late romantics. According to Kravitt:

> it explained why instrumental lyricism came, in the nineteenth century, to be called "free declamation" by Liszt and others; why the term *declamatory style*, certainly in use before Liszt, found its way into the Riemann-Einstein lexicon as a chief characteristic of tempo in the second half of the nineteenth century; and why late romantics—Mahler, for example—in their desire for intense expression, wanted even the timpani to sing.[19]

Wagner was so consumed with the issue that he wrote emphatically that "our conductors so frequently fail to find the correct tempo because they are ignorant of singing."[20]

There is little doubt that these four principles influenced the late-nineteenth-century performer's concept of tempo. The application of the first principle for expressive purposes overpowered performers in the late nineteenth century. For unlike their immediate predecessors, the late romantics insisted that tempo be flexible, that it change with the emotional content of the piece. Accordingly, most works were performed in an elastic manner, even the choral works that the early romantic conductor generally had performed strictly in time from beginning to end.

The difference in concept between the late-romantic and a twentieth-century approach to tempo is tied very closely to their individual conception of rhythm. For the late romantic, rhythm was placed at the service of feeling. To contemporary performers, basic rhythm and motion, not the element of feeling, are the foundations of musical art. This reversal is obviously not a simple shift of emphasis, but a complete change of orientation regarding tempo. With rhythm today considered a primary factor of musical performance, the training of musicians and the traditions of performance have been vitally influenced. This is the age where purism in performance is honored; late-romantic rhythmic practices, especially the extravagant ones, are now generally considered in poor taste.

Naturally, such an orientation creates a dilemma for the choral conductor who is performing late-nineteenth-century music—that of being sympathetic to its rhythmic principles, but at the same time doing full justice to them when interpreting that music. The solution is often a compromise, one in which the rhythmic principles of late-romantic music are realized partly according to the aesthetics of its time and partly according to those of our own. These sharply differing attitudes make one aware of how closely tempo as an expressive element is to be associated with Romanticism, a point made quite clearly by Dorian in the *History of Music in Performance:*

> What the artist feels becomes the decisive factor in the rendition. Obviously, one cannot expect to set an inflexible, mathematical standard of art; if ideas of the composer are subjective and their directions relative (in spite of such mechanical aids as the metronome), the interpreter's knowledge is likewise subjective, and therefore his ways of performance are subjective too. We conclude, then, that the ego of the interpreter and the score of the composer provide the very combination through which creative inspiration may be translated into musical reality.[21]

PHRASING, ARTICULATION, AND DYNAMICS

The early years of the nineteenth century were still very much under the influence of the Viennese classicists; in the second half the performer broke with many of the older rules and conventions that were established in the writings of C. P. E. Bach, Quantz, and Leopold Mozart. It was inevitable and entirely appropriate that in an era dominated by individuality and expression, an entirely new system of phrasing, articulation, and dynamics would develop.

One of the first examples of this new freedom in performance was found in the changing system of accentuation. The Leopold Mozart adage "The meter makes the melody" was no longer valid in the second half of the century. Conventional accentuation, which in all pre-Romantic styles formed the structure within which the melody unfolded, disappeared, and the melodic line now became a dominant and independent factor in interpretation. Prior to the nineteenth century, performers were required to observe the accentuation indicated by the time signature; now they were able to give free reign to their imagination and perform a work with two or three accents within a given bar—or perhaps none at all.

This new freedom of interpretation, while suitable for much of the music that was written in the last half of the century, was also applied to editions of older music; eighteenth-century music, for example, was edited in a manner that eliminated the important tradition which emphasized the beginning of each bar. The absence of traditional accentuation caused works from an earlier period to be performed evenly and at a much faster tempo than was intended.

In the nineteenth century every aspect of music was expanded. This may be seen in the phrases that are characterized by broad lines, widely spanned curves, and uniformly flowing single notes. Compare the regular two- and four-bar phrases of the Classical period to the length of the following melody from the Mahler *Eighth Symphony:*

Example 21

Here we have a ten-bar phrase which has no breaks except for the single rest. For reasons of dramatic shape and the way in which Mahler makes it possible (through the use of all vocal sections) to sustain this extreme range (two and one-half octaves), it is clear that this phrase is to be performed without further articulation.

As the function of the orchestra was broadened, and as musical performance moved from the Viennese salon to the major concert halls of the world, there was a constant and growing need for increased clarity, precision, and dependability in dynamics.

Beethoven's dynamic markings generally follow the pattern established by Mozart, although he uses more *ff* and *pp* markings. His use of crescendo and decrescendo  signs instead of descriptive terms is radically different from the practice of the Viennese composers. This is especially true when he extends these wedges over several bars. One other dynamic sign, $<>$, appears in the late piano sonatas of Beethoven, as well as in music of other composers, and signals with unsurpassed accuracy the peak of the crescendo swell.

The development of dynamic markings in the second half of the nineteenth century presents nothing radically new, but a few items should be noted. Chopin and Brahms show extreme care in their indications. Chopin's works often show the entire flow of the music accompanied by an almost uninterrupted chain of dynamic wedges, all very accurately placed and sensitively proportioned. Brahms is economical and precise, which is typical of every aspect of his writing. The conductor and performer will do well to follow his markings with special care.

In the late nineteenth century dynamic markings reach an extreme in the works of Verdi and Mahler. The *ppppp* in the aria of the "Princess of Eboli" in the fourth act of Verdi's *Don Carlos*, and similar markings in the symphonies of Mahler, are an indication that the composer attempts to place increasing controls upon the performer and conductor.

Gustav Mahler, 1860–1911 (The New York Public Library Picture Collection)

SUMMARY

The interpretation of nineteenth-century choral music is dramatically shaped by the individualism and subjectivity of the performer. As the period progresses the "performer" of the eighteenth century becomes the "reproducer" in the nineteenth century and the conductor emerges as the primary force in the musical product. With personalities like Berlioz, Liszt, and Wagner leading the way, an entirely new concept of tempo evolves; the objective standard of the metronome and similar methods is replaced by the emotions and feelings of the performer. The vast instrumental and vocal forces that composers require to express their musical ideas create a new tone color, and the public concert replaces the church and court as the patron of the arts. By the end of the century the intellectual understanding and formal clarity of the Age of Reason has succumbed to the will of the performer. The Romantic period has signaled a new era: the individual has emerged triumphant.

NOTES

1. Philipp Spitta, *Robert Schumann, ein Lebensbild* (Leipzig: Brietkopf, 1882), p. 22.

2. Ignaz Moscheles, *Recent Music and Musicians*, translated by A. D. Coleridge (New York: Henry Holt, 1873), p. 203.

3. Richard Mackenzie Bacon, *Elements of Voice Science*, rev. edition (Champaign, Illinois: Pro Musica Press, 1966), p. 100.

4. Eva Badura-Skoda, "Textual Problems in Masterpieces of the 18th and 19th Centuries," *Musical Quarterly*, 51 (1965), p. 317.

5. Louis Spohr, *Violinschule* (Vienna: T. Haslinger, 1832).

6. Richard Wagner, *On Conducting*, translated by Edward Dannreuther (London: William Reeves, 1887).

7. Frederick Dorian, *The History of Music in Performance* (New York: W. W. Norton, 1942), p. 199.

8. Elliott Forbes, rev. and ed., *Thayer's Life of Beethoven*, 2 vols. (Princeton: Princeton University Press, 1967), 2:687–688.

9. Carl Bamberger, editor, *The Conductor's Art* (New York: McGraw-Hill, 1965), p. 21.

10. George Henschel, *Personal Recollections of Johannes Brahms* (Boston, 1907), pp. 78–79.

11. Dorian, op. cit., p. 280.

12. *Lettres de Claude Debussy à son éditeur*, October 9, 1915 (Paris: Durand, 1927).

13. Dorian, op. cit., p. 205.

14. Frederick Niecks, *Frederick Chopin*, 2 vols. (London: 1888), 2:102.

15. Eric Blom, editor, *Groves Dictionary of Music and Musicians*, 5th edition (New York: St. Martin's Press, 1954), vol. 7, p. 290.

16. Dorian, op. cit., pp. 206–207.

17. Wagner, op. cit., p. 20.

18. Ibid., p. 51.

19. Edward Kravitt, "Tempo as an Expressive Element in the Late Romantic Lied," *Musical Quarterly*, 59 (1973), p. 503.

20. Wagner, op. cit., p. 19.

21. Dorian, op. cit., p. 30.

Chapter Fourteen
RECOMMENDED READING LIST

Badura-Skoda, Eva. "Textual Problems in Masterpieces of the 18th and 19th Centuries." *Musical Quarterly* 51 (1965): 301–317. This important article is required reading for the interpreter of music of the eighteenth and nineteenth centuries.

Blume, Friedrich. *Classic and Romantic Music.* Translated by M. D. Herter Norton. New York: W. W. Norton and Company, 1970. A survey of the development of style charcteristics of "classic" and "romantic" music in relation to their historical contexts.

Dorian, Frederick. *The History of Music in Performance.* New York: W. W. Norton and Company, 1942. Here is a book that is devoted to the performer's approach to musical interpretation. Of special interest is the discussion of revisions and "corrections" of famous musical scores.

Einstein, Alfred. *Music in the Romantic Era.* New York: W. W. Norton and Company, 1947. An approach to the music of the nineteenth century that emphasizes the impact that music had on the Romantic movement.

Longyear, Ray M. *Nineteenth-Century Romanticism in Music.* Englewood Cliffs: Prentice-Hall, Inc., 1969. A short but comprehensive survey of nineteenth-century music.

Chapter Fifteen

The Twentieth Century

Contemporary music, especially, is created to waken you up,
not put you to sleep. It is meant to stir and excite you; it may
even exhaust you. But isn't that the kind of stimulation you go
to a theater or read a book for? Why make an exception of
music.—AARON COPLAND[1]

IN THE RAPIDLY SHIFTING cross-currents of twentieth-century developments in music,
three main trends may be discerned: toward tradition, toward control, and toward
freedom. Some works, composers, or schools of composition may be classified with
a fair degree of certainty under one of these trends; others, perhaps the majority,
show influences from two or even all three of these trends. To some extent this
threefold division of musical trends corresponds to Whyte's division of social or
personality types into tradition-directed, other-directed, and inner-directed, in *The
Organization Man*.[2] But any such comparison should be regarded not as providing
exact parallels, but rather as evidence of the fact that music is a form of human
behavior and as such is subject to the same general principles as other forms of
human behavior.

      The trend toward tradition in music embraces not only such clearly tradi-
tion-oriented movements as neo-Baroque, neo-Classic, and neo- or post-Romantic,
but also, at least in part, other movements such as nationalism, and various individual composers and works. As in preceding stylistic periods, we find that much,
though by no means all, religious music is written in a conservative style that looks
back to the techniques, materials, and attitudes of the past. Popular music from
Broadway musicals to jazz and rock is also likely to be conservative in such aspects

as melody, harmony, and form; innovative aspects would be found in timbre and performance styles. It is understandable that the general public would find it easier to accept and appreciate music written in a musical language that is more or less familiar to them. At the same time it is understandable that some members of the public, and even more so some composers, would seek new solutions for old problems; indeed, that they would seek new problems and challenges which would demand fresh techniques and materials.

The trend toward control in twentieth-century music may be seen as a reaction to some of the excesses of freedom and subjectivity in the preceding century. The idea of submitting the musical process to the rigors of some form of intramusical or extramusical control is not new. Examples may be found in a variety of sources from the mensuration canons of Ockeghem to the numerological references in Johann Sebastian Bach. In the twentieth century this trend toward control found

Robert Shaw Chorale, Robert Shaw Conducting

full expression in the strict twelve-tone writing of the second and third decades and even more so in the mathematically or computer-controlled music written in the years following the Second World War. Whether the trend toward control is a symptom of twentieth-century man's increasing reliance on and fascination with technology may be left an open question, but one that we would tend to answer in the affirmative.

The trend toward freedom was a counterreaction both to the rigidity and complexity of serial music and to the conventions and stereotypes of neo-Classic and other tradition-oriented schools. Freedom is to be found, not only in the abandonment of traditional forms and harmonic procedures, but even more strikingly in "chance" or aleatory music. The term *aleatory* is derived from the Latin word for dice player, and it is interesting to note that one of the earliest examples of aleatory music was Mozart's *Musikalisches Würfelspiel* (Musical Dice Game), a composition, or perhaps more accurately a game, in which a number of phrases were to be played in an order that was determined by throws of dice. The element of chance may be used in music in aspects of composition or aspects of performance. Chance elements in contemporary music may be regarded not only as a reaction to the overemphasis on control in music, but also, to an extent, as the result of influences from non-Western cultures, such as John Cage's work with the Chinese *Book of Changes*.

GENERAL CHARACTER AND STRUCTURE

It would be impossible in the short space of this chapter to review all of the significant schools, trends, and styles of composition in the twentieth century. Instead we shall concentrate on the developments of twelve-tone and aleatory technique as two representative directions. Our description will try to emphasize those aspects that have relevance to the performer, rather than those that are only of importance to the composer or the listener. At the same time we must gain at least a fundamental working knowledge of the compositional technique as a basis for our performance understanding.

Twelve-tone technique may best be understood in the words of Arnold Schoenberg, the first composer to systematize the technique.

> I call this procedure *Method of Composing with Twelve Tones Which are Related Only with One Another*.

This method consists primarily of the constant and exclusive use of a set of twelve different tones. This means, of course, that no tone is repeated within the series and that it uses all twelve tones in the chromatic scale, though in a different order. It is in no way identical with the chromatic scale.[3]

The basic set referred to by Schoenberg may also be called a *tone row* or a *series*. The tone row for a choral composition of Schoenberg is given below. You will notice that this row begins with an obvious and intentionally parodistic reference to traditional music—the C-major triad. Normally, however, the composer attempts to construct rows without any such references to traditional pitch patterns. Secondly, you will notice that we have numbered the row with the Mod 12 numbers, with C as O.

Example 1

Schoenberg, *Tonal oder Atonal*, © Belmont

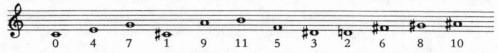

The row or basic set is the source material for this entire choral composition. Other works would have other rows as their source material. The row may be heard in any one of four forms—*prime* (original form), *inversion* (upside down), *retrograde* (backwards), or *retrograde-inversion* (upside down and backwards). Any one of these four forms may be heard in any one of twelve possible transpositions, that is, beginning on any one of the twelve notes of the chromatic scale. Thus there are 48 possible rows (4 forms × 12 transpositions), and these may be conveniently represented in a matrix or "magic square" as shown below. Example 2a shows the matrix with Mod 12 numbers; Example 2b shows the matrix with pitch names. In both cases the prime (P) forms may be read from left to right, the inversion (I) from top to bottom, the retrograde (R) from right to left, and the retrograde-inversion (RI) from bottom to top.

Example 2

(a)

Prime (P) →

I	0	4	7	1	9	11	5	3	2	6	8	10	↑
n	8	0	3	9	5	7	1	11	10	2	4	6	R
v	5	9	0	6	2	4	10	8	7	11	1	3	e I
e	11	3	6	0	8	10	4	2	1	5	7	9	t n
r	3	7	10	4	0	2	8	6	5	9	11	1	r v
s	1	5	8	2	10	0	6	4	3	7	9	11	o e
i	7	11	2	8	4	6	0	10	9	1	3	5	g r
o	9	1	4	10	6	8	2	0	11	3	5	7	r s
n	10	2	5	11	7	9	3	1	0	4	6	8	a i
(I)	6	10	1	7	3	5	11	9	8	0	2	4	d o
↓	4	8	11	5	1	3	9	7	6	10	0	2	e n
	2	6	9	3	11	1	7	5	4	8	10	0	(RI)

← Retrograde (R)

(b)

Prime (P) →

I	C	E	G	C#	A	B	F	D#	D	F#	G#	A#	↑
n	G#	C	D#	A	F	G	C#	B	A#	D	E	F#	R
v	F	A	C	F#	D	E	A#	G#	G	B	C#	D#	e I
e	B	D#	F#	C	G#	A#	E	D	C#	F	G	A	t n
r	D#	G	A#	E	C	D	G#	F#	F	A	B	C#	r v
s	C#	F	G#	D	A#	C	F#	E	D#	G	A	B	o e
i	G	B	D	G#	E	F#	C	A#	A	C#	D#	F	g r
o	A	C#	E	A#	F#	G#	D	C	B	D#	F	G	r s
n	A#	D	F	B	G	A	D#	C#	C	E	F#	G#	a i
(I)	F#	A#	C#	G	D#	F	B	A	G#	C	D	E	d o
↓	E	G#	B	F	C#	D#	A	G	F#	A#	C	D	e n
	D	F#	A	D#	B	C#	G	F	E	G#	A#	C	(RI)

← Retrograde (R)

By supplying any one of these forms with rhythmic patterns, the composer may create a melody as shown in Example 3. Notice that it is possible to repeat pitches directly; what the system in its purest form prohibits is the return or restatement of a pitch before all twelve pitches have first been stated.

Example 3

Schoenberg, *Tonal oder Atonal,* © Belmont

To - nal o - der a - to - nal? Nun sagt ein - mal in welch-em

Stall in dies-em Fall die gross - re Zahl dass

man sich hal - ten, hal - ten kann am sich - ern Wall.[4]

Other lines may be created from other forms of the row. It is also possible to construct chords from the row simply by sounding some of the pitches of the row simultaneously instead of successively as shown in Example 4. Schoenberg does not use this technique in this particular work since it is a strict canon but he employs it frequently in other works.

Example 4

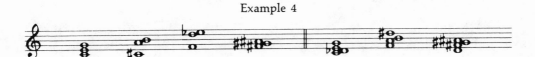

Many other special techniques may be used to transform the raw material of the tone row to the sounding fabric of a completed composition. Sometimes the pitches of the row are distributed among two or more parts, sometimes only seg-ments of the row like hexachords (six notes) are used, and sometimes the composer will take other liberties with the distribution of the pitches of the row. Indeed, it might be said that in most compositions the composer seeks to conceal the presence of the row rather than to expose it. The treatment of the row should lead to the same balance of unity and variety that is the goal of compositions in almost all styles. Handled properly it can lend a strong sense of underlying unity to the composition; at the same time the skillful composer can derive from it a great variety of melodic, contrapuntal, and harmonic material.

What are the ramifications of twelve-tone or serial technique for the choral conductor? Must he laboriously trace the usages of the row through every single measure of the composition and then teach this to his chorus members, or should he ignore the row construction and treat the composition as if it were not written in serial technique at all. The answer would seem to lie between these two extremes. Though the choral conductor himself, as a matter of interest, may wish to study the row usage in an entire work, he need not demand that his chorus members know the work in this great detail. On the other hand, he certainly should make sure that the chorus members know the row on which the composition is based and should have at least some knowledge of the way the row is used in some parts of the music.

Knowing the row can be of very practical assistance to the singers in learning to sing the composition. Joseph Flummerfelt, in describing his rehearsals with the twelve-tone sections of Penderecki's *Passion According to St. Luke*, has said:

> I began rehearsals . . . by teaching the tone rows in their several permutations. Once the choir is able to sing these absolutely in tune, the sight reading of the sections to which they apply is obviously much faster and, perhaps more importantly, a structural awareness comes into the performance.[5]

In the interpretation of sections of twelve-tone compositions where the row is hidden through distribution between several parts, it is usually not necessary to bring out the row as an entity, rather the newly created melodic lines should have an integrity of their own. An exception to this would be instances of so-called *Klangfarbenmelodie*, where a melodic line is deliberately broken up between several instruments (the technique is rarely used with voices) and yet intended to be heard as a unit. A typical and easily understood example of this technique is shown below. Notice also the characteristic wide leaps or octave displacement.

Example 5

Webern, *Symphonie*, Op. 21, I, © Universal

It may also be helpful to drill some on the three-note, four-note, or larger chords created from the row, if these are an important part of the composition. When the singers have gotten used to these sonorities they may be more comfortable, confident, and accurate in performing them.

The classic twelve-tone works, including such choral masterpieces as the two cantatas of Webern and several works of Schoenberg and other later composers, do present the singer with great problems in the performance of pitch. On the other hand, some of them present relatively few difficulties in other performance aspects such as rhythm, and they are usually meticulously marked in such aspects as dynamics, articulation, and tempo. In view of this it would be regrettable if amateur choruses never attempted the performance, or at least the reading, of these works. That a high school chorus, albeit a superb one, can perform works such as the Webern cantatas has been proven by the Princeton (New Jersey) High School choir under the direction of Thomas Hilbish.

Aleatory technique may, as we have said, be applied in both the composition and the performance of twentieth-century music. In composition, the aleatory influence may be reflected in such devices as using the skyline of New York to determine a melodic curve or changing the specks and slight deformations on a blank piece of music paper into notes. On a more complex level, composers like Iannis Xenakis use formulas for random distribution and advanced computer techniques to achieve chance effects in the composition of their works. Knowledge of the technique used may be interesting but it is usually not crucial for the performance of the work. This is, instead, subject to the normal demands that would obtain if the work had been written by traditional means. Granted, the resulting work may be marked by a high degree of variety and a strong tendency toward disorganization and may confront the conductor with the choice of either emphasizing this disunity or attempting somehow to introduce elements of unity into the performance. Still, he would be faced with this decision no matter how the work was originally conceived.

Aleatory or chance elements may be introduced into the performance aspect of a work in many different ways. We should begin by stating that all music involves some degree of chance in performance. No matter how carefully the composer indicates his intentions and no matter how carefully the performer tries to follow these, there is always some variation from one performance to another. As we have seen in the previous chapters, this chance element, this contribution on the part of the performer, was especially strong in the Renaissance and Baroque periods. The performer was expected to be a collaborating co-creator, not merely a faithful re-creator. In the Classical and Romantic periods, however, this tendency was reversed, and in early twentieth-century works like those of Stravinsky, for example, the performer is expected to refrain from any added interpretation of tempo, dynamics, and articulation, and is forbidden to change or add any notes.

In a way, aleatory performance constitutes a reaction to the preceding strictness and a return to earlier practices. Realizing, however, that most performers would be somewhat timid or uncertain about adopting a co-creative role, composers of aleatory music have, to a greater or lesser extent, spelled out those aspects of the composition in which the performer is invited to make his contribution. In some cases the composer will specify the rhythm and invite the performer to choose the pitches; in some cases he will specify the pitches and invite the performer to choose the rhythm. In some cases he will specify both pitch and rhythm, but will allow the performer to determine the order in which sections of the piece occur successively or the way in which the elements of the composition are presented simultaneously. In other cases the performers may be given almost complete freedom in their choice of materials.

Performance of such works may demand special approaches on the part of the conductor. His main problem will be to encourage his singers to use their new freedom with a sense of conviction and without falling into the clichés of traditional pitch and rhythm patterns. If singers are told, for example, that they are to invent a rhythm pattern they may very easily fall into traditional patterns like

To avoid this it may be effective to practice some more unusual rhythms, especially those involving the prime numbers 5, 7, 11, etc. Patterns like the following may be suggested.

Example 6

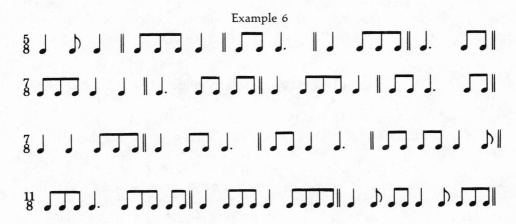

Although it may seem opposed to the spirit of aleatory music to drill on such patterns, it is paradoxically true that most singers need this kind of discipline if they are to be led to freedom and to exploration of rhythmic ideas beyond those of traditional music. Similarly in pitch, it may be advisable to drill on some patterns drawn from tone rows in order to open up the aural imagination of the singers. Eventually, of course, the sense of freedom in the selection of materials must be emphasized in the performance of aleatory music.

THE USE OF VOICES AND INSTRUMENTS

The problems connected with the use of voices and instruments in twentieth-century music are not those of trying to interpret composers' intentions and to recreate archaic sounds. In most cases the composers are quite specific and the instruments are readily available.

Rather, the problem is the willingness and ability on the part of conductor and singer to explore to the fullest the new world of sounds presented by many composers. In various works and styles these composers call upon singers to produce an incredible variety of timbres from whispering to shouting, from tongue clicks to whistles, from a white sound to an extremely rich vibrato. Timbre, indeed, becomes an essential aspect of the music, sometimes even surpassing pitch and rhythm in its importance for the meaning of the music. To neglect or compromise this aspect would be unfortunate in any music but especially so in contemporary music.

PROBLEMS OF NOTATION

After many decades of music literature in which the reading of the text was relatively unproblematic, some compositions of the twentieth century have reintroduced problems of the interpretation of notation, involving the use of new signs or terms, or in some cases the reinterpretation of old symbols. Most compositions using new terminology or symbology have introductory sections in which these are carefully and specifically explained. However, some new notational conventions have been used with sufficient frequency that they should be generally understood by the conductor. In the following sections we shall emphasize these more widely used signs, but shall include some other less frequently used signs and terms because of their characteristic interest.

The new signs and terms may be associated with new aspects of control or with new aspects of freedom in twentieth-century music. For ease in reference, we have divided this section into subsections on pitch and rhythm. Each subsection treats first signs and terms associated with greater control and then those associated with greater freedom. Signs and terms relating to tempo, dynamics, and timbre are treated under separate headings later in the chapter.

The Interpretation of Pitch Notation

There have been countless attempts to reform the notation of pitch, but only two of them have had any extensive acceptance among musicians, namely Klavarscribo and Equiton. Klavarscribo, as the name suggests, is based on the keyboard. The alternating groups of two and three black lines represent the alternating groups of two and three black keys on the piano; the white spaces represent the white keys. Most Klavarscribo scores are meant to be read from top to bottom; some are adapted versions in which the keyboard is, in effect, laid on its side and then the music is read in the traditional manner from left to right. Equiton is based on a staff of just two lines per octave. Notes are represented with leger lines and with a differentiation between black and white notes. Example 7 shows a chromatic scale and the first few notes of the Schoenberg row transcribed into Klavarscribo and Equiton.

Example 7

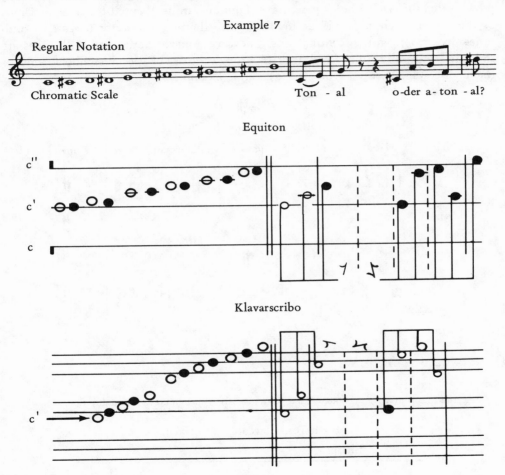

It can easily be seen that either of these systems has clear advantages over traditional notation in terms of clarity, especially for more chromatic music. In both systems no distinction is made between enharmonic notes; F sharp and G flat, for instance, would have the same notation. Whether or not either of these systems ever achieves total acceptance, it is still interesting and helpful for those performing modern music to become familiar with these efforts at notational reform.

Both Klavarscribo and Equiton are notations dealing with the traditional pitch system of twelve notes per octave. Equiton can be adapted for finer divisions of the octave, such as would be involved with the use of quarter tones and sixth tones. In most twentieth-century music, however, quarter tones and sixth tones are indicated with the regular five-line staff through the use of special symbols. Some of the more commonly used symbols are given in Example 8.

Example 8
QUARTER TONES

Sharp	Haba	Penderecki	Bussotti	Zimmermann	Kagel*	Kopelent
1/4	↓ or ↄ	+	+	♦ or ⇑	♮♯♭	⇑
2/4	♯	♯	♯			♯
3/4	♯	⇑	⇑			♯
Flat 1/4	d or ♯	♭		♦ or d	♮♯♭	↳
2/4	♭	♭	♭			♭
3/4	↗♭	d				

*This means to move the note (natural, sharp, or flat) ¼ tone in the indicated direction.

Sixth Tones (according to Haba)

Sharp		Flat	
1/6	↓	1/6	ↄ
2/6 (1/3)	⇑	2/6 (1/3)	♭
4/6 (2/3)	♯	4/6 (2/3)	♭

Tone clusters (chords made up of major and/or minor seconds) are difficult to notate efficiently in traditional notation and so contemporary composers have developed the following special symbols to represent them.

Example 9

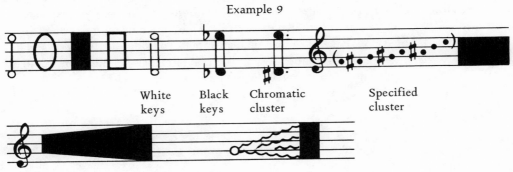

White   Black   Chromatic   Specified
keys   keys   cluster   cluster

Gradually emerging clusters

Turning to aspects of freedom in pitch notation, probably the most widely used technique is that of *Sprechstimme* (speech-voice) or *Sprechgesang* (speech-song) used by Schoenberg and others. Alban Berg describes the technique as follows:

> The melodies in the vocal part which are distinguished by special notes are not to be sung. The performer has the task of changing them into a spoken melody while taking into account the pitch of the notes. This is achieved by:
> 1. adhering very precisely to the rhythm (and note values), allowing no more freedom than in normal singing;
> 2. being aware of the difference between the tone of the singing voice and of the speaking voice; in singing the performer stays on the note without change; in speaking he strikes the note but leaves it immediately by rising or falling in pitch, but always bringing out the relative pitches of the notes.
> The performer must take great care not to fall into a singing manner of speaking. This is not what the composer intends; nor does he desire a realistic, natural manner of speaking. On the contrary, the difference between ordinary speech and speech that can be used in music should be clear. On the other hand there should be no suggestion of singing.[6]

Some works have a full spectrum of possibilities including natural conversation with no indicated music notation and with no attempt to structure either the pitch or rhythm; *Sprechstimme* indicated with notes having a double crossbar or "x" through the note stem and intended to be performed as indicated above with exact rhythms but with only approximate relations between pitches; *Sprechgesang* indicated with a single bar on each note stem and intended to be performed like *Sprechstimme,* but with somewhat more of a sustained songlike quality and somewhat more accurate pitch reproduction; and finally normal singing represented with regular music notation and intended to be sung with exact pitches and rhythms. These four possibilities are illustrated below.

Example 10

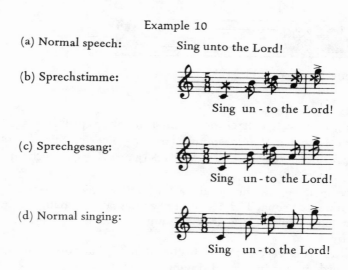

(a) Normal speech: Sing unto the Lord!

(b) Sprechstimme:

Sing un - to the Lord!

(c) Sprechgesang:

Sing un - to the Lord!

(d) Normal singing:

Sing un - to the Lord!

Some conductors recommend practicing *Sprechstimme* and *Sprechgesang* by first singing the melody with exact pitches and then gradually moving away from them. These techniques, when performed properly, can have a very striking effect in both solo and choral music. In some music other methods of symbolization are used to indicate approximate pitches, aleatory order of pitches, and various types of glissandi. A representative sampling of these is given in Example 11.

Example 11

APPROXIMATE PITCHES

1) *Sprechstimme* (Ligeti)

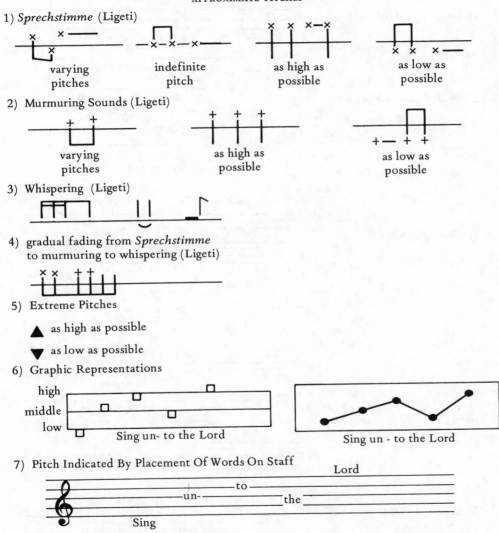

varying
pitches

indefinite
pitch

as high as
possible

as low as
possible

2) Murmuring Sounds (Ligeti)

varying
pitches

as high as
possible

as low as
possible

3) Whispering (Ligeti)

4) gradual fading from *Sprechstimme*
to murmuring to whispering (Ligeti)

5) Extreme Pitches

▲ as high as possible

▼ as low as possible

6) Graphic Representations

high
middle
low

Sing un- to the Lord

Sing un - to the Lord

7) Pitch Indicated By Placement Of Words On Staff

Lord

to

un-

the

Sing

8) Pitch Indicated By Height Of Letters

SING UN **TO THE LORD**

ALEATORY ORDER OF PITCHES

1) Pitch Box—Definite Pitches

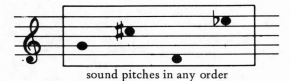

sound pitches in any order

2) Pitch Box—Indefinite Pitches

sound pitches by following the
dotted lines in any route

GLISSANDI

1) Nine Line Staff

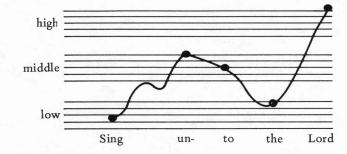

Sing _ _ _ _ _ _ _ _ _ _ _ _

2) Fifteen Line Staff

Sing   un-   to   the   Lord

3) Glissando With
   Time Span
   Designated

The Interpretation of Rhythmic Notation

In both Klavarscribo and Equiton the color of the notes (black or white) specifies pitch level and therefore cannot be used to represent rhythmic durations. Instead duration in both systems is shown by means of proportional distance between notes. Various types of lines are used to mark beats and bars, and the notes are placed at the point where their sound is to begin. Beams or curved lines may be used to show which notes belong together in a single melodic line. Neither beams nor note head color show anything about duration: this is indicated solely by position and relative distance. The following example in Equiton should make these principles clear.

Example 12

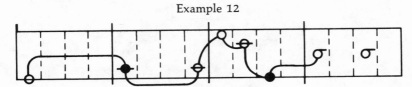

John Cage has applied a somewhat similar system of "proportional nota-tion" to the traditional symbols of rhythmic notation. In other modern works musical "events" are coordinated precisely with chronological time; a stopwatch replaces the beat in the performance of passages like those shown in Example 13.

Example 13

1. Browne, R., "Chortos"
   "The clock is set at 0:00 (facing the chorus) and left unplugged until the piece begins. It runs for five minutes during the piece, establishing the time for all the actions."

    0:00 Begin humming sound*
    0:15 Stop. Silence.**
    0:16 Ten singers speak one word each, ad lib, during this time.***
    0:25 Thirty singers speak one word each, ad lib, during this time.
    0:45 Every singer speaks five words, ad lib, during this time.
    0:55 Stop. Silence.

    * Toneless, uncentered, slowly fluctuating in pitch, quiet, but dense, and low is the range of each singer.

    ** All stops and starts should occur without emphasis, but with precision.

    *** All words should be stated clearly, audibly, and conversationally. Don't act, compete, or call attention to your word or your time. . . .

2. Staggered entrances

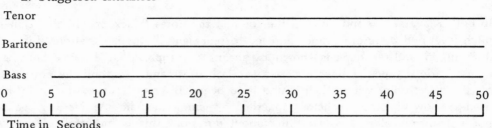

Tenor

Baritone

Bass

0   5   10   15   20   25   30   35   40   45   50

Time in Seconds

3. Numbered fermatas (numbers referring to seconds of duration)

4. Special rest signs

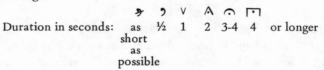

Duration in seconds: as   ½   1   2   3-4   4   or longer
                       short
                        as
                      possible

Turning to examples of freedom in notation, probably the most frequently encountered method of indicating this is to find verbal indications like "free" or "in free rhythm" placed over traditional rhythmic notation. Other means of indicating relative degrees of free rhythmic performance are indicated in Example 14.

Example 14

(a) Duration lines

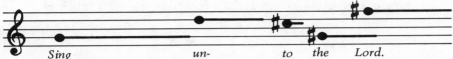

Sing   un-   to   the   Lord.

(b) Duration indicated by length of words

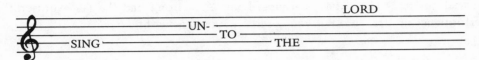

(c) Frame notation (Kagel)

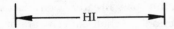

Perform within the indicated
time at any desired point.

ORNAMENTATION AND IMPROVISATION

In a sense we have already touched upon some aspects of ornamentation and improvisation in our discussion of aleatory techniques in the preceding sections. It is interesting to note that much twentieth-century music exhibits one of two extreme approaches to the aspects of ornamentation and improvisation. Either they are completely forbidden as in many works of Stravinsky, Webern, and others, or they are lavishly encouraged as in aleatory compositions.

    There is, however, one type of music which can be said to occupy somewhat of a middle ground as regards ornamentation and improvisation, namely the performance of jazz and some other popular styles. It would be beyond the scope of this text to try to summarize all of the stylistic aspects of jazz, rock, and other popular schools. These are well discussed in books by David Baker, Jerry Coker, and others. Probably the most satisfactory way for singers to learn the various styles of ornamentation and improvisation is to listen to recordings by such artists as Ella Fitzgerald. In listening to these some aspects will be quite obvious like the slight flattening of certain scale degrees (blue notes), or the substitution of

$$\overset{\ulcorner 3 \urcorner}{\eighthnote\ \eighthnote} \quad \text{for} \quad \dotted\eighthnote\ \sixteenthnote,$$

a practice we have already discussed, incidentally, in the Baroque period. Beyond this, however, the ornamentation and improvisation of an outstanding jazz performer almost defies codification in a simple set of rules or representation with musical notation. Ultimately, perhaps, Louis Armstrong had the last word on the performance of jazz, "Man, if you got to ask, you'll never find out."

INTERPRETATION OF TEMPO

The interpretation of various new symbols for rhythm has already been discussed in the section on the notation of rhythm. In this section we shall concentrate on the question of interpretation of tempo. In many ways this is less of a problem in modern music than it was in earlier music. For one thing we frequently have recordings made by the composer or under his personal supervision by which we can determine such interpretive matters as tempo. A word of caution is in order here, however. Sometimes the composer is not the best interpreter of his own music. Some composers have admitted that they have found interpretation by other conductors to come closer to the realization of their intentions.

Another factor that makes the interpretation of tempo in modern music less problematic is the fact that composers more and more rely upon the metronome to give exact instructions for the rate of speed at which their music is to be played. But again we must suggest that the metronome marking can rarely be taken as a totally infallible guide. Personal performance styles and architectural acoustic conditions must be taken into account. The same metronomic speed may sound lively and clear performed by one group in one hall, and lifeless and muddied when performed by another group in a different hall. In brief, the given metronomic marking should be a starting place and a very important factor in the choice of tempo, but it can never wholly replace the sensitive intuitions of the conductor.

In addition to the standard use of metronomic markings, some contemporary composers have invented new methods of indicating tempo or more particularly change of tempo as shown below.

Example 15

(a) Tempo indicated by wedge

Accelerando Ritardando

 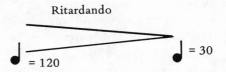

(b) Tempo indicated by wedge-shaped beams

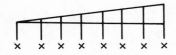 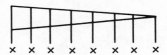

(c) Tempo indicated by arrows

 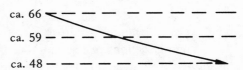

(d) Tempo indicated by slant of the staff

(e) Tempo indicated by arrow and spacing.

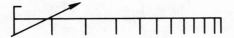 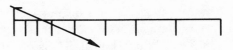

One of the most interesting aspects of tempo in twentieth-century music is the technique of *metric modulation* usually associated with Elliott Carter but used by other composers. According to this technique changes in meter and tempo are given a certain sense of unity and logic by virtue of the fact that a given value in the old tempo and meter is made equal to a given value in the new tempo and meter. This principle dates from the Renaissance system of prolations and it may be found that tempo transitions within music of all periods are sometimes more logically and easily performed in this manner.

Example 16
Metric modulation

Some twentieth-century music presents the challenging problem of having two or more sections of the choral or instrumental ensemble required to play in two or more different tempi. Though some conductors have attempted to conduct such "polytempi" alone, most find that the most satisfactory solution is to use two or more conductors, one for each section. This could be regarded, interestingly enough, as a return to the earlier tradition of dual direction. Turning to aspects of freedom in tempo we find that the most usual way to indicate this is by verbal instructions, such as "free in tempo," "in recitative style," etc. Occasionally composers will use brackets or boxes to enclose the areas in which free tempi are to prevail.

PHRASING, ARTICULATION, AND DYNAMICS

Phrasing, in the specific sense of deciding which notes should be grouped together and which should receive slight differences in terms of weight or importance, is, or at least should be, just as much an important part of the interpretation of twentieth-century music as of earlier music. All too often performers are content with having mastered the technical details of pitch and rhythm in their performance of difficult twentieth-century works and do not take the trouble to consider those details of phrasing that distinguish a vital and meaningful performance from a merely adequate performance. The same general principles of tension and release or of grouping according to such factors as contiguity in pitch or duration apply just as appropriately to twentieth-century music as to earlier music but they must now be accommodated to new materials, techniques, and forms.

There are a wealth of new techniques and symbols signifying them in the realm of instrumental music, but we shall not discuss these. In vocal music it is probably fair to say that the choral singer of today must be prepared to make almost any sound imaginable, not only with his voice, but sometimes with other parts of his body or even with instruments. Some of the possibilities are given in Example 17.

Example 17

▶ ✗	Inspiratory sound: Sprechstimme while breathing in (Ligeti)
o	Falsetto (Bussotti, Berg, and others)
O	Open mouth
⊖ or –o–	Half-closed mouth
⊟ or +	Closed mouth
Я or ✗↑	Clicking sound with tongue
▼	Quasi-hiccup (breathe in quickly)
▲	Swallowing sound
▶◀	Audible breathing

Dynamics in contemporary choral music are still generally indicated with the traditional Italian abbreviations. There have been some experiments in indicating dynamics in decibels or in percentages with 1 representing the softest level, 50 a medium level, and 100 the loudest level.

Westminster Choir in a recording session with Leonard Bernstein
and the New York Philharmonic.

VISUAL ASPECTS

One of the most vital trends in contemporary art is toward multimedia expression. In a sense this is really nothing new—medieval man experienced multimedia art when he attended the mass on Sunday and *saw* the beauty of the architecture, the statues, the paintings, the candles, and the elaborate costumes of the celebrants; *heard* the varied sounds of chanting, singing, and instrumental playing; *tasted* the communion wafer; *felt* the coolness of the stone cathedral; and even *smelled* the burning incense. The renewal of this tendency in modern multimedia art takes various forms.

In choral music this has meant that some works call upon as much visual or physical participation as aural participation, and the choral conductor who wishes to bring his chorus a varied experience must be sure that visual aspects are just as correctly performed as sounding aspects. Pauline Oliveros, for example, in her composition "O-Ha-Ah" calls upon the chorus to perform yawning or stretching gestures and instructs the chorus to sit down when the conductor stands up after

Charles Ives, 1874–1954
(The Bettmann Archive)

having bent down to tie his shoe lace. Other choral works call for rhythmic movement of various types.

SUMMARY

The case for incorporating twentieth-century music in the choral program has been
well stated by Val J. Hicks in *Innovative Choral Music Notation.*

> Five philosophical justifications for the inclusion of avant-garde
> music in the curriculum are:
> 1. Much new music calls for active *involvement* instead of passive
>   cooperation; therefore, it tends to bring into play new physio-
>   logical and psychological reactions which form the basis for more
>   effective and enduring learning.
> 2. Contemporaneity of subject matter makes for more compelling
>   learning situations for youngsters, and avant-garde music appeals
>   to the students' natural sense of exploration and curiosity.
> 3. The performance freedom found in much avant-garde music

tends to create more personal involvement than does traditional music, because when one is free to make rehearsal-performance choices, there is likely to be more learning *interest* present.

4. Avant-garde music can help make music more *inclusive,* rather than exclusive because it often demands musical effects which the *untrained* student can perform adequately.

5. Innovative choral music helps bridge the present with the past and learning is usually more effective when it proceeds from the present to the past.[7]

Hicks made these remarks in specific reference to the use of innovative or avant-garde choral music in choral organizations in the schools. We believe they would also apply to other choral organizations. Further, we would add one other reason to his list of justifications for performing music of the twentieth century, whether it be oriented toward the new concepts of freedom and control or toward the tradition of the past. This is simply the fact that some of the most interesting, effective, compelling, and worthwhile choral music has been written and continues to be written by composers of our own time.

In all of the performance chapters we have been stressing those aspects which make one period of choral literature different from other periods. It is, however, one of the sublime glories and mysteries of music that it ultimately resists assignment to any closed chronological or geographical category. The power to move men's hearts and to fascinate men's minds is common to all enduring music regardless of place or period, and it is the realization of this potential that is the essence of the choral experience.

NOTES

1. Aaron Copland, "A Modernist Defends Modern Music," *New York Times* 25 (December 1949), p. 11.

2. William Hollingsworth Whyte, *The Organization Man* (Garden City, New York: Doubleday and Company, Inc., 1957).

3. Arnold Schoenberg, *Style and Idea*, trans. Dika Newlin (New York: Philosophical Library, 1950), p. 106.

4. "Tonal or atonal? Come on and tell us which stable in this case the greater number can be kept."

5. Joseph Flummerfelt, "Passion According to St. Luke—Penderecki," *The Choral Journal* 13:8 (1973).

6. Alban Berg, *Wozzeck* (Vienna: Universal, 1955), quote from the score.

7. Val T. Hicks, "Innovative Choral Music Notation," (Unpublished Ph.D. dissertation, University of Iowa, 1971, pp. 15–21.

INDEX